Far from Home

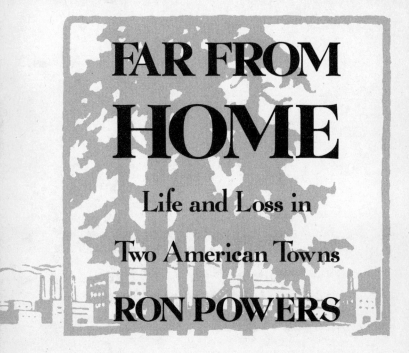

FAR FROM HOME

HOME

Life and Loss in

Two American Towns

RON POWERS

ANCHOR BOOKS
DOUBLEDAY
NEW YORK LONDON TORONTO SYDNEY AUCKLAND

An Anchor Book
PUBLISHED BY DOUBLEDAY
a division of Bantam Doubleday Dell Publishing Group, Inc.
666 Fifth Avenue, New York, New York 10103

ANCHOR BOOKS, DOUBLEDAY, and the portrayal of an anchor
are trademarks of Doubleday, a division of Bantam Doubleday Dell
Publishing Group, Inc.

Far from Home was originally published in hardcover by Random House, Inc.
in 1991. The Anchor Books edition is
published by arrangement with Random House, Inc.

Library of Congress Cataloging-in-Publication Data

Powers, Ron.
Far from home: life and loss in two American towns/Ron Powers.
1st Anchor Books ed.
p.   cm.
I. Title.
[F549.C2P88   1992]
974.6′1—dc20   92-13986
CIP

Acknowledgments

Many wise and generous people aided me in the writing of this book by contributing information, analyses, opinions, anecdotes and data about Cairo, Illinois and Kent, Connecticut; or about the changing prospects of American town life in general. I have acknowledged most of them within the text. Several others have wished to remain anonymous. To all, I extend my sincerest gratitude.

For certain valuable insights into the history of community development in America and the Third World, I am grateful in particular to Professor Jnan Bhattacharyya, director of the Department of Community Development at Southern Illinois University.

For Cairo's cultural and political history I relied on several locally and regionally published books, anthologies, commission reports and civic brochures, and one nationally published volume—*The Other Illinois*, by Baker Brownell (Duell, Sloan and Pearce, 1958). An important regional source was *A History of the City of Cairo, Illinois*, by John M. Lansden, first published in 1910 and reprinted in 1976 by Southern Illinois University Press.

Also of historical value were *A History of Cairo*, by M. B. Harrel, published locally in 1864; *The Attractions of Cairo*, first printed in 1890 and reprinted in 1975 by the graphic arts students of the Cairo-Egyptian Adult Center and *Alexander County Profiles*, printed by the Commercial Press in Cairo in 1975. My understanding of Cairo's economic and racial struggles was enhanced by the volume, *Toward a New South? Studies in Post–Civil War Southern Communities*, number 97 in the Contributions in American History series published by Greenwood Press of Westport, Connecticut; and by a comprehensive study by the journalist Paul Good that centered on testimony given at hearings held in the town of Cairo in March 1972 by the United States Commission on Civil Rights.

In addition, I relied on current and past editions of the *Cairo Evening Citizen*, and of the *Southern Illinoisan*. Cheryl Frank of the *Southern Illinoisan* was particularly helpful. I extend my gratitude to the courteous staff of the Cairo Public Library.

For the history of Kent and of early town life in Northwest Connecticut, I am indebted to several works. They include *One American Town* by Donald S. Connery (Simon & Schuster, 1972); *Democracy in the Connecticut Frontier Town of Kent*, by Charles S. Grant (W. W. Norton, 1972) and *A New England Town: The First Hundred Years*, by Kenneth A. Lockridge (Norton, 1970).

Other sources of Kent history included: "Kent 1776," a bicentennial pamphlet edited by Ann Soper Davis; *Stories and Recollections of Kent*, a collection of essays by Phil Camp published in 1988 by Pocketknife Printworks in Lakeville, Connecticut; the 1986–87 Kent School catalogue; the Annual Reports of Kent covering fiscal years 1987 and 1988 and the *Reader's Digest* of November 1940.

Several regional and local newspapers in Connecticut supply excellent coverage of the changing socioeconomic face of that state. Among the most valuable for my purposes were the *Litchfield County Times*, the *Kent Good-Times Dispatch* and, until it ceased publication, the *Kent Weathervane*. Ed and Laura Rapp, the publishers of the *Weathervane*, were generous with their time and comments. I also found *The New York Times* a reliable source of information on shifting population patterns and the transformation of town life in the Northeast. *Yankee Magazine* provided a useful overview of rapid growth in small New England towns during the 1980s.

Many scholars and other specialists in the study of American town life supplied me with texts of their monographs, surveys, speeches and policy papers. These include Professor Don A. Dillman, Department of Sociology, Washington State University; Professor Darryl Hobbs, Department of Rural Sociology, the University of Missouri; Willis Goudy, sociologist, Iowa State University and Kenneth P. Wilkinson, Department of Agricultural Economics and Rural Sociology, Pennsylvania State University.

I also drew information from "Small Town Triage: A Settlement Policy for Rural Kansas," a monograph prepared by three professors of regional and community planning at Kansas State University: Thomas L. Daniels, John W. Keller and Mark B. Lapping.

Organizations and agencies that responded to my queries with essential information include: the National Main Street Center, the National Trust for Historic Preservation, Partners for Livable Places, the Lower Mississippi Delta Development Commission, the media relations department of the Colonial Williamsburg Foundation, and the National Register of Historic Places, whose inventory nomination form of December 1977 told me much about Cairo's historic buildings.

Finally I would like to thank my dear friends at the Bread Loaf Writers Conference for their valuable responses to the work-in-progress, and my wife, Honoree Fleming, for her unfailingly perceptive reading and criticisms of the text.

Far from Home

Chapter I

Toward evening of a late-winter day, late in a dark decade in the fortunes of American city life, I rented a car at a small airport in western Kentucky and started driving on a two-lane highway toward Illinois.

I was headed for a town—a violent and sorrowful little town that lay wedged between two rivers at the southern tip of the state, a place of cruel secrets and gothic ruin, which bore the tragically hopeful name of Cairo.

Cairo was dying. But that fact hardly set the town apart. In a time when America's cities were disintegrating—under a hideous blight of incivility, poverty, rage, drugs, gang criminality, racism and the random play of semiautomatic weapons—the deaths of small American towns were scarcely noticed.

But towns were dying. Certainly towns of Cairo's tiny size and age and isolation were dying in one way or another, or were dead, or were lingering in a kind of cataleptic trance, dreaming their histories like the mostly aging people who lived on in them.

American towns had flourished and died, like trees, throughout the history of the nation, of course. There was nothing novel about a dying town. It was the suddenness of the blight (a factory closing) and the virulence of its spread (to the "rust belt," the Lower Mississippi Delta) that marked town death in these times. The litter of dead and dying towns had begun to form a kind of calligraphy on the surface of the country, a coded message that seemed to announce the final closing of some old system, the final corrosion of a set of agreements about the very nature and function of civic life.

PARDON OUR DUST, the messages seemed to say. RELOCATING TO SERVE YOU BETTER. COME VISIT US AT THE MALL.

And yet this was not the full extent of the message. America was not yet quite finished with its towns. On the ever-widening perimeters of the dread-soaked cities, certain sleepy, forgotten villages had suddenly found themselves jolted awake, bathed in the searchlights of rediscovery: their senescence arrested, their atrophy jazzed back into a kind of hyperlife by a reverse tide of colonizers—the urban monied class, fleeing the urban terror, for weekends if not for a new life.

Rezoned, subdivided, sanded down, defoliated, relandscaped, refaçaded, rewired, boutiqued, marqueed, malled, condoed, satellite-dished, barn-converted, commuter-routed, solar-energized, BMW'd, cocained, hand-gunned, X-rated, their Main Streets and sewer systems gridlocked, haberdashed with the latest in gourmet ice-cream parlors and oil-on-masonite galleries and squid-ink pasta bistros and real-estate chalets, these old burgs stood stunned and gasping in their spruced-up state—a little exhausted perhaps by the tremendous enema that had flushed their vitals to clear the way for the new gastric rush.

Either way, the decade has been a grim one for towns.

Within this drunken zigzag between oversaturation and rot, Cairo, Illinois, was a special case, a connoisseur's choice—worth a detour. Cairo was dying, but it wasn't simply dying, it was dying slow and it was dying mean. Cairo had in fact been dying for a hundred seventy years, dying since the moment of its breech birth in 1818, and dying of every disease, human and economic and elemental, that could be conjured and called down upon a town. Its capacity to cling to a kind of life did nothing to ennoble Cairo, but only reinforced its sinister aura. The town's sulphorous legacy of corruption, wretched luck and murderous temperament made it seem cursed; a locus of evil. From what I had learned of its present agony, Cairo had the aspect of a crushed snake, waiting for the setting sun to still its thrashes. That sunset seemed to be approaching.

But I was not driving to Cairo to witness its death throes. I was drawn there by the rumor of a last-chance grasp at life, an impossible scheme for redemption. That sort of thing interested me. I was a fugitive from American town life. I had departed my own Midwestern rivertown nearly thirty years before, against my will, and had been trying to make myself feel rooted in a succession of cities ever since, with decreasing hopes of success. Eventually I joined a tide of colonizers in a village on the perimeter of an eastern city. I bought some squid-ink pasta, rented some videos. In the meantime the town I had left began to wither, and then to grasp at life. Like a son visiting a stricken parent, I journeyed back and watched some outside professionals try to restore my hometown to its former vitality. The professionals brought in scientific marketing techniques. Their plan was to reposition the town as a theme-park "attraction" based on its authentic past. The plan failed. The "attraction" became a gaudy parody, and then the parody itself faded. The town was left stunned and bitter, aware that it had participated in its own violation.

And now I'd gotten wind of another outsider at work in another dying town, a town worse off than my own, a town at the nightmare edge of American life. No professional this time, just an old man with some theories. I'd heard that this man had been promising the people of Cairo, in effect, that he could help them unshackle the town from its history of wretchedness and create a prairie version of John Winthrop's *City on a Hill.*

The fugitive in me wanted to believe that. A notion had been growing in me for several years that if town life in this country was indeed over, so was an essential culture rooted in obligation and the perception of a common good. The withering of this culture—however narrow and corrupt it might have tended to be in its extreme logic—had provoked a moral blight that had spread upward and outward through the life-system of cities.

If an old man could redeem Cairo, redemption could happen anywhere. If he could not, then at least the scale and the terms of his failure might in themselves provide some clue as to what lay ahead, some sense of how much time was left for the very notion of town life.

I rolled warily toward Cairo in the day's last light, half-expecting to be halted, challenged, turned back, shot at. I fully expected to be scrutinized—by men in Polaroid sunglasses, perhaps, slowing alongside; by faces turning to stare at the outsider from street corners, storefront windows. I was conscious of my alien license plates and the make of my car, conscious of my beard, of the tape recorder I'd left in plain view on the passenger seat beside me. I imagined looking in my rearview mirror and finding a car with a red dome-light behind me.

I left Kentucky and turned north onto U.S. Route 51 on the Illinois end of the Ohio River Bridge. A quarter mile outside town, I passed a welcoming billboard that reinforced my sense of time out of kilter. Its message read: CIGARETTE BOOTLEGGING: IMPRISON-MENT, FINE.

U.S. 51 was a two-lane concrete slab that crowned a high-banked ridge. A plowed soybean field spread below it on the left. Down on the right the Ohio eddied into scrub oak. Not far beyond the bean field but invisible under the amber glare of the setting sun, the Mississippi curled; it humped once and then joined the Ohio half a mile behind my back to form the southernmost dagger-tip of Illinois. Cairo lay wedged between the rivers and their floodwalls just ahead.

It was the region's bloodthirsty past that prompted my dark ima-ginings. The high road was a good spot for an ambush. And this was the ambush cradle of the nation. I crept toward the city limits feeling the guns of two centuries scoping my progress, leading the target: I felt the murderous sights of the innkeeper Billy Potts, an early American brigand who took poor travelers in—and took the rich ones out, including, one night, his own son, unrecognized, come home to flash his bankroll for the family, never a prudent impulse around Cairo. I felt the long rifles of the flatboat robbers of the 1820s; the musketry of Union sentries at Fort Defiance on the southern tip of the town, where Ulysses Grant schemed his siege of Vicksburg from the second floor of the Halliday Hotel. I felt the drawn horse-pistols of swamp bushwhackers and the derringers of pimps and card sharks from the packet boats; I felt all the nighttime ordnance of the Vigilantes and the Copperheads and the Flatheads and the Regulators and the Klansmen and the bootleg gangs, the Shelton brothers and the Wortman boys, and the boozy shotgun duck hunters every fall: all the fusillades cut loose across Cairo's two violent centuries. A good deal of blood had seeped into this old clay floodplain and the town at its tip that was founded as an American El Dorado, a center of river trade, even a possible new site for the nation's capital—but was then abandoned to an epoch of failure, disease, murder and the corrupting flow of time.

The first outsider to remark on Cairo's peculiar ambience was Charles Dickens. Dickens steamed past Cairo in April 1842, twenty-four years after the settlement's founding, when it claimed two thousand inhabitants. His impressions, published in his *American Notes,* haunt the erstwhile civic boosters of Cairo to this day.

"At the junction of the two rivers," Dickens wrote, "on ground so flat and low and marshy, that at certain seasons of the year it is inundated to the house-tops, lies a breeding-place of fever, ague, and death. . . . A dismal swamp, on which the half-built houses rot away; cleared here and there for the space of a few yards; and teeming, then, with rank and unwholesome vegetation, in whose baleful shade the wretched wanderers who are tempted hither, droop, and die, and lay their bones; the hateful Mississippi circling and eddying before it, and turning off upon its southern course a slimy monster hideous to behold; a hotbed of disease, an ugly sepulchre, a grave uncheered by any gleam of promise; a place without one single quality, in earth or air or water, to commend it; such is this dismal Cairo."

Those were the good times. Not even Dickens could have imagined what lay ahead for this town. No one could have foreseen the floods, the epidemics, the bankruptcies, the failed grasp at the twentieth century and its receding beacons of progress, and then the long, seething half-sleep in the residue of what remained: the gambling, the whorehouses, the racketeering, and the mutually loathing stare of two trapped races: the blacks up from the Deep South, the whites coming west from Appalachia, each a reminder to the other of the stalled journey, the paralysis inside the flow of time.

Cairo's last great civic event, in fact, had been a shooting war between its whites and blacks—a war that went on for more than four years and brought the town to its present point of near death.

Cairo is connected to Illinois by roughly the same accounting that connects it to the twentieth century. In every real sense the town is part of the South, lying lower in the country than Norfolk, Virginia, and in the dispersal cone of the Cumberland Gap. But the South to which Cairo belongs is extinct and has been for fifty years, maybe a hundred: the shopping malls of Paducah, thirty miles to the east, with their Dead Kennedys T-shirts on sale in the craft arcade, have bled Cairo, not offered it cultural reinforcement.

What the town retained—what could not be bled out—were the ancient memories, the dreams of an extinct South.

There were racial lynchings at the turn of the century; a race riot in 1937; a firebombing and cross-burning in 1952. In 1962 the city's swimming pool closed rather than integrate. In 1964 blacks were beaten with clubs and chains when a group of them tried to integrate a roller-skating rink.

And then the organized shooting began. In July of 1969 a nineteen-year-old black soldier died in a Cairo jail cell. The police reported it a suicide by hanging. The soldier's body was embalmed before there could be an autopsy. The street-fighting and burning lasted three days. A committee of armed white males formed; it decorated itself with Nazi insignia. Its members called themselves the White Hats. They offered themselves, six hundred strong, as volunteer deputies to the city. A counterforce of blacks, the United Front, centered around a young minister named Charles Koen. The shooting echoed through Cairo nights. Outsiders drove through town with their heads hunched down, their children flattened on the floorboards.

The shooting folded itself into the rhythms of town life with a sort of macabre rationality. By day, the white and the black males of Cairo worked at their jobs, if there were jobs to work—or picketed, or hung out, or drank. Toward evening, the men would return to their houses or apartments and collect their shooting stock. Then the White Hats would set up perimeters or launch patrols in cars equipped with radio communication. Most of the shooting took place along "Sniper's Alley," a two-hundred-yard corridor between the police station and St. Columbia's rectory, a black redoubt; or in the streets surrounding a fortified black public housing project called Pyramid Court.

The night patrols and gunfire never seemed to cease. The town's population diminished—not from casualties so much as from terror, bankruptcies, arson, despair. As the nation's other racial war zones cooled—Watts, Detroit, Newark—forty-two hundred Cairo whites faced off against thirty-eight hundred Cairo blacks in a town built for a population of twenty thousand.

In time, the Reverend Charles Koen and the United Front organized a boycott of white businesses that gutted the town's economy. The main function of civic life in Cairo became the shooting. Eventually the shooting involved automatic weapons of the type used in Vietnam. Witnesses recall tracer rounds. Squads of young black men went sniping in Army combat fatigues; their siblings and children huddled in cast-iron bathtubs as protection against a slumberland bullet. The governor sent in National Guard troops, an armored truck. The shooting went on; nearly two hundred episodes over four years. There was burning, too. Storefronts, houses, glowed in the night; only their husks were left standing.

And there were more intimate expressions of the rage. A local white Baptist minister, Rev. Larry Potts, gained brief national attention for his Old Testament response to sin. One January afternoon the reverend took a baseball bat and caved in the skull of a seventy-two-year-old black gardener named Marshall Morris. Potts explained to the authorities that he had beheld Morris sexually attacking Mrs. Potts. The state's attorney, a seventy-five-year-old lion of Cairo society and founder of the White Hats by the name of Peyton Berbling, was shocked by the gardener's wantonness and ruled the slaughter a justifiable homicide; no indictments. Rev. Larry Potts and Mrs. Potts were hospitalized for a week after the incident. They were later divorced.

Incredibly, Cairo suffered only about a dozen casualties in all—half of them fatal, one death self-inflicted, nearly all of the victims black. In its rage and despair, the black community split into factions: Rev. Charles Koen, vilified by whites, became a pariah to many blacks, a presumed cynic and profiteer. He went on a hunger fast of forty-eight days that nearly killed him, and eventually receded in visibility; he became a shadowy presence in the town. Visiting journalists called Cairo a war zone, a madhouse, America's Vietnam. Finally, in the early 1970s—with the economy prostrate, the middle-class gone, most of the town's commercial district burned to the ground or gutted—the shooting faded into silence.

This was the recent history of the town I was approaching, the town that dealt harshly with cigarette bootleggers.

And yet curiously, perversely, Cairo clung to its old obsession of El Dorado: to the boosters' assurances of natural resources, natural assets; to its deep anemic superstition, crazed and lucid as any belief in astrology or ESP, that it would one day rise up and present these assets to redeem its destiny and take its place among the necessary cities of the world.

And now an old man had come to tell the people that the time to claim their destiny was at hand. An old man named Poston, a professor of some sort. A man with theories about the incantatory power of town meetings. I wanted to meet this Poston, and learn something of his theories, before he was shot, hanged, burned, beaten or otherwise made familiar with the nuances of the local community temperament.

It was Poston who had secured a room for me in the truckstop motel on the northern side of Cairo—the one room with a commode big enough to stand up in, he had assured me on the telephone—and who had agreed to meet me there on this March evening. But to get there I had to survive the drive through the length of town.

A Nabisco warehouse on the left, falsely reassuring; how evil could a town be if it housed graham crackers? A population sign, outdated and overstating, on the right: 6300. And then the town.

Cairo was barely visible above its own tree lines. The town seemed to have sunk down into the silt below its foundations. I had expected a tight little suffocation of tank-town architecture, however vacant, but here was a tabletop of building blocks swept level by a child's arm. A couple of distant church steeples gave the only evidence of skyline.

Route 51 widened into a grand boulevard, a straight line to the horizon called Washington Street, whose lack of traffic exaggerated its surplus width, and whose width further reduced the dazed and peeling little buildings on either side.

To the right there was a cinderblock liquor store; a CITY MOTEL FREE TV, the white lettering nearly vanished into the bleached blue marquee; and a desperate little capsule of 1950s aluminum and plate-glass called the Nu-Diner, Famous for Steaks and Farm-Fed Fresh Catfish. To the left, a few wooden shanties yawed forward on stilts. I drove several blocks, past the buildings with half their roofs burned away, past shattered windowglass on the sidewalks.

I turned right on Eighth Street, toward the Ohio River.

Here lay the shell of Cairo's old center, the remnants of a downtown life that had last flared in the drugstore years after the Second World War. A gorgeous plumed canopy of beryl blue in the middle of the block caught my eye. It cascaded down across two stories of a three-story brick storefront, and the custardy white lettering proclaimed THE GEM. This would be the movie house, the picture show; and indeed the place seemed to have cast its aura of good times across the entire block. Looking around, I saw a chipped red-and-white Elks Club marquee, the remains of Lee's Coffee Shop and Lounge; a jewelry store; a flower shop; a Hair and Body Works; even a prescription drugstore that still seemed to be in business.

But the Gem had died, and from the evidence, it had not been a stately death. The marquee beneath the vertical plume, in identical white lettering on beryl blue, read: GEM VIDEO. Below that were chained doors.

What I had not seen in town, it suddenly struck me, were people. A few cars, a figure on a shanty stoop, but no hint of what I had dreaded on the way in: locals, denizens, a population to stare at the outsider with the silent authority of citizenship. The absence of scrutinizing faces now seemed more eerie than their presence would have been.

I drove the rest of the way east on Eighth Street, to the corner where it joined Commercial Avenue. Eighth and Commercial. I looked at the desolate intersection and recalled something I'd read about from Cairo's history. A man had been lynched here once. A black man, in 1909. The details were ironic and gruesome. The man had been accused of strangling a white woman. Fleeing the town, he'd been tracked down with bloodhounds. A sheriff had escorted him out of Cairo on a train to spare him a lynching, but the accused man had leapt from the train, the sheriff on his heels, and made a run for it on foot. This turned out to be a regrettable impulse. He ran into the arms of the very mob he had nearly escaped. A history of Cairo published the following year recorded the consequences: "They . . . brought him to Cairo and to the intersection of Commercial Avenue and Eighth Street, and there, after trying to hang him to the steel arches spanning the intersection of those streets and finding it slow and difficult work, they shot him to death, and then dragged the body to the place of the crime, a mile distant, and there burned it."

The decorative steel arches were gone now. A sign on a storefront door at the corner read: UNITED FRONT LEGAL SERVICES. A little pocket of the living past. I could not resist stopping to peer through the window. Rev. Charles Koen did not seem to be in. On the far side of Commercial stood the gutted remains of a three-story masonry building, an old bank from the looks of it. An orange cat flickered from the collapsed plywood window boards and darted into the dark carcass of the building next door.

I let my gaze trail northward and took in a baleful sight. I was looking at the spine of a great dead thing, a broken but recognizable skeleton that stretched parallel to the Ohio River for a dozen blocks. This was Commercial Avenue as it remained from the previous century. Not one building in the ranks could have been erected later than the immediate post–Civil War period. Now the avenue formed its own sarcophagus, an unconscious shrine to Cairo's mercantile zenith: brittle hulls of warehouses, balconied hotels, saloons, storefronts, the dangling remnants of iron lace and figured cornices, the friezes and the woodworking worn nearly smooth by weather.

The twentieth century had denied Cairo the means of bulldozing

this architectural fossil. Preserved by poverty, it had grown decrepit by stages. The hotels had turned into whorehouses, tapping
a high-volume market of barge pilots and duck hunters. The storefronts were converted into gambling joints and honky-tonks. For
a time it seemed that Cairo might fulfill its economic destiny after
all. But then a new kind of blight descended, called civic reform.
The pleasure houses closed down. The burnings of the 1970s took
their toll. On one of the few intact windowpanes some vanished
hippie had painted a "Peace" sign and four hands stretching into the
center. Next door another sign, possibly ironic, suggested, SHOP
CAIRO STORES.

A kind of anthill commerce seemed, incredibly to sustain itself
in the bowels of a few of these buildings: a cable-vision office; a
bowling alley; an exchange store, one third of which had been
blackened in a bygone fire (electrical wiring hung from the ceiling
like entrails).

And still I saw no people. The town felt evacuated. The silence
was galactic, and the United States of America seemed a long way
away.

On a storefront, with utterly nothing behind it, was a message
elegantly stenciled in black paint on a white surface:

HOLY GHOST BARBER SHOP

Darkness was settling on the town. I decided it was time to find
Richard Poston.

In the pinewood office of Glen's Mid-America Motel I overheard
my first conversation among Cairo citizens. Two members of the
service staff, identical squat women with vast rippling hips, were
in the process of resigning, possibly to form a tag wrestling team.
"I'll rip your motherfucking mouth out," one of them was explaining to the desk clerk as I entered.

My presence had the startling effect of triggering institutional
grins from everyone. "May I help you?" the desk clerk asked; he was
a thin man with badly stained teeth, which lent a macabre note of
dental plausibility to the woman's threat.

I thought of Renfield entering Castle Dracula. "I'm just passing
through," I blurted before I could stop myself; my garment bag was
a dead giveaway. I grinned, too, to show what a kidder I was, and
the four of us stood there grinning at one another for a few ambiguous moments. Then I hurriedly checked in.

The terms were payment in advance, all phone calls collect. Glen's Mid-America was a two-story barracks of saliva-colored brick that looked solid enough to withstand a tactical nuclear exchange. It hunkered half a mile from an interstate in the middle of what might once have been a field, now it was loose gravel and mudholes. The place was half filled, judging from the number of eighteen-wheel rigs outside. Between the office and the motel out back was a small swimming pool. I counted nine tubeless thick-tread tires floating on the surface, and I tried to imagine them as vacationland props, each supporting a sun-lotioned trucker, sipping a Budweiser and scanning the latest edition of *Guns and Ammo*.

I was pleased enough with my room—pleased that I could indeed stand upright in the commode, pleased that the odor of vomit in the corridor did not buckle my knees once the door was closed. I hooked my bag on the clothes bar and stuffed my tape recorder deep inside the pocket of my outer jacket. When I returned to the motel office, Richard Poston was outside, leaning against the door of his car.

"I go around with this music all the time," Poston told me as I got in, indicating the noise thumping from his dashboard cassette deck—a John Philip Sousa march. "It gives me a little pep. I still go in for the Glenn Miller stuff, though. I guess I'm kind of old-fashioned, Ron." We lurched over potholes in his old four-door sedan, headed for the motel's all-night truckstop coffee shop, a free-standing bungalow about a hundred yards across no-man's-land.

At seventy-three, he looked as old-fashioned as Carl Sandburg: a slight gray-haired man with a thin, deeply lined face. His black eyes were set close together under a wild tangle of brows. They seemed to rake in anyone in their sight. He was smaller, more sucked-in and more fierce than I had anticipated. The dust jacket photograph on a book of his that he'd sent me showed a jowly, complacent-looking academic. But that photograph was twenty years old. Something besides age had happened to Richard Poston in those years. Hunched forward at the wheel, puffing sparks from a filter cigarette, he seemed to have pared himself down for something; jettisoned the nonessentials; trimmed himself for action.

His wardrobe fascinated me, and would continue to fascinate me as I saw it in all its careful combinations. He was always spruced up. On this evening he wore a burgundy cardigan sweater with navy trim; a blue dress shirt and tie; pressed gray slacks and gray suede lace shoes. This careful coordination of color and cloth must have turned a few heads (and curled a few lips) in Cairo. But if Poston's clothes weren't current, neither were they conspicuously out of date. I could not place them in time. The tie and the belt were of a thinness that recalled the early 1960s, but on Poston, they seemed freshly unwrapped. Scarcely an hour in Cairo, I was already feeling the traces of a time warp; this clothing enigma of Poston's pushed me a little further out of time.

But he was more than some natty crackpot, some moonstruck prophet off the road to bawl his visions into a handy catatonic town. I had not yet learned much about Richard Poston, but I knew this: in a little more than a year of extended visits to Cairo, he had managed to coax white and black citizens into the same room to talk about their poisonous differences. He had accomplished this without the aid of a sidearm. More than that, he had organized some of these antagonists into a committee, equipped them with a rakish title—"Operation Enterprise"—and sent them on a mission to recover a weed-choked, refuse-strewn thicket known officially as Fort Defiance State Park. This historic wedge of land, south of town, formed the precise tip of Illinois, where the rivers joined. In the 1860s it had been the site of the encampment for Ulysses S. Grant's army, the launching point of the Vicksburg Campaign.

The park cleanup had been a famous success. There was not a single casualty. A National Guard unit was called in, but to wield chain saws instead of tear-gas grenades. Within hours of a spring morning, General Grant's old tenting ground had been raked clean of its rotted trash and its beer bottles and its spent prophylactics; its driftwood had been burned, its weedy jungle mowed down to the tolerances of lawn, and the five hundred black and white Cairo volunteers stood contemplating what now lay at their feet: a park. A veneer of public grace. In the very mundaneness of a city green, Cairo had reforged a link with the century and the culture. This crucible of American decay and self-annihilation now had a place where people could go for picnics. And Richard Poston had a constituency.

I had noted his public-relations-man's way of inserting my first name into his sentences. Now, as we settled into a booth at the coffee shop, a place so hard up that the plastic menu covers bore the name of another town, he used the same trick on the glassy-eyed waitress, and the woman dimpled and almost curtsied. I declined the special of the day—calves' brains—in favor of a cup of coffee, and complimented Poston on his touch with the ladies.

His gray face flinched in what I took to be a highly economical smile. Richard Poston darted his narrow black eyes at me and delivered an astonishing speech.

"My relationship with this town now, Ron—I'd call it a mass love affair. It's intimate. Businesspeople open their books to me. Women tell me about their problems with their husbands. Husbands tell me about their problems with their wives. I walk into a meeting, it's not unusual at all for three or four women to come kiss me on the cheek."

All this might have been a little hard to take had it not been for the peculiar detachment I sensed in Poston's delivery. He was not conversing, he was orating; it had the whiff of rehearsal, like his clothing. I was to learn that spontaneity was not something that one could expect in Poston; he inventoried his ideas and kept them carefully sorted in his mind, like cassette tapes. And yet he was never oblivious of the moment. The set speeches were his way of organizing a prodigious storehouse of knowledge about Cairo and its people. Richard Poston had mentally inventoried the town.

He was a research professor emeritus in a field of study called community development, a field largely improvised nearly half a century before, as a consequence of a Rockefeller Foundation project, the "Montana Study." His pursuit of this discipline, a blend of intense local fact-finding and diagnostic intervention in the life of a town, had centered mainly in the Pacific Northwest.

He had happened on this arcane field after a career that spanned counterintelligence in the Second World War and forestry in Montana. In 1953 he arrived at Southern Illinois University in Carbondale, about sixty miles north of Cairo, and created a community development field service there. "I saw it by this time as a function that every university in the country should perform," he said, his voice rising a little. "If this were done by every university in the United States, Ron, we could *change the face of America!*"

As the years went on, Poston was allowed time to travel the world as a consultant for such programs as CARE. He kept his affiliation with the university until his retirement in 1974.

But a little more than a year ago, Richard Poston had been coaxed out of his retirement. A new university president wanted to reactivate the old field service, which had fallen into neglect. "I recommended to them," Poston said, "that instead of looking into several towns, we start with just one town, that we could maybe build into a new model—or help the people build into a new model," he amended, heedful of his own dogma.

One of his first applicants was an Illinois state senator named Glenn Poshard, who had begun to fear that Cairo's many lingering afflictions were finally about to extinguish the town. Poston agreed to take Cairo on as his model project.

Now Poston was talking about that model's afflictions as they flowed, or bled, from the shooting years of the 1970s.

"The arson, the property damage, the bankruptcies—all this is awful enough," he was saying. "But the more long-lasting damage, and what was even worse in some respects, Ron, were the mental scars. And these are very deep, festering psychological scars that have given this town a sense of utter defeat. Absolute hopelessness.

"When I came here, that's all I could hear from people all over town. Everywhere I went, in restaurants, on street corners, no matter who I talked to, it was—'You're wasting your time. It's impossible. Nothing can be done. Cairo's gone, it can't come back.' And the blanket of defeatism—it was awful, Ron. I mean awful."

Poston lighted another cigarette—he chain-smoked a brand called Now—and I took the moment to glance around the coffee shop. A black busboy bumped through a pair of swinging doors. The two or three other customers wore seed caps, overalls—garb as timeless as Poston's cardigan. Under one cap curled unwashed shoulder-length hair. Black militants and hippies. I recalled the titles I'd glimpsed on the audiocassettes for sale on the cashier's counter as we'd walked in: "Black Sabbath," "Gene Autry."

Like Poston, Cairo seemed to have been skipped by a decade or two. And now Poston was talking again, drawing me farther back in time.

"What we have out here is a 'republican' form of government," he was declaring. "Where somebody *represents* the people and they decide *for* the people. Well, but the thing I'm trying to incorporate into this community development format that we're workin' on is, in effect, *your old New England town meeting*. Because I want everything we do to be determined by the people at large. They come to the town meetings and they vote." Poston leaned toward me. "The only difference between these town meetings and the old town meetings, the American town meeting of New England, is that we break into these discussion groups, which they didn't do in those days."

I asked Poston exactly what it was he intended to accomplish with his town meetings in Cairo.

"My job, Ron," he said, eyeing me through cigarette smoke, "is to work myself out of a job." Once again, I had the feeling that I was the beneficiary of a set speech, perhaps to an imaginary crowd of which I was a part. "I don't look upon what I'm doing here as a public service—I look on it as a *genuine educational enterprise* in which you get the population of a whole town educated about itself and what it can accomplish for itself. This is what I see, Ron, as *one of the purest forms of old-fashioned American democracy.*" The imaginary crowd burst into applause, and Poston waited until it had died down. "And that can only be preserved in the small town," he went on after a moment. "You use the term, 'town,' I use the term, 'democracy,' we're talking about the same thing."

"But in practice," I prodded gently from deep in the audience, "what does that mean?"

Poston's eyes got crafty over his coffee cup. "I've often compared this type of work," he said in a lowered voice, "to the relationship between a patient and a psychiatrist. Now, I've devised a lot of action projects for these people who come to my meetings. But in the end the action projects, in themselves, don't mean anything. What counts is the *inter*action among the people; and it's up to me, as the psychiatrist, to get that interaction going.

"When a patient goes through analysis, at first there's sort of a stand-offishness between the patient and the psychiatrist. The analyst's trying to get inside the patient and the patient doesn't want to let him. And that was the case with me here in Cairo. I had to get accepted.

"Gradually we go past that, and the town bares everything. As a patient does to a psychiatrist. You've told your innermost secrets. You've laid all your dirty linen out. The guy knows everything there is to know about you. That's what I mean when I say my relationship with the town right now is a mass love affair.

"So, anyway, this is gonna evolve to a point where there becomes a state of dependency, where they're dependent on me. They feel that they can't get along without me. My job then will be to work myself out of a job. I've got to wean them. I've got to build this town into a *self-determining, self-sufficient unit.* That's my job."

Again, respectful applause from the imaginary crowd. In my mind, they—we—had somehow become an audience from the past, from the New Frontier; spruced-up people in yearbook haircuts, the men in dapper little thin ties. Asking not what our country could do for us. Already I was beginning to pick up in Richard Poston's cadences, his syntax, a subtle analogue to the vintage of his clothing. His rhetoric was an artifact, as perfect in its representation of another age as an old newspaper or the marquee of a picture show.

It contained an innocence that I found attractive but also disturbing. Doc Poston was bringing his old-time religion to a town drowning in its past. The armed combatants of fifteen years ago had not gone away; they were still around. Some of them occupied positions of power, and power in a small southern town did not always respond to cries for democracy in America.

What would happen when Doc Poston's grass-roots crusade for a resurgent Cairo—a crusade that implied its own power base—scraped up against the vested interests that lay half-submerged, like the town skyline? What resources would this old man draw upon when the town started to close on him?

I was about to get some notion of Poston's ability to deal with those unsentimental prospects. He had arranged for us to have dinner with a man who was once a leading firebrand of the White Hats—and who was currently the mayor of Cairo.

It was dark when we parked on the street near Harper's Restaurant, where Al Moss was waiting for us. Harper's was an island of bright lights and cosmopolitan finesse in a sea of flatness, closed-down filling stations and franchise-food logos so faded they seemed to have lost blood. Inside was an unexpected treasure: a curving art deco bar of teakwood and mahogany that dated from 1935. The barstools were empty; all the patrons sat at small white-clothed tables under gigantic wall photographs of Cairo's forgotten duck hunters, depicted frozen in various attitudes of shotgun ecstasy, baring their teeth as they snatched high their prey.

There exists a photograph of Allen E. Moss on the hunt, but his quarry is not ducks. It is not on display at Harper's. The photograph was made by a news cameraman sometime in the early 1970s. It shows a chubby Moss on Commercial Avenue, splayfooted, his arm drawn back, a thick object in his hand. He is cocked to throw. His target is a line of black demonstrators from the United Front. His comrades, arrayed beside him, are the White Hats.

Al Moss, child of Cairo, was a high commando in the White Hats, and a political protégé of the group's founder, the attorney Peyton Berbling. After the group was disbanded by the governor's order,

Moss was elected to the city council. He was appointed commissioner of public health and safety. In the course of testimony before the U.S. Commission on Civil Rights, which came to Cairo for hearings in March 1972, Commissioner Moss was asked by the general counsel whether there was, in the city of Cairo, a building code. Moss's reply was enshrined in the public record:

"There must be, sir. As I explained when I first sat down at this table, I do not make that my specialty. I'll be glad to research the subject if you'd like a complete detail on it."

Al Moss was standing to greet us at our table, his small feet pressed together. In his mid-fifties now, and in his fourth term as mayor, he looked like what he was, an aging altar boy who has done well. His grooming and dress announced his pure-vanilla citizenship: his suit was sensible to the point of rebuke and quivering with synthetic fibers and service-club pins; his striped tie in gunmetal tones was bolted deeply into his throat. His silver pompadour, which called to mind the swirl on a Dairy Queen ice-cream cone, bore the treadmarks of a recent combing.

I stared at Moss—I couldn't help it—and waited for him to stare back, to unleash the hard insider scrutiny I had been expecting since I crossed the Kentucky-Illinois line. I didn't imagine that writers from the East were Al Moss's top choice for dinner partners. But the mayor was not making eye contact. He kept his blue-eyed gaze slightly above me and to my right during Doc Poston's introductions, as if he were trying to identify one of the duck hunters on the wall. The pose gave him a pious look; I half expected him to lift a hymnal and begin singing the first, second and last verse of some mighty Republican anthem. I suspected he had numbed himself to this encounter, and for the first time I began to sense that Richard Poston was an arm-twister of some talent.

We took refuge in our menus. Harper's proved to be a basic prairie small-town eatery: steak, chicken and Mandarin Chinese. I was personally inclined to try something safe and top-sirloiny, but Moss pointed with civic pride to the Chinese section of the menu. He said it had been one of Cairo's chief attractions for many years. I said I had no doubt that was so. We all ordered heaping canisters of iridescent orange-and-yellow-colored food soaking in dark pools of monosodium glutamate, served up by grandmotherly occidentals in crepe-soled shoes. This being Cairo, there were no fortune cookies.

Mayor Moss and I spent the meal crashing heavily around one

another, striking a series of self-flattering poses. Moss was the homespun public servant, the former newspaper boy abashed by his high office but sworn to do right by the people who put him there. "Hell," he told me with a nudge, gazing over my shoulder, "I haven't got any secrets. I learned a long time ago: if you got half of 'em chasing ya, half of 'em following ya, you're lucky. The trick is to stay out in front and make it look like you're leadin' 'em all." I leaned back in my chair and let out a hearty guffaw over that one, a friendly reporter who wouldn't think of asking about Negroes. Across from this mutual audition, Doc Poston leaned forward on his elbows, his red lids turning his eyes to sleepy slits, a deceptive lizard, taking it in.

The check arrived, the mayor said our credit cards weren't any good here, and I began thinking of what sleep might be like at Glen's Mid-America; would I have to count truckers floating by on treaded tires? But Al Moss had a suggestion. He would take us on a tour of the town in his car. The offer startled me. Moss's ordeal of hospitality was over; from every indication at the table, he would have been only too thankful to escape this company of outsiders and vamoose into the night.

But something quite the opposite happened. Belted behind the wheel of his silvery late-model sedan, Al Moss became a changed man. He flipped on the ignition switch and the dashboard panels blazed alive with lights—red warning lights, green winking lights, yellow glowing lights, digital flashers; the lights of dials, gauges, indicators, factory options. Al Moss had the biggest dashboard I had ever seen. The colored lights of his panels cast their green and red glow on his face, his suit, his pompadour, and suddenly Al Moss was in charge, the ruler of the universe.

With Doc Poston in the backseat and me beside Moss, riding shotgun, as it were, we glided through the dark ruined streets of Cairo. The houses and buildings had lost their distinct shapes in the night, and upon this black canvas Al Moss began to paint the town, paint it in the colors known only to the people who lived there, the insiders, the dreamers of El Dorado.

We drove along Commercial Avenue, which Moss pointed out was wide enough that you could turn a team of horses around in it. Time slipped away. Moss took us along the sycamore-shaded streets of his paper route; he pointed to the long trains heading north out of town on the Illinois Central, trains filled with Cairo men, soldiers bound for Europe and the legions of Eisenhower. We crossed the Mississippi bridge into Missouri and made a wide arc on a flatland interstate from where we could look back at the town, all but lost on the horizon, just a few lights glowing like embers to mark its mass.

The dashboard panels flickered, and the ribbons of light painted Moss's face. Doc Poston was forgotten in the backseat. "We have so many natural assets here," Moss was saying. "The two waterways. *So* many natural assets." The sky was the limit, the nighttime sky, and there was suddenly no legacy of hopelessness or evil, no Negroes, only the unchanging present, as perfect and as powerful as the American dashboard that now pointed us back to Cairo.

Chapter II

Not many weeks before my introduction to Doc Poston and Mayor Moss in southern Illinois, my wife and I attended a small dinner party in an early nineteenth-century farmhouse a few winding miles north on U.S. Route 7 from the village of Kent, in northwestern Connecticut, where we had kept a small house for several years.

The occasion was our introduction, long deferred, into the town's social life. Our peerage in Kent—population 2640—rested mainly on paper: deeds of property, tax rolls. We were weekenders—an increasing, and increasingly dubious, nomadic tribe at the fringes of this 250-year-old hamlet's shifting ecology. (Kent was incorporated in 1738, nearly fifty years before the ratification of the U.S. Constitution.) Like most of our immediate neighbors on a rural blacktop road south of town, we pounded up weekly in an eighty-mile stream of traffic from New York. Disembarked, pulsating, from our cars, grateful for the temporary release from subway atrocity and panic-button burglar alarms, we lugged sacks of clothing and groceries into our redoubts. Then we set about to claim for a few hours within these rounded Berkshire foothills a trace of what must be a kind of American tribal memory: fields and rivers; of the color and scent of agriculture; of openness and stillness; of freedom of movement for children; of the progress of a day as measured by the changing qualities of light rather than by wristwatches and electronic warnings; of the profundity of country night as opposed to the vaporlit menace of urban darkness. A unity with older cycles and seasons. Our timetables read forty-eight hours and counting.

We had purchased our house, a white-frame modified Cape that nestled into a gently sloping forested hill four miles south of Kent, in the early spring of 1983. A pair of whitetail deer had long-legged it out of the woods and across the macadamized driveway below us on the March afternoon we closed the deal. Their visitation had seemed a happy promise to us. If nothing else, this glimpse of brown wildlife had helped mollify our displeasure at having to bid against a rival buyer to the full list price of the house.

Without fully comprehending it, we had joined a New England land-rush boom that by the decade's end would project many of the region's old colonial towns and communities into the suburbanized heart of middle-class, late-twentieth-century life. A great deal of this projection had already happened, in Maine and New Hampshire and Vermont and in other reaches of Connecticut. Kent—owing partly to its isolation from interstate arterial routes out of New York—had thus far been shielded from the process. We had arrived as part of the wave that would offer Kent its turn.

All we knew then was that this place would offer us and our small son—Dean was then a little more than a year old—some sanctuary from our fortressed lives on the Upper West Side of Manhattan.

Our newly bought weekend house was perhaps thirty years old. A small but comfortable white woodframe, it sat on a wooded hillside above a two-lane road. Our hill rose past a flower garden on one side of the house and a fenced vegetable garden on the other. A small sun porch faced a trim back lawn bordered by woods and shaded by a gigantic old oak tree. On clear nights the rural sky burst with stars; bugs with veined wings beat against the picture window; and in wet summer nights we could lie in the sun porch and smell the rain.

Between the house and the road below, an acre of sapling trees and underbrush gave us an illusion, not entirely false, of woodsy isolation. The campus of the South Kent School, a small private prep school, covered several hundred acres on the far side of the road. Across from us was a meadow that served as the school's lacrosse and football field. I could walk my young son, and later his younger brother, Kevin down our driveway to watch afternoon football games in the fall, dreamy intimate games that seemed as suspended in time as the land on which they were played. There were no stands of any kind—spectators and dogs drifted up and down the sidelines with the action—and framing the gridders were the hills, fir and spruce trees, a lake beyond the meadow and, between the field and the main road, the mid-nineteenth-century frame residence of Bernie, an unreconstructed hippie and the school's baker, who kept a goat pen at the rear of the house, not far from the fifty-yard line.

That goat pen became, at least for our sons, the central experience of our weekends in South Kent. Bernie kept it stocked with life—furred, horned, feathered. Dean and Kevin could always count on a couple of goats to feed handfuls of grass to, and a sheep, and sometimes a lamb or two. From time to time there were geese, a disputatious bantam rooster, even a Shetland pony. Cats and kittens roamed the premises and allowed themselves to dangle, warm and humming, from my sons' arms. Just as Kent was for my wife and me a microcosm of a nearly vanished America, the goat pen was for the boys a little citadel of the sort of childhood they could not even know was practically extinct.

We came to understand that history formed a kind of living atmosphere here. It hovered like a pocket of quiescent air upon us. It lived in the names of roads and ponds and mountains that were the names of first-settling families—Skiff, Geer, Stone, Hatch, Bull, Swift, Pratt. History lived in the town clerk's office, where maps and property deeds and minutes of town meetings dating to the eighteenth century were bound and filed, without ostentation, alongside those of the present. It lived in the outdated, nearly useless, sometimes abandoned buildings that the town accommodated, like so many great-aunts and great-uncles, in their doddering dignity: a swallow-infested community house, a converted railroad depot, a quixotic empty lumberyard smack in the middle of Main Street. It lived in the Historical Society and in the Grange and in the myriad histories preserved in the minds of the town's elders. It lived on a plaque affixed to an ancient oak tree south of town:

UNDER THIS TREE
GENERAL GEORGE WASHINGTON
HELD COUNCIL WITH HIS STAFF
SEPT. 20, 1780

Implicit for many of us jaundiced city-dwellers in these sensory longings, but not so easy to express (or fulfill), was the wish to rebuild some kind of lost affection for our fellow man, some affirmation of community. In this wish, as in no other, the week-ender's paradox—isolation within the small hive—was revealed.

The town wanted more than affection and affirmation. In the opaqueness of a teenaged checkout clerk at the Kent Market (making change for a copy of *The New York Times*), beneath the calibrated good cheer of a service station attendant (glancing at the license plates), lay an aura of the withheld. Weekenders brought in money, yes. But they brought in something else, something less welcome. They brought in a voyeur's stare; they had a way of turning the authentic and the necessary (checking the oil, ringing up change) into a sort of performance. It was all in their goofy grateful grins; it was all in their clothes, which were a little overwrought; a little too Banana Republic for town requirements. And it was all in the way the weekenders never got involved in anything, never joined any of the organizations, never took responsibility. In that detachment, however unavoidable, the weekenders transformed the real business of town life—the obligations and the services, the Memorial Day parade—into a pageant, an ongoing operetta. A lot of the townspeople resented that, especially the teenagers, who didn't necessarily think all that much of the operetta in the first place.

And so the weekenders were left with their goofy grins, holding their *Times*es and their change, wondering why the kid behind the counter had never bothered to learn their first names.

But none of those tensions permeated this February evening. The night was cold and cloudless, and in the few minutes before we were due at our hostess's door, my wife and I found a small dirt road that took us up and beyond her yellow-lighted farmhouse to the crest of a hill. There we watched a cadmium moon work its way up above the dark palisades on the far side of the Housatonic River. It was easy to believe, just then, that we belonged here, in this rational and timeless winterscape.

Our hostess, Carol Hoffman, was a warm and gracious townswoman who managed without noticeable effort to float at the center of town life—quietly indispensable to its web of obligations and ceremonies. Like many of the town's leading citizens, Carol Hoffman was technically an outsider herself. She had arrived in Kent several years before with her husband John and their three daughters to establish the Kent House of Books—first in their farmhouse and later, as inventory expanded, in an old two-storied, white-frame building on Main Street that had served variously as the town hall, a filling station, the post office, an ice-cream parlor and a store that sold coffins.

John Hoffman had been a gentleman bookseller in the old tradition. Jug-eared and rotund, with a mild but speculative gaze, he was a lover of and teacher of literature; a scholar-proprietor whose stock reflected his tastes and standards and not the transitory whims of blockbuster marketing. After John collapsed and died of a heart attack on a Kent tennis court in 1984, Carol Hoffman gathered herself—with the help of her daughter Kathy—to the task not only of continuing the House of Books, but of continuing it according to the standards her husband had valued: the American and English classics; good contemporary literature (including a John McPhee Shrine); plenty of children's books; and at least one or two scrupulously displayed copies of the works of every local writer, no matter how long the works might have been out of print or how tempting the display space might seem for more salable merchandise.

Seated now at Carol Hoffman's dining table, sipping a crisp white cabernet and tucking into an elegantly sauced breast of chicken, my wife and I became aware that we were in the midst of a fair microcosm of Kent town life, as it had begun to redefine itself midway through its third century.

No one in our small group had been born in the town. On the other hand, all, except for my wife and me, were now permanent residents. All had reached middle age. All were white; most were mildly to the left of center politically; all were professionals. The company included Donald Connery, a former foreign correspondent for Time magazine, and his wife, Leslie, a teacher. There were also a real estate executive and his wife, a former dancer and now a photographer; a teacher at one of Kent's two private schools; an oil company executive. All of us felt an intense and proprietary fascination for the community. Donald Connery had published an elegiac book about the town and its cycles some twenty years before; Leslie, a hearty and quick-witted woman, was a leading member of the local volunteer fire and ambulance department— she made a joking point of showing everyone the electronic beeper attached to the waistband of her skirt.

And all were preoccupied, with varying degrees of concern, by the evening's main topic: the process of escalating and potentially transfiguring change that was well under way in the small town—a process in which each person at the table, ironically, had played part.

The 1980s had brought a wave of real estate trading and speculation to rural New England. The activity reached into towns and villages that had considered themselves immune (or, in the case of de-industrialized mill towns in Massachusetts and New Hampshire, hopelessly inaccessible) to the rapid infusion of new capital, new shopping concerns, new house-building—in a word, development.

Modernizing change was not, in itself, a novelty in New England. The process of administering touristy "quaintness" had been going on in certain Maine fishing villages and Vermont skiing towns since the early post–World War II years; and in northwest Connecticut, a steady trickle of writers, artists, movie actors and TV/advertising aesthetes had been finding its way into the hills and hollows for at least that long. (Fredric March was one of the first Hollywood stars to discover the seclusion of northwestern Connecticut; James Cagney would hotfoot it across the continent to his rural New York State retreat, just a few dozen miles to the west, on completion of every film.)

In the mid-1960s the Green Mountains of Vermont and the White Mountains of New Hampshire began to absorb another, equally colorful, sort of subculture, or sub-counterculture: hippies, rock musicians, urban and collegiate dropouts, who settled into communes and sent their amplified Grateful Dead sounds twanging into the deep pine forests and the ungrateful Yankee farmhouses for miles around. Many of these cultural refugees remained on into middle age, spawning families of their own and creating remarkably stable, if remote, communities rich in arts, crafts and intellectual ferment.

But none of these tinkerings and leisurely migrations even began to prefigure the sudden incursion of massive urban wealth into the original Colonies at the dawn of the Reagan administration.

Suddenly, coastal fishermen who had figured the worth of their houses at $25,000 were flabbergasted to receive offers of six times that figure. Rural farmers, whose parents or grandparents might have paid $600 for a family cabin a generation ago, were selling those cabins for $100,000. Waterfront houses on islands off the Maine coast were going for half a million—the cost of a Manhattan condominium. Middle-class houses in central Connecticut towns that sold for $20,000 two decades ago were being listed at $600,000.

In the historic western Connecticut town of Litchfield, settled in 1719, a real estate firm recorded, in 1985, the highest price ever paid for a house there: $440,000 for a colonial estate on two acres. Two years later, within six weeks of one another, two houses near the town center sold for $1 million each. The least expensive house in Litchfield was listed at $127,000.

"Growth surge" became a term of common use to describe towns in the process of doubling or tripling their size. And drivers on rural access blacktops began to experience a new kind of traffic phenomenon: gridlock, flanked by cornfields.

Journalists in the region began to notice this onslaught of what New Englanders called, with curt understatement, "fresh money." And they began to brood on some of the darker consequences that "fresh money" might imply for deeply rooted local people who were, putatively, its beneficiaries. A columnist for the *Litchfield County Times* portrayed the process in the Puritan tradition of the cautionary tale.

"I keep thinking," he wrote, "of a little old lady in one quiet neighborhood. All about her were nice old homes. Then one day developers got their claws on it and tore it down. Others followed. Then she was offered big bucks for her own lovely old house with its high ceilings, marble mantel, and conch shells.

"She stoutly refused. 'I was born here. I love it. I want to die here,' she said. Then suddenly her taxes exploded sky-high. Tall new buildings around here, she was told, 'are making your property more valuable.'

"And suddenly her own swollen tax bill forced her out. She surrendered her house to rent-payers. Last we knew she was living in a tiny back room, in her daughter's house, miles away."

Writing in the *Boston Globe Magazine*, reporter Peter Anderson struck a similar note regarding the illusory benefits of fresh money: "When a fisherman's $25,000 house suddenly becomes worth $150,000, no one blames him when he sells and moves inland to a trailer. But real estate inflation makes it difficult for a young fisherman to stay and difficult for the retired fisherman to pay his property tax. At this rate, those of the old money and those of the fresh money will own the [Maine] coast, all the pretty parts of it, all the way to Calais. Nothing can stop it short of an invasion by the Khmer Rouge."

Anderson recapitulated the rising price of some prime Maine

shorefront property over twenty-five years: $10 a front foot in 1960; to $12 and $15 in the early sixties; then increasing by $10 a foot a year to $40 and $50 and—by the mid-seventies—to $200. A decade later that price had doubled. By 1986 the price stood at $500 a foot; one year later it had doubled again, to $1000—a hundredfold increase in one generation.

Meanwhile, reported Anderson, the number of dairy farms in Vermont had fallen from four thousand ten years ago to twenty-seven hundred in 1987. "Farming," he wrote, "is an old industry, as are fishing and logging, and the old industries are less a part of the New England landscape than they once were. The industries that thrive are insurance, banking, and real estate."

And speculation. Edie Clark, a senior editor at the traditionally affable and boosterish *Yankee* magazine, compiled a withering series of articles dissecting the voracious land-brokering by such fast-rising firms as the Patten Corporation. Formed in the late 1960s by a former vacuum-cleaner salesman, Patten opened its first regional office in Maine in 1982. Within a few years the company had become the largest marketer of undeveloped land in the Northeast.

Patten's formula—a formula generally followed by the dozen or so other speculators operating in New England—was simple and remorseless. The firm would target a town so small and so remote that its boards of selectmen had never thought it necessary to enact a master zoning plan. Unobtrusively, the company would buy, at bargain rates, large tracts of woodland or lakefront acreage within the township. Then it would subdivide the land into building lots. Then it would advertise the little parcels in urban newspapers, targeting stockbrokers, corporate-merger lawyers and other high-income dreamers of rustic getaways. Four years after it opened its first regional office, Patten was the biggest gainer on the New York Stock Exchange. Its assets stood at $80 million.

As Ms. Clark noted, the speculators were able to camouflage their high-volume activities through a sophisticated arsenal of marketing euphemisms. For instance, the firms were not real estate companies, in that they did not act as sales agents. This technicality gave them a certain invisibility. Their newspaper advertising unfailingly carried a variation on the line "For Sale by Owner," and a column of such ads in a regional newspaper's real estate section—further localized by a wide assortment of telephone numbers—effectively erased the picture of a centralized corporate-development Wehrmacht.

And so a tragicomic tableau began to be enacted, and reenacted, across the bosky woodlands and the rugged coastline of New England: selectmen and planning-board volunteers, having awakened to the wrenching realization that, say, one hundred new house lots were suddenly in the works near a hamlet of five hundred residents, frantically flipped through mail-order planning handbooks as city-slicker lawyers in power suits purred legalese at them in town meetings—their own town meetings.

The city had come to the countryside, to get away from it all. And yet somehow "it all" had not been left behind. The city was transforming the countryside in its own image.

What combustion of forces had unleashed this fusillade of "fresh money" into these remote and essentially defenseless towns? Who were these fresh faces that followed the fresh money? What were the consequences to town life?

The soaring stock market in the early 1980s generated the economic power. The new cultural/political climate, a romanticizing of private wealth and accumulation, created an aggressive and self-aware class of urban money-makers who would give the decade its defining sensibility.

Among this class's most conspicuous—and most satirized—avocations was its compulsion to improvise, largely through purchase, its own gentility. Essential to any image of gentility was the second home. But where? Not in the crowded and cacophonous cities. Not in the banal, déclassé suburbs. Where then?

The country, of course. A second home up in the country. Or Down East in Maine. It gave a gracious tone. It said status. It said taste. Not to mention its advantages as an investment. In the northeastern megalopolis belt especially, the young managers and brokers and entrepreneurs began to imitate the rustic tastes of the artists and actors and intellectuals who had preceded them into Arcadia. They became instant weekend squires.

One very rapid physical sign of this onrush was the barn-depletion crisis in eastern New York State.

The rehabilitation—"rehabbing"—of ancient barns quickly became a second-home motif (not to say a fad) for the new country-dwellers in western Connecticut and Massachusetts. It was not long before every available unused, dilapidated barn in the region had been claimed by intense young accountants wielding T-squares and power drills.

But still the wealthy weekenders arrived, and demanded barns. And so a new kind of middleman arose in the lower New England countryside: the barn broker. Fanning out westward, these enterprising locals scouted out suitable relics across the New York State border. If a buyer agreed that a certain barn was suitable to his or her "rehab" fantasies, the building would be bought, disassembled, transported to some freshly sectioned-off building lot and reincarnated as a weatherized, dormer-windowed, hardwood-floored, butcherblock-kitchened, pine-paneled, sanitized and satellite-dished travesty of its former self.

Young urban professionals were not the only invaders of the Eastern seaboard countryside, nor was the upturn in the stock market the only impetus for the surge of town growth. Many other late-twentieth-century forces were adding momentum to the process: a wave of highway improvements followed by the increase in rural speed limits in several states, which shortened commuting time from cities; the new linkages in computer communications, which freed many kinds of workers from their inner-city offices; and, finally, the outward march of those very offices from the central city into suburbia.

Westchester County, the rolling expanse of woodlands and tony suburbs north of New York City, began to experience a new kind of building boom: not in housing subdivisions or shopping malls, but in corporate headquarters, as companies fled the high tax structures and the anxieties of Manhattan. These headquarters, in turn, created a new outer radius of residential possibilities for their employees. An office worker conditioned to a thirty-five- or forty-mile commute to work and back now found that that distance could place his or her family in a charming, unspoiled farming community with affordable real estate. Very quickly those communities became less charming and conspicuously spoiled (and less affordable), as a sudden surge in the population put unforeseen stresses on sewer systems, service roads, schools and municipal services.

But congestion was far from the severest consequence of the population surge into the small towns. The most ruinous costs were to the spirit—the very marrow and essence of town life. The urban flood tide was turning ancient New England communities into garrisons of strangers. In northwestern Connecticut, where my family and I were among the invaders, the symptoms of town dissolution in the midst of prosperity intruded almost daily.

Illegal drugs—marijuana, cocaine (including "crack"), heroin— could be purchased in any of Litchfield County's twenty-six communities, the state police reported early in 1988. Drug-related arrests in the state had increased from 8,494 in 1983 to 11,154 just two years later, and much of that increase had occurred in the county's smallest and most rural towns. The patterns of distribution did reflect a certain home-cooked sensibility. Instead of urban-style drug rings, enforcement officers found themselves tracking more modest systems of refinement and packaging. "Kitchen laboratories," these systems were called, an ironic reference to the fact that they flourished in the private homes of "respectable" people.

New Milford, a charmingly situated river village of steep hills and white clapboard that had been settled in 1670, found itself dealing with, among other unfamiliar problems, a crack epidemic and nighttime packs of young boys who sometimes harrassed the elderly walkers on the town streets. (It was a further symptom of dissolution that two thirds of New Milford's thirty-nine-member police force could no longer afford to live in the same town as the youths whose behavior they sought to restrain. Nor could more than half of the 309 public school teachers who tried to educate them in class. Like the old lady in Litchfield with her conch shells, the cops and the teachers had to surrender their home ground. Their salaries were not in the same economic universe as the new prices of houses in the town—a $150,000 minimum, in the late 1980s—nor the escalating property taxes that flowed from these prices. Much of New Milford's working class had retreated farther out into the countryside, commuters to their own communities.)

In Woodbury, population seven thousand, the selectmen began considering whether to hire a second resident state trooper, and residents began organizing metropolitan-style neighborhood crime-watch programs. Criminal incidents in the town had increased by 45 percent from 1983 to 1985. The selectmen cited "unprecedented development"—new houses near the town and new shops inside the town—as the key factor in the crime surge. The need for a second trooper was also debated in the hamlet of Morris, population two thousand.

Torrington, one of western Connecticut's larger towns, began to launch organized raids against drug dealers. The police department turned to computerized data to analyze patterns of crime, and later debated whether to use stun guns.

Nor were towns the only arenas in which law-enforcement issues threatened to overtake the more traditional observances of etiquette and neighborly consideration. A newly arrived man not far from the village of Cornwall drew noise complaints from his neighbors by firing his machine gun at targets during parties on his estate property. The man expressed displeasure at the complaints, drawing attention to the fact that he was an American citizen.

The spread of anxiety over lawlessness was not limited to dry land. The thirteen patrolmen who ventured out on small boats to enforce the laws on Lake Lillinonah, a 1,900-acre body of water that once was a sleepy retreat for flatboat fishermen, were authorized in 1988 to carry firearms—for the first time since law enforcement was established on the lake in 1955. One of the patrolmen, William Bechtold, justified the need to the *Litchfield County Times:* "Society's changing and more and more people and a different type of people are using the lake. Just this year we had two incidents involving long guns where people on the water were shooting at and around people's docks."

Wanton speeding became a problem in the region—again, not only on dry land but on the lakes. The governing body of Candlewood, another large recreational lake in the region, voted to set a speed limit of forty-five miles an hour on the water surface, but not before an emotional public hearing of boaters pressing for the right to travel as fast as they pleased—eighty miles an hour, say.

Near the 230-year-old village of Winstead, Highland Lake was dying—dying of overdoses of various kinds, all supplied by man. The lake's immediate problem, one that had developed in the last years, was a rapid increase of algae and weed growth, which choked off oxygen necessary to the life-support systems of fish. The algae "growth surge" was caused, paradoxically, by a fish—the alewife, dumped in large numbers into the lake in the 1970s by the Department of Environmental Protection as a food-fish for trout and bass. The problem was that the alewife itself needed food, and fed greedily upon zooplankton, an organism that in turn was a devourer of algae.

The second kind of overdose that was killing Highland Lake was more dolefully familiar: pollutants, contaminating the watersheds flowing into the lake—septic sewage, detergents, the pollutants that accompany new development.

These strange new discontents were hardly confined to the state's northwest corner, of course. In Westport, a once secluded artist's colony on Long Island Sound that grew into a bustling city of twenty-nine thousand, could be seen perhaps the most grotesque example of fragmented civic identity: the Compo Beach playground war. Learning that a group of parents—newcomers, mostly—had planned to finance and build a collection of modernistic wooden swings and ramps and jungle gyms, designed by a famous architect of children's play-spaces, in a park near the beach, a contingent of three hundred more-established citizens formed an angry protest group.

The protesters turned out at a hearing of the town's planning and zoning commission armed with slides, petitions and stickers inscribed with the slogan "Not That Spot." The opponents—who had filed two lawsuits to block construction—denied to a *New York Times* reporter that they were "anti-playground." They just wanted the project built somewhere else. Among their objections were that the swings would be too tall, the design too ugly, the construction too amateurish, and that the wooden planks would contain too much strychnine.

Some conflicts and discontents would no doubt have reached into the towns and wildernesses of the Northeast whether the urban population boom had detonated there or not. Drug abuse, for example, is a national scourge that has seemed to spread like pollen into every crevice of the continent. But other changes—such as the economic uprooting of stable families from the communities where they had lived for generations and their dispersal into the isolation of backroad farms, or houses, or trailers—were the direct result of an invading culture of superior resources and might. Certain fundamental town bonds were rapidly dissolving—bonds that had held towns together in a system of shared goals and duties and agreements first knitted in pre-Revolutionary times. Such agreements helped form the principles of American democracy, as well as the communal myths from which Americans to this day derive their sense of unique history and special purpose in the world.

Perhaps no tradition better defined those bonds than the tradition of volunteerism. Small New England towns (like small towns in many regions of America) depended on volunteers to keep alive their vital systems. Fire departments, ambulance units and rescue squads, snow-removal teams, hospital auxiliaries, library associates, planning and zoning officials, fund-raising chairpeople, Scout leaders, lifeguards, churchworkers, groups who furnished hot meals to elderly citizens and even managed activity centers for them—these were the province of volunteers.

Volunteers enriched the life of Kent. The volunteer planning and zoning chairman at that time, a retired marketing executive named Paul Moroz, put his snowy goatee and ruddy features to triumphant use each Christmas season: in the classic red suit, and with a leather strap of harness bells dangling from his neck, he held court as an uncannily convincing volunteer Santa Claus in the recreation hall of the Congregational church, while his wife, Norma, directed the gingerbread-decoration contest as Mrs. Claus.

Eighty percent of Connecticut's fire departments were run by volunteers. One small-town selectman estimated that the cost of replacing his community's volunteer fire department with even a partially professional cadre would cost the village half a million dollars a year.

But volunteerism became one of the most conspicuous casualties of the new population surges in the towns. The weekend visitors, the summer residents and the new commuter families were not necessarily more selfish than the townspeople; very often the new-comers were simply oblivious of the volunteer chains. Even if they became aware of them, their intermittent presence in the communities reduced their capacity to serve: volunteering was not so much a hobby, or a sporadic gesture, as it was an integrated function of one's identity—as inextricable from the yearly cycles as one's job or family.

But if newcomers did not volunteer, and if their crowding of the New England countryside was accompanied by an abrupt increase in land prices, shopping malls, traffic congestion, urban-style crime, drug abuse and general incivility, and an evaporation of the simple and ancient ability to recognize one's neighbor by face and name, it did not follow that the newcomers—the "fresh money"—were indifferent to the ambience of the towns they were invading.

To the contrary. The newcomers tended to be quite starchy about the unwelcome changes in the quaint villages they had chosen as refuges from the city. Newcomers were not at all sure they approved of other newcomers coming in and cluttering up their bucolic paradise. This attitude provided endless satiric fodder for the locals, who on the whole—and despite abundant provocation—remained considerably more tolerant of the upheavals than their arriviste neighbors.

There even emerged a maxim, invoked almost exclusively by the locals, to describe the newcomers' philosophy: "The last one aboard—pull up the ladder!"

The future of Kent—its capacity to withstand the tumultuous forces of urbanity—was a topic that circled the dinner table that February evening at Carol Hoffman's farm.

None of Carol Hoffman's guests opposed growth; that proviso was stated and restated. On the other hand, the village had absorbed a succession of nasty jolts within the last two years, jolts that had jangled the nerves of every transplanted outsider in the vicinity, and a few of the longtimers as well.

Kent's recent traumas were scarcely noticeable as one entered the town. At the crest of a low rise above the Housatonic floodplain a northbound motorist is greeted by an electric four-way signal close to a Civil War obelisk. Given a green light, one would drive past a Sunoco filling station; a gray stone Episcopal church; a smattering of Victorian and Gothic Revival houses converted into clothes and craft shops; the House of Books; the Kent Market; a couple of storefronts (more converted residences); some empty space where the Lions Club held its annual baked lobster sale in the summer; the Villager Restaurant; the fire station; the library; a disused railroad crossing; the Fife 'n' Drum restaurant, where the Bonanza bus took on passengers and where Dolph, the owner, played piano each evening; the old Congregational church; the community house (site of harvest fairs and antique shows); a guest house; an antiques shop—and that was it. The trip through town took perhaps half a minute.

This sparseness was deceptive. Kent people lived invisible as Hobbits beyond the village center. They lived along the latticework of blacktop roads that threaded through the hills and hollows and along the riverbanks of the township's forty-nine square miles. A fairly substantial number of these people bore family names that were duplicated on the local roads, bridges and mountains: names of people who began settling the area as early as 1720.

Life in Kent had its disadvantages—hard work at low wages, a steady dwindling of the region's farm economy—but it was ordered and peaceful. Despite the regular trickle of newcomers, Kent's longtime residents had almost allowed themselves to grow comfortable with an astonishing possibility: that Kent would manage to slip through the development surge of the 1980s unnoticed by the hordes.

The floodtide had washed up perilously close to Kent's boundaries—New Milford was only twelve miles south—but somehow the town had not been inundated. Maybe it was the roads, some of the residents told one another. Maybe it was the access—or the lack of same. Route 7, which began in Norwalk, on the Connecticut shoreline, and meandered north through Massachusetts and Vermont to the Canadian border, was for most of its length a beautiful but remote and tedious strip of old two-lane concrete. Originally mapped out in 1919 as part of Connecticut's highway system, and extended in the late twenties as a connecting trunk to the north, Route 7 had not changed all that much in sixty years—but the roadside around it had. The eighteen miles connecting Danbury to New Milford, for example, were an almost unbroken accretion of auto-age glut: car washes, shopping malls, drive-thru burger chains, filling stations, branch banks, computer stores. And besides being traffic-choked, Route 7—at least the Kent part of Route 7—could be damnably hard to find. To reach Kent from New York required a number of road changes, veeroffs, alertness to rustic landmarks (including for many years a three-story-high wooden kitchen chair) and, using the most direct approach, negotiation of a covered bridge. Bad roads had been among Kent's greatest assets.

Carol Hoffman's dinner party drew toward its murmurous close; the guests put aside their coffee cups and began to make contented remarks about the food and companionship. Leslie Connery's electronic beeper emitted a burst of sharp tones. Half in amusement—she had after all made a jocular point of showing it off earlier in the evening—Leslie flipped the speaker switch on as the guests sorted out their overcoats and handbags.

A dispatcher's voice, the voice of a very young man, was summoning volunteers to the site of a collision on Route 7, just a few miles south of town. Two cars, head-on. At least one serious injury. No further information, the young voice said.

Donald and Leslie made hasty good-byes and left quickly in their car for the scene of the accident. A few minutes later, as my wife and I drove through the mostly darkened village toward our turn-off, we saw that a highway patrol car had blocked off all southbound traffic on 7.

We did not learn the full extent of the horror until the following day. The accident had indeed been a head-on collision, and it had resulted in a fatality. The dead person was a seventy-two-year-old Kent woman named Dorothy Gawel. A passenger, Mrs. Gawel absorbed the full impact of the crash of her daughter's car and a pickup truck. Mrs. Gawel, in a sense, had been a victim of the outdated road system that was sheltering her town. Used mostly by local people, the section of Route 7 between Kent and New Milford was becoming a fairly notorious deathtrap, having claimed twenty-nine lives over a fifteen-year period that saw 1,422 accidents. (The Highway to Heaven, locals were beginning to call it.)

A little bit of Kent's intricate community webbing came loose that night. Dorothy Gawel had been one of the town's most beloved citizens, a member of an old-line family, and a volunteer in the old tradition. The crash that killed her had the eerie effect of casting a harsh and fleeting light, like a headlight beam, upon a whole sector of Kent society that was rapidly receding into the shadows: the working-class families, established for generations, who were being priced and crowded off their native ground by the affluent, visible newcomers. That receding society had intricate ties indeed: the voice of the youthful dispatcher who had called for ambulance volunteers belonged to Dorothy Gawel's unsuspecting grandson, Alan.

Kent grieved for Dorothy Gawel, and looked for ways to express its anger at her death: forty citizens turned out the following week for an open meeting sponsored by Mothers Against Drunk Driving at the community house.

Meanwhile, the forces of urban progress were creeping closer to Kent from the south. Not three weeks before Dorothy Gawel's death, serious lobbying had begun for state funding to construct a "Super 7" highway, an eight-mile strip from Brookfield up to New Milford, a divided stretch that would relieve some of the congestion on the old road there.

And a strip that would, in time, deliver more fast-track New Yorkers from the roaring I-87 almost to Kent's doorstep.

Chapter III

I am a town boy. I am of the old confederacy of towns. I came of age in midcontinent at midcentury, during the final throes of a true town ethos in America—a dissolution foreordained half a century earlier, when cement highways began to pave over the frontier. I grew up at the end of an era, a fact of which I was clam-happily unaware. The Town, for me as a boy, was what I believed eternity must look like.

But why did I believe this? And why mightn't the same be believed of a city, by a city boy? Doubtless it might; doubtless it has been. I can't say whether I or my friends would have made equally ardent city boys. (Could the absence of nature—pushed back beyond the curve of the earth—have been compensated for by the proximity of a big-league baseball team?) The very attempt to imagine it, these thirty years after I left the town behind, fills me with a kind of seasickness, a sense of the void—as if I were embarking on some lunatic voyage, having left my Self standing abandoned on the shore.

At any rate the question is moot: I was not able to live alternately in a city and a town. I have no well of comparative experience.

But I think I understand something of the hold that town life had on me, and perhaps on my friends (a good many of whom live on in our dazed and atrophied town to this day). I believe that it derived from the radiance conferred upon our most mundane daily cycles and enterprises, upon our sorrows and bereavements as well as our ecstasies, upon our odysseys through the seasons and the rituals of the year and upon our most primitive sense of connectedness to one another and to the physical town—a radiance that was itself derived from our consciousness of the earth, vast and unpopulated, beyond our town's borders, the tilled and electrified vestiges of wilderness.

There was the prairie, dark and boundless under the moon, and there at its center was Hannibal—a fragile membrane of vapor lights and telephone lines, tavern and lawn, the insinuating river abrading its skin. Our isolation had a paradoxical effect: it absolved us from anonymity. Disconnected as we were from urban power, urban celebrity, urban wickedness and urban transcendence, we bred our own hierarchies of incredible purpose and drama.

Our town was filled with vivid characters. Nearly everyone was important. (My own father was something of a town archetype, the Fuller Brush Man.) In childhood it was possible to actually be famous—for wealth, for wisecracks, for fists. Among adults, we had statesmen and a family of outlaws; we had an aristocracy—the country-club "well-to-do"—and we had the Wedge, a black ghetto in the center of town. We had a radio disk-jockey and we had tag-team wrestlers at the Armory; we had a town crazy, mustard-gassed in World War I, and we had a whore. Our leading merchants looked exactly like the photographs we'd seen of leading merchants everywhere; and our leading hotel, a couple of blocks from the railroad station ("In the Heart of Downtown!"), with its Special Banquet Rooms, its Hofbrau Cocktail Lounge, its facilities for Rotary and Kiwanis and Optimists and Hi-Twelve, its free parking lot in rear, seemed to us as cosmopolitan as anything advertised in the *Saturday Evening Post.* We had everything we needed. We were a town.

What we needed principally was one another. I don't intend that observation as sentimental. The people of my town were bound to one another as often by bigotry, jealousies, class hatred and blood feuds as they were by brotherhood, loyalty, friendship and blood ties. The point, I suppose, is that we were *bound.* We were cells in a biological stream, flowing through an organism surrounded by the void. We knew, all of us, exactly, what was expected of us within this organism. We knew our functions, our limitations, our taboos—our place.

And we knew that the stream implied a history and a future, just as the big river brushing past the town's skin implied a living continuity of time. There had been other cells similar to ourselves functioning inside the fragile membrane before our time; there would be other, similar cells functioning after us. Eternity.

If all that sounds like a paean to repression, an ode to orthodoxy's oblivion, it may well be. Yet consider this: I left that town thirty years ago to freely invent my destiny in the erupting ethos of urban America, and I still wake up in Hannibal's hive, panting from a long blind dash along its darkened streets. The vapor lights have gone out, and I cannot find my way. A central condition of my adult life is that I can go anywhere I please, except back.

I recognize that it was necessary for me to leave the town and invent my destiny, free from the town's delimiting opinion, its Aunt Polly civilizing stare. I recognize that it was necessary to put behind me what was, after all, a protracted state of innocence.

But I also believe that the innocence was necessary. The story of America is at once a story of a new Eden claimed and of the inevitable departure from that Eden. The Republic's first native philosopher, Ralph Waldo Emerson, recognized this tension. "When men are innocent," he wrote, "life shall be longer, and shall pass into the immortal as gently as we awake from dreams." And yet it was Emerson who insisted that the new American man must push outward from paradise; that he must free himself from the comforting doctrines of traditional Christianity and reinvent himself through fearless immersion in personal experience—a plunge outward into "Chaos and Old Night."

When Americans remain beguiled by their own divine innocence for too long, they tend to visit holy mayhem on the less anointed: the nations of Sioux and Crow and Blackfeet; the "little brown brothers" of the Philippines; the domino-toppling communist devils of North Vietnam. But when Americans shed their innocence too quickly, or pass ungraced by it into their adulthood, they are capable of other dark escapades: a virulent and remorseless plutocracy founded on predatory capitalism; a passionless acceptance of technology as a substitute for human intuition; a flight from native place toward the artificial community of the bedroom suburb, the corporation, the demographic.

The crucible of necessary American innocence has always been the Town.

"We are talking now of summer evenings in Knoxville," wrote James Agee in 1938, invoking the sweet lost neighborhoods of 1915.

In his images of those remembered fathers who set out leisurely in crossed suspenders, following their hell-bent children through the dewy grass in the softly shining daylight after supper, Agee expressed the profound and mysterious attachment between Americans and their towns—and also the ache of ambivalence, the preparation for flight: the mature Agee understood that his former self was living in Knoxville only temporarily, "successfully disguised to myself as a child."

This ambivalence hovers at the edges of even the fondest literary visions of American town life. Perhaps no writer was ever more annealed in his craft by his native town than Samuel Clemens. His Hannibal, Missouri, became "St. Petersburg" in his most enduring novels—with all the intended connotations of heaven. "After all these years," Mark Twain wrote near the beginning of *Life on the Mississippi,* "I can picture that old time to myself now, just as it was then: the white town drowsing in the sunshine of a summer's morning; the streets empty or pretty nearly so; one or two clerks sitting in front of the Water Street stores . . . [and] the great Mississippi, the majestic, the magnificent Mississippi, rolling its mile-wide tide along, shining in the sun . . . "

As his biographer Justin Kaplan notes, Mark Twain spent his career writing in one way or another about Hannibal, "about what began to seem the most memorable boyhood ever lived." And yet he left—left at seventeen, as soon as he was able; and his works drew as deeply on the horrors of the town—its torpors and its brutalities, its drunks and its murderers—as they did on the sunshine sweetness.

And Clemens recognized—perhaps bitterly—the rigid orthodoxies of his town's class structure. In his autobiography, he wrote:

In the small town of Hannibal, Missouri, when I was a boy everybody was poor but didn't know it; and everybody was comfortable and did know it. And there were grades of society—people of good family, people of unclassified family, people of no family. Everybody knew everybody and was affable to everybody . . . yet the class lines were quite clearly drawn and the familiar social life of each class was restricted to that class. It was a little democracy which was full of liberty, equality and Fourth of July, and sincerely so, too; yet you perceived that the aristocratic taint was there. It was there and nobody found fault with the fact or ever stopped to reflect that its presence was an inconsistency.

Mark Twain was born on a farm, spent his boyhood in a small town, and closed out his long life as an habitué of the great cities of America and Europe. He was thus almost a living embodiment of the nation's progression along these three great venues of experience. And his torn sensibilities, which drove him both to satirize the urban Gilded Age and to force himself into its society, mirrored the nation's own dilemma—its sense of loss within its lust for gain—as its inevitable journey to the city took on momentum.

Before there was the city there was the town; before there was the town there was the farm. "The first farmer was the first man," wrote Emerson, "and all historic nobility rests on possession and use of the land." The Old World immigrants savored the New World first for the sheer purity and endlessness of its land—the new Eden—and only secondarily for its settlements. "Some few towns excepted, we are all tillers of the earth, from Nova Scotia to West Florida," boasted Crèvecoeur in 1782, in his *Letters from an American Farmer.* "We are a people of cultivators, scattered over an immense territory, communicating with each other by means of good roads and navigable rivers, united by the silken bands of mild government, all respecting the laws, without dreading their power, because they are equitable."

But even in their scattered state, the early Europeans-cum-Americans found another bounty that the Old World, with its orthodoxies of class and religion, could not permit: the bounty of spontaneous intimacy. "A traveler in Europe becomes a stranger as soon as he quits his own kingdom," exulted Crèvecoeur, "but it is otherwise here. We know, properly speaking, no strangers; this is every person's country; the variety of our soils, situations, climates, governments, and produce, hath something which must please every body."

Crèvecoeur's epistles thrum with a boosterish euphoria that in the balefulness of the late twentieth century sounds almost hysterical. And yet a far less excitable Frenchman, visiting the new republic nearly half a century later, drew essentially the same impressions—of a pervading tranquility, order and contentment, founded on a sympathetic relation to the land itself.

"Americans love their towns for much the same reasons that highlanders love their mountains," Alexis de Tocqueville remarked in *Democracy in America.* "In both cases the native land has emphatic and peculiar features; it has a more pronounced physiognomy than is found elsewhere. In general, New England townships lead a happy life. Their government is to their taste as well as of their choice."

That, of course, was the point of the American exercise in the first place. The civic stability and contentment that Tocqueville observed in 1831 already had two-hundred-year-old roots, and those roots had been fiercely planted: by English Puritans escaping a century of discordance with the Church of England—a discordance paid for in repression, civil war and martyrdom.

The Puritans had wanted to move closer to a more pristine form of scriptural worship by paring away the accumulated layers of church bureaucracy: its labyrinthine rituals, its authoritarian bishops in their imperial vestments who temporized the Word of God as they preached it. They insisted on a simpler and more communal form of worship that extended into home and family life and that depended on rigid self-discipline and on work as a vocation. These utopian visions, so intolerable to the institution of the English Church (and to most of English society) could be implanted without resistance in the new Eden wilderness. And beginning in 1630, with the Massachusetts Bay Colony, the Puritans began that implantation.

Soon these waves of immigrants began to coalesce into settlements. But this first progression—from farm to town—did not imply a disharmony with the wilderness or a retreat from its brutal bounties. The early New England town, rather, was an affirmation, the very embodiment of the communal ideal—perfection through love, cooperation, hard work, and tranquility—that had been denied to the Puritans in England.

"In the depths of the American experience lies a craving for peace, unity, and order within the confines of a simple society," writes the historian Kenneth Lockridge, who traces the roots of that craving to what he calls "the conservative foundation" of this Puritan legacy. (Lockridge goes on to point out that, regrettably enough, next to this craving "lies a willingness to exclude whatever men and to ignore whatever events threaten the fulfillment of that hunger.")

Professor Lockridge notes that what the Puritans established in the New World was itself more ancient than modern: "For decades life in this part of America was intimately linked in all its phases to the intellectual and social traditions of medieval Europe and to a worldwide peasant tradition dating from the origin of recorded history." And other modern scholars have argued that, the industrial revolution notwithstanding, this rural and peasant community tradition is in fact the natural state of man.

"[The] symbiotic relationship of man and growing things called rural life is normally the seat of the small community and, as I shall try to show, of the true community," wrote the sociologist Baker Brownell in 1950. "All human life, of course, is eventually dependent on this relationship. . . .

"Rural life is the normal milieu of the human community. Thousands of years of human culture confirm it. I do not know whether the community must be rural to exist, but the evidence of centuries seems to indicate it. Cities have come and gone. Their cultures and philosophies have been epiphenomenal, as it were, upon the deep permanence of their rural background. But the human community as a sustaining, many-functioned, organic pattern of life has rarely, if ever, been in them. The community is rural. It belongs to rural culture, philosophy, and life."

This reading seems to make rather short work of the Mesopotamians. And the Sumerians. Likewise the citizens of Changan, or Teotihuacán, or Ur. Some density of denizens seems to have been necessary to have satisfied certain fundamental human longings for trade, defense, aggression, worship, and the more rarified nuances of vice, for artistic expression and the pursuit of knowledge (at midcentury in America it was estimated that one million people were needed to support a university; no corresponding figures were given for the number needed to support a slum).

The question is: how high the density? Athens managed to transform the Western world's notions of politics and aesthetics while drawing from a population pool of fifty thousand. In 1922 Le Corbusier estimated that the ideal city would accommodate three million, a figure remarkably consistent with the population of Paris (three million) in 1922.

Those who crave the city's orgiastic multisensory burn aren't counting heads, of course: to them the city is self-creating, self-defining, self-evident, absolute. In 1949, in an age when people still bothered to reflect on the balancing tensions between urban and rural life—when there still was something of a balance to reflect on—a country-born architect named Joseph Hudnut issued a kind of city-lover's manifesto. "We are held in the city," he asserted, "neither by pleasure nor by economic necessity but by a hunger which transcends both practical and sensuous experience, a hunger seldom revealed by appearances, seldom acknowledged in our consciousness. We are held in the city by our need of a collective life;

by our need of belonging and sharing; by our need of that direction and frame which our individual lives gain from a larger life lived together."

The high priest of urban sovereignty, Robert Moses, was, typically, a good deal more coldly to the point. "The urban trend," he wrote in 1956, "whether we like it or not, is undeniable. The shift from country to town is steady. There is little wavering in the graph." Baudelaire, of course, surpassed them both in probing to the terrifying core: "I love thee, infamous city; Harlots and the hunted have pleasures of their own to give, The vulgar herd can never understand."

Perhaps none of the arguments mattered. What mattered was the Darwinian rush, the inevitable accelerating onslaught of industry and technology and world war that obliterated the balance, that diminished the importance of the small American town and vested the city as the authoritative center of the national life.

And the transformation happened rather suddenly. The historian William Leuchtenburg, in *The Perils of Prosperity*, notes that America in 1914 was not profoundly different from the America of just after the Revolutionary War. "There were men still living whose fathers had known Jefferson and John Adams," he wrote. "In prairie towns women remembered the day Ralph Waldo Emerson had alighted from the train to talk to the local Chautaqua."

Only eighteen years later, Leuchtenburg argues, it was all over. "The task of industrialization had been essentially completed. . . . In 1932, Americans no longer had the same sense of confidence either in themselves or in the efficacy of reform. . . . As Newport mansions and Fifth Avenue homes were dismantled, social authority was diffused. If it passed anywhere at all, it passed to Hollywood."

Leuchtenburg acknowledged that America had been rapidly industrializing since the 1880s, "and with industrialization had come a raft of problems—city slums, factory reform, unassimilated immigrants, and class animosity. . . . The experience of World War I made matters much worse. The war and its aftermath killed much of the humanistic, cosmopolitan spirit of 1914."

What was lost by all of this? A kind of Arcadia, Leuchtenburg believed: "Men remembered county fairs and church socials, spelling bees and sleigh rides, the excitement of the circus train or the wild dash of firehorses from the station house. . . . They recalled the sound of peanut whistles and the hurdy-gurdy, the clang of the trolley, the cry of the carnival pitchman, the oompah of the military band on a summer evening, the clatter of victrolas and sulkies, the shouts of children playing blindman's buff and run-sheep-run. They remembered people: the paper boy with his off-key whistle, the brawny iceman sauntering up the walk with his five-cent cake of ice, the Negro stable boys, the printers and devils in the newspaper offices . . ."

But those memories began to darken. In 1922—sixty years before the rapid urbanizing of New England—Babbitt came to town, a genially monstrous creature of his changing times, "nimble in the calling of selling houses for more than people could afford to pay." American novelists were beginning to take note of business as a transforming force—almost as a literary character. When Babbitt "laid out the Glen Oriole acreage development," reported his creator, Sinclair Lewis, "when he ironed woodland and dipping meadow into a glenless, oriole-less, sunburnt flat prickly with small boards displaying the names of imaginary streets, he righteously put in a complete sewage system. The only flaw was that the Glen Oriole sewers had insufficient outlet, so that waste remained in them."

And a few years later, when Thomas Wolfe's alter ego George Webber renewed his acquaintance with his hometown in *You Can't Go Home Again,* "it was a disconcerting experience. The sleepy little mountain village in which he had grown up . . . was now changed almost beyond recognition. The very streets that he had known so well, and had remembered through the years in their familiar aspect of early-afternoon emptiness and drowsy lethargy, were now foaming with life, crowded with expensive traffic, filled with new faces he had never seen before. . . .

"On all sides he heard talk, talk, talk—terrific and incessant. And the tumult of voices was united in variations of a single chorus—speculation and real estate.

"Everyone bought real estate; and everyone was 'a real estate man,' either in name or practice. The barbers, the lawyers, the grocers, the butchers, the builders, the clothiers—all were engaged now in this single interest and obsession. And there seemed to be only one rule, universal and infallible—to buy, always to buy, to pay whatever price was asked, and to sell again within two days at any price one chose to fix. It was fantastic. Along all the streets in town the ownership of the land was constantly changing; and when the supply of streets was exhausted, new streets were feverishly created in the surrounding wilderness; and even before these streets were paved or a house had been built upon them, the land was being sold, and then resold, by the acre, by the lot, by the foot, for hundreds of thousands of dollars."

The Great Depression put an end to that sort of recreation, of course; and as the Depression began to wane, an entirely new agent of change began to trace its patterns on the landscape. The new national system of highways was nearly complete. Already, since the 1920s, a skeletal system of paved roads, each affixed with its heroic name, had connected several remote points on the continent: the coast-to-coast Lincoln Highway, the Dixie Highway, the Yellowstone Trail, the Ponchartrain Road, all bore their Model Ts filled with begoggled adventurers trying to taste some of the wildness of the recently vanished frontier. Already these few exploratory tendrils were yielding their first strange blossoms: motor hotels, gas stations, roadside cafés, billboards, boosters' coats of arms, and a burgeoning riot of roadside attractions.

By 1928 the nation had endured a bloody initiation to the open road; nearly thirty thousand Americans had died on it. In 1932, as the highway historian Phil Patton notes, President Hoover's Committee on Recent Social Trends reported that the automobile "had erased the boundaries which formerly separated urban from rural territory and has introduced a type of local community without precedent in history." Writers for the *WPA American Guide* series noticed the same thing. Fanning out across the country in the late 1930s to compile a composite portrait of American life, these writers discovered—often to their distress—that the automobile had reshaped the nation's towns and cities, blurring them into the countryside, and had advanced an unromantic new mode of standardization into the far hinterlands. (Ironically, highway building was another job-creating thrust of that same WPA.)

The Roosevelt administration (according to Patton's research) had spent $4 billion on highways by 1942, and Franklin Roosevelt was already dreaming of a grand system of superhighways.

The paved highway truncated the classic American progression from farm to town to city: once the lifetime journey of a few statesmen, scholars, artists and captains of industry, the trip could now be made routinely in a day. As if in answer to Thomas Wolfe's elegiac call of the twenties—"For we are all so lost, so naked, and so lonely in America. Immense and cruel skies bend over us, and all of us are driven on forever, and we have no home"—came Jack Kerouac's shriek back from the fifties: "Madroad driving men ahead—the mad road, lonely, leading around the bend into the opening of space towards the horizon of Wastach snows promised us in the vision of the West, spine heights at the world's end . . ."

Now the fate of towns had passed out of the passionate consciousness of writers and into the tempered calibrations of sociologists.

Rural sociology in the United States was simple enough in the days when rural society itself was stable and untraumatized by rapid change. In 1911 a sociologist named Charles Josiah Galpin was able to identify community boundaries in a Wisconsin county merely by charting the patterns of wagon turnings on local roads. Galpin observed that wagon tracks along the county's dirt highways tended to be, in effect, a reliable script from which he was able to posit conclusions about the county's religious habits, its politics, its volume of farm production, its maintenance needs, and its rituals of celebration and bereavement.

Galpin is considered by many academics to be the "father" of rural sociology in America. He predicted the dissolution of boundaries between city and town, and between town and countryside, that accelerated with the century. He created methods of study and research—techniques for identifying social patterns—that would later become standard among the various "community development" movements around the country.

But perhaps the most significant thrust of Galpin's work was his inquiry into how social groupings affected people's behavior. He was an early proponent of the *Gemeinschaft/Gesellschaft* model (the construct was advanced by the German psychoanalyst Alfred Adler) for distinguishing between rural and urban manners and modes of conduct. *Gemeinschaft* behavior is intensely personal, and is grounded in a pervading awareness of obligation to the surrounding community ("What will the neighbors think?"). *Gesellschaft* behavior tends to be impersonal, utilitarian, prompted by an assumption of transience. Galpin understood the interdependence of rural and urban people, and the necessary integrity of their cultures. He warned of the dislocations inherent in reducing the sense of control in small communities, in undermining *Gemeinschaft*. The decades have proved his warnings prescient.

Rural sociology has grown infinitely more complex as the object of its study has grown complex—as those early wagon tracks of Galpin's eroded, were paved over, and finally gave way to the new electronic "tracks" of telephone wires and broadcast waves and data-processing currents. And yet many of its early concerns remained legitimate as the century proceeded, as urbanization, mobility and technology eroded the old necessary integrities, and replaced them with ambiguity and diffusion.

The contemporary sociologist Don A. Dillman, of Washington State University, has pointed to one fulfillment of Galpin's prophecies that nearly everyone grasps instinctively: that the rural-to-urban mergings of the twentieth century have constituted an assault on *Gemeinschaft* behavior, not to mention the very identity of rural and small-town life. Citing the automobile and the telephone as early agents of the assault, Dillman traces the accumulating elements in the wave.

"The rise of the national corporations," he writes, "assured a regular turnover of local managers with whom less mobile segments of the population then interacted. The expansion of diverse educational opportunities and military experiences brought rural people in contact with other sections of the country and other countries of the world to an unprecedented degree. The increase in women who worked . . . brought still other interactions. Television and other media of the mass society bombarded the countryside with messages. On a society-wide basis, the mass media promoted homogeneity."

In 1942 the sociologist Arthur Morgan wrote, "Many an American small town or village is no longer a community. Too often it is only a small city, the citizens largely going their individual ways. This progressive disappearance of the community in present-day life is one of the most disturbing phenomena of modern history. It constitutes an historic crisis."

In other words, rural America was being pureed by progress—blended into an increasingly diffuse, culturally ambiguous and urban-influenced mass; a sort of *Gemeingesellschlop*.

Other sociologists have drawn finer distinctions within these movements and trends.

"There are two rural Americas," Darryl Hobbs has claimed. Hobbs is a professor of rural sociology at the University of Missouri. Of the two, he suggests, one is real and the other imagined. The imagined rural America is the stuff of national myth: an enduring region of one-room schoolhouses and Main Streets, and a constant wellspring of purity, innocence and character-building experiences. (This mythic place is familiar to at least one generation mainly as a stagelighted backdrop for telemarketing beer, cars, presidential candidates, "just-like-fresh" ready-mixes and concentrates, and other consumer products of dubious authenticity.)

The other rural America—Hobbs's vision of the real one—is quite a bit less fetching. Instead of small towns warmly encircled by family farms, its dominant images are cold, rotting, meretricious, cheap—and, most tellingly, imposed almost arbitrarily upon the land by outside forces; colonies. They include the garment factory, the mobile home park, the dilapidated mining town, the migratory worker camp, the retirement community, the ski resort—or the suburban bedroom community.

"A commitment to place is an important feature of rural life," Hobbs has written. "It's an essential feature of preservation. [Yet] a nation of movers is unlikely to produce the sustained commitment to place necessary to preserve rural ways and places. While we have been mobile, a lack of attachment seems to have become embedded in the national psyche."

Given these new realities, American towns—as the centers, the critical mass, the communal souls, of their host rural environments—appear to be in danger of inevitable extinction by drought (except for those few sustained as curiosities, by urban dilettantes) as the tides of history recede farther and farther from them. Certainly the statistical trends are far from encouraging.

In 1880—to consider one portentous barometer—agriculture and manufacturing, the traditional life-systems of towns, accounted for 86 percent of American jobs. By the year 2000, it is projected, that percentage will have dropped to 24 percent, and urban, information-age jobs (data-processing, education, technology and science) will have risen from 2 to 66 percent.

Or to consider another: population analysts have projected that at the same millennial turning, the twelve largest population centers in America, resting on one tenth of the land area, will contain 70 percent of the population. Furthermore, the most typical immigrants to these centers from the vestiges of rural America will be—as they have been for many decades—the young, the well-educated, the dynamic, the ambitious.

These interlocking transformations accelerated in the 1980s. The catastrophic drop in farm prices virtually shut down town after town across the Midwest. Iowa, the traditional cornucopia of American farm prosperity, lost 63,000 residents between 1980 and 1986. In fact, through the first half of the eighties, nearly half the country's rural counties lost population. The Midwest as a whole suffered the greatest decline—it lost more than 3 percent of its people in those years.

As economic opportunities vanished and the middle-class young followed, the very structures of town life began to atrophy like disused limbs.

Businesses failed, manufacturers folded or went elsewhere. Nearly half the small-town gas stations in Iowa that existed in the 1970s were gone by the end of the eighties. The Ford Motor Company lost 400 of its smaller outlets in the same timespan. (Just as often, it was the decision to close down a plant deemed expendable at a stockholders' meeting that plunged a community into desolation.)

Hospitals shut down—more than 300 during the decade, and more than half of those in small towns; and at least 300 more were threatened. Local public schools folded or consolidated into regional educational plants. (Missouri boasted 8,607 school districts in 1945; by the end of the eighties that number stood at 545, and that same decade had seen a 20 percent drop in the state's enrollment.)

Churches closed their doors, or were converted into seldom-used "community centers." The town grocery store, the town dry-goods store, the town variety shop, the town sporting-goods store, the town barbershop, beauty parlor, bakery, coffee shop—all were replaced by the shopping mall, the Wal-Mart, the K mart. (By the late 1980s there were 1200 Wal-Mart centers in America, nearly all of them at the fringes of municipalities of under 25,000 people.)

Kansas was on the brink. Kansas was a state of small towns, more than 600 of them; and of these, 532 had fewer than 2,500 people. During the slavery/free-soil battles of the 1850s, and the bloody border wars that followed, Kansas towns had been prey to some of the most brutal episodes of violence in American history (John Brown's massacre of five proslavery settlers at Pottawatomie Creek is among the most notorious). But after the Civil War the state settled into a century of quiet, stable farm prosperity that, along with Iowa's, became a symbol of the nation's fathomless prosperity.

That changed in the 1980s. The world glut of grain and oil diminished prices for those commodities in Kansas; land values and rural incomes lost their underpinnings. Young people left the towns and farms for Wichita, or left the state altogether, looking for work. Of the remaining population, 13 percent were over sixty-five—15 percent in many counties—compared with the national average of 11 percent. The towns' economies began to wither. Thirty-three rural banks failed between 1984 and 1988. Those that survived virtually stopped making farm loans. Retail trade sales patterns reflected the gathering constriction: between 1985 and 1986 they dropped $52 million (12.6 percent) in towns under 5,000, and $101 million (12 percent) in towns between 5,000 and 10,000. But in towns of 10,000 to 15,000, retail sales grew $19.9 million, or nearly 6 percent.

So critical was the prospect for many—perhaps most—Kansas towns by the end of the 1980s that a group of sociologists at Kansas State University proposed a radical strategy of rescue, which they termed "triage." (This was a reference to the selection process used by French battlefield medics in World War I, in which the mortally wounded and the slightly wounded did not receive immediate help—the former because there was little hope of survival; the latter, because there was little threat.) The sociologists hoped to promote the use of limited public funds for towns between 2,500 and 5,000. By implication, Kansas towns under 2,500—more than 500, or five-sixths the total—would be left to die, or to survive as best they could.

But no place in America suffered as badly in the 1980s as the Lower Mississippi Delta, a narrow belt of 8.3 million people living in 214 counties clustered near the Mississippi River in Arkansas, Louisiana, Mississippi, Missouri, Illinois, Tennessee and Kentucky. At the top of the belt was Cairo, Illinois.

As the eighties began, the Delta had already overtaken Appalachia as the poorest region in America. More than a fifth of its people lived in extreme poverty (compared with 17 percent in Appalachia). In 1988, per capita income in the Delta stood at $10,192, compared with $13,577 nationally. The region's unemployment rate was 8.8 percent, compared with the nationwide rate of 5.5. (In Alexander County, where Cairo lay, the figure was 18.51 percent.) Federal, state and local "transfer" payments to poor people totaled almost $2 billion in 1986—not counting Medicare and Medicaid payments. This was an increase of more than 800 percent for such purposes in 1969.

These figures, compiled by a bipartisan group of Delta senators and U.S. congressmen that was formed under public law in 1988— the Lower Mississippi Delta Development Commission—suggested that massive and decisive action was required. But no one seemed to know what to do.

Its unique historical problems aside, Cairo suffered from the same symptoms of decay that were attacking the vitals of similarly isolated towns all across America. Its population was declining, and aging, and growing poorer—its unemployment rate, 14 percent, was twice that of the state of Illinois. Its downtown business district, vitiated by the racial wars and boycotts of the 1970s, eventually had been bled nearly dry by the satellite ring of large shopping centers in larger towns thirty-five and forty miles away, in Missouri and Kentucky. Its middle class was nearly nonexistent.

And finally, in 1986, Cairo lost its hospital.

Southern Medical Center had been founded during the Civil War by an order of nuns, the Sisters of the Holy Cross, under the name St. Mary's Infirmary. A civic brochure published during the 1880s, "The Attractions of Cairo," cited the infirmary as one of the ornaments of the town: "A Model Institution. It Combines the Benefits of a First-Class Hospital With the Comforts of a Home."

The brochure went on to assert that the infirmary "is situated in one of the best and most pleasant portions of the city. The buildings are surrounded by a luxuriant growth of shady and ornamental trees and shrubbery. The entire grounds and surroundings are cheerful and homelike, and eliminate, as far as possible, all depressing ideas of an infirmary. The street cars pass every few minutes from the different railroad depots and steamboat landings."

The brochure promised that "the class of cases taken in this Institution covers the whole field of disease, except Insanity and Infectious Maladies. Special attention will be given to Surgical Cases, including Deformities, Laceration of Cervix and Perinaeum and troubles affecting the Genito-Urinary organs; also Rectal troubles . . . the physicians in charge are equipped with the most complete and modern Electrical Appliances known . . . and Electric, Vapor and Turkish Baths and Massage, which have proven remarkable curative agents . . ."

The original infirmary, depicted in etchings of the period as a balconied wood-frame building surrounded by trees and shrubbery, gave way to a more institutional brick structure near the turn of the century. That structure, renovated in 1952, survives to this day. The Sisters of the Holy Order continued to administer St. Mary's well into the 1970s, when rising debt forced them to sell it to a nonprofit corporation. Under the post–Civil War care of the sisters, the hospital had accommodated seventy patients. In the 1920s, when the region's population numbered more than 20,000, the facility mustered forty-four beds.

What happened to the hospital was fairly representative of what happened to hundreds of similar small-town hospitals around

America. Its pool of patients shrank as the population declined, after the Second World War, and the number of patients able to pay for their own care shrank even more radically. (Most patients transferred their bills to Medicare or Medicaid, and in the 1980s, reimbursement for these funds began to decline, even as operating costs for hospitals increased.) By the spring of 1986 the average daily census of the hospital was eight patients. The nonprofit owners had incurred severe debt and had turned over the management of the facility to a medical center in Paducah. This center filed for bankruptcy in June 1986, citing debts of more than two million dollars.

The State of Illinois and some neighboring universities tried a variety of subsidization and reorganization plans, but the odds were hopeless. The building itself was in violation of several safety-code standards. There was no obstetrical care available. Most doctors were referring their patients to hospitals outside the community. The hospital's license was due to expire at the end of the year, and recertification was in grave doubt. The hospital closed its doors on December 1, 1986, except for an emergency room, which survived until August of the following year.

After that, people who got seriously ill or were injured in Cairo were simply out of luck. They faced a thirty-five mile ride by ambulance (or, if they were lucky, by helicopter) to one of several neighboring towns in Illinois, Kentucky or Missouri. A calamity that would have been unthinkable even a generation before had come to pass: the town had lost its hospital.

A blight of slightly less catastrophic proportions had attacked the Cairo school system—as it had attacked many other systems in towns across America.

In 1890, "The Attractions of Cairo" was able to boast that Cairo's public schools were "Crowning Monuments to the Zeal, Liberality and Culture of Her People." The proclamation continued: "There is no institution in Cairo in which its citizens take more pride than its public school system. . . . The school buildings are large substantial structures. . . . The class rooms are all large and airy, and have every comfort and convenience to be found in first-class school buildings of the present day.

"The studies embraced in the curriculum of the grades are reading, writing, spelling, arithmetic, language and grammar, geography—local and general, drawing—synthetic and analytic, United States History, physiology and hygiene and calisthenics, a systematic development of the physical being of the child.

"There are two courses in the High School—one covering the English language, mathematics and sciences; the other, the English language, mathematics and Latin, through grammar, Caesar, Cicero and Virgil—designed particularly to fit the student for colleges or higher institutions of learning.

"Good schools," the brochure concluded, "are the bulwarks of liberty, progress and civilization. Cairo is proud of her schools, liberal in supporting them and progressive in their betterment."

Public school enrollment in 1890 stood at 1,600 pupils.

By the late 1980s, no educators in Cairo were talking about Caesar or Cicero or Virgil; in fact, very few spent much time talking about United States history or physiology, or even mathematics and sciences. What had become the new symbol of hope in the Cairo public school system was a sort of crisis-intervention educational plan called the At-Risk Program—the risk being the risk of categorical failure, which touched perhaps half the 1,300 children enrolled from primary grades through high school. At-Risk, in its essence, was designed to motivate children to stay in school, and thus to assure a large enough enrollment to keep the school system functioning.

It was not consolidation that threatened the integrity of public education in Cairo. The town was too isolated, at the narrow tip of Illinois, to consolidate with any other district. Nor was it a strong alternative system within the town. There was a small Catholic elementary school, St. Joseph's. There was a small Montessori preschool program run by a townswoman. And there was the "alternative" school established in the late 1960s by the Baptist minister Larry Potts, now reduced to only a handful of students.

What threatened the integrity of public education in Cairo was something more basic than any of that. It was the accelerating decline of a population acculturated to the need to learn—a middle class.

But population loss, economic loss, were hardly the only afflictions threatening to destroy American town life. Nor did population gain, even economic gain, guarantee any real restoration of town unity, of *Gemeinschaft*—as the suddenly prosperous and repopulated small towns of the rural Northeast were quick to discover.

Enlightened New England sociologists did not condemn out of hand the sudden migration of urban dwellers; they recognized the communal, as well as the economic, potential of town growth. At the same time, they lamented certain tendencies among these new-comers, tendencies that were as ominous to the long-term health of towns as abandonment and decay. "Metro-imperialists" was a label that gained a certain Yankee currency as the 1980s wore on.

The problem was best articulated by a pair of Vermont sociologists who also participated in the electoral politics of their state, Frank Bryan and John McClaughry.

"More and more people are living in Vermont in spite of Vermont," the two men complained in their 1989 political manifesto, *The Vermont Papers*. "They are spinning technological cocoons to protect lifestyles that are more appropriately practiced elsewhere. They don't want to be Vermonters as much as they want to look like Vermonters."

These people, Bryan and McClaughry went on, were the very "metro-imperialists who stay in the outback and do their best to make it conducive to urban living—who apply the technologies of the city to the country."

These new "unsettlers" of Vermont, the authors charged, "are turning Vermont into an artificial, systemized techno-suburbia at the cost of the human-scale community life which beckoned them originally. The final indignity is 'quainting' the landscape to cover their tracks, the building of postcard villages and the creation of artificial scenic vistas. Meanwhile the native population is moved onto reservations (called trailer parks) or are otherwise zoned away from the places where the urban unsettlers might want to be."

And so a new and grotesque prospect seemed to emerge for the American town, that sacred entity so celebrated by Tocqueville and Agee and Thomas Wolfe and Mark Twain: death by atrophy, or death by renaissance. It began to look as though the American town, in all its maddening orthodoxies and all its ennobling unity of purpose, was headed for the same oblivion as the military band on a summer evening, or the peanut whistle, or those wagon tracks in the dirt of those lost Wisconsin county roads.

And yet not so. For America was not quite ready to surrender its towns, at least not in what remained at the core of its mythic imagination.

Most Americans wanted to live in towns, even as they squeezed themselves ever more tightly into megalopolis. Nearly every survey of attitudes revealed that wish. Even as reports of depression, alcoholism and suicide began to permeate the mass-media picture of the farm crisis and the rust-belt crisis of the eighties, the majority of Americans interviewed said that if they were economically free to do so, they would live in small towns.

"There are in excess of two million farms in the country," noted the sociologist Darryl Hobbs. "But only one fourth of the farmers account for most of the production. Three fourths of the farms generate only a small fraction of the production. Most of these are operated by part-time farmers, hobby-farmers, rural residents or whatever we end up calling them. They not only are not earning income from farming, they're subsidizing their farm income from off-farm income.

"We generally assume that people's quality of life is related to their standard of living," Hobbs continued. "But some recent studies don't show such a correlation." He cited an eighteen-month study by the University of Michigan's Institute for Social Research. "Among persons in all parts of the country, from all walks of life," he wrote, "those people with a 'lower standard of living' express the greatest satisfaction with their lives. Furthermore, those most satisfied of all are living in rural areas."

Even the skeptical Vermont sociologists Frank Bryan and John McClaughry could respect the essential human yearning that has prompted the migration of those whom they call "the unsettlers," the "metro-imperialists."

"The new settlers saw promise in Vermont," they wrote. "They saw an opportunity to establish a place to be, one final attempt to live close to the earth again, one last chance to verify the hope that marks the human race—we are each other's keepers."

And yet the twin afflictions of town life in the last decade of the twentieth century—atrophy and hyperprosperity—seemed almost perversely at odds with that hope: these very people, who loved towns so ardently, were the agents of their gathering doom.

Chapter IV

The night Doc Poston came to Cairo is an event that certain towns-people (not to mention Poston himself) recall with the heightened clarity that approaches myth. Small personal details remain il-luminated in their memory. For Angela Greenwell, it was the night she invited Miss McBride to lean on her.

The night was a cold one in the stunned town—February 11, 1987. The occasion was a small gathering in the home of a Cairo attorney. The organizer was Glenn Poshard, the state senator who had prevailed on Poston to end his retirement and apply his theo-ries of community development to Cairo.

Poshard had invited fifteen of the town's leading citizens to as-semble in the attorney's living room. Black and white, they were an uneasy convocation that included people who had never thought of one another as anything but enemies—if in fact they thought of one another at all. Poston himself would later describe the occasion, with characteristic modesty, in a pamphlet covering the origins of Operation Enterprise:

"Sitting there in the pleasingly furnished front room of a Cairo private home," he wrote, "I watched with a sense of unease the expressions of those fifteen Cairo citizens as the senator glowingly introduced me. . . . The applause was spontaneous. All eyes focused on me."

Two of the eyes belonged to Angela Greenwell. The wife of a

wealthy farm-owner named John Greenwell, Angela was one of the town's few links with aristocracy. The link was direct. Mrs. Greenwell was what a previous era had admiringly called a clubwoman. She had given herself almost entirely to community service.

She was the president of the Chamber of Commerce, operating out of a small and narrow office adjacent to the shut-down Gem Theater. In addition, she directed a Montessori-style program for dyslexic children and gave swimming lessons at the pool on her farm.

A stately woman in the fullness of her middle years, Angela Greenwell wore her golden hair in a swirling bouffant. She never appeared in public without a careful application of eye-makeup, even when her ensemble of the day was a cashmere sweater and fashionable jeans. She drove her silver Cadillac to St. Patrick's Catholic Church and to the several charity projects that she spearheaded each year. And yet despite her endless service, Angela Greenwell seemed to the ordinary people of Cairo about as approachable a figure as, say, Nancy Reagan.

"Angela was like many of the good citizens of Cairo; she never realized it existed," remarked a man who knew and liked her. "When you're in your clique, when you go to Bill Wolter's party, when your husband's on the board of trustees of the bank, when you run in all these crowds—well, it's a little closed society, see. And Angela was in it."

The night Doc Poston came to town was the night Angela Greenwell's perception of Cairo—and her life—began to change. A year after that pivotal evening, Mrs. Greenwell still became misty-eyed as she reconstructed it.

"I had been in the country all day," she recalled in her most mannerly public-speaking voice, "and when I came my normal route into Cairo there was an accident, so I had to go all the way back home and come around a different route. So when I arrived at the meeting Senator Poshard had called, I was late. And when I walked around the corner I saw a movement, and I thought at first, What is this?—it wasn't so well lit. And then I saw Miss McBride."

Angela Greenwell's encounter with Jenolar McBride—Miss McBride was her universal honorific—at the edge of the attorney's house was as symbolic, in its way, as the confluence of the two rivers at the edge of the town. As Mrs. Greenwell embodied the highest social possibilities of white Cairo, Miss McBride embodied the cultural aspirations, such as were able to survive, of black Cairo.

Jenolar McBride was seventy-seven years old. She had begun her teaching career more than half a century before, in 1932, while still a student at what then was called Southern Illinois Teachers College (later Southern Illinois University, Richard Poston's affiliate institution). After taking a master's degree in education at the University of Illinois in 1942—"I was the first black girl in my hometown to get a master's"—she had arrived in Cairo with her husband, also a teacher, in 1953 to begin teaching English and the social sciences. She had retired in 1980, a widow, after rounding out her career in the Cairo school system's administration. A tiny, bespectacled woman in neatly marceled hair, moving along painfully behind a large wooden cane, Miss McBride was one of the very few blacks remaining in Cairo who could, by word and example, command a consensus in her community.

"I didn't realize at the time that Miss McBride had had hip-replacement surgery a couple of years before," said Angela Greenwell, recalling their encounter. "I'd known Miss McBride—not intimately, like I've come to know her, but I knew her casually throughout the years. I didn't even know what was to be presented that night.

"What I *did* know was that there was one large step up to the porch that had to be navigated by her. So I said, 'Miss McBride, why don't you lean on me?' And she—well, at that point we were both late, and she thought maybe she'd turn around and go home. And I said, 'Oh, if you do, I will too! Why don't you just lean on me and I'll help you?'

"So we went on into the house and into the front room, where the extra chairs had already been arranged in a circle. And there were two right together where Miss McBride and I sat down."

Jenolar McBride agreed with Angela Greenwell's version of the story.

"It was too tall, that step up," she said, chuckling. "It was pretty high for me, with my cane. I didn't even know what Senator Poshard wanted to talk about that evening. He'd done me so many school favors I figured I should come when he called. But that step up looked pretty tall. And I said, 'I think I'll just go back home.' And Angela said, 'Oh no'; says, 'I'll he'p you in.' Otherwise, I'm not too sure I would have gone on."

The two women's decision to proceed, supporting one another, into the meeting may have been indispensable to Doc Poston's most fundamental hopes for Operation Enterprise. It was the first spontaneous gesture of conciliation between the two races since the shooting war of a decade before. Angela Greenwell and Jenolar McBride would become the twin pillars of the small group of bold loyalists who sustained the operation through its first, edgy, risk-laden year.

What they and the others heard in that room was an astounding torrent of ideas: ideas they would never have thought to associate with their fading and forgotten little town; ideas that formed the core of Richard Poston's forty-year obsession with the restoration of town life in America.

Several of the people who witnessed that performance attempted to recapitulate it for me, with varying degrees of bemusement or respect. No one savored the task more than Poston himself. More than a year after he had turned that roomful of grudging, dubious Cairoites into a spellbound gallery, he reprised it for me, nearly word for word, in his small apartment.

It was the morning after our dinner with Mayor Moss at Harper's Restaurant. Poston was red-eyed from a typically sleepless night, but neatly turned out, as always—the burgundy cardigan again. I sensed he was even a shade euphoric, perhaps over the windfall of a fresh audience. Whatever else Doc Poston might call himself— professor, historian, community developer—he was at the very base of his instincts a storyteller, a mythmaker. This thought occurred to me again and again as I watched him acting the generalissimo among the people of Cairo, the master of tactics and strategy. His most valuable legacy to them, I came to believe, would be an imparted sense of the *story* of themselves, as characters in a drama.

"The senator started out, and he introduced me," Poston recalled. "A very glowing introduction. I almost had stagefright after listening to it. So then I outlined this program, in which the people of Cairo would study in depth and thoroughly analyze *themselves as human beings.* As a community. It would be like mass psychoanalysis! So that they would really know themselves as a community.

"I told them it would require the active participation and support of every membership organization in town: Rotary, Kiwanis, women's clubs, the Jaycees, et cetera, et cetera. Every business establishment in town, every trade union, the city and county government, and every church in town, bar none.

"It would have to be both black and white, and include people who didn't belong to any organization. It would mobilize the entire community in one vast, overall effort to really examine itself.

"I said we'd hold biweekly town meetings in which we'd organize committees for each of the different areas of community life. We'd have a census committee to gather all statistical data. This is not just the taking of a census. This is the people going into *every household in town:* conditions of the house, whether it has toilet facilities, whether it has heating—so they'd really *study themselves,* dig out their internal shortcomings and problems, and really get acquainted with each other."

Doc Poston paused for breath, and to hold a match to a fresh cigarette. I glanced at the drab trappings of the tiny alcove that served as his living room and study. Everything in it had been scavenged for him by the women of Operation Enterprise, a fact that deeply gratified the active streak of roué in him. ("I'm the only fella in town with five females who have the key to my apartment" was a line he liked to pull on the nuns and new acquaintances.) I was sitting on one of two easy chairs of marginal upholstery. Poston was perched elflike on the small swivel chair that faced a cheap office desk, on which rested a portable electric Smith-Corona typewriter and a scarlet telephone. The other piece of furniture was a sofa covered in an orange brocade so rich it brought water to the eyes. A cramped bedroom, furnished with a single-mattress iron bed, a kitchenette and a closet-sized bathroom completed his apartment. In the bathroom I had noticed a pair of circular plastic styling combs and a can of hairspray.

Poston's library consisted of a cracked-spined *Webster's New Collegiate* and a 1936 edition of *Roget's.* The bookcase that housed this collection also supported a black-and-white General Electric television set, unplugged. The walls were decorated with some commercially hand-tinted nature photographs, a sentimental watercolor of a Revolutionary War fife and drum, and three utterly contemporary cheesecake calendars. A pair of plastic sunglasses had been Scotch-taped to the wall near one of the calendars, along with the handwritten legend: "Dark Glasses for Viewing this Calendar— Marge." Marjorie was Poston's wife, to whom he had dedicated his first book, *Small Town Renaissance,* thirty-eight years before, and who remained at home in Carbondale, sixty-five miles to the north, awaiting her husband's weekend visits.

"Then we'd do this attitudes survey along with that," Poston continued, picking up the presentation exactly where he had left off.

"Where they'd really examine how human attitudes affect the life of a community. That probably is a major psychological force that determines everything a community does. *The levels of suspicion in this town, Ron, are in the sky somewhere.* Everyone thinks everyone else is a crook. Just a very high level of suspicion. Along with that there's a general attitude of *We can't do anything. We're helpless.* A blanket of defeatism hangs over this town."

The imaginary audience murmured and rustled. Poston noted that, and hurried on.

"All right. Then we'd have to have committees on such things as environmental improvement, to examine the physical appearance of the town. Its aesthetic features, its needs for landscaping, beautification, that sort of thing. We'd need committees on government and public service, to build two-way channels of communication between the government and the people, and pave the way for people to become more actively involved in participatory citizenry, that sort of thing. We'd need committees on economic development, industrial development. We'd look into the possibility of industrial recruitment *after proper preparations,* because industrial development is one of the most *highly competitive businesses there is.*"

The Holy Ghost Barber Shop flashed before my mind's eye. The vacant streets of Cairo, so numbingly barren of committee material. Government and public service? I wondered—not for the first time—how much of a chance Doc Poston's mythmaking stood against these desolate realities.

Poston was gesturing, his cigarette hand upraised. "We'd do a thorough inventory of every existing industry in town to try to figure out the possibilities for expansion and new spin-off industries that could be built. We'd examine every possibility for starting new home-grown business through local entrepreneurs—guy with an idea for a better mousetrap and how we'll help him get started, or *her* . . . we'll look into possibilities for agricultural diversification, food processing, vegetable, meat and fish products. We'd get into the subject of potential tourism." (Here I am afraid that I subjected Doc Poston to a rather nakedly incredulous stare.) "We'd have a retail trade services committee to examine the consumer buying habits of the town. Figure out the total effective buying power—Ron, there's approximately *twenty-five million dollars in gross retail sales in this town,* and the town's losing probably 75 percent to other towns. Shopping malls in Paducah! So if twenty-five million gross retail sales is only 25 percent of the total effective buying power, we're talking about an awful lot of new money. We couldn't get it all back, but s'pose we could recapture *20 percent of it . . .*"

From across the street outside Poston's bungalow apartment building came the tinny peals of electric chimes from the neighborhood's Baptist church. My mind drifted to the image of the church that I had glimpsed as I got out of my car that morning—a low-slung sickly yellow stone, or fake stone, building. I recalled that a cannon was pointed at the church, or seemed to be, by a trick of perspective; a commemorative Civil War cannon. It struck me that I had seen a lot of cannons pointed toward a lot of institutional buildings during my brief time in Cairo.

And then, as the electric chimes tonged their irritating accompaniment to Doc Poston's oration, I shifted my mind's gaze to the edifice that truly dominated the neighborhood just down the block from the little church, diagonally across the street from Poston's peeling front door. This was one of Cairo's most venerated historic landmarks, a three-story white mansion of solid brick, built at the close of the Civil War, in 1865. Its formal name was Riverlore, though Cairo people tended to refer to it as the Wolter place, in reference to its present occupant.

Riverlore quite simply existed in a separate sphere from the rest of the town. It hung in some self-generated fantasy of magnolia trees and parasols above the surrounding desperation and blight. Historical brochures of the town pridefully pointed to Riverlore's eleven high-ceilinged rooms, its floor-length windows, its slate mansard roof and its double-doored entrance of carved poplar. The pamphlets drew admiring attention to its period chandeliers, its ceramic-tiled fireplaces, its landscaped gardens and its redbrick walks of herringbone pattern. Notice was paid to the old English clock in the entrance hall (two sets of chimes, Westminster and Whittington), to its ship's stair from the third floor to the roof, to its weathervane and sundial.

None of the brochures mentioned the enormous Confederate battle flag that was tastefully displayed at times from Riverlore's mansard roof.

"We'd need committees on recreation, education, the school system, public and parochial," Doc Poston was declaring. "We'd look into a committee on housing, delinquency prevention, social welfare. We wouldn't leave out anything. And the committees would all be local people. And I would supply a research outline for each committee. But then they would elaborate on 'em. Because you have to tailor-make 'em to fit the local situation, always."

I let half my attention linger on the big white house a little longer. Since the 1960s Riverlore had been inhabited by a tough and reclusive businessman named William Wolter. Wolter's presence in Cairo loomed over Richard Poston's plans for the town as surely as the shadow of Wolter's mansion loomed over Poston's bungalow. As chief executive officer of Waterfront Services Co., a tugboat and mooring service for commercial river traffic, Wolter controlled the wharfage rights to most of the Ohio River shoreline that fronted Cairo, a stretch of nearly two and one-half miles. These holdings made him perhaps the wealthiest, and surely the most powerful, citizen of the town, a potentate who held Mayor Al Moss (humble owner of Al's Boat & Trailer, a small-boat outfitter) deeply in his thrall.

Bill Wolter was invisible to most Cairo people most of the time. One of the few times he came to public attention, in fact, was an occasion of tragedy: in 1978 his fifty-six-year-old wife, Helen, died of asphyxiation caused by the smoke of a fire in her bedroom. The fire did not spread throughout the mansion, and Wolter, who was in the house, escaped without harm. Wolter—who had earlier divorced Helen, married again, divorced his second wife and then remarried Helen—was married once again after Helen's death, to a younger woman whose father owned considerable riverfront property on the Kentucky side of the Ohio River.

Although he moved in the same narrow social circle as the Greenwells and was in fact a close friend of John Greenwell, Bill Wolter showed none of Angela Greenwell's interest in community service. People who had seen him described him as a portly man of harsh temperament ("Looks somepin' like a bullfrog," was one resident's dry appraisal) who affected silk smoking jackets and ascots. He gave a couple of parties a year—one at Christmas, one on Derby Day. The guest list was tightly limited.

A woman who found herself on the inside at one of those Christmas parties recalled it with a sort of bewildered amusement.

"A lot of us people went just because we wanted a chance to see the inside of the house," she said. "And it really didn't work—as a party, I mean. We ate in one room, and then it was 'Now we will retire to the next room.' And we didn't get to see anything but the couple of rooms the Wolters wanted us to see. It's like he keeps it like a museum."

Poston had described for me, in icy indignation, his one meeting with Bill Wolter, at a Christmastime reception at another, lesser, Cairo landmark home. Poston recalled that when the two of them were introduced, Wolter stared at him but did not offer his hand.

Perhaps Wolter had already got wind by then of a plan Doc Poston had begun to hatch for Cairo's economic resurgence—a plan that moved ever closer to his grand design for Operation Enterprise. The plan involved creating a historic theme park down at Fort Defiance, complete with a riverboat, moored on the Ohio, that would house a combination cabaret and restaurant.

Such a venture would thrust Operation Enterprise smack up against Bill Wolter's wharfage empire. Wolter, in a sense, was fashioning his own story of Cairo. It may not have been as bardic as Poston's, but Wolter had begun telling his first. Sooner or later, the two narratives seemed destined to collide.

Now, perched on his swivel chair, Doc Poston was winding up the chapter of his triumphal debut in Cairo. His gray and narrow face was quivering with pleasure.

"Well, when I got through explaining this, Ron, there was a . . . just a *dead silence.* You could hear a pin drop. People looked like they were stunned. 'How could we ever mount such a monumental effort?'" Poston began to shake his shoulders in silent mirth. "They were just literally . . . as if they'd been carried away. There wasn't a word spoken. It seemed like"—here Poston broke into a brief fit of coughing—"*eternity.*"

This sounded a little hyperbolic. But when I asked Angela Greenwell, some time later, to give me her best recollection of the group's response, her answer was strikingly similar.

"He spoke about forty-five minutes, and then everybody was just . . . there was an aura there that . . . you could *hear a pin drop,*" she told me. "People were in a trance. I thought, *Gosh,* this is wonderful. This is spectacular. I'm inclined . . . I lean toward community, like Doc does. I believe in self-help. But this just sounded like it was too good to be true. I thought, *Finally, a group of people were alive,* you know, *in Cairo.* A whole group!"

Even Miss McBride, a woman not given to breathless hyperbole, admitted to me that she'd felt something special in the room that night.

"When he got through readin' what he wanted to read to us," she said, "and tellin' us what the program was all about, we women didn't open our mouth. But the men, they spoke up. Some said, Yes, and some said, Well, I don't know. But yet ever'body agreed to go along with the program. Ever'body, looked like, was in agreement that night."

"Ever'body" included Mayor Al Moss. Angela Greenwell—who could not have dreamed on that euphoric evening that one night some months later, her dignity in disarray, she would be dragged, shouting imprecations at His Honor, from a Cairo City Council meeting—was pleased to see that the mayor was the first member of the group to find his voice.

"He said, 'I think this is a wonderful idea,' " she remembered. " 'I approve of it, I support it.' And then after him, the representative for the labor union said the same thing. And after him, one of the mayor's council members, who was black and who had been in conflict with Al, you know, from day one. And then behind him, one who had run for the council but was defeated, but who stayed involved with politics.

"Here they were, people from different political parties, different races, the winners and the defeated—but here they're all saying the same thing."

Poston moved quickly that night to consolidate the hopeful mood he had created. "I told 'em," he said, "if you're really serious about this, if you really want to do this, form yourselves into a temporary ad hoc steering committee. And then you go to work to promote the idea, all over town. Then, once there is a certain level of interest, we'll begin the town meetings."

Town meetings were the structural bedrock of Doc Poston's community-development philosophy. As he emphasized to me many times in our conversations, the town meeting, though it typically bristled with agenda items and committee reports and citations of accomplishment and action projects for the future, was, in a profound sense, an end in itself. Its overriding function was psychological. The town meeting reinforced a *sense* of accomplishment, of forward movement, even though the stated objectives in any given meeting might be marginal to the needs of the town.

"At each town meeting," Poston said, "there would be a report from one of the committees. It would show its findings, the problems it had dug out, and then make recommendations for action. Very specific, concrete recommendations for action.

"I make sure we have a battery of discussion leaders, and also note takers, to keep things moving in a lively and productive fashion. I even have training sessions for the discussion leaders and note takers. Then at each town meeting, the committee makes its presentation, the crowd disperses into discussion groups, each with its own discussion leader and note taker. Then they reconvene, and the note takers form a panel in front and report back the recommendations."

As labyrinthine as such proceedings might seem as a model for grass-roots democracy in action—although I hated myself for it, I could not entirely suppress the image of Chinese peasants conscripted into Chairman Mao's Cultural Revolution—they apparently stirred the blood of the people assembled in that Cairo living room.

"One of the men—the superintendent of schools, in fact—jumped up and said, 'Well, I think we all oughta take a solemn pledge here,'" Poston recalled, chuckling at the memory, "'that we will definitely see this thing through. That no matter what, we will stay with it and see it through.'

"And they all agreed. And they all stood up. And they all pledged. It was like a group of people in court"—he chuckled again—"being sworn in as new citizens."

Poston recalled driving back up to Carbondale that night, along with Senator Poshard, in a state of ecstasy. "We both said, 'My god, this Cairo thing really is a possibility,'" he remembered. "But I said, 'Glenn, that pledge—don't get carried away by that. At least half of 'em won't live up to it.' And he said, 'Well, these people are pretty sincere.'" Poston paused and shook his head. "Glenn's a very idealistic person," he said. "I have a great respect for him."

As dramatic a piece of theater as it was, Richard Poston's performance before the leading citizens of Cairo was, in most important respects, the easy part. He had won a beachhead in the town for his operation. Now, his years of academic in-fighting told him, he must strike quickly at Southern Illinois University to ensure that there would be an operation to land on that beachhead.

"I said to Glenn in the car on the way home, I said, *Glenn, we gotta get a press release out on this thing.* The acting president at SIU (a man named John Guyon, later the university's president) had been telling me that we couldn't have a press release until—he kept using the term—'we get our act together.' I never could figure out what he meant by 'get our act together.' I'd already written three papers for him on what we were gonna do, and the philosophy behind it, and how we'd get started, and how it would work, and the relationship between the university and the community, and the relationships that would be developed between the university and agencies of the federal government, and with the politicians of both parties, and so on, and how it would all have to be rooted together, and we'd form an alliance and so on—but he kept saying we had to 'get our act together.' "

As John Guyon was very soon to learn, Richard Poston had *his* act together. Poston well understood that without a rapid and specific commitment for funding from SIU, his reactivation as a community developer would dissipate into an empty ceremonial gesture. He also understood the leisurely manner in which such requests usually passed through a university's many bureaucracies. The flanking movement he plotted out that night in Glenn Poshard's car was characteristically simple, and swift, and precisely preemptive.

"I drove it home to the senator how important this would be, this press release, in getting the community thing started. I told him the SIU news service knew all about it, and they had a press release written." (Composed by one Richard Poston.) "All they were waiting for was Guyon's authority to release it.

"He said, 'I'll take care of that.'

"So the next morning in Carbondale my phone rings, and it's Glenn Poshard, and he says, 'You and I have a meeting with the chancellor!' "

Poston was in the thrall of his own story again, smoking joyously, building the cinematic scene.

"It wasn't more than a few minutes till the phone rang again, and it was John Guyon." Poston waved some cigarette smoke into the scene. "He said, 'What's this about a meeting with Lawrence Pettit?' I said, 'I don't know, John, I just got a call from Senator Poshard about that very thing.' See," Poston said, leaning over to explain, "you're not supposed to see the chancellor without going through the president! Gotta have some respect for channels, although I don't have much respect for channels. So John says, 'Well, the chancellor called and asked me to be there too.' I said, 'That's fine, John, I think we ought to all get together.' " Poston paused to indulge a small fit of laughter. "They have a slight problem with me now, because I don't act like a normal professor. I don't respect any of the channels and I call 'em all by their first names. It's crazy."

Yes, it was a movie. One of those pearly black-and-white, Warner Brothers vintage comedy-dramas produced, directed by and starring that irrepressible rascal "Doc" Poston as Spencer Tracy, a fast-talking can-do Joe, come to get things rolling for a certain burg that's been handed a raw deal, but still has a date to keep with a dame called Destiny.

"So we get to Pettit's office, and Senator Poshard lit into him like gangbusters," Poston was almost crowing. "He said, 'We've got these people in Cairo all ready to go. There's a very high level of expectations. The university's the only instrument we have for development in this area. Are you gonna do this or aren't ya?' And Pettit says, 'Well, sure, we're gonna do it.' And then Dr. Guyon says, 'Yes, sure, we're gonna do it.' And I said, 'Well, we need to get this press release out.' And Pettit said, 'Well, why don't you go ahead?' And I said, 'Well, the news service already has a press release written, but they're waiting for Dr. Guyon's authority to release it.' John says, 'I'll call 'em right now.'" Poston paused to laugh again. Then he cut to the next scene, a spinning headline.

"So a big press release comes out: PIONEER DEVELOPER RETURNS!"

Fade to Doc Poston, armed with his mandate-by-press-release, headed back to Cairo to begin the reclamation of his America.

He came back to a crisis-in-progress. The optimistic aura generated by his grand entrance was evaporating fast. Torpor, doubt, cynicism, had reclaimed most of the citizens who had attended that inaugural meeting. Cairo had begun to have second thoughts about its date with destiny.

"At each of our first few meetings, the number of people on the steering committee went down," Poston remembered. "And it continued to decrease. And decrease."

One of the first absentees was the superintendent of schools —the very man who had issued the emotional call for the "solemn pledge" to see Poston's idea through.

Another dropout was a men's clothing merchant, the former president of the Cairo Retail Merchants Association, who had found it necessary to move his own business across the Mississippi River to Cape Girardeau, Missouri.

A prominent Democratic party woman began to make herself scarce. "She's a woman who talks big, everything's lovely, everything's rosy . . . and she disappears," groused Poston, still galled by the memory.

Perhaps the quickest dropout—aside from those who did not bother to attend even one subsequent meeting—was Mayor Al Moss. "He came to one meeting, stayed for about fifteen minutes," said Poston, "and that was it."

Within weeks after its birth, Operation Enterprise lay at the point of death.

It was saved from extinction by the two women who had steered one another into the living room the night Doc Poston came to town: Angela Greenwell and Jenolar McBride.

"You can put a gold star beside their names," Poston assured me. "Those were the two keys. By the very force of their personalities, they saved Operation Enterprise from going under."

The keys Mrs. Greenwell and Miss McBride provided unlocked something that even Doc Poston, with his vast theoretical resources, was helpless to summon on his own: a knowledge of Cairo people, and their dependability.

Gradually, the two women began to repopulate Senator Poshard's steering committee with people who wanted to steer. Mrs. Greenwell worked her contacts in white Cairo, Miss McBride hers in black Cairo. Their task required a good deal of patience and perseverance—phone calls and follow-up calls, personal cajoling, nighttime strategy meetings. But it required something more than that, something not associated with the people of Cairo, certainly in this century. It required what might be described as secular faith: in this case, an ability to imagine and communicate a vision of the town's redemption.

In the late winter, Doc Poston announced the first significant operation of his overall scheme: a census of every man, woman and child in Cairo, to be taken on May 16, 1987.

"Now the whole thing began to come alive," declared Poston. "With Angela's and Miss McBride's help, we got these two census co-chiefs, a white woman named Carolyn Mayberry, and Priscilla Williams, who's a black schoolteacher in the junior high. She's working on her master's degree now, and working on two-three jobs, raising money to send her children to college. Boy, talk about the work ethic!"

This core group of women began to recruit volunteers. Eventually, two hundred twenty-five Cairo citizens responded. Poston set up a week-long training program—three sessions a day leading up to the actual canvass. "I wrote a thirty-page manual on how to take the census for them," he said. "Then I'd have 'em practice their interviewing technique on one another. By the time May 16, 1987, rolled around, they were ready."

The day before the census-taking, Poston organized a community religious service in front of the public library. Two black ministers and two white ministers led the worship. The high school band played, and some five hundred people who had assembled joined hands to sing "Amazing Grace." It was almost certainly the largest public display of civic good will, to that point, in Cairo's history.

The following day, Poston's volunteers fanned out through Cairo's broken streets with their survey forms and their pencils.

I asked Poston whether the census volunteers encountered any hostility in the town. His dark eyebrows shot up.

"Doors slammed in their face. People grabbing their questionnaires and tearing them up. Oh, yes, they did encounter some hostility. There are certain districts in this town that wouldn't give the right time of day to you if you were the wrong color. I'm talking about on either side. So we very carefully arranged it to make as certain as we could that the person working a given block would be a person likely to be accepted by the people on that block. When they'd come to somebody who would refuse to cooperate, then we'd get a different somebody who thought, Well, I can get to them. And in most cases that worked. Now, there'd be a few where nobody could get any information; they wouldn't respond to anybody. So in that case, we'd take somebody who knew the inside, knew the family completely, how many rooms, knew everything about it, and would fill out the questionnaire anyhow. So at the end we had an accurate, complete count."

Along with the population and housing questionnaires, the volunteers handed out another form to be filled out: a kind of public opinion poll that Poston had devised, called the Cairo Community Attitudes Survey. When the returns were added up, it was found that 1,430 of the town's 5,000-plus residents (a figure that included children) had completed the questionnaire.

The population data were undoubtedly valuable to Poston. But the real harvest of the census drive, for him, lay in the responses to the Community Attitudes Survey questions—which the respondents were allowed to answer anonymously. The results did not betray his florid imagination.

"If you look through this questionnaire, you'll see that it has some very delicate questions," he said to me. "What are the things you like most, dislike most, most important problems, how do we get along with each other, who are the most influential people in town . . . And Ron, *they tore this town apart.* I'd made up my mind to write this report up in such a way that it would produce constructive, positive results rather than negative ones. If I hadn't been careful, Ron, *that report could have blown this town to smithereens.*"

The fact that Cairo already lay, to some extent, in smithereens was perhaps temporarily lost on Poston. Flipping through a copy of the Attitudes Report, he showed me some examples of the town's opinion of itself.

"No work, no jobs, nothing here" . . . "Trash, litter, weeds, torn up sidewalks" . . . "Downtown Cairo, ugh!" . . . "No shopping mall" . . . "No swimming pool" . . . "The throwing of trash, beer cans and bottles in the street" . . . "Politicians in cahoots with people of influence" . . . "Cairo's blacks and whites will never get together" . . . "Too much petty crime, homes not safe day or night" . . . "Loud mouths" . . . "Rotten politics" . . . "A closed society."

Richard Poston wrote an eleven-page summary organizing the complaints into categories, each followed by a "discussion question." This would form the agenda for the town meetings of Operation Enterprise. Poston held the first of his town meetings on November 30, 1987. Cairo High School allowed him the use of some classrooms. Before long, a regular coterie of more or less faithful followers began to assemble. The name Operation Enterprise had itself sprung from a citizen's suggestion at one of these meetings, Poston insisted—although, like so much of what Doc would attribute to "the people," it had a distinctly Postonian ring, at least to my ears.

Attendance was lower than the many hundreds Poston assured me had "jammed the rafters" at his town meetings of yore—a typical turnout might range from forty to sixty. Nor were the attendees necessarily a cross section of the town. At one town meeting I attended I asked a middle-class resident, the owner of a radio station, what sorts of people he saw around him. "I see nuns, day laborers, some retired schoolteachers, some people who may own a car," was his reply. And who don't you see? I asked him. His answer was immediate, and faintly tinged with contempt: "I don't see people like me." And yet a sense of purpose—even a mystique—began to radiate, however sporadically, from Poston's presence in the community.

"I have a love affair with Cairo," Poston had declared in a kind of stump oration at the inaugural town meeting. "Tonight, we mark a new milestone in Cairo's history. We come together tonight to begin mobilizing our brain power. This is the beginning of a full-scale organization from within the ranks to march forward for Cairo's future." Addressing the assembled onlookers, he said, "You are making a statement. Your presence shows that you care about Cairo."

As the weeks went by, and attendance languished well below one hundred, Poston came to suspect privately that intimidation—not to say paranoia—was among the factors preventing the meager ranks from swelling. But he allowed himself to be inspired by the beguiled enthusiasm of the people who did venture forth. Perhaps his storyteller's sense of strangeness was even gratified by the ambiguous testimony of one lifelong resident. The night of the first meeting, the woman stood up to declare that after listening to the opening-night presentations, she felt the urge to go to the river and put her foot in it.

Chapter V

I drifted around Cairo in Doc Poston's wake for a few days. I saw the town in the forgiveness of morning light. With eighteen-wheeler rigs dieseling along Washington Street, up from Kentucky and headed deep into Illinois, the flattened townscape borrowed some rough tremors of life.

We had breakfast at a variety of worn little nondairy-creamer cafés. The aluminum marquee outside one of them had slipped a letter: OPEN 5 A.M., LOSE 8 P.M. Poston talked, smoked, talked, never unattentive to the overweight waitresses, who adored him.

His mind was fastened almost obsessively upon Operation Enterprise. The most significant function in the group's brief history—its public debut, in a sense—was scheduled to unfold in just a couple of days: The Quinstate Forum was coming to town, and Operation Enterprise was to be the host organization.

The Quinstate Forum was an annual convocation of sociologists and community developers from towns in Illinois and four nearby states—Missouri, Kentucky, Tennessee and Arkansas. Each year representatives of these communities, along with a few social science professors from nearby colleges and universities, held a day-long meeting "to share their ideas, frustrations, failures and successes with other communities so we may learn from their experiences," as the Quinstate Forum brochure explained it.

This year the Forum had decided to come and review the year of progress ignited in Cairo by Operation Enterprise. Mayor Al Moss himself would make an appearance to welcome the delegates.

Doc Poston had been gearing up for the event like a Broadway impresario. Typing away beyond midnight in his small apartment after long workdays at Angela Greenwell's Chamber of Commerce headquarters, he had written and produced what amounted to an old-fashioned community pageant. His Enterprisers would present it for the Forum at its meeting site, the gymnasium of St. Joseph's Grade School on Walnut Street. For weeks he had been directing rehearsals—drilling his "battery of committee chairmen" in their speaking roles, coaxing each fiercely concentrating participant through his or her excursion into the florid Postonian syntax.

The Quinstate Forum would be more than Operation Enterprise's debut. It would be Richard Poston's formal reemergence, after more than ten years of seclusion, before his peers in the community development world. The Operation's pageant would kick off the Forum's conference in the morning, the Big Finish would unfold that night. All the delegates to the Quinstate Forum would be invited to remain in Cairo to observe and participate in an actual town meeting. Poston envisioned a packed house, regional television cameras—it would be a grand bazaar of boosterism; it would be Araby.

Under normal circumstances it was difficult to lead Richard Poston into areas of conversation beyond his immediate fixations. He had a storyteller's natural contempt for small talk—he bantered less than almost anyone I had ever met—and paradoxically, given his considerable ego, he showed almost no inclination at all to discuss his personal or family history.

In the days leading up to a major Poston production my efforts to learn more about Poston, the man, bordered on the hopeless. Finally, one morning at Glen's restaurant, as George Jones sang "The last thing I gave her was the bird" on the jukebox, Doc Poston picked up a book of matches to turn over in his hands, and launched in.

"Well, I was born in Farmington, Missouri, on December 31, 1914—five minutes of twelve midnight. I've always said, Ron, that if I'd been born six minutes later, I'd be a year younger!" He gave his little guffaw.

"My father was a lawyer. My mother was a schoolteacher. They left Farmington when I was a year old, and they went to, uh, well, we lived in several towns. We lived in Joplin, Missouri, and then my father had a law office in Kansas City, Kansas. I actually grew up in Kansas City, Kansas. That's really the town I remember.

"My father died when I was ten years old. His name was Felix. Felix Oliver. So, when he died, it left my mother with—there were three boys, and my two sisters were twins; they were eight years older than I was. One of them died of MS—she was bedridden for about twenty years. The other, who is now eighty-one, lives out in San Jose, California, and she acts like a kid of thirty-five. And then my brother, who is five years younger than I am, he lives out in Arizona. Near Phoenix. He was the manager of Harrah's, the night-club, and restaurants out in Las Vegas, before he retired.

"My other brother—he died when he was four years old, of pneumonia. They didn't know how to treat the pneumonia in those days. So my mother had these five children. And my father had had a lot of serious business reverses; they'd just gone through what they called the panic of 1924, and '25. And he was just getting going again, had bought a house there in Kansas City, Kansas, when he had this heart attack. And that was the end.

"And so we didn't have much money. If we had five dollars in the house, it was a lot of money. We were really floating in wealth with a five-dollar bill! My mother's relatives talked her into movin' to St. Louis. So we went there for a year and we didn't like it. So we went back to Kansas City."

He tried a sip of the cold coffee, made a face, and set the cup back down.

"I remember one time in the thirties when I wanted to join the CCC, the Civilian Conservation Corps. I'll never forget this. Your family had to be on welfare to make you eligible for the CCC. I went down there, and they said all I had to do was get my mother to sign a piece of paper saying we were on welfare, and they'd let me in. So I went home with this piece of paper, and I'll never forget this as long as I live—*my mother had a fit.* She said, 'That's tainted money. Government money is tainted money. We will never accept tainted money if we starve to death.' And yet here she was, a life-long Democrat."

Poston's narrow eyes were nearly closed under the thatch of his brow. There was silence for a moment—the waitress filled our cups and set down a bonus fistful of nondairy creamer—and then I told Doc Poston that it was a funny thing, but since I'd met him, I'd been trying to figure out his own politics. It was true: his missionary-like taste for organizing collectivist town projects had struck me as the hallmark of do-gooder liberalism; yet his contempt for government social-assistance programs, his constant romanticizing of individual enterprise, sprang directly from conservative ideology.

"I can't tell whether you're a Republican, or a Democrat, or what," I said.

This pleased him; his gray face came alive again with a short guffaw. "Well, I usually try to keep that a secret from people," he said. "In this bidniss you obviously have to work with both parties, be able to go in and out of all factions, and get along with all of 'em." And then Poston began a story that sounded at first like a different conversation entirely.

"My mother was a teetotaler," he remarked, a little dreamily. "She was superintendent of the Sunday school in the Methodist church. She believed everybody should stand on their own feet. She drove those principles into her kids. We were a very close family. Very close."

He lit a fresh Now.

"I got so deeply involved with the federal bureaucracy during the 1960s," he went on. "Johnson's War on Poverty. Sargent Shriver wanted me to be director of training for VISTA. The domestic version of the Peace Corps. And I told him, "Sarge, I'd be more than happy to serve as a consultant, but I don't want to work for the federal government.'

"So he got me to Washington as a hundred-dollar-a-day consultant. That was in 1965 or somewhere along in there. Ron, I went there—they were in a building that was, as I recall, eight stories high." Now Poston's voice began to take on some of its oratorical pitch. "All day long, people just kept running up and down the elevators! Except at noontime they'd all go out for lunch and have two or three martinis—*and they'd be smashed for the rest of the afternoon.* And I spent the whole week there, and I didn't do any work. So on Friday I came in and said I was gonna go home, and they thought I meant back to the hotel. I said, 'No, I'm going back to Carbondale. I just want to collect my five hundred dollars and go home.' "

The imaginary audience was back in its seats, and Poston was at the podium. I became aware of a few diners at far tables, turning their faces to survey Doc.

"And they wanted to know, 'Why are you doing that?' I said, 'Look, I have been *stealing from the taxpayers for five solid days.'* I said, 'I'll take this money now that legally you owe me, but which

I've really siphoned off of the—it's gone down the drain. But in this case, I'll accept it. But that's all I'm gonna steal from the taxpayers!' "

Poston stared off into space for a moment, still scandalized at the memory. Behind him in the restaurant a man laughed out loud at something, and a waitress rang the cash register bell.

"Ron, *I wasn't doing any work.* I was on a *bureaucratic treadmill.* I flew back home, flew into St. Louis, took a commuter flight into Carbondale. The next day, I got in my car and drove over to Murphysboro, the county seat, and changed my registration from a Democrat to a Republican. It's been that way ever since."

After a moment or two his voice softened again.

"I'm not really either, I guess," he said. "You know . . . I just think that we've gotta have more self-help in this country."

I asked him if he would pick up the story of his childhood in Kansas City, Kansas.

"We—we were very poverty-stricken, Ron. My two sisters, who were then eighteen years old, got jobs with the telephone company. One of 'em kept working till the other could go through bidniss college, and then *she* worked while the other one went through. They supported the family, those two eighteen-year-old girls. My mother's total life was wrapped up in taking care of this younger boy, Charles, our brother who died."

Of all the conceivable options a fatherless, nearly destitute Midwestern family might consider in the Depression year 1934, relocation to the state of Montana might have ranked in probability with a tour of the Balkan states. And yet a series of impulses led exactly to that opportunity for the Postons. More improbably still, the move led young Dick Poston quite by accident into contact with an experimental field of municipal sociology that would form the theoretical core of his life's work.

"I had the notion I wanted to study forestry," he said. "One of the most highly recognized schools in that field in those days was Montana State University in Missoula, which is the headquarters of Region One of the U.S. Forest Service."

One of Poston's sisters was married in 1934. By coincidence, she and her new husband chose to spend their honeymoon in Glacier National Park, in northwestern Montana.

"They took my mother and me and my brother Robert along. We all rode out with my sister Virginia and her husband on their honeymoon," Poston said, and chuckled. "They dropped us off in

Missoula. That's how I got to Montana. That's where the university was. We didn't have the money to send me away to college, so we just all moved out there."

"And there my mother set up a private kindergarten, which she operated till she was eighty years old. She took twenty-five kids in the morning and twenty-five kids in the afternoon."

In Montana Poston's boyish fantasies of life as a forest ranger became transmuted into a more sophisticated concern for the reclamation of land.

"I got out of forestry and took a degree in botany," he told me that morning at Glen's. "I'd gotten interested in range management, which involved the scientific study of grasses, edible plants—so botany became my field of study."

The degree took six years to achieve. Poston found it necessary to drop out of school for long periods and find work to support his mother, brother and sister.

"I went to an employment agency one time," he told me. "Got a job on a ranch, running a stacking rack in a hayfield. Guy asked me if I'd ever worked on a ranch before. I said, 'Oh, I come from Kansas. Kansas is full of wheatfields.' What I didn't tell him was that I came from *Kansas City,* Kansas." Poston stopped to chuckle, still abashed at his own mischief.

"So I got a friend to take me down to a farm implement store to see how these machines worked. I learned that, but I also had to drive a team of horses. I'd never done that before. We found a fellow driving a junk wagon through the streets; we stopped him and asked him to let us drive his horses. He said, 'Git outa here!' " Poston was convulsed for a moment, helpless to continue. "So we got back to the ranch, and there were the horses I had to drive to load the stacker. Boy, were they monumental animals! Guy told me to take the horses and unharness them. I'd never unharnessed a horse before in my life. Boss came up and said, 'Migod, you've practically taken the harness apart!' Said, 'It'll take me two days to put it back together!' But he was a nice guy. He let me get away with it."

Even more vivid were Poston's memories of his days as a worker on the U.S. Government's Western Range Survey on the plains of eastern Colorado, near the Kansas line.

"It was during the height of the dust bowl," Poston said, leaning back a little in his booth and staring at something beyond the confines of Glen's coffee shop. "Two-mile-high clouds of billowing dirt coming across the plains. The land had been overplowed—the tractor'd just replaced the team of horses—and in the drought cycle there were no wheat roots to hold the soil in place.

"We were measuring the carrying capacity of the range. The square-foot density of every species of plant growing there. Each plant had an edibility factor. We had to figure how many cow-months you could graze a given piece of ground.

"And, Ron, the dust storms had blown the ground down to absolute hardpan! Blown the soil clear out to the Pacific Ocean. You could strike a match on the surface of the ground. Dunes of dirt piled up over the second-story windows of houses."

In this crucible of waste and ruin—80 percent of the surrounding farm families were on public relief—the small young man, the college student and part-time soil conservationist, began to improvise his first rough notions of community enterprise.

"See, the Soil Conservation Service was setting up these demonstration projects to show farmers how to bring their land back," Poston explained. "Get their grasses and wheat to grow. Well, Ron, what I did was, I got to going out there and organizing these farm families into discussion groups. I figured that if the farmers and their wives could discover these things for themselves—if it was *their* idea instead of some Soil Service bureaucrat's—then they'd have the will to get something accomplished.

"I did the organizing on my own—weekends, evenings. I truly believed that if these ideas for reclaiming the range came from the farmers themselves, they'd act. And they did! They motivated themselves."

An inspiring, and quintessentially Postonian tale—harboring one small, crucial, and quintessentially Postonian hedge: it was of course Poston, and not the farmers, who supplied the "discoveries" and "ideas"—and also the genius for getting the farmers to believe the ideas were their own.

Montana in the 1930s was not quite the uncorrupted Rocky Mountain wilderness that the calendar art and the postcard tintypes of the period might suggest. The state had inherited an uncommonly lawless and bloody legacy from the fur-trading epoch of the early nineteenth century, a legacy compounded by the gold-rush era of the 1860s and then the buffalo-herd bonanza of the 1880s. Prospectors, speculators, railroad barons, stickup men, prostitutes, gamblers and waves of kindred get-rich-quick artists had fought, pillaged, used, swindled and murdered one another for more than a hundred years, helping themselves in the process to the territory's precious ores, its pelts, its hides, its grazing land—not to mention the native habitats of the Crow, Blackfeet, Gros Ventre and Assiniboine. By the end of the nineteenth century a new source of riches was being gouged out of the mountains: copper.

In 1911 the Anaconda Copper Mining Company emerged, after a decade of brutal entrepreneurial warfare—sabotage, bribes, mob violence, lawsuits—as the preeminent economic colossus in the state. A year later the Montana Power Company was organized. Soon the two corporate leviathans became intertwined, having common interests, officials, political aims and social policies. Together, they became known by Montanans simply as "the Company." Their combined holdings included mines, timber, stores, dams, power plants, and many of the state's influential newspapers.

Among the most telling social effects of the Company—compounded by the wounds of Montana's violent, exploitative history—was the repression of local initiative and public dissent. This, in turn, had the effect of creating the venue for a radical new form of laboratory experiment in community dynamics—an experiment whose populist assumptions would seize hold of Richard Poston's imagination. The experiment was called the Montana Study.

Richard Poston caught up with the Montana Study in 1945, after a stint in New Haven as a government bureaucrat. He did not participate in the study itself but attached himself to it as a kind of self-invited chronicler (magazine articles, later a book) and trailed in its wake until it shut down its operations in 1947, under a cloud of skepticism and academic hostility.

The Montana Study changed Richard Poston's life. He fell under the spell of the men who had created it; he traveled five thousand miles across the state, revisiting the towns it touched, interviewing the people who had participated in it, prevailing on them to describe their experiences, conversations, feelings. He heaped all of these impressions into a book of euphoric, almost desperate celebration, *Small Town Renaissance*, published in 1950, when Poston was thirty-six years old. Among its other attributes, the book is a lexicon of Richard Poston's habits of thought and speech, which still reflect, in their peculiar mix of innocence and obsession, the common American vernacular during those few postwar years of overwrought faith in, and longing for, the perfectibility of the nation. On one of my visits to Cairo, Poston gave me his only surviving copy of the book. I read and reread it for months afterward—sometimes engrossed, frequently dubious, always a little awed in the presence of Poston's own palpable, enigmatic yearning. And always hearing his young-old voice resounding off every page.

The Montana Study had its philosophical genesis in 1943, with the appointment of Ernest O. Melby as chancellor of the state university system. A product of Minnesota farm life, Melby was temperamentally disposed to view America as a vast organism connected, nourished and biophysically balanced by its tissue of towns and small rural communities. He saw the great population trend of his time, the war-accelerated shift from farms to cities, as a kind of pathology: a glut of cells in certain sectors of the organism, a resulting deficiency in the great remainder, with a disastrous prognosis for the organism entire.

Poston would write in his book that Melby interpreted the swelling of cities as nothing less than a threat to the postwar balance of international power. "He had seen this movement into the cities accentuated by . . . still more loss of independence in political and social thought," Poston asserted. ". . . When the guns of World War II ceased firing, America would be thrown into conflict with Russia, which would be the leading exponent of state collectivism and communism, and if America failed, the world would say democracy does not work. . . . If the University of Montana could do something to help people in its towns and rural areas to live more fully, more richly, and more creatively—then, thought Melby, Montana . . . might actually introduce a stabilizing influence on the entire nation."

Ernest Melby did not have to scour the fringes of academia for a pedagogical underpinning to these visions. He could draw upon affirmation from within his own respected institution, Northwestern University, in the person of a professor of philosophy named Baker Brownell.

This was the same Brownell who wrote, in 1950, "Rural life is the normal milieu of the human community. Thousands of years of human culture confirm it. . . . Cities have come and gone."

Ernest Melby's dream of Montana—radical and even dangerous, given the entrenched political interests and the quasi-colonial economies of the state—was to revitalize Montana's small towns through an aggressive interventionist extension of the university into Montana town life. Shortly after he became chancellor of the University of Montana, Melby was able to persuade the Rockefeller Foundation that such an outreach was worthy of funding. Shortly after that, Melby tapped an old colleague at Northwestern, ruralist philosopher Brownell, to help him conceive a master plan.

On April 28, 1944, Melby, Brownell and David Stevens, director of the humanities division at Rockefeller, together drafted the outlines of the Montana Study.

Doc Poston was well diverted into his personal reverie now. The waitress had given up the pretext of filling his cup. He sat with his long jaw resting in the palm of his hand, his elbow braced on the table—the attitude of a college kid; cigarette smoke plumed up from the side of his skull. He had given himself up completely to the pleasures of this excursion.

"When I graduated, Ron, there were no jobs in my field," he said. "This was 1940. They weren't hiring any botanists. I'd gone back to Montana, to Helena, to join the forestry service. Didn't know what I was going to do next.

"Well, in 1940, the U.S. Census Bureau was gettin' ready for the decennial census. They had their enumerators, with their big portfolios—this was before the age of computers. They'd go into every household and take down information on great big census questionnaires. Then in Washington, at the Bureau, they had a room with about four hundred coding clerks. Their job was to code the questionnaires, then put them on a keypunch card and run them through IBM sorting machines. That's how they counted the population.

"So in 1940 the U.S. Census Bureau sent telegrams to civil-service people all over the country, inviting them to tabulate the census. Well, I was in the civil service. And I'm sitting up on a lookout tower in Helena National Forest in Montana when they called me from the ranger station telling me I'd got a telegram offering me a job in Washington." The memory put Poston at a loss for words for a moment. His eyes went a little shiny.

"The notion of going to the *Nation's Capital*—why, that was just unbelievable! Think of it—going to the *Nation's Capital!*" He was a young man again. "The way you went to Washington in those days was on the train. Or a bus. I took the train."

It was in the Nation's Capital—as the Flames of War Licked their Way across Europe, and a Mighty Democracy Prepared for the Grim Task of Preserving Freedom—that Dick Poston met, wooed and won the woman of his dreams.

"I got there, and there were four other fellows and I—we jointly rented an apartment. And we were all lookin' for a date. I had the name of this girl. The pastor of the Methodist church in Missoula, Montana, had told me to look up his niece, Marjorie Atkinson. So

I said, 'I'll show you fellas how to get a date!' I called up the War Department. That was where she worked. And I gave her this big line. She said later she'd never got a line like that."

The night Dick Poston met Marjorie Atkinson, it was just like in the movies.

"I'll never forget—she was living in a girls' boardinghouse. They had a parlor there where you could sit on a couch and talk to your girlfriend. We sat and talked there for a long while. And then finally we said good night and she closed the door behind me. I stood out there in front of the boardinghouse and lit a cigarette and said, *I'm gonna marry that girl.*"

It took Poston five months, by his own reckoning, to get his first kiss from Marjorie Atkinson. "But I plotted a well-organized campaign," he assured me. Eight months after that kiss, they were married. "We had a lot of plans," Poston recalled, almost out of the side of his mouth. Bogart-like, he stubbed a cigarette into the saucer of his coffee cup as a thin trail of smoke escaped his nostrils. "I was going back to the Soil Conservation Service. I'd had an offer from 'em to go to Albuquerque for two thousand dollars a year." He squinted. "That was a lot of money then."

The Land of the Rising Sun had other plans. As of December 7, 1941, America and Dick Poston had an offer to go to war.

Poston's contribution to the war effort turned out to be less than cinematic, but it was at least consistent with his predilection for exhaustive detail. He worked in the Investigations Division of the Civil Service Commission—counterespionage. He trained with a unit that was being groomed to work with the FBI and the Secret Service to look for spies dropped off German submarines on the coast of Maine and the eastern provinces of Canada. "I worked with the Royal Canadian Mounted Police," he told me with pride in his voice. At the end of the war he and Marjorie headed back to Montana.

The Montana Study commenced operations in the fall of 1944 on the state university campus at Missoula, funded by a three-year Rockefeller grant. Baker Brownell moved his wife and children to Montana from Evanston, Illinois, and set to work defining objectives.

Ernest Melby resigned his chancellorship. The study's funding had triggered jealousy within the university system's other campuses and made his position untenable. He was reappointed president of Montana State and became chief executive officer of the Rockefeller grant. Melby added another Northwestern man to the study's staff, the sociologist Paul Meadows, and the three men began canvassing the state, explaining their objectives to townspeople, hoping to be invited into a community.

"Brownell made it a strict policy never to go into a community to organize a study group without first being invited," Poston wrote in his book. "And this policy was never violated."

The model for Baker Brownell's study groups was the New England town meeting. His aim was to keep the groups nonpartisan and nonpolitical. Ideally, the groups would comprise a cross section of the community. Their agenda would be self-analysis (guided subtly by Montana Study volunteers, who in turn had digested a 50,000-word study guide drawn up by Brownell), followed by an organized pursuit of whatever objectives—economic, social, cultural—had been identified through that analysis.

"The idea of community study groups," wrote Poston, "was based on the belief that frank and friendly discussion by the people themselves is the best way to get at community problems, and that so long as people will talk together as neighbors in the communities of America the democratic way of life will endure."

The first town to accept a study group was Lonepine, a general store ringed by about ninety families scattered across a valley northwest of Missoula. Lonepine's problem was that it was about to die of old age: its settlers were genuine pioneers, homesteaders who had staked out claims forty years earlier. Now the town was losing its children and grandchildren to the twentieth century. They followed the new highways to Missoula, San Francisco, New York. Those who remained were in the mood to hear anyone who thought they could help.

The people of Lonepine, in their overalls and cotton dresses, fell dutifully to their first assigned task: filling out their questionnaires. Brownell's study guide, which served as a basis for the questionnaires, placed strong emphasis on a consciousness of community history: How many families do we have? How many have been here ten years or longer? How have the families in our community changed in the last two generations? It also urged a certain dialectical attention to even the most lighthearted matters: "Recreation should be an important part of our community life," it primly prompted the volunteers to propose, "but in America, recreation has often taken the form of commercialized entertainment. Most of us have become mere spectators. This kind of recreation may be relaxing, but it does not provide an opportunity for creative self-expression. . . . Can play opportunities, both for young and old, be increased? How?"

Once a week for ten weeks Brownell, Meadows and the Lonepine people convened their "town meetings" to collate and analyze the responses to these questions. The results, on the whole, were . . . ambiguous. True to Brownell's fondest expectations, a few "action projects" did indeed spring into being. The Women's Club was inspired to organize a community library. A folk history of the town got under way. A historical play, researched, written and acted by Lonepine citizens, was produced, under the supervision of a visiting professor of theater.

Groping, perhaps, for the most positive light available, Poston, in his book, quoted one citizen as declaring: "As a result of our Study Group we've noticed a big difference in the part young people are playing in our Grange."

The Montana Study moved on.

Another community drama, produced in the played-out logging town of Darby, featured a cast of 125. All the good lines went to the Devil (representing Outmoded Thinking), who strutted about in horns and a cape, chiding the Good Woodsmen, "Beat the land, cut the trees, beat it, beat it" until the Woodsmen had had quite enough of this and hurled the Devil cathartically from the stage. Shortly afterward, Poston's book noted, some townspeople formed a corporation and worked out a rational logging plan. A new sporting-goods shop opened, and a dress shop, and a restaurant, and a farmers' trading center. "We never dreamed," one Phil Twogood told the inquiring young Dick Poston, "that our Study Group would lead to so many wonderful things for our community."

Another study group–inspired community pageant, in Stevensville, a cow town of seven hundred, confronted the sensitive issue of relations between white settlers and the Flathead Indians—and moved the local American Legion chapter to brand the study group as communistic. The charge did not stick.

And so it went through the small towns of Montana. Conrad suffered from a lack of recreational facilities. Enter the study group. Fighting off random charges that they were "idle dreamers" and a "radical element," the group generated a recreation committee that in turn produced an eight-point program to meet community recreational needs, including the construction of a modern gymnasium, an auditorium, a swimming pool, and special rooms suitable for arts, crafts, music and other recreational and educational activities by the public. They even passed a bond issue for a new high school. "Our country is in a dangerous state," one resident opined to the scribbling Dick Poston, "because our destiny is too often governed by pressure groups. A group like ours is a bulwark against the danger!"

In all, the Montana Study had implemented study groups in fourteen communities and had begun almost fifty related projects when its time of reckoning came.

Ernest Melby's hope had been that the project would be accepted by the state legislature and the university system, and would pass from its three-year experimental status into permanence. It was not to be. The university system never united behind the project; the presidents of the various campuses viewed it as unwelcome competition for funding and prestige. As for the state's politicians, many had never heard of it. Many of the rest suspected that it was a communist front.

"Despite the success of its community study groups and the invaluable research conducted through its special projects, the political impact of the Montana Study upon the state as a whole has been small indeed," wrote Poston.

In January 1947 the state legislature voted against a $50,000 appropriation that would have kept the study alive. And yet the study did not vanish without a trace. Its literature formed the models for programs that were soon developed in twelve American states and five countries. Some of its pioneering techniques for surveying community demographics and attitudes became institutionalized in various departments of rural sociology and university extension services, where they survive to this day.

And of course there was the work of Richard Poston.

He became an apostle of the study. In the course of researching *Small Town Renaissance*, he sent out magazine articles on the topic to several publications, including the *Reader's Digest*. "They held it for quite a while," he said. "Finally they sent it back to me with a letter saying how much they wanted to use this, but they couldn't fit it into their schedule right at this time. But, they said, we hope the enclosed check will in a small way express our unhappiness." Poston guffawed. "There, Ron, was a check for three hundred bucks!"

Beyond its revenue value, *Small Town Renaissance* gave Poston cachet in the field. He became a kind of Mr. Community Development—first at the University of Washington, where he established a bureau, and then, in 1953, at Southern Illinois University in Carbondale, where he founded the department that still exists.

"He was part of the coincidences of history," an admiring professor at SIU remarked to me once. "You see the Montana Study, then the civil rights movement, then the Great Society programs and the community action projects that followed. They were all tied together by a common impulse. The impulse was—you'll pardon me if this sounds corny—democracy. There was a tremendous resurgence of interest in democracy and 'community' in that era—not just in America but globally. It stirred people, and to that extent at least, it was successful: people fanning out from the district towns in India, to teach the principles of community action.

"Since then," the professor went on with a shrug, "it has gone down. In India, the Philippines, it became overly refined. Instead of the whole picture, it got bogged down in increased agricultural production, that sort of thing. In America, the major explanation for the decline is the bluntest one: namely, the funding ran out. Academically, we became a problem of taxonomy. What *is* 'community development'? Is it sociology, anthropology, philosophy—what? Right now the department here is under the academic vice president—we are in no college. And this is happening everywhere. Even at a time when, as Edward Said has said, the world is filling up with refugees."

And yet the professor refused to concede that community development in America had had its day.

"You don't hear about them in the mass media," he said, "but the numbers of community organizations that exist right now—it's just phenomenal. *Thousands* of groups right now. Locally active. Staving off the clear-cutting of forests. Fighting utility rate increases, telephone rate increases, watchdogging the coal-mining companies. Greenpeace. Amnesty International. SCAM, the Southern Counties Action Movement.

"Dick Poston has been a model for this sort of work. He's very, very well recognized." The professor chuckled. "Who can write like him? Who can work like him? And he has no fear!"

Poston spent the next two decades working out of the SIU department. He wrote three more books; he did consulting work for other universities. He accepted community-development assignments in Saigon and Colombia for the Kennedy administration. Finally, in 1975, he retired.

"And went to work the next day," he triumphantly told me, "for the Southern Illinois Power Cooperative as their director of area development. They needed a high-pressure sewer system—took four years to get that done. And then the chairman of the board of the Tennessee Valley Authority called me . . ."

The achievements, the summonses, the calls back to action were endless. And so it was hardly an interruption of his retirement when state Senator Poshard prevailed on Doc Poston to come down and save the dying town of Cairo.

The breakfast check had been lying on our table for perhaps an hour. I finally reached for it. The depletions of remembering, and of talking, and of nicotine had begun to show on Poston's thin face. His skin seemed grayer, and his narrow-set eyes, rimmed with redness, had begun to blink rapidly. I assumed he was tired; perhaps I had overextended him, drawn his energy—which I still thought of, at that point in my knowledge of him, as limited—away from more pressing tasks, such as last-minute preparations for the Quinstate Forum.

But as we left the restaurant—it was midmorning on a sunny but raw March day, and the sudden sunlight made Poston squint and blink some more—he repeated a remark he had made the previous night. Its vehemence made me realize how fiercely alive he was. What was not so clear was whether Poston was living, at that moment, in the past he had just re-created for me or the present.

"If this sort of thing were to be implemented by every university in the United States, Ron," he was saying, "*we could change the face of America.*"

Chapter VI

FOR SALE

PROPERTY OF KENT SCHOOL

KENT, CONNECTICUT

The Hill Campus of the Kent School, including over 200,000 square feet of buildings—dormitories, classrooms, gymnasium/auditorium, dining hall and a first-class riding facility—is located on 588+ acres on the top of Skiff Mountain (1300+ foot elevation) in Kent, Connecticut (see photo). . . .

. . . Representatives of the school have met with members of the Kent Zoning Commission and, with their encouragement, have presented a preliminary master plan for the property. This plan proposes up to 350 dwelling units and includes conversion of some of the existing facilities into multi-family units. . . . Kent has in recent years attracted a number of wealthy and famous New Yorkers including Henry Kissinger, Meryl Streep and Oscar de la Renta, and now appears to rival the Hamptons on Eastern Long Island as a weekend haven for New Yorkers. . . . The property is offered for $12,000,000, all cash. . . .

> —From a brochure issued by the
> real estate firm of Hayden,
> Tolzmann & Associates, Inc.,
> of Bloomfield, Connecticut

It was by this notice in the late summer of 1986 that the people of Kent discovered, to their dumbfoundment, that their small town had suddenly been thrust into the preliminary stages of flash-growth. Three hundred fifty new "dwelling units," in the charming parlance of the times, would abruptly swell the town's population by a third.

The notice amounted to a shock in a season of shocks to the town's self-image. In 1986 it was no longer possible to pretend that the big-stakes development washing through the rural Northeast would somehow bypass Kent. Outside money had found the town, bigger money than even the town's most prominent local developers, Gordon Casey and Bill Litwin, had to spend. For instance, a local developer who was backed by New York investors was moving toward a multimillion-dollar deal on a 138-acre family farm north of town on Route 7, the Conboy property: just the sort of transaction that had ignited the rapid suburbanization of countless New England villages already.

And now came this news from a putatively local institution, a symbol of permanence and restraint in the community: the Kent School.

The Kent School, a prep boarding institution, enjoyed an excellent reputation throughout New England. It had been established in 1906 as an academy for boys by an Episcopalian order. The school's most distinguishing landmark was St. Joseph's Chapel. A slate and stone shrine with a cloister, a garden and an elongated Norman bell tower, it was positioned against the steep wall of the tree-covered Skiff Mountain, and on clear autumn days its formal ringing lent the entire town an almost medieval aura. (By contrast, the annual cost of room, board and tuition—$12,600 in the late 1980s—tended to evoke the present.)

The school's regimen was spartan, disciplined, rigorous and tony. Attendance in the Episcopal St. Joseph's chapel, three times during the week as well as on Sundays, was expected of students not specifically Jewish or Roman Catholic. (The Catholics had their own chapel, and the Jewish students had van service to the nearest synagogue.) It was the sort of place that liked to describe itself as "a community of teachers and students," a place that invited prospective students and their parents to "reflect" on its way of life.

Now, the Kent School was giving its host town the opportunity to reflect on *its* way of life, and the prospects of continuing that way of life.

. . .

The reasons for selling, according to the school's headmaster and rector, a man named Richardson W. Schell, were strictly economic and logistical. In 1959 Kent School had begun admitting girls. But the Episcopalian sensibilities of the place—which at the time still insisted on a quasi-monastic routine for its male students—were not yet prepared to tolerate the admixture of young women and men on the same grounds.

The school created a separate campus for its girls on the site of a six-hundred-acre farm atop Skiff Mountain, a steep, winding four-mile journey from the original grounds. As time went on, the Hill Campus added five dormitories, an observatory, several hockey, soccer and lacrosse fields, some tennis courts and a working stable of eighty horses, half of which the students owned.

But this arrangement proved awkward from the start. Winters tended to isolate the girls on top of the mountain; the steep and narrow macadamized road, so enticing in the leafy seasons, could be brutal under ice and snow. Slow-moving Kent School buses transported the girls down and up the mountain to attend joint classes; the daily haul was hazardous and exhausting.

And so in 1986 the trustees of Kent School decided to end the decades of risk and inconvenience, even if it meant ending the segregation of the sexes. They announced plans to consolidate the entire student population on the Valley Campus. The consolidation would cost $13 million. To help meet that cost, the school fathers would place the Hill Campus on the real-estate market for commercial development—350 residential units, as prescribed by the school's own "preliminary master plan."

Headmaster Schell, a blond and roundish man with degrees from Harvard and Yale, who had been appointed in 1980, had a blandly reassuring palliative for local consumption.

Noting the school's eighty-year presence in the "fabric" of the town, Schell told a weekly newspaper that "we are not about to embark on any arrangement, relative to the possible sale and future use of the Skiff Mountain Campus, without giving full and thoughtful consideration to all environmental, economic and social issues. Nothing," he added, perhaps just a shade self-evidently, "would give us more pleasure than to have the town and its citizens give full approval and support to whatever plan eventually evolves."

Evidently the headmaster's assurances were enough for the Kent Planning and Zoning Commission. After a meeting with some of the school's trustees, the commission encouraged the development of the master plan. "This town is ready to go," declared the commission's chairman, a dapper science teacher of South Kent School named Paul Abbott, to local newspaper reporters. "It's going to happen." Asked by a reporter whether conservation easements should be placed on some of the property, so as to blunt the shock of development, Abbott replied: "I don't think the town needs any more conservation areas. I'm really worried about the amount of untaxable land. We better develop what we've got."

The town's first selectman and highest elected official, a woman named Maureen Brady, seconded this opinion. It seemed that, as far as official Kent was concerned, the Kent School plan was right in line with the village's progressive interests.

And yet this uncritical view was by no means universally shared in the community. The first notes of skepticism sounded almost immediately. At the counter of the Villager restaurant, at coffee hour after services at St. Mary's or St. Andrew's or the First Congregational Church, in the bar at Filippo's, in weekly newspaper columns, in backyards and on tennis courts, townspeople started wondering aloud.

They wondered about the meandering old Skiff Mountain Road and its capacity to accommodate the sudden glut of cars and jeeps and vans (not to say motorcycles) generated by as many as 350 new families. "The same factors that make access to the girls' campus difficult, especially in winter, would make a possible 350-unit housing development there a nightmare for town services," editorialized the nearby *Lakeville Journal*.

They wondered about strains on sewer and water systems; they wondered about access by fire and ambulance crews. They even wondered whether the Kent School was as much a part of the town fabric as Headmaster Schell imagined. ("A private school like that is almost a town in itself," muttered one young townsman who had done some maintenance work on the trimmed grounds.) But beyond these specific and technical concerns, the people of Kent pondered a less tangible question, but one always at the edge of their consciousness in the 1980s: was their town on the verge of change beyond recognition, by forces beyond their control?

There was that matter of the "wealthy and famous New Yorkers," just for starters. The idea might have excited the souls of the sorts of people who wrote real-estate brochures, but to the ordinary resident of Kent, it was not exactly the element that made life in the town worth living.

Henry Kissinger's, for example, was an exceptionally undiplo-matic choice of names to drop—at least from the viewpoint of many Kent natives. Near the beginning of the 1980s Kissinger had purchased a 350-acre estate, known as the Henderson place, on Route 341, a few miles from the village. Subsequently no one could recall spotting Dr. Kissinger or his wife Nancy standing in line with a Sunday paper at the Kent Market, or shopping for a pair of hedge shears at the True Value Hardware outlet in Kent Green, or volun-teering to help out with Meals on Wheels at the Kent Grange.

What people did remember, and bitterly, about the Kissingers' relationship with the town was the destruction of the blueberry bushes.

Blueberry bushes had grown wild on some fifty acres of the estate the Kissingers had purchased. The previous owner had permitted townspeople to come onto his property and pick at will, and for many years, blueberry picking on the estate had been one of the community's pleasant spring rituals.

The Kissingers discouraged this sort of familiarity with the lower orders. They discouraged it by ordering the blueberry bushes uprooted.

The town was aghast. The imperiousness of it left many people in a kind of mild shock. Kissinger allowed volunteer workers to salvage some of the bushes by replanting them on Kent School grounds and along the rights-of-way of local back roads. But a cherished tradition had been ripped from the fabric of the commu-nity, and some ancient, deep-seeded grudges against outsiders had been virulently revived.

One manifestation of this revival was vandalism. "If there is one subculture that's a good model of the community as total town, it's kids," a Kent minister once told me. "Unfortunately, in some ways it's an unhealthy model. They have definite allegiances, friendships, places to be, and they know one another better than anyone else. The sad thing is that many of the things they do are sort of destruc-tive."

And much of the destruction, particularly as the 1980s moved along, was aimed at outsiders. No weekenders' house was entirely safe from the attentions, however cursory, of weeknight visitors. Our own house, removed as it was from the main road by a thicket of screening trees, escaped serious damage during the time we owned it. We suffered only one break-in, a surgical and profes-sional job that thankfully escaped the notice of our young children; it was achieved by knocking out a basement windowpane behind the cord of firewood that we kept stored underneath the front porch. The intruders took only a small portable television set—we noticed a radio-cassette deck that had been unplugged from its outlet, but ultimately left behind. The neatness and selectivity of the robbers, of course, did nothing to soften our inevitable anger and disillusionment; our make-believe paradise had been exposed for the fragile artifice it was.

An "outsider" neighbor of ours just down the road, an elderly, retired and widowed banker who lived in his house year-round, was not so lucky. This quiet man had landscaped the small grounds around his early nineteenth-century house, through which a brook flowed under a willow tree into a simple and elegant rock garden. But someone in the sparse neighborhood couldn't stand it. The old man's sapling trees were repeatedly split in half, his rocks overturned, his fence rails wrenched from their sockets.

The newcomers and the outsiders made a predictable response to the vandals, one that had long since gained currency in cities: they rigged their houses with elaborate alarm systems. As the eighties wore on, the nocturnal hills and hollows of northwestern Connecticut resounded with the beeps and peals and shrieks of detonated automatic devices from within darkened, fashionable houses—the devices set off, as often as not, by wind, rain, electricity in the air, or, as one local resident mordantly put it, "a mouse farting against the windowpane." It fell to the state Highway Patrol and the Kent volunteer fire department to respond to these colonists' crises. Alan Gawel, the fire marshall, told me that in a typical year his office alone answered thirty-one automatic alarms. Of those, about seven were genuine emergencies.

The most extravagant and oddly bloodchilling instance of vandalism—if that is the precise word—that our family observed was perpetrated not upon a house or a lawn or a stand of trees, but upon the road itself, the very road that brought most of the outsiders and weekenders into Kent from the city.

Four miles south of Kent, spanning the Housatonic River as it flows parallel to Route 7, is a covered bridge, called Bull's Bridge. The original structure was built in the propitious year of 1776, across a spectacular boulder-strewn waterfall. Its architect was Jacob Bull, the great-great-great-grandfather of Eugene Bull, the retired Kent postmaster and a member of the Planning and Zoning Commission as recently as 1988. George Washington crossed the bridge on his way to a tavern while it was under construction. Its descendant, dating from the mid-nineteenth century, remains a conduit to Kent for motorists approaching the town from New York State on Route 22.

As we approached the bridge on the winding blacktop road one autumn afternoon we noticed that the road had been painted with tire-rubber. And not simply a succession of linear skid-marks, either, but thick savage loops and curlicues—the kind of loops achieved by spinning a car in a tight, screaming circle with the accelerator floored. The loops proceeded, at closely spaced intervals, nearly interlocking in places, to the entrance ramp of Bull's Bridge. On the other side they resumed again: up the short steep incline to the intersection with Route 7, across Route 7, and on up the mile-long rise to the crest of a hill that overlooked our South Kent valley. The looping skid-marks continued on the other side of the rise, down the mile-long descent past other weekenders' houses, past our driveway, and across the railroad tracks to the intersection of Route 341 into town—a macabre, hateful and death-mocking mural of some black obsession, like the circular scrawls of some giant child with a felt-tip pen in its fist.

The following morning, when I drove into Kent for a newspaper and groceries, I found to my horror and fascination that the evil markings continued on, looping and looping again, up and down hills and around curves, for most of the four miles into town. I tried to imagine the gunning engine, the shriek and tear of rubber, the blue smoke, the driver's face, the reactions of oncoming traffic. Had there been one car, or several? Had the driver, or drivers, returned like dutiful workmen each night—I imagined it had been done at night; nights on Kent's back roads belonged to what the minister had called "the subculture"—to continue their sinister graffiti? Or had it all been accomplished in one monstrous, suicidal, alcoholic marathon?

More to the point: if this was indeed some kind of colossal Morse code aimed at newcomers, what kind of atavistic rage might be unleashed by an instant saturation of perhaps twelve hundred new strangers?

From the very first, Kent was meant as a haven from the pressures of growth and density that attended the settlement of the New World. The town had been founded along the classic lines of the closed Puritan society, a century after the formation of the Massachusetts Bay Colony in 1628. By that time some twenty-five towns clustered along the New England coastline and its largest river valleys. A second wave of settlers had already pushed west into the interior. Beginning around 1734, land speculation and the exhaustion of planting acreage had forced yet a third outward push, into what one earlier traveler had described as "a hideous, howling wilderness"—the present northwest corner of Connecticut. Within this hilly territory were laid out, midway through the eighteenth century, fourteen new towns, including Kent.

"Orderliness," "loyalty," "steady habits," "harmony" and "mutual respect" are terms prominent among historians' descriptions of early life in the town. Of the forty-five adult males who brought their families to the site in 1739, after the Windham Auction of the previous year, thirty-two were land proprietors. The proprietors had risked capital in competitive bidding for the privilege of their positions in the town, and like proprietors elsewhere in the New World, they guarded those privileges—surveying, road- and school-building, the setting of tax rates—closely. The agreements they had signed were rigid: each original landowner agreed to build a house not less than eighteen feet square for each lot of fifty acres. He agreed to "subdue, clear and fence" six of those fifty acres for dwelling purposes. He agreed to certain matters of conservation, cleanliness and civil conduct. Reliability and constancy were survival considerations in the Yankee wilderness. Each member of the hive was expected to contribute his or her share. There were no weekenders.

There was, undeniably, a flurry of speculation in Kent land in the first decades after its settlement. But the buying and selling was transacted largely among relatives. The town's population remained remarkably constant over the years: from the initial 440 in 1739, it took seventeen years to reach a thousand. It took three quarters of a century to double that number, an event triggered in the 1830s by the first real labor-force immigration, when the town's ironmaking industry began to expand.

The second wave of newcomers appeared at the century's end as the ironmaking era played itself out, and it was greeted with cynical calculation by the locals. "We can all get some benefit when deserted farms are taken over by gentlemen to whom farming is a fad," one writer of the times advised. "They are sure to spend money and benefit the laboring people. This class of purchasers should be welcomed and encouraged."

By 1930 Kent's population had sagged back to 1054; the local people got by on small farms, raising dairy cattle and tobacco. It was about then that the third influx of outsiders started arriving—the influx that would continue, in small increments, for the next half-century, until the era of flash-growth.

This group consisted of artists and writers—the forerunners of the weekenders, the summer people, the "wealthy and famous New Yorkers." The artists came because the land was cheap and beautiful and life was peaceful. As they stayed, the artists inevitably became interested in local government affairs. This did not necessarily mean that the locals had a corresponding interest in the artists. The artists attended the town meetings. They voiced their opinions along with the locals. Sometimes their opinions differed from those of the locals. Sometimes these differences had to be mediated by the police.

But as the years went on, and more and more newcomers trickled into Kent, and as the affluence of the newcomers increased, and as they grew older and retired from their professions and made the gradual conversion from "weekenders" or "summer people" to "permanent residents," a metamorphosis of town politics occurred: at some point, the newcomers-turned-permanent-residents began to take over the political governance of the town.

Some became selectmen. (The bylaws provided for three.) Maureen Brady, the first selectman and only full-time elected official, had moved to Kent from Long Island. She had been a longtime secretary to a beloved, local-born first selectman named Bob Ward before his death in 1984, and had then succeeded him in the office.

Another body of government that typically attracted a lot of these people was the Planning and Zoning Commission.

Planning and zoning had not existed in Kent until the mid-1960s. Like most New England townspeople, heirs to the Puritan values of orderliness and harmony and mutual respect, Kent residents had always regarded zoning as mildly totalitarian, if not downright blasphemous—an outrageous constraint on the sacred right of property owners to husband their land as they saw fit. (It was this plausible philosophy, exploited by distant development-speculators, that turned many unzoned New England villages into strip-developed monstrosities in the 1980s.)

The people of Kent beat back four separate campaigns to establish local zoning before they finally approved a master code in 1965. What turned local sentiment around, as it happened, was not the abstract threat of rapid expansion, but the clear and present prospect of a junkyard. An outside firm had applied for a permit to open up such an enterprise in the history-laden hills north of town.

Even then, the town's selectmen held out as long as possible. They defied a court order to permit the junkyard. A Planning and Zoning Commission formed only as a last resort, and it quickly approved the necessary restraints.

Now Kent at least had a legal mechanism for dealing with the onslaught that was still unforeseen, although inevitable. But for years, and in fact well into the 1980s, the commission remained temperamentally disinclined to obstruct the sovereign wishes of property owners.

The P&Z, as it was known, remained dangerously ineffective in more subtle ways as well. Its membership was blithely and obliviously in over its collective head. There were no qualifications beyond getting elected, on slates that were generally unopposed—although members were expected to take a look at the master regulations. There was no pay. Service on the commission was part of Kent's "volunteer" tradition. Expertise in land use was simply not part of the equation. But perhaps not even that was the root cause of the risk. Perhaps the root cause lay in the emerging new temperament of the town itself.

As the 1980s progressed, the pre-Revolutionary village of Kent, Connecticut, seemed increasingly to hold these Truths to be self-evident: that all Men are created equally interested in Real Estate, that they are endowed by their Realtor with certain unalienable Rights, that among these are the Adjustable Rate, Rising Property Values and the Pursuit of the Top-of-the-Market Turnover.

Real estate dominated the town's political life, defined its social classes, saturated its consciousness. A new town hall, completed in 1989, was situated on land donated by a real estate agent and developer, and formed a sort of faux-civic backdrop to that same developer's new shopping area, called Kent Green. Some less-than-reverential Kent citizens privately referred to the building as "the town hall boutique." Real estate display ads bloated the pages of Kent's two local weekly papers. Real estate shingles (nearly always of white clapboard, hanging from a Colonial-style post and chain) decorated an astonishing proportion of the trim lawns along Main Street, as well as those less conspicuous to the transient traveler.

Real estate, in fact, seemed to blossom as the industry of choice in the area: the 1989–90 New Milford telephone directory, which covered Kent and a scattering of nearby towns, listed no fewer than ninety-two separate real estate agencies (well over a hundred if one included the separate offices of such corporate firms as Merrill Lynch, Robert Mark, William Raveis, RealTech Realtors and Century 21), followed by twenty-six real estate appraisers, thirteen commercial real estate specialists, eleven real estate consultants, ten real estate management firms, five real estate title services, four real estate developers and one real estate maintenance contractor. (To be sure, there was some overlap here, as a few firms defined themselves under more than one category.) This was not to mention the listings for related businesses, such as security-guard and patrol agencies and real estate inspection services.

The real estate people did their work well. During the eighties Kent, which for most of its history had been a self-contained village of merchants, tradesmen and innkeepers surrounded by small dairy farms, drew property taxes from a population almost equally divided between permanent residents and weekenders. Many of the permanent residents, moreover, were people at midlife who had come to settle in Kent from somewhere else.

"And it's changing every year," observed one real estate agent. "All the property we're selling is going to New Yorkers, probably 95 or 96 percent. The average townsperson here can't afford to buy a damn house in Kent." The realtor shook his head, as if wondering when all this irrational buying and selling would end. "It's kinda sad, in a way, you know," he said.

Another broker, equally scandalized by the rampancy of it all, pointed out that six hundred building lots remained for sale in Kent. "Within five years those lots will be sold," he said. "I know they will. Now, if you put six hundred more families in Kent in the next five years, it will have a tremendous impact. Roads, sewers, schools. We can't keep providing these services. We don't have any real commercial tax base. So taxes will keep rising." The real estate agent sighed a "what are you going to do" sort of sigh. "We've got to work something out," he said.

The preeminence of the real estate culture was incarnated in Kent's two leading citizens. They were not manufacturers, not owners of established retail businesses, not clergymen, not doctors or lawyers, not famous artists or writers, not retired entertainers or sports stars, not even—strictly speaking, at least—political figures. The two leading citizens were none of these. They were real estate men. (However, one of the two—the largest individual property-owner in the town—had served as chairman of the Fire District's Planning and Zoning Commission; and although the town's nominal political leader was its first selectwoman, many residents looked upon this broker as Kent's de facto mayor.)

Much of Kent's ongoing folk drama during the eighties flowed, in fact, from the proximity of these two men, and from the fact that they nourished a mutual loathing and were each capable of wrenching the town's commercial landscape violently in one direction or another for reasons that depended heavily on one-upmanship.

Their names were Gordon Casey and William Litwin.

Gordon Casey was an authentic baron of the town, perhaps the wealthiest and most powerful native son that Kent had produced. The Caseys were immigrant stock, like the Gawels, and like the Gawels their roots in the town ran deep—into the nineteenth century, although it beat Gordon Casey as to exactly when. The niceties of genealogy were not particularly suited to Gordon Casey's tastes.

Unlike the Gawels, the Caseys—at least Gordon's generation—had struck it rich. The medium of exchange was land.

Gordon Casey ran the town's biggest real estate agency, he owned the most land—about 250 acres within and peripheral to the town borders—and he controlled much of the town's politics. At sixty-four he showed the remnants of the swarthy young business bull and general hell-raiser that many of his acquaintances remembered with clarity, if not for the record. His hair was still anvil-black, and his brows were two violent slashes. His suitcoats strained under his bull shoulders, and his broad, thin mouth took many dips and rises from the left side of his face to the right.

He was known, among some of his friends and most of his enemies, as the Godfather; or, if they were feeling more charitable, as Chairman Casey. Nicknames like those rolled off his back. If he felt like it, Gordon Casey could come back with an aphorism or two that would shut everybody the hell up. One of his favorites was short and sweet: "Owning," he liked to rumble with terrible joviality at his cronies, and sometimes his adversaries, "is zoning."

It was Gordon Casey who had sat as head of the Fire District's Planning and Zoning Commission for a number of years, irrespective of his status as a land broker. It was Gordon Casey who had donated (or ponied up, depending on one's point of view) the two acres at the foot of a picturesque little gumdrop of a mountain that were the site of the new town hall. (The building turned out to be a rather strenuous-looking redbrick edifice that might indeed have been mistaken as one more specialty shop among the other mock-Colonial specialty shops on Casey's Kent Green: the Body Image, the Cobble Cookery, Sweet Violets, the Orient Express, Je-Lang Tile.)

"My father's father came over from Ireland, stayed in New York maybe a couple of weeks. Had some connection in Kent; I've never been able to find out what that was," Gordon Casey told me, in a rumbling, distracted growl, in his office one Sunday afternoon. "Came up to Kent and bought this house on Lane Street, which is an in-town house. And was married, and then he had—" Casey squinted out the window for a moment; his lips moved "—one, two, three, four. Had two boys and two girls. One was John Edward, that was my father; the other was Harry J., that was my uncle. A daughter Francis and another daughter Margaret.

"My father went to school to the eighth grade in Kent. Then he had to go to New Milford to high school. He went down there; he used to take the train or some damn arrangement. And he went four years to New Milford High School. And that"—Casey flipped a hand over, palm up, on his desk—"was it."

That was all it needed to be. John Edward Casey came back home and went to work as a clerk at a general store, near the center of town, known then as Watson & Morehouse. Morehouse died. "My father somehow accumulated enough money, borrowed enough money from his father, to buy out Morehouse's share. They changed the name to N. M. Watson & Co. Then Harry—my father's brother—started to work in the store. My father expanded the business to include lumber as well as the general store."

In 1935 John and Harry Casey bought out N. M. Watson. Their purchase included the store, an adjacent lumberyard and, directly across Route 7, a graceful old two-story Victorian house that was used as an inn to accommodate the railroad trade. It was known then as the Petite Chalet. (Among the young women of the town who worked as waitresses in the Petite Chalet's dining room was Dorothy Gawel.) Later the inn became known as the Golden Falcon. The building remained a town fixture until the Casey family tore it down in the mid-1950s.

At the close of World War II John Edward Casey gained absolute control of N. M. Watson: the general store, the lumberyard, the inn across the street. At about this same time Gordon Casey, his son, returned to the town after several years at Fort Bragg, North Carolina. Gordon joined his father's business.

More than forty years later Gordon Casey reflected on how close he had come to missing out on his entrepreneurial rise in his native town—how narrowly he had escaped a college education.

"I figured I'd go to Syracuse," he recalled, glancing out his office window with the hint of a private grin. "Guess I was gonna take a business course or some damn thing like that. But then I got back here, and—Syracuse never happened. A mistake, in a way," he said, in a tone that did not convey deep regret. "I started to work in my father's lumberyard as a laborer. I gradually advanced from being a laborer up to buying stuff, and so on, so forth."

When his uncle Harry died at age forty-nine, Gordon Casey joined his father as a partner in N. M. Watson & Co. One year later, almost to the day, John Edward Casey died. And Gordon Casey, twenty-five, freshly married, found himself the chief executive officer of a lumber company.

"I didn't know anything," he rumbled. "It was a question of, do I keep the business or sell it off. I elected to keep it and learn the lumber business. Which I proceeded to do. I worked like hell on it. I built the business up. I ran it for nineteen years."

In that time Gordon Casey increased the annual gross revenue of N. M. Watson from about $800,000 a year to $8 million. "That would translate to about $25 million in today's economy," he pointed out. He accomplished this by learning lumber. He learned when to place his order on twenty carloads of 2-by-4H plyscore sheathing: not when the load started out from the Pacific Northwest, but when it reached Chicago and the seller was more eager to strike a deal.

At the same time, Gordon Casey began to acquire land.

"I sold out the company in 1972 because I heard the railroad was gonna go out," Casey recalled. "The Penn Central line. I could see what that was gonna do to my lumber business. I couldn't remain competitive if I had to have all the lumber trucked in. This outfit called Gettman and Judd offered me the best price, so I sold it to them. I retired. I was forty-eight then.

"That didn't work. I was extremely restless. So I said I gotta do something. So I took a real estate course. 'Principles and practices,' anybody can take it. You gotta work for somebody else for two years. So I did that. Then I opened my own agency. That happened in 1978." Casey shrugged, glanced out his office window. What else did I want to know?

Kent, Connecticut, in Gordon Casey's father's time, was essentially the same town it had been at the end of the Civil War, when the perfection of the Bessemer steel-making process ended its hundred years as an iron mining and forging center. When the last furnace was shut down in 1895, Kent reverted to its pre-Revolutionary character: a farm hamlet. Dairymen, grain farmers and tobacco growers kept the economy alive. For the next half century after John and Harry Casey established themselves, Kent would change only in response to the most insistent of outside pressures and trends: the telephone, the power line, the fading of the railroads, the ascension of the paved highway and the automobile.

It was a town shaded by elm trees and laced by the whistle of the midnight freight. Its storefront buildings were a Hobbits' world of shifting and layered functions: the post office moved back and forth across Main Street depending on the political party in power; the legendary E. W. Bull Building sold ice-cream cones and coffins and gasoline downstairs, while upstairs it provided meeting-space for town meetings, school plays, and suppers put on by the Masons, the Eastern Star, the Grange.

Kent's citizens had their own brand of New England flintiness: the town clerk, asked to speak louder after muttering the minutes of the last meeting, would always fire back the same rejoinder: "Dig out your ears!"

The circus came in the summer, and the rodeo, and the auctioneer. Passenger trains connected Kent with the laticework of similar hamlets around the northwest corner of Connecticut. Visitors could disembark at the northern end of Kent Station and stroll easily into Kent's tiny midway: to Fiengo's Pewter Mug, a bar and restaurant (a barber shop was in the back); to Chase & Giddings, with its newspapers, cigars and soda counter; to Mosher's Store for dry goods, shoes, dress patterns; to Boyd's Store for a frosty soda pop, licorice, jelly beans, bib overalls, men's underwear and, outside Boyd's a stem-winding gas pump.

"Maybe the nicest thing about the town," wrote Donald Connery in his appreciation of Kent, published in 1972, "and the most old-fashioned, is the way those citizens long in years grow old so gracefully and so naturally continue to play valuable roles in the workings of the community. Not only are there some three-generation households, but there are grandparents and even great-grandparents serving most usefully in local government and in the church and social organizations. Retired people still earn money superintending the tool museum, looking after the maintenance of the library, playing the church organ and taking on jobs that fit their experience. By their presence they strengthen the roots of the young."

That observation was unquestionably as true in 1872, or in 1772, as it was in 1972. It was however, to prove dramatically less true in 1982. The fact is that within a year after Connery's book was published, Kent's two-and-a-half-century-long era of bucolic continuity and contentment began abruptly to end. Within a decade, Kent had all but ceased to be a haven for indigenous "citizens long in years." These people found themselves crowded aside by the newcomers, who were short on years, perhaps, but long on cash.

Perhaps the single person most responsible for thrusting Kent out of its cocoon and into the late twentieth century was Gordon Casey's nemesis, William Litwin. That, at least, was what the nemesis himself enjoyed thinking.

"I would like to take the credit as being the individual who put Kent on the map," allowed Litwin, tilting back in his cushioned swivel-chair, when I visited him in the study of his South Kent farmhouse home one day. "Kent used to be a sleepy little village up here that nobody knew anything about. It was just sort of . . . there."

Not after Bill Litwin hit town, it wasn't. After Bill Litwin, Kent was, irrevocably—whatever else one might say of the town . . . well, it was *There*.

If the aging Gordon Casey was the town's quintessential insider, Bill Litwin was its most ambitious parvenu. Despite his arsenal of personal advantages—he was younger than Casey by perhaps fifteen years, muscular from years of military training, glib where the older man groped for a sentence, audacious where Casey was cautious, flamboyantly public where Casey was private—despite all of this, Bill Litwin had not as yet, after nearly twenty years of trying, quite managed to supplant Gordon Casey as the chief arbiter of the town. All he could claim for his efforts to date were one bankruptcy and one wickedly finagled trophy from the old man's personal archives: the deed of title to the land, which Casey had leased to a trust company, on which the old N. M. Watson general store and lumberyard had once stood—the Casey family's druidical shrine.

"Litwin's little bit of underhandedness," as he joyfully admitted, involved a tax-free exchange of properties through a third party in another town: Litwin then ripped down the remnants of the shrine: three or four empty lumber barns that had stood for half a century, with charming incongruity, in the center of the village. In their place Litwin erected a new complex—"Railroad-Era Victorian" was the formal architectural description—that he called Kent Town Center.

The center, a small two-story maze of shops and office space, was completed in 1989. It stood not fifty yards from Gordon Casey's real estate office at the northern end of town, throwing the townscape ever so slightly out of scale, so that Casey could contemplate, if he chose (or perhaps even if he did not choose) its Railroad-Era Victorian lines every day on his way to and from work.

"That's bullshit," Litwin cheerfully conceded of the Center's designer description. "It's neo-mall."

And yet even this masterstroke of audacity left Litwin feeling a little unfulfilled. Gordon Casey remained the town's kingpin. Bill Litwin may have had the stamina, the gall, the imagination, even a certain vision, necessary to engineer Kent's destiny in a way that would forever bear his imprint. Gordon Casey, however, had the land. And the political influence. The town hall was in his shopping center, not Bill Litwin's. "Owning," as Gordon Casey might have reminded Bill Litwin, "is zoning."

Certainly Bill Litwin had started out as though he intended to own Kent—or at least sweep the town and everybody in it, including Gordon Casey, toward a destiny that would surpass George F. Babbitt's most florid visions of Zenith.

Litwin had hit Kent in 1970 with his second wife, Marcy, in search of nothing more than that same quality he would later dismiss out of hand—a quiet country retreat. He was a commercial airline pilot then, for Pan American Airlines, and a veteran of twelve years as a Navy pilot in the Mediterranean, having reached the rank of lieutenant commander. He had grown up in Southern California, and retained that region's prevailing politics—libertarian conservatism—and its clear, open-voweled way of speaking. But his roots had been severed in considerably darker, less bountiful circumstances: Litwin's parents had fled Nazi Germany, their small son in tow, not long before the outbreak of the Second World War.

Once established in Kent, the Litwins decided that Marcy needed something to do while Bill was in the air for Pan American. They rented some space on the ground level of a storefront in town and Marcy began selling small potbellied stoves. (The storefront was the same one from which E. W. Bull had once dispensed ice-cream cones, coffins and gasoline, and where John and Carol Hoffman would eventually put their House of Books.) Litwin himself puttered contentedly about the store during his hiatuses from flying. Years later, he would look back on those uncomplicated times with a certain wistfulness.

"The town had some real characters back then," he recalled. "We had Bart Seger, sort of a mountain man—he and his brother used to sit up on Fuller Mountain Road in their outdoor privy, door open, waving to people as they drove to work. Bart was the town drunk. He used to stand outside the Episcopal church on Sundays and shout obscenities." Litwin allowed himself a nostalgic smile. "When we ran the Country Stove, Bart used to come in and just sit around until we'd kick him out. He'd sit by the woodstove. He smelled bad. And he looked so awful. He would go into the laundromat and take all his clothes off except his long-johns and run 'em through the wash. He was a real character." Litwin paused a moment, lost in reverie. He shrugged. "And then one day he froze to death in back of the Chevrolet dealership."

Those halcyon days ended abruptly when Litwin stumbled on the commodity that for a few years made him one of the fastest-rising entrepreneurs in the Western world.

The commodity was a small Japanese-made kerosene-burning space heater. Litwin came upon one, between flight assignments, in the home of a California friend. Litwin was immediately struck by the device's mass-marketing possibilities. Americans, in the early 1970s, were still suffering the aftershocks of anxiety over the OPEC-induced oil shortages. Here was a cheap alternative to both home heating oil and woodstoves—and no one had yet seized on it.

Bill Litwin seized. He moved quickly to form a contractual agreement with a Japanese production firm, Toyotomi Kogyo, that gave him the sole right to distribute its kerosene heaters in the United States. Then he opened his own company in Kent. He called it "Kero-Sun." His payroll, at the outset, covered two employees.

Within three years Litwin was a former airline pilot and an industrialist of the future. His payroll quickly expanded to three hundred in Kent alone, and his company brokered a product for a U.S. distributorship that grew to fourteen thousand.

Sales totals reached $200 million. "We were international," Bill Litwin remembered. "We had a Swiss company, we had a British company, we had salesmen and a sales office in France. We had a New York advertising firm, Young and Rubicam. Hill and Knowlton was our advertising firm. Kero-Sun had worldwide publicity. Huge spreads—I mean, every time you opened the paper, every time you read a business magazine, there was something about Kero-Sun.

"That's how we put Kent on the map. All these people—plus all the salespeople, plus all the people from all over the world who were trying to get us to sell them and get distributorships and so forth—they all came to Kent. A lot of these people you see around here now, people who are now retired, getting near retirement—they came here because of Kero-Sun."

Meanwhile, the entrenched power structure of the once-quiet little town, a structure headed by the arch-druid Casey, sat and silently watched the newcomer flash his roll.

"For a while there, I was the golden boy of the business community," said Litwin. "My prominence in that community transcended Kent. I'd risen above all this. You know, I was somewhere else, flying my Lear jet around and all sorts of crazy things.

"Well, the fact is, at that point I was feeling very magnanimous. And I was giving a lot of things to the town. I planted all the trees along Main Street. I paid for most of the town's new fire truck. I paid for a good deal of the town ambulance. These are the kinds of things that I was doing."

Well, not exactly *all* the kinds of things. It was during this flush period—in 1981, just before his equally spectacular crash—that Bill Litwin felt brazen enough to whisk Gordon Casey's ancestral turf out from under his nose.

"Look," said Litwin, "the property had gone to seed. Everything had decayed. It became worse and worse and worse. I came along and said, *What a great spot for a conference center! And a hotel!* Which we fully intended to do. We thought it was right on target. Perfect for Kero-Sun.

"I tried to buy it from Casey. But he didn't want to sell it to me. He didn't like me to begin with. He considered me a threat to his power base, because of Kero-Sun. So I had to get it through the tax-free exchange with this third party.

"When Gordon found out about it, he went crazy. Really furious. He was furious. So, from that point on, Gordon did really strange and sort of bizarre things."

One of those things was Casey's announcement of the revival of the Golden Falcon Inn.

"When he heard that we were gonna put up a conference center," said Litwin, "he put up a sign directly across the street—right where the Lions have their lobster thing—that said, Future Site of the Golden Falcon Inn." Litwin paused and shook his head.

"Everybody knew that was bullshit. Pardon me, but there was no Golden Falcon Inn going in there, especially if we were gonna go ahead with our thing. Ours was gonna be a *big thing*. A forty-five-room hotel, and conference rooms, and all kinds of things. Two stories. Now, if you'll recall, the original Golden Falcon was one of the inns on Main Street that the Casey family *tore down!* The Casey family tore down a lot of historic buildings in this town. But build another one? No way."

History would never record the extent to which Gordon Casey was willing to maintain his Golden Falcon gambit alive against William Litwin's hotel and conference center. People abruptly stopped buying Japanese kerosene space-heaters. In 1983 Kero-Sun went bankrupt.

Litwin insisted, in the years that followed, that it was the mild winter of 1982 that caused the drastic decline in kerosene heater sales. But equally as damaging, surely, was a famous Consumer Reports article, published in the fall of 1982, which asserted that kerosene heaters were potential fire hazards. Whatever the precise cause, Kero-Sun evaporated from the world business scene as abruptly as it had appeared.

Litwin himself escaped ruin by the grace of bookkeeping: he kept his salary and personal finances separated from the company's ledgers. But his days as a corporate Golden Boy had come to an end.

"When Kero-Sun collapsed," he said on that afternoon in his study, "the plans for the inn and so forth collapsed with it. One of the major users of that complex would have been Kero-Sun. So that thing went on ice."

Litwin bared his teeth in something like a grin as he remembered the capping detail of the whole debacle.

"The minute that happened," he said softly, his gaze focused on something beyond his booklined wall, "Casey's sign came down."

Chapter VII

> We judged that three nights more would fetch us to Cairo, at the bottom of Illinois, where the Ohio River comes in, and that was what we was after. We would sell the raft and get on a steamboat and go way up the Ohio amongst the free States, and then be out of trouble.

With the publication of *The Adventures of Huckleberry Finn* in 1885, the unprepossessing village of Cairo, Illinois, found itself lifted into the pages of world literature for a third time: Samuel Clemens had joined Charles Dickens and Anthony Trollope in citing the town. Trollope had visited Cairo twenty winters after his countryman Dickens, in 1862, to observe "the sheds of soldiers . . . bad, comfortless, damp and cold," at Ulysses S. Grant's army barracks at Fort Defiance; and the native American, Clemens, would steam past yet again, several years after his river-pilot days. Known by then as Mark Twain, he would blandly remark in *Life on the Mississippi* that "Cairo is a brisk town now and is substantially built and has a city look about it. . . . "

But in literature, as in its melancholy life, Cairo was mostly a travesty of American community ideals. A compendium of dreams gone wrong. An object-lesson. By the time Al Moss got back home from the air force in the early 1960s and opened a business and worked his way into the favor of the town's elders and got himself put forward in public life—as a leader of the White Hats: then as fire commissioner; as commissioner of public health and safety; as city councilman; and finally, when a man named E. J. Walders slumped over and died in office in 1974, as mayor of Cairo—by that time, the town was essentially finished. Like so many other towns along the Mississippi Valley, towns that a century and a half ago had been founded in the brilliant dawn of the westward rush—that Emersonian thrust of self-invention, of eternal renewal—Cairo now lay in the thickening amber of its past.

A new century had passed it by; had passed them all by. As their transportation-based economies—their reasons for being towns—receded, vanished, these congealing places were defined proportionately by their communal memories, their secrets. Their curse was to remember. And Cairo, like many of these towns in the decaying light of the late twentieth century, had a great deal to remember.

Dickens had seemed to recoil from the village by sixth sense—"a detestable morass," he'd called it on his return upriver in 1842, having branded it "a dismal swamp" on his way down. And even Twain, in selecting the town for its cameo fictional turn, gave it an eerie, almost prophetic function: the point of Huck's and Jim's brush with Cairo was that they *failed* to fetch up in it. They slid past its dozen houses in the Mississippi fog, in the night, into slave territory, and got their raft smashed by a steamboat in the bargain. Even to *wish* to intrude onto this baleful ground, it seemed, was to play dice with the forces of evil.

Centuries before the site became a town, in fact, the best experience anyone could hope for there was no experience at all.

Perhaps the first European to set foot on the riverbound peninsula was Father Louis Hennepin, the French explorer and missionary priest, in March of 1660. He did not care for the experience. Floating down what was then known as the Meschasipi, his party came to "a river within forty leagues of the Tamaroa; near which, as the Illinois inform us, there is a nation of savages called Quadebache. We remained until the 14th, because one of our men killed a wild cow as she was swimming over the river, whose flesh we were obliged to dry with smoke to preserve it . . . We left that place the 14th, and saw nothing worth observation. The banks of the river are so muddy and so full of rushes and reeds, that we had much to do to find a place to go ashore."

Another French Canadian priest, Father Jean François de St.

Cosme, halted at the site for one night in December 1699. He later recalled that "nothing special befell us nor did we find anything remarkable until we reached the Acansias [Arkansas]."

Fathers Hennepin and Cosme were ahead of the odds. Something special did indeed befall the next prelate to pause there. Father Jacques Gravier, journeying with a canoe party down the Mississippi, reached the mouth of the Ohio around October 15, 1700. What befell him and his companions was a nauseating fever that washed over them every three days. Fortunately, the priest improvised an excellent remedy: "A small piece of Father François Regis' hat, which one of our servants gave me, is the most infallible remedy that I know of for all kinds of fever." Father Gravier also reported that his party saw fifty bears moving from the south to the north, and killed four of them.

Sieur Charles Juchereau de St. Denis, an entrepreneurial Frenchman emigrating to Canada, enjoyed even better hunting near the site a couple of years later, and in the process, attracted the attention of the prevailing zeitgeist. Juchereau, along with about thirty of his countrymen, built a fort and a tannery a few miles from the confluence of the Ohio and the Mississippi. Within a year or so the party had killed and skinned thirteen thousand buffalo and had stored the skins for shipment back to France. The Frenchmen also had tremendous success with the abundant deer, bears, turkeys, ducks and geese. The indigenous Cherokees, deeply impressed by this entrepreneurial energy, waited discreetly until Juchereau had accumulated a large stock of skins and furs, and then, "selecting a convenient occasion and with united forces," as a local historian later put it, "they made an attack upon him and his men and killed almost all of them and seized the whole of their valuable collections." Juchereau escaped, but died a few years later in the nearby settlement of Kaskaskia.

The first man to recommend settlement on the site had the prescient instinct to also recommend fortifications. Father Xavier de Charlevoix, arriving in 1721, wrote in his journal that the countryside near the conjunction of the Mississippi and the Ohio "consists of vast meadows, well watered, where the wild buffaloes feed by the thousands . . . A fort with a good garrison would keep the savages in awe."

It was not until nearly a century later that anyone actually tried it. Illinois, its population growing fivefold with the great westward migration of the early nineteenth century, was admitted to the Union in December 1818. The territories of the Louisiana Purchase were starting to absorb an influx of settlers from the former colonies, coaxed outward by the cheap land and the allure of fantastical promotional schemes. The notion of *progress* was taking hold in America. Many of the onrushing adventurers were not farmers but speculating townsmen, eager to throw up new cities in the wilderness: imagining hotels and dry-goods companies and right-angled boulevards where only prairies, dotted with buffalo droppings, unfurled to the horizon.

It was an age of almost delirious preoccupation with cities' propensity to generate either moral influence or poisonous evil and squalor. Scientific and pseudoscientific theories abounded, overlapped, contended. Cities were the repositories of intellectual and moral beatitude. No—cities were by nature unwholesome, unnatural; witness the European plagues. Thomas Jefferson developed a scheme, late in his presidency, to drain cities of their noxious vapors. "Take, for instance," he wrote, "the chequer board for a plan. Let the black squares only be building ones, and the white ones left open, in turf and trees. Every square of house will be surrounded by four open squares, and every house will front an open square. The atmosphere of such a town would be like that of the country, insusceptible of the miasmata which produce yellow fever. . . ." He wanted New Orleans to be built according to such a plan. It was not.

It was this phobic dread of vast, crowded cities as agents of foulness and disease that led, indirectly, to the creation of Cairo and other "New Babylons" along the great inland waterways of America. A theory arose that such rotted capitals as Memphis, Nineveh and Carthage had succumbed to their own interior decay; to the "exhalations" caused by waste at their centers. One commentator predicted that the emerging American metropolises would escape this degeneracy by virtue of being built along the Mississippi River valley system. Their impurities, the visionaries concluded, would be safely swept away on the current.

Reinforcing that theory was the notion of William Gilpin—a notion adapted from Germany's Alexander von Humboldt—that the great civilizations of the world had flourished within the "Isothermal Zodiac," a belt, circling the globe, that embraced the climate most congenial to man. The global apotheosis of the Isothermal Zodiac, Gilpin felt, was the Mississippi Valley. "The Great Basin of the Mississippi is the amphitheatre of the world," he declared. "Here is supremely, indeed, the most magnificent dwelling marked out by God for man's abode."

. . .

Early in 1818, several months before Illinois's admission to the Union, a group of speculators headed by a Maryland-born merchant named John Gleaves Comegys had secured a charter from the territorial legislature to incorporate, on two thousand acres, a city and bank near the very heart of this great natural amphitheatre at the confluence of the two rivers. The city that would arise there would be named—in reference to its command of a Nile-like fertile basin—Cairo.

In harmony with the spirit of the times, Comegys flourished grand plans. He envisioned streets eighty feet wide and up to two miles long to accommodate trade in this forthcoming American collossus of trade and navigation. He decreed four distinct market-places, each occupying a city block. He called for a total of 4,032 lots platted in a rectilinear pattern on 290 blocks. He immersed himself in plans for levees, a city square.

So many resources . . . !

But for all its projected grandeur, "Cairo was then only a paper city," as a markedly morose marker at the present entrance to Fort Defiance State Park observes. John Gleaves Comegys died in 1819. Without him, the trust group foundered, went bankrupt, and the paper city was forfeited to the United States government.

And so the first New World edifice to be erected on the site turned out to be not a town hall or a statue or a cathedral, but a tavern: the Mouth of the Ohio, put up by two brothers, Moses and Thompson Bird, in 1828. (Thompson Bird was an active impressario up and down the Mississippi in that era. A decade earlier, a few years after the legendary New Madrid earthquake had sent the Mississippi and Ohio rivers foaming backward and created thousands of refugees from the southern Missouri Territory, he had speculated in the U.S. land certificates that had been granted to the dispossessed. Some of the paper he held was for the first building lots of the village that became known as Hannibal, Missouri, the town of Mark Twain's youth and, later, my own.)

As things turned out for Cairo, a tavern proved a fitting symbol of its destiny.

Aside from the Mouth of the Ohio, the "paper city" between the rivers lay unimproved for nearly twenty years. During that time, the townsmen from the eastern seaboard accelerated their great immigration into the American interior. The population of Illinois swelled from 11,000 in 1809, to 55,000 in 1820, to 325,000 in 1836. Progress beckoned the immigrants. The Black Hawk War in 1831 brought the economies of scale (annihilation) to the prevailing techniques of Indian-slaughter (a $50 bounty for every hostile Indian hide). Robert Fulton's paddlewheel steamboats, those flat floating wedding-cakes, smashed and routed the small canoes and keelboats and flatboats that had made up the bulk of river traffic until then.

Cairo lay invisible for a while, a desultory spectator to progress. Its site at the Mississippi-Ohio juncture, barren except for the tavern, served as a wood-yard for the steamboats' furnaces, and the Mouth of the Ohio grew notorious as a watering hole for their famously thirsty captains and crews.

And then quite suddenly, progress burst upon Cairo, in the form of the El Dorado dream.

In 1835 six Illinois men purchased the Cairo site. Their names were Judge Sidney Breese, Anthony Olney, Alexander Jenkins, Thomas Swanwick, Miles Gilbert and David Baker. Four months later these same men formed the original incorporating group of the Illinois Central Railroad.

One year after that, the Illinois legislature appropriated ten million dollars to clear the channels of rivers, build turnpike roads and construct railroads—twelve hundred miles of railroads. The legislature forced the Cairo buyers to surrender their charter to the state, but then granted corporate status to Jenkins, Gilbert and a New York man named Darius Blake Holbrook, and conferred on their company, the Cairo City and Canal Company, the power to construct a city on the land—to be known as the City of Cairo.

Jenkins, Gilbert and Holbrook began expanding their acquisition of land. They acquired the land on credit. As collateral they offered the written promise of a vast railroad system lancing upward through Illinois, connecting ultimately with Galena on the northwestern Mississippi shore, and having Cairo as its southern terminus.

The prospect of a link, near the center of the American continent, between railroad transportation and the conduits of two giant waterways seemed colossal; progress incarnate. *(Unlimited resources . . . !)* It was about this time that people started mentioning the unbuilt Cairo as a possible new site for the capital of the republic.

On the 26th of June, 1837—the same day as the incorporating agreement between the State of Illinois and the Cairo City and Canal Company—the company launched one of the century's most flamboyant and far-flung promotional campaigns. Its goal was capital. Among its targets were several English investors, in particular the London banking firm of John Wright & Co. Its technique was the one destined to become a combustive engine of American growth: unsupportable hyperbole, or hype.

Wright & Co. attempted caution. They hired two investigators from Philadelphia, William Strickland and Richard Taylor—men whom the firm understood to be knowledgeable—to go and investigate the site. Strickland and Taylor went willingly, their knowledge of Cairo stemming partly from the fact that they were on the payroll of the City and Canal Company. The report they prepared for Wright & Co. contained the following assurance, among others:

> There is not in any quarter of the globe a situation so commanding and replete with every kind of produce and material to promote the prosperity of the merchant, the skill of the mechanic, and the growth of a great city.

That was good enough for Wright & Co. The London firm doled out loans to Cairo City & Canal totaling $1.25 million. To cover its own bet, and attract investors, Wright & Co. indulged a little hype of its own. It published "florid lithographs," as one Cairo entrepreneur later recalled, "portraying a metropolis at the junction of the Ohio and Mississippi [that] appeared in the pubs, halls and squares of London. Pounds and shillings flowed into the coffers of John Wright & Co., and thence to Darius Holbrook."

Now an actual city began to replace the invisible "paper city." Workers began constructing levees, a dry dock, a shipyard, brickyards, sawmills, an iron works, a warehouse, residential cottages. By the end of 1840 Cairo had a population of 2000.

And yet this eruption of a tangible town concealed a terrible flaw, which was to retard Cairo's character like a malign gene down through all its decades. In one important respect Cairo remained a paper city. The people who had come to live there—the people who were building the shipyard and the levees—could not own the land they lived on. The land belonged to the corporation, to the City & Canal Company. The populace rented. That condition was the recipe for a catastrophe that very soon ignited.

The State of Illinois had overextended itself with its ten-million-dollar Act for Internal Improvements. By late 1839 the state faced bankruptcy. In February 1840 the legislature repealed the act, effectively nullifying its agreement to build a railroad down to Cairo.

The first casualty of this decision was John Wright & Co. of

London. Unable to stem a withdrawal of investors, the firm collapsed in November of that year. (This collapse was on Charles Dickens's mind when he surveyed Cairo from his steamer in 1842—"vaunted in England as a mine of Golden Hope," he could not resist mocking in his journal.) Then, in December, the Cairo Bank failed. On the heels of that failure, Cairo's populace—without proprietary ties to the town or its land—fled. Later that winter the rivers flooded the nearly vacant town, crashing through its new levees and coating its remnants in muck.

The rivers flooded the town again in 1844. They flooded it again in 1849. During these years the arrested embryo of El Dorado lay in a kind of undeath: mosquito-infested, overgrown, mud-caked, teeming in summer with poisonous snakes and wild boars, frozen and exposed in winter.

And yet not utterly expired. The stunted shells of the aborted building-boom provided shelter for assorted itinerants, fugitives, squatters and hermits. (In February 1847, the demi-town actually petitioned the state for permission to construct a building—as it happened, a jail.)

More improbably still, the dream of El Dorado survived. Darius Holbrook refused to acknowledge the finality of the disaster. He maneuvered obsessively to keep his devastated corporation alive.

In March 1843, Holbrook was able to reorganize his firm into an entity called the Great Western Railway Co. The state granted him permission to begin work on a new railroad extending north from Cairo. Capital formation proved slow. In March 1845 the state repealed Great Western's charter. Holbrook and his group sold their holdings. In 1848, a land grant bill for a central railroad system passed the United States Senate and narrowly missed clearing the House of Representatives. Holbrook, gambling on the mood of the times, reincorporated Great Western. But by then the growing inevitability of an Illinois railroad had widened the pool of interested players. Holbrook suddenly found himself in competition with two powerful adversaries indeed—a Chicago financier named Samuel Staats Taylor, and Taylor's ally, the United States Senator from Illinois and the future debating opponent of Abraham Lincoln, Stephen A. Douglas.

Douglas and Taylor had decided to mount their own thrust to organize a railroad. (Douglas's interest stemmed from a wish to see a rail line linking Chicago, rather than Galena, with the mouth of the Ohio.) The senator was able to block land-grant appropriations for Holbrook's enterprise.

Once again Darius Holbrook found his dream thwarted. In December 1849 Holbrook—whose indomitable persistence over nearly fifteen years had prevented the notion of a Cairo-linked railroad from evaporating—surrendered to the combined forces of capital and politics. He gave up his claims to a charter for the last time, and in February 1851 the state legislature granted incorporation papers to the Illinois Central Railroad, with S. Staats Taylor the effective chief officer. (Holbrook was mollified with a thousand shares of stock in the new company.)

Taylor also directed the third—and, finally, the successful—attempt to found a genuine city. Building lots were platted and offered for sale. By 1854 the Illinois Central reached from the town to the Illinois shore opposite St. Louis. Thirty-seven hundred steamboat dockings were recorded in that year. Now people were speculating that Cairo might become the largest interior city on the continent. The town was officially incorporated in 1857; its population stood at 1,756.

But the advancing civilization could not dislodge, or soften, the essential brutality that hung in the river mists about the region; that had predated the town itself by at least two centuries. Rivermen were hard, violent men, and its railroad origins notwithstanding, Cairo was from the beginning a riverman's town.

A local newspaper publisher, writing during the immediate post–Civil War period, recalled with nostalgic affection a certain tradition that had been in vogue among rival groups of adolescent males on the riverfronts during his youth at mid-century. The tradition was known as "tweezering."

"They never quarreled," the memoirist wrote. "They simply 'tweezered' one another; that is, if a single individual was caught by two of an opposite party, he was thrown flat upon his back, and by the use of tweezers, the hairs were pulled from his nostrils.

"We have often seen," the editor continued mirthfully on, "a single young man fly from crowds of cronies, all over the wharf, jumping logs, and hazarding his neck and all to save the one or two remaining hairs that his nose contained. This was capital fun to all but the victim. If he kicked and 'cut up' during the tweezering operation, the hairs were extracted very slowly. This inflicted so much pain that the captive would speedily become quiet and submit to the further manipulations of his captors uncomplainingly. To such an extent," he concluded, "was this folly carried on at one time, that but few young men in Cairo could boast of a single well-developed hair in his nostrils."

. . .

With the railroad open between Cairo and Chicago, the brutal little town at the mouth of the Ohio was at last shouldering its way into the economic vitals of the Midwest. In 1859, Cairo shipped six million pounds of cotton and wool northward, and seven thousand barrels of molasses, and fifteen thousand hogsheads of sugar. And then came the Civil War.

The war seemed at first to consolidate Cairo's aura as a city of destiny. Within two days of the surrender of Fort Sumter in April 1861, a special train carrying a brigadier general, six companies of infantry and four batteries of artillery came hurrying down the new Illinois Central line from Chicago. The soldiers rushed out of their coaches in time to secure the grimy little town—the southernmost point of the country loyal to the Union—just hours ahead of a Southern force advancing from Kentucky.

In September of that year Ulysses S. Grant arrived to take command. On the hastily improvised campground called Fort Defiance, at the rivers' confluence, Grant built the great army that would spill its mass down into Tennessee and then Mississippi on a ponderous and bloodsoaked campaign that would end with the seige and capture of Vicksburg in July 1863.

The disastrous long-term effects of Grant's occupation did not seem disastrous as the army gathered in Cairo: boom times were in.

Tinhorn merchants and building-owners made sudden fortunes on rents and prices, exploiting a transient military population that totaled two hundred thousand over the course of four years. (The rents and prices would come crashing back down after Appomattox.) Refugees—runaway blacks and displaced whites—poured through town from the South; more than forty thousand during the war. (Those who stayed would form the origins of a biracial, mutually hostile underclass in the town.) Prostitutes, gamblers, con artists—the inevitable detritus of an army encampment—worked their way into the burgeoning community fabric and bred a hardshelled subculture of Midwestern vice that regenerated itself well into the twentieth century. *("So many resources . . .")*

The Union military command took control of the city government almost as an afterthought, further weakening Cairo's already feeble political fabric. Other nascent institutions also suffered. "The two newspapers here then received from time to time friendly suggestions from the generals commanding the post," wrote a local historian, "who for the most part were treated as editors in chief."

But the most vitiating effect of the Civil War on Cairo was scarcely noticed in the bustle of the flush times. The town ceased to be a hub of mid-continental trade. A Union flotilla—assembled, forebodingly enough, at Cairo—commenced a blockade of the Mississippi River to cut off supplies to the South. The Mississippi would never regain its importance as a transportation conduit. Newer railroad lines, commencing further to the north and east of Cairo, in the heart of the Illinois farmlands, began to ship pork and corn north to Chicago. It was Chicago, in fact, that would expand into the great Midwestern trade colossus—that would enact the consummation of Cairo's El Dorado dream.

Cairo continued to grow, even to prosper, for about a generation after the war's end, a great onrushing animal as yet unaware of the bullet that had struck. Its population was 8,500 and growing. More than 3,500 steamboats docked there in 1868. Iron works came in, and a sewing-machine cabinet factory, and a massive Illinois Central grain elevator. Seven railroads were based there by 1887. Here was the "brisk town now, substantially built," that Mark Twain noticed from the deck of his passing steamer.

These were the years in which the elegant mercantile buildings sprang up along Commercial Avenue, parallel to the Ohio, the palaces of bracketed cornices and dentils and wrought- iron balconies: the same buildings that sagged, brittle and hollow, in Al Moss's time, facing one another, eyeless, across an empty boulevard wide enough to turn a long-vanished team of horses around in.

For perhaps three decades the white and black races regarded one another uncertainly in Cairo; they even felt their way toward a rough accommodation. The town had simply grown so fast, and with such a scatterquilt mixture—destitute Southern whites, runaway black slaves, and a later influx of black laborers, German tradesmen, Irish roustabouts, English merchants—that a kind of social incoherence prevailed for many years, forestalling the drawing of rigid lines of territorial claim and exclusion. (Besides, European immigrants were busy brawling with other European immigrants, and the European immigrants in general picked fights with the native-born whites for much of that time.)

Black and white families lived in the same neighborhoods—sometimes in the same buildings. Black people were accepted, if not exactly welcomed, in white-owned hotels, theaters, restaurants, barbershops, saloons. Black doctors could practice in the town, and blacks could be elected to judgeships, or the city council; they could join the police department, or work at the post office. There were racially mixed marriages.

Had someone like Richard Poston come seeking to implant community-development ideals in Cairo in the waning years of the nineteenth century instead of the waning years of the twentieth, he would have found a community that worked, in its own rough and bloodletting way. But then, had that someone come to Cairo in those years he would have been lucky to escape with tweezered nostril-hairs and a dunking in the Ohio River. Like Chicago, its expanding sister-city up north, Cairo wasn't ready for reform yet.

But the post–Civil War bullet had struck, had lodged, and the hemorrhaging, irreversible, had begun.

The criminal subculture that had seeped into town during the war spread its stain, nurtured by the needs of whoring, hard-drinking riverboat men and fractious immigrant laborers. By the 1870s tiny Cairo claimed mention among the nation's urban vice capitals: a midlands mecca of murder, drunkenness, professional sex, gambling, vigilante violence, and predatory opportunism. "One of the most wicked places in America," a missionary worker assured his supervisor in New York.

Now, too, the effects of the wartime blockade were starting to leech the town. The steamboat trade thinned out; the rail traffic shifted elsewhere. As Cairo's legitimate economic base ebbed away, its dependence on illicit windfalls deepened.

The races and the classes began to distance themselves from one another. The building boom of the 1880s pulled the shrinking but wealthy class of owners and merchants northward, into small but elegant neighborhoods of brick-paved streets and gingko and magnolia trees. Left behind were the increasingly impoverished families of black and white laborers, who crowded into separate areas of the southern sector, inside thin-walled wooden shanties built on stilts over the porous, flood-prone soil down near the confluence.

A more hopeful segment of the black working class leapfrogged the fashionable white merchants entirely. Its leaders ventured beyond the town's northern border and cleared out a settlement in a lowland thicket near the Mississippi. They named this place, with appalling optimism, Future City.

Future City survives to this day. Or at least the junk-strewn, weed-choked, fire-blackened, skeletal traces of Future City—still inhabited—survive in the canebrake, below the elevated roadbed of the old Illinois Central line, a necrosis attached to a larger scrofula.

. . .

Why did white Cairo grind its heel into black Cairo? Perhaps it would be as sensible to ask: what took white Cairo so long?

Some historians believe it was frustration: the helpless whites making the equally helpless blacks the scapegoats for Cairo's economic decline. Others believe it was more a matter of simply prioritizing the meanness that had floated like a phosphorescent haze over the little dagger-tip of land since the time of the French Jesuit explorers: the whites just needed a few decades to beat and bloody and murder *one another,* first, over their ethnic and religious and class differences.

At any rate, the first racial-purity leagues made their appearance in the town at about the century's turn. The Illinois National Guard arrived in Cairo too late to prevent the 1909 lynching of a black man who had been suspected of raping and killing a young white shopgirl. Three years later the guard just managed to prevent another lynching, this time in retaliation for the snatching of a woman's purse.

By 1915 Cairo was a virulently segregated town. Its population peaked in 1920, at just over 15,000. By 1938, a guide to Illinois cities and towns found it necessary to report that "the street fronting the levee (Commercial) is lined with hotels, shops, and taverns, many of them deserted and falling to ruin." The guide was too genteel to report that Cairo's prostitute population in that era numbered more than a thousand, and climbing. The chief legitimate industry in town was the processing of cottonseed oil, but that was failing, as were the remaining lumberyards and the railheads. The Great Depression had Cairo in its grip—a grip that had not loosened by the time Doc Poston arrived in 1988, the latest visionary to invoke El Dorado.

By the 1930s Cairo had long since ceased to be a port of entry to the North. By then it had become the end of the road—or, as Huckleberry Finn and Jim had fictitiously enacted it more than a century before, a hooded and stygian gateway to the South.

Chapter VIII

These were the memories that stirred dully in the town that Allen E. Moss inherited, virtually as the gunfire died down, in 1974. These memories had long since annealed Cairo's political character: male, grim, suspicious of outsiders, authoritarian; a political character given to patronage, secret allegiances and hard retribution. The pale men who had preceded Moss as bosses of Cairo—elective and otherwise—had been of a paternalistic temperament that was severe even by the standards of small Southern towns. I studied their faces in the black-and-white photographs along a dim hallway wall at the Cairo Chamber of Commerce. Hard faces. The faces of men in starched white shirts and narrow ties and rimless glasses and service-club pins, the expressionless faces of men who preferred to be known by the initials of their first two names.

Like most of the men on the hallway wall, Moss was a Republican. People in town who had known Moss from his childhood found nothing astonishing in that fact, and nothing particularly political, either; at least not in the ideological sense. Allen Moss had always been the type of fellow who wanted to please his elders. And in Cairo, for a century, a fellow—certainly a white fellow—who wanted to please his elders joined the Republican party.

The Republican party had risen to dominance in Southern Illinois during the Reconstruction. These foundations cast an ironic shadow over its generally separatist influence in the twentieth century. The GOP's rise in the 1870s had been augmented by newly enfranchised black voters, who saw Lincoln's party as their best hope for a full-fledged entry into the common flow of American life.

The blacks' very success within this party (in 1870 their votes were decisive in electing a white Republican to the Cairo school board) worked against them. As white Republicans grew increasingly nervous about this new monolithic bloc of influence, they found it convenient to disassociate themselves from their black allies. In the edgy first years of the twentieth century, white GOP party regulars tried a number of ways to disenfranchise the black vote. In 1913 they hit on a masterstroke, one that virtually guaranteed the political invulnerability of Allen Moss and men like him. They changed the rules of the game. The new device was the city commission form of local government.

City-commission abolished the procedure of voting for council representatives by wards. Instead, all candidates ran "at large," subject to the entire city's vote. This meant an end to a black candidate's hopes of getting elected, at least so long as the town's racial majority was white and that majority voted as a bloc—which it did: for nearly seventy years half-black Cairo was without a black City Council representative.

It was Charles Koen, the hunger-striking United Front leader and lifelong nemesis of Moss, who resurfaced from years of lassitude in 1981 to repeal that system. Koen ran for a city council seat. Along with several associates, he used this device to file suit in federal court to restore the aldermanic system of ward representation. Directed by Moss, the City of Cairo rose to the bait. It spent nearly a quarter-million dollars fighting the suit before agreeing to a consent decree that established five wards. A sixth council representative would run at-large, as would the mayor. Koen served one symbolic term; but since that time, there have always been at least three black Cairo councilmen.

Not that this victory necessarily broke down the political/business power elite that had ruled the town for most of the century. In a small town, there was more than one way to grip the loyalty of a man, even a black man, and Allen Moss and his patrons in the business community understood those ways.

A man in town who followed local politics ticked off the surviving mechanisms of control.

"One of these guys is a dentist with no independent political thoughts at all," he told me. "The mayor made him Commissioner of Finance. That makes him the most powerful member of the council outside the mayor—and a mayoral cohort. Then, one of the black councilmen is a guy who tries to do right, but he has a political patronage job. He's a guard up at the state prison. Now, Moss is a Republican, and the governor is a Republican, and Moss isn't above reminding him of that fact. This guy's got a wife and kids to support. In a town where the unemployment rates are that high, if you lose your job, what are you gonna do?

"Then there's another member of the council who has a lifelong business contract with Bill Wolter"—the town's wharfage czar. "A lot of us can't see where Bill Wolter's interests stop and Al Moss's begin. This guy votes on issues like the leasing of city-controlled wharfage rights to Wolter for *twenty cents a lineal foot.* How do you think he's gonna vote?"

So much for half the city council. Two of the remaining three, working men, operated under a different set of allegiances: to a local labor-union leader named Eddie Smith. Smith, a Democrat, had priorities that sometimes conflicted with Moss's. Frequently, they did not. In any event, that left exactly one city councilman whose votes could be considered immune to the pressures of vested interests. This was the at-large member, a young schoolteacher named Darryl Hoppe who worked across the river in Missouri.

But the mechanisms for preemptive control, should the mayor care to use them, extended beyond the potential to influence votes in the city council. There was the mechanism of controlling community opinion, or at least the conduits of its information: the editor of the local newspaper, the *Evening Citizen,* was the wife of the chief of police. And there was at least one parliamentary mechanism that Moss's few vocal opponents accused him of using again and again during council meetings: a selective and arbitrary interpretation of a "pass" vote.

Under the rules, councilmen could choose to vote "pass," if they did not wish to vote "yea" or "nay" on a given issue. Mayor Moss, it was widely claimed, interpreted "pass" votes as whim, or predilection, struck him—sometimes as abstentions, but other times as votes on the side of the issue that he wanted to carry.

Mayor Allen Moss was a true child of Cairo.

"A goody two-shoes," was the way one woman of the town remembered him: the sort of boy who never got his fingernails dirty, who looked after his mother, who never stepped out of line. His teachers had all adored him; he'd had no real friends. He worked his paper route, finished high school, got a glimpse of the world picture in the air force (he made staff sergeant), lived a little while in California, decided it wasn't anything like Cairo and came back home. He got squared away—he married, started an outboard-motor-supply business (he and his wife continued to live in a modest little apartment above the showroom), raised a son, Allen Jr. and followed the St. Louis Cardinals on the radio when he had time.

A small-town paragon. A civic-minded fellow. A good old boy.

And something a little extra.

"Al has more going for him than you might notice at first," a man who had known the mayor a long time observed. "You wouldn't think it, maybe, but he has strong ties to what I call 'the invisible society' in this town. There are some legitimate millionaires here, even though you never see them around. They're isolationists by nature, and they can afford to do their socializing elsewhere. But they're the ones behind the Cairo Women's Club and the Historical Association. They dispense the money to the charities and the foundations.

"These people like the town a certain way," the man went on. "They like to control things. They put Al Moss along in his political career—saw that he got appointed mayor when Jim Walder died. Al Moss is the one they rely on to see that things are done in this town the way they want them."

And what were the attributes that endeared Moss to this "invisible society"?

"He has a certain amount of guts," the man said. "He was the buffer between these people and the niggers during all the trouble back in the seventies."

Certainly the young Al Moss was the apple of Peyton Berbling's eye. Berbling's is one of the expressionless pale faces on the hallway wall in the Cairo Chamber of Commerce. Berbling, now dead, was born at the century's turn, and in the early seventies reigned as the town's uncrowned monarch—longtime state's attorney, arbiter of local society. It was Peyton Berbling who decided that the young Baptist preacher, Larry Potts, had performed "justifiable homicide" in bashing the seventy-four-year-old gardener, Marshall Morris, about the sewing room of the Potts household with a baseball bat until Morris stopped moving. It was Berbling who organized the White Hats, the vigilante committee that stalked black Cairo in white construction helmets, provoking the armed resistance, led by Koen, that led to the shooting years.

Al Moss quickly rose in the White Hats, a flattopped field leader. He led the patrols; he got himself photographed ready to heave a brick at a black picket on Commercial Avenue. These gestures did not go unappreciated within the ruling circles of Cairo. It wasn't long before Moss found himself embarked on a political career. He was elected to the city council, and even awarded an area of special responsibility in keeping with his particular talents and interests: commissioner of public health and safety.

In that capacity, Al Moss offered some memorable testimony during the 1972 hearings conducted in Cairo by the U.S. Commission on Civil Rights—hearings that had been prompted by the racial shooting, arson and mercantile boycotting.

The hearings had already established that Larry Potts's segregated Camelot School had begun operations in two public school buildings that the city had sold to Potts's group at dirt-cheap prices. (The larger building, a twelve-room brick structure, sold for $4400.) Now the commission was examining official Cairo's degree of willingness to move ahead on making low-cost housing available to people, including black people, who lived in that 50 percent of the town's buildings officially described as "dilapidated."

As later recorded by the civil-rights journalist Paul Good, Moss was asked specifically why he had opposed a biracial, nonprofit housing development project that would have been funded by state and federal money.

Moss: "There was a lot of local opposition because they felt like the program—it was a 235 or 236 program, I'm not clear on that. My memory doesn't serve me that exact. But there was a lot of opposition because it hadn't worked anyplace else. And I still think it's fashionable nowadays to do what the taxpayers and the people who elected you want you to do."

General Counsel: "What, if any, steps is the city council taking to provide low-income housing for people in the city?"

Moss: "As far as I know, there are no immediate steps or nothing that's being pushed, but the city does have a Housing Board that is trying to get funded."

Commissioner Mitchell: "Is there a building code?"

Moss: "There must be, sir. As I explained when I first sat down at this table, I do not make that my specialty. I'll be glad to research the subject if you'd like a complete detail on it."

Staff Director: "Mr. Moss, you testified earlier that the basis for your opposition to the 235–236 program was because it didn't work anyplace. Am I correct?"

Moss: "That's right, sir."

Staff Director: "Could you tell me where you got that information?"

Moss: "There was a lot of adverse publicity. I think one of the major networks done an hour special on it. Some of the areas was in Detroit and some on the East Coast, and the West Coast. It just didn't work."

Staff Director: "Mr. Moss, the 235–236 program is the most successful program HUD has ever had."

Moss: "Well, I'm not a housing expert, sir. Maybe it is. But the literature I have read was adverse to it."

This was a humiliating exposure, and there were plenty of other moments like it—the despised civil-rights bureaucrats in their Washington suits, shuffling their papers and whispering to one another and making the local civic leaders look like a bunch of damned thugs and fools—but eventually it was over. The local leaders simply out-waited the Washington bureaucrats, and eventually the commissioners went away, and the town, its ammunition spent, lapsed into its post-armaggeddon siesta.

It dreamed its memories.

The memories survived inside the Cairo Public Library, a two-story brick building erected in 1883, where Jefferson slept undisturbed, and Carlyle, and Conrad (and even Dickens); and where local luminaries were enshrined on microfilm or peeling poster paper. Luminaries such as Mrs. C. L. Keaton, a longtime organist at Cairo Baptist Church who, in 1925, designed the famous redbird logo that to this day perches on the front of the St. Louis Cardinal uniform jersey; and Malvin M. Franklin, the melody-writer whose hits had included "Come Take a Dip in the Deep With Me," "I Was Born in Michigan" (a one-step novelty song) and, "The Jingle, Jingle, Jingle of Money In My Pocket (Is the Sweetest Music to Me)." "Cairo isn't what it used to be," the librarian, a stately woman with swept-up hair, confided to me one afternoon. A memory brightened her face. "It's not like back when we had all the prostitutes—" she put a hand to her mouth.

"Cairo was a good town back in the old days, before the trouble," a grandmotherly woman remembered softly, in the parlor of one of those houses. "It had a lot of good restaurants. It had the largest auto auction in the world going on. There were gobs of drugstores. Men's shops. It had nightclubs. Strippers. We had a town that darky didn't dare go into."

Now there was no place for a respectable grandmother to go, and besides, darky outnumbered whitey—which didn't seem to matter anymore, except in the vaguest of exploitable-opportunity terms: a black person's vote cost five dollars in the local elections.

On the barren surfaces of all these memories, in the amber light, Moss spread his quieting reign.

So many natural assets . . .

He ran a town profoundly dedicated to its status quo. His most important constituents—the white small-businessmen and their wives from Larry Potts's Cairo Baptist Church; Bill Wolter, the Waterfront Services boss who controlled the lucrative Ohio riverfront through a comfortable lease agreement with the city; the other members of the invisible society—all had their reasons, whether economic or emotional, for keeping outsiders on the outside, maintaining a steady keel, consolidating what was already theirs.

The town's energy—such energy as there was—flowed inward. The president of the First Bank and Trust Company, which held the city's assets, was the city treasurer. "A lot of money sits in that bank that belongs to the city," complained a local man. "They don't get the same interest on it as if it were in a bank in Chicago. They have an audit each year, but if they give a report of that audit, I'd have a problem knowing where it is."

"Wolter's responsibility is to maintain his levees and the riverfront," complained a city employee of twenty years' standing, "which he doesn't do. Of course this also applies to Bunge" (a ghastly-looking and -smelling skeleton of a soybean processing plant a mile or so upriver from Wolter's operation, the local colony of a large and distant corporation). "Bunge hasn't maintained theirs either. City workers clean the levees, on the city payroll."

I asked Al Moss one day about the city's relationship with its two largest employers. On the subject of Bunge, he gave me his sincerest local-boy, what-can-you-do-about-it shrug.

"Bunge," he said. "You go over there and start taking a picture on that street, there'll be a guard ask you what you're doing. That's just the way they are. We went for months here when they first came to town—*we didn't even know what that plant was gonna be!* We accepted a local man's word, fellow who was the manager then, that everything was gonna be okay. We took him on blind faith. But big companies in this day and age, they're just defensive as hell."

I asked Moss about Bill Wolter—pointing out to him that many Cairo citizens, not to mention Richard Poston, were convinced that Moss and Wolter ran the town like a fiefdom. We were in Moss's wood-paneled office off the main showroom at Al's Boat and

Trailer, as it happened, and when Moss replied, after a moment's reflection, it was in his role as heads-up businessman and pious civic booster.

"I met him through my connection with the river bidniss," Moss declared, as if otherwise he might never have heard of the man. "And by virtue of the fact that we'd take orders from him. We had shortwave radios and things at the store. Sometimes we'd go down there to deliver orders or whatever.

"Bill Wolter has been good for the river industry," Moss forged ahead. "He's past president of the Propeller Club. Bill's very well educated. He's been in the merchant marine. When we have a drowning, which we have three, four a year here, and we need his boats, he never thought anything about taking that boat off of a seventy-five-dollar-an-hour thing and going out, helping pick up the body. He's just that kind of guy: 'What do ya want, we'll do it,' see.

"Well, that means somethin' to me," said Al Moss, shifting now into his official role as mayor. "I mean, that's the guy that belongs in the community. That's the guy that knows he's got a stake here. Now, he's not a diplomat. But most river people aren't. They're very blunt. If they believe it, they say it. And a lotta folks don't know how to take 'em. But he's successful, too. And in small towns, there's a natural inclination to resent success. How many times have you seen this? The same people that put you on this pedestal will be the first bastards tuggin', tryin' to pull you off."

Some other Cairo citizens were not so dewy-eyed about Wolter's legacy to the community, especially regarding his effect on community growth in general and, in particular, his control of the Ohio levee.

"A riverfront is kind of like a public highway," one man observed. "You don't have a right to keep everyone from using it. It's a good question, who owns those wharfage rights to begin with."

As for Wolter's bluntness, it was legendary, and it seemed to increase in proportion to perceived encroachments into his sphere of influence. After Angela Greenwell, the president of the Cairo Chamber of Commerce, joined forces with Richard Poston's Operation Enterprise, Wolter began to cut her short in social encounters—even though he remained on good terms with Mrs. Greenwell's wealthy husband, John. I heard several eyewitness descriptions of a corrosive scene between Wolter and Mrs. Greenwell at a country club near the town about a year after Poston had begun his town meetings. Spotting Mrs. Greenwell at the bar, sipping a soft drink, Wolter was heard to bellow—"in exactly these words," as one onlooker put it—"Listen, you bitch, you know you're not welcome here. Get your ass out of here." A moment later, as Mrs. Greenwell fled the bar, Wolter added, to the room in general, "That bitch doesn't run the town; I do."

Whatever the realities of Moss's and Wolter's feelings about openness and growth in Cairo, the general assumption in the town was that they were allied against it. A woman who assisted Angela Greenwell at the chamber of commerce described her efforts to *conceal* from the mayor the fact that an outside company had shown some interest in building a plant there.

"Our office got a phone call from this fellow up in a small town north of here," the woman remembered. "He said some people from Denver wanted to put a recycling plant in Cairo. They wanted a site with a railroad siding and a riverfront. He asked for an appointment at ten A.M. the next day with one of us. He'd already been warned to deal with the Chamber, not City Hall.

"I went out and found some Chamber board members. One of them told me, he said, 'You go find Bill; he works at the Cairo railroad terminal. He owns some property.' So I did. I found him at his warehouse. He was selling lottery tickets. I told Bill that these people had asked for a hundred and sixty acres. Well, this Bill and two other men owned some acres on the Mississippi side of town. He said he might be willing to sell it.

"So the next morning," the woman went on, chuckling, "I put on a nice little conservative suit and met with the gentlemen. The Denver people had flown in, and there were five of them in all, dressed up in suits!" The woman paused to laugh. "Walkin' right down the main street in Cairo! And you know what? Somebody up above was lookin' out for us, because they weren't noticed! That was the day the TV crews were in town to cover Al Moss throwing Charles Koen in jail and tearing down one of his buildings!"

This was Al Moss's Cairo as it stood when Doc Poston came to town.

Chapter IX

While the town fathers of poverty-stricken Cairo seemed perversely dedicated to stifling economic growth, the leading citizens of prosperity-stricken Kent seemed mostly hellbent on keeping the economic onslaught unchecked. The consequences were oddly similar for the core populations of each town, the entrenched, generational families. The results in each case were drift, hardship, disenfranchisement.

During my visits to Cairo, I got acquainted with a cross section of its people largely through Doc Poston and his Operation Enterprise town meetings. In Kent—where, as a weekend resident, I could not escape an awareness of being a part of the problem—my connection with the long-term population came to center more and more on the bereaved Gawel family.

I followed the fortunes of that family as discreetly as I could after the night of Dorothy Gawel's fatal automobile accident. It seemed to me that her death had produced at least one redemptive seed: it regenerated, however briefly, a sense of community among her peers—the native-born, working-class people who were being inexorably pushed to the far peripheries of their ancestral town by the influx of prosperous strangers.

The Gawels themselves, while far from the oldest clan in Kent, formed a luminous example of this stratum. The family could trace its heritage in the village to the beginning of the century.

The father of Dorothy's late husband Joseph, a Polish immigrant named Andrew, had come to Kent in 1901 and established a productive local lineage indeed: farmers, carpenters, schoolteachers, building contractors, merchants. Community service, in fact, seemed to be a part of the Gawel gene pool. Nearly all the male Gawels had served in the volunteer fire department. Dorothy's brother-in-law Walter, who was to die six months after Dorothy at age eighty-two, had been, variously, a Kent selectman, a chief of the fire department, a member of the Republican Town Committee, a town assessor and a member of the tax review board. He also founded the town's Chevrolet dealership and supervised construction of its building, which still stood on Route 7 across from the Fife 'N' Drum Restaurant. One of Dorothy's three sons, Thomas, was currently a member of the sewer commission.

And of course there was Alan, Susan's son and the family's pride, appointed the town's fire marshall at age nineteen—the youngest such appointment in Connecticut's history—who a year later had dispatched the call for ambulance volunteers, unaware that the victims were his mother and grandmother.

The Gawels—including Dorothy—had even gained enshrinement, however pseudonymously, in that Holy Grail of Americana, the *Reader's Digest.* Up in the attic of Susie Gawel's house there was preserved a yellowed copy of the November 1940 issue that contained an article titled "Peasant's Progress," written by a Kent resident named Edwin Muller.

It described the saga of Muller's sixty-year-old neighbor "Nick Janeski" (Andrew Gawel), and how this hearty blue-eyed owner of 250 acres had arrived in the United States nearly forty years before with four dollars, a small bundle and no English. He had carried a card bearing the address of his cousin who worked on a Kent dairy farm. Directed to the right train in New York City, "Nick" had fallen asleep onboard and missed his stop, so he had to walk 20 miles through the sleeting November Housatonic Valley night, stealing a few hours' sleep in a pigpen. The next day he discovered that the cousin had left the region to work in the factories. "Nick" spent the winter in a farmer's barn, eating scraps of bread and looking for work. He picked up English on his own and eventually found work on a dairy farm, laboring from five in the morning until seven at night, seven days a week. He did this for four years. Then, with the money he'd saved from his eighteen-dollar-a-month salary, he bought thirty adjoining acres and summoned his bride-to-be from Poland. The two of them worked the small farm for many years until the farmer who'd let "Nick" stay in his barn retired to live in Ohio, and sold the property to "Nick."

Dorothy Gawel made her cameo appearance near the end of the piece, which surveyed the family of the now-prosperous "Nick": "His younger brother, who married a girl of the old Yankee farmer stock, is his partner." (In the margin near this paragraph some Gawel had drawn a careful circle around the notation: "DOT.")

The article—published a year before America's entry into World War II, and not long after Hitler's invasion of Poland—finished up on a note of patriotic affirmation.

> He looks around at the good things that have come to him. Not only the material ones; more important is his standing in the community, his right to be a free and equal citizen of the land. . . .
> Then the chuckle breaks out. Hitler has said that this country will fall apart because of the strains and cleavages between the different classes and races of which it is composed. When you observe Nick Janeski and his American children, when you see how they have built themselves into this community, you know that Hitler is wrong. If the United States ever falls apart it will be because Nick's grandchildren—and those of the native stock—will drift into assuming that good things come as a matter of course, good things that were created by the toil and courage of Nick and his like.

As I read this passage, I found myself wondering whether a true prophecy might not have fallen somewhere between Hitler's dark predictions and the author's own sunny blandishments. America was not "falling apart" in the time of "Nick's" grandchildren—not in the sense of any Eastern European state's collapse, at any rate. But there were strains and cleavages being felt between its classes and races, and strains and cleavages being felt right here in "Nick's" adopted American town. Nor was it the case that "Nick's" grandchildren, or those of native stock, had drifted into assuming that good things come as a matter of course. On the contrary, that particular generation had drifted into precisely the opposite malaise: an assumption that things had gotten quite beyond their control.

In the span of Kent history, even the Gawels were newcomers. Eugene Bull, the retired postmaster and still, in 1988, a member of the planning and zoning commission, could trace his ancestry in Kent back before the Revolutionary War.

These established families were by no means the wealthiest residents of Kent. In fact, the depth of familial roots in the town was more likely to be in inverse proportion to income level. (The job of town clerk, a roughly indicative standard of local salaries, paid $21,000 in 1988; by contrast, some of the newer property-owners in the forested hills outside town were Wall Street corporate-merger specialists earning upwards of one million dollars a year.) Many of the older native-born residents—Dorothy Gawel's peers—lived on fixed incomes. With each passing year of increasing property values and a higher tax base, their sense of connection to their ancestral community began to slip away.

It was this enclave that felt the loss of Dorothy Gawel most acutely, and angrily. An irreplaceable piece of Kent's fading agrarian history, of its tapestry of inherited customs and folkways and obligations, had died with her. Among this group were people who had gone to school with Mrs. Gawel fifty-five years previously; who had sipped morning coffee with her every day for forty-nine years; who recalled her as a first-prize winner at the State Grange (for a crocheted tablecloth); who observed her singular rapport with animals—she was said to have fed a fox and a raccoon from her backdoor. And there were people who had worked alongside Dorothy Gawel as she performed volunteer service in the community, at the Kent Nurses Association, which she had founded, and as secretary of Kent Village Elderly Housing.

In trying to expiate their pain over Dorothy Gawel's death, her friends and contemporaries turned reflexively to a forum that harkened back to town life as they had known it before the transformations of the postwar years: they called an open meeting of the Grange.

The Kent Grange was an artifact of Kent's old inner enclave. It may not have been a center of community power like the volunteer fire department, with its fund-raising capacities and strong bonds of male comradeship, but it was a refuge for the native-born oldtimers in a community being diluted by strangers. The Grange had been formed in 1900. Like granges throughout America, in those days it was a farmers' organization, but unlike many granges of the westerly states, it did not function as a cooperative for bulk buying of commodities at lower rates than local merchants charged. The Kent Grange was never at odds with the town. To be sure, it had a legislative committee that kept an eye on state road-building and rural electrification plans, and other issues of interest to farmers, but mostly the Grange was fraternal and social.

Old-timers in the town could still remember the festive husking-bee trains that puffed up from New York on the New Haven line in bygone autumns, starting in the late 1930s. The trains carried four or five hundred city-slickers up to the Kent Grange for a few hours of the rustic life: singing, dancing hoedown, eating roast turkey and husking the local corn. The old-timers remembered when *Life* magazine sent some photographers to cover the doings one year.

The husking-bee trains carried on for several decades, until the Pennsylvania Railroad took over the New Haven line. Then the tradition died.

The Grange survived, as an organization, into the late nineteenth century, although as one farmer after another in the township sold his land for real estate development, it began to lose membership, as well as much of its original reason for existing. By the late 1980s it could claim ninety-five members, about half the total at its peak. Many of these members were women, and many of these women were what the American society had taken to politely calling "seniors." "You can join up at age fourteen," Marie Naboring, a long-time member, had told me once, "but we don't get the younger kids anymore." Now the Grange was mostly a social and service organization, holding three-dollar breakfasts each morning at the Community House behind the Congregational Church and using the revenues to buy "Lifeline" electronic-warning systems for the elderly people of Kent to wear around their necks at home.

But on the clear, cold night of Wednesday, March 2, 1988, the Kent Grange was in session with a vengeance. The group had called an open meeting at the Community House—"The public is urged to attend," thundered the *Kent Weathervane*—and had invited to the meeting the New Milford chapter of Mothers Against Drunk Driving. Although it was not explicitly stated, most people understood that the event was a response to the traffic accident that had killed Dorothy Gawel and injured her daughter Susan, the driver. (The pickup truck that had plowed into the Gawel car had been driven by a twenty-seven-year-old man named John McGuinness, of the nearby town of Sharon. McGuinness, superficially injured, had refused to submit to an alcohol test at the site of the collision, which was his right under Connecticut law.)

About fifty members of the public showed up for the 7:30 meeting. Not one of them was a Wall Street corporate-merger specialist. (Nor was one of them a Gawel.) By dress and by attitude, those who gathered declared themselves as lifetime residents of the town. They wore plaid shirts with string ties, and shiny jackets with service-club pins, and ski sweaters, and they kept their glasses on chains around their necks. Most were old. There were two young families; two children.

They took their seats around four rows of formica tables in the basement of the center, which still displayed its Christmas wreath on its outside door. There was a stainless steel coffee urn on a table against one wall, and a plastic tray heaped with egg-salad sandwiches on white bread. A faded American flag hung from a pole near a corner, and the posters on the wall advertised the upcoming Daffodil Festival (sponsored by the American Cancer Society) and the Grange's breakfast program ("Why Eat Alone? Your Friends are Waiting For You").

The MADD representatives—a New Milford barber named Joe Martin and his wife Loretta, the parents of a twenty-year-old killed in an auto crash—had set up a card table at the front of the meeting hall, and they handed out baseball-type MADD caps and bumper stickers that said, DON'T LOSE TO BOOZE and GET HIGH ON LIFE. The moderator, a Kent woman named Carolyn Chase, got things started by expressing what must have been the consensus feeling of the group: "We see these things on television, and wonder—with all the proof that *20/20* has, and *60 Minutes,* and they just can't seem to do anything about it."

Loretta Martin told the group that the drunk-driving laws in Connecticut were among the worst in the nation. She recited some statistics: one person in five in their lifetime will be involved in a drunk-driving crash; seventy people a day are killed by drunk drivers; "as far as teenagers in 1986, three thousand five hundred thirty-eight died in alcohol-related crashes."

She talked about "the lighter side": "If you think our drunk-driving laws are tough, here's what they do in other parts of the world. In El Salvador, your first offense is your last. It's execution by firing squad." (*Wooooooooooooo!* gasped the Kent citizens.) Then Loretta's husband Joe took the floor. He was the sort of fellow that civic groups warm up to, a soft-spoken man who might have been playful at one time. He wore an honest open-collar shirt and blazer and had gentle, expressive eyes. Joe launched into a discussion of legislative strategy, and at once there was a flurry of notepads and pencils. Then the talk drifted a little—to poster contests, to the effectiveness of bumper stickers, to the symbolic value of a red ribbon tied to rearview mirrors.

"Wouldn't it be a good idea to put it on a tree?" asked a woman in the audience.

"Uh, the red ribbon on the tree is for POWs," explained Loretta Martin.

It was halfway through the question-and-answer session when I realized that Dorothy Gawel's accident had not been brought up. Nor was it likely to be brought up. This was not a confrontational crowd. This was the Kent Grange. Its members were not conditioned, by experience or temperament, to mount crusades, to petition, picket, demonstrate, to demand "rights" or signal their frustration in any of the rituals familiar to anyone who had watched television news over the past quarter-century.

"The old people of Kent were not brought up to protest, to object," said a townsman. "They have their feelings, but they don't display them in public. You don't rock the boat. You don't stir up tensions around you." I mentioned the absence of Gawel family members at the meeting, and the man's eyes hardened. "If it had happened to me, or any member of my family," he said, "I'd have been there screaming at them to do something."

But these citizens had been born, most of them, into a prior culture; a culture of reasonable redress, in which people aired their grievances in open meetings, with their townsmen adversaries in attendance, and a moderator to sort things out.

Somewhere in the course of this indignantly organized Grange meeting, it seemed to me, the awareness had settled in that Dorothy Gawel's death could not be avenged. A question from the floor conveyed this resignation: "What good does it do even if you can take their licenses away? Most of them will go ahead and drive anyway." And Joe Martin could only nod his head and lift his dark eyebrows in agreement.

Yet this Grange meeting did not seem to be ending in futility. By ten minutes of nine o'clock, the questions from the floor had begun to peter out, and yet no one seemed in any hurry to leave—not the Kent citizens, not Joe and Loretta Martin. People got up singly to tap the coffee urn, go to the bathroom, and return to light a fresh cigarette, get comfortable again in their chairs. In some subtle and unstated way, the gathering had shifted in its intention, from a militant planning session to a kind of wake, a shared memorial, not only to a mourned member of the community, but to a mourned way of community life.

. . .

Not every native-born citizen responded to the regenerative opportunities offered by the meeting of the Grange. For many, the dislocations of rapid change had engendered a pessimism so acute that the very notion of community was now a bitter obscenity. Some families who felt this pessimism most severely had gone so far as to isolate themselves from the town, burrowing in to the hills and hollows with a dark defiance that amounted, in extreme cases, to a kind of social regression, a throwback to nineteenth-century subsistence living. In my travels around the remoter stretches of macadamized roads beyond the town center, I occasionally glimpsed a hand-built wood-and-stone shanty gouged so tightly into the hillside that it had the effect of a cave. In the dirt driveway would be several lean, yelping hounds, a rusted tractor or other piece of heavy machinery, and a pickup truck rigged with rack headlights and, inside the cab, the inevitable brace of high-powered rifles. Some of the weaponry I saw was of the assault variety currently making headlines in the hated metropolis to the south. If the man of the household was visible in the midst of all this—usually bearded, ball-capped and clad in some combination of work clothes and military camouflage—he would never look up as my car passed. I never stopped.

Backwoods people had been fixtures in the New England countryside since before the Revolution, of course. But some of these denizens bore the surnames of Kent's oldest families, the same surnames that had been affixed to the roads and the hills themselves.

The powerfully built young man—call him Ben—whose farmhouse I visited some time after the Grange meeting was not nearly as alienated as the people in the shanties. Articulate, college-educated, sophisticated in town concerns, he was married and successfully employed. And yet he had not been among the native-born townspeople who had gathered to mourn Dorothy Gawel and ponder ways to cope with the social ills that had led to her death. While sympathetic, he'd had his own preoccupying list of social ills to reckon with, and his concerns kept him inside his mountaintop farmhouse, save on those occasions when he confronted one or another of the town's public committees to argue policy.

Ben's views, distilled to their essence, were probably not that different from those nurtured by the people back in the hills and hollows—or from native-born Kent people in general. They began to pour out, reluctantly at first, when I asked him what he thought had gone wrong with the town.

"Well, I'll tell you what went wrong," he said from the kitchen of the farmhouse. He was cutting warm wedges, for himself and me, from his wife's freshly baked apple pie, and the scent of cinnamon filled the bright room. It was a clear afternoon in winter, and through the picture window beside the small dining-room table where I sat, I could look out on a sun-dazzled vista that might have inspired a painter of the Hudson River School, except that there was no river. The old brown farmland fell abruptly into a deep plunging valley, then rose again on the other side into another high ridge. Beyond that ridge were more hills and valleys, until the delineations blurred in the hazed blue distance. At the bottom of the nearest valley a pond shimmered whitely in the hard light. A lone deer stood motionless above it, in a brown open field on the far hill. The only other entity that drew the eye swelled a few hundred feet above the deer, near the crest of the far hill, facing the burly young man's farmhouse: a gabled and turreted mansion, 7500 square feet in volume, built by a corporate executive.

"I'll tell you what went wrong," Ben repeated, returning to the table with the slices of warm pie. "Basically what you've had in the eighties is people coming in from the outside with a lot of money. Developers. They have access to all kinds of legal professionals and engineering professionals, and they come up here and it's easy pickin's. Because the local people—" Ben, seated now, with one ankle resting on a blue-jeaned knee, paused, and stared out the bright window, and shook his head. He was not comfortable speaking his thoughts aloud to an outsider—which I most assuredly was, my house in South Kent and the pie in front of me notwithstanding—and he chose his words with a cautiousness bordering on hostility.

Strapping, denim-clad, he was a local person himself. The wood-frame farmhouse he and his wife lived in had been owned by his parents, and their parents before them, and their parents before them. He was a local person, and he had lived on this hill up above the town in peace until what he would only call "a dispute" prompted him to make himself something of an expert in local zoning matters. He continued to live in the old farmhouse above the town, but now he lived with a deep and abiding anger.

"The local people—first of all, they don't think anybody's going to do anything bad to 'em," Ben continued. "I mean, somebody comes up here to develop land, and the local folks are taking 'em at face value. The person comes in, he's friendly, he's shaking their hand, and they think, 'Boy, what a great guy.' And all the while, the guy's planning to slip something by 'em. But they're not suspicious." He paused. "Oh, they are now. But three or four years ago they weren't suspicious."

Our conversation took place many months after the shocks of 1986. As we spoke, the six hundred acres of Kent School property on top of Skiff Mountain still lay on the open market, its destiny still unresolved. But the 138-acre Conboy property sale had indeed gone through, and it had triggered the very chain-reaction of farm divestments that local people, including my companion at the table, had feared.

"Conboy Flats," Ben was saying, almost under his breath. "Fifty-eight lots, all of 'em on a side hill, and when that's done—have you driven up Route 7? You've seen the one house that sticks up above the tree line? Kind of over the original farmhouse? That's a three-story house. And every story shows. There's gonna be fifty-seven more of those just like it. The whole hillside is gonna look like a condominium complex in some suburb.

"That guy who did that," he went on, still looking out his window into the bright winter glare, "also just did one on the road that you probably drove by on your way here. He did a lot in the town to the north before he came to Kent. He came in here in a big way and just started buying up land like crazy, with his backers in New York. Just tried to push everything to the maximum. Just tried to find every loophole, twist every regulation that he could find to maximize his profit, and that's all he cared about.

"This is the kind of person Kent was not prepared to deal with. The planning and zoning wasn't ready for him. A subdivider like him comes in with a complicated plan, sheafs of maps, drainage comps this thick—and everybody on the commission dearly wants to believe that everything is in order so they can simply say, 'That looks good.' Because who's got the time and the knowledge to go sheafing through all this and looking for things? It's a full-time occupation, really. And these people are amateurs."

I pointed out to Ben that, before the developers could come in with their complicated plans and their sheafs of maps, they had to have claim to the land they wanted to develop. This could not happen without the complicity of Kent people—namely, the family farmers with huge acreage who were willing to sell to the developers.

Ben nodded. He'd heard this argument before.

"The farmers here were never rich people," he said in measured tones. "They were always very poor, regardless of the size of their land. Sure, it's a tough decision to sell. It's very emotional. These people are living on land that's been in their families for two hundred years. On the other hand, you can say that it's land that didn't cost them anything; or if it did, it was paid in dollars that are meaningless today.

"Almost anybody you can name around here who's thinking of divesting will become rich. Overnight. I could divest this land here and become rich. Not rich like some people. But I'd never have to work again. So everybody wrestles with that."

As Ben talked, I thought of a conversation I'd had a few days before on the same topic—the dilemma of Kent farmers—with a minister in the town. "This place is simply not, if you have a conscience," the minister had said to me, "an idyllic rural haven. I suppose that you can still come up here on a weekend and get that. You go into town and get your supplies and go back to wherever you are, and if you're surrounded by enough trees or fields, you can really get that illusion.

"But it is an illusion. The appeal of this place to outsiders, over the years," the minister had gone on, "has derived from being in close proximity to work that has never made money for the people doing it—farming. Farming was the theme park, if you will, of this town for the city folks. So in effect part of the charm of Kent has always depended on a certain level of sustained poverty. No farmer has ever gotten rich here, except by selling his farm."

Now, to my host seated across the dining-room table from me, I asked what I knew was probably an unwelcome question. It's clear, I said, that you want to see Kent continue as a rural community. But do the people who are truly rural—the farmers—want to see it continue as a rural community?

His answer was instantaneous: "Absolutely."

Rural, meaning dairy farms? I prodded.

Now Ben hesitated, but when he spoke, his answer was forthright.

"No. Rural meaning—" he spread his hands. "We're talking about aesthetics. We're talking about what you see out the window. This attitude is *overwhelming.* When they're asked to give their opinion, the people of Kent say, 'Let's keep Kent rural.' Their opinion is that they want to keep the rural look of the place."

As tactfully as I could—because I shared that opinion—I pressed

Ben a little further: If you want a rural look, but there is no longer any real rural economy—isn't that inherently false?

Ben's mouth tightened; he dug his chin into his chest and considered. "It comes down to being totally aesthetics and visual," he said after a minute. "Nobody is saying let's keep the rural lifestyle; we're just basically saying, let's keep the *appearance* of a rural lifestyle. Let's keep the development patterns looking rural. Otherwise, it's just—" he looked out the window again. "It's just a crime against the topography of Kent."

I reminded him that in the wake of Conboy Flats and similar experiences, Kent had sought some professional backup for itself: it had hired a planning consultant from a larger Connecticut town to review and analyze all future development proposals. Without taking his eyes from the bright windowpane, he nodded slowly.

"Now what becomes the challenge," he said, "is the interpretive part of the regulations. Let's say the town decides they're not going to allow any more development along exposed ridgelines. To protect the vistas. Like that house over there. That's the kind of thing they have to review a plan for, and make judgments on. But even then," Ben said, digging at his pie-crust with the tines of his fork, "the negative forces always win. That's become my philosophy; the negative forces always win. The negative pushes first. You may push back, but you're never gonna get back what the negative has already gotten. You may win a victory, but you're gonna lose the war."

I asked him to give me an example of that.

"A developer comes in with a plan and says, 'Well, I'm only going to cut the trees I have to cut in order to approve this subdivision.' Okay, so you approve the plan. This sounds good to you. So he goes in there on a rainy day, and he tells his cutting crew, 'Clear-cut the side of the hill.' The Zoning Enforcement Officer shows up and says, 'Hey! What are you doin'?' 'Oops,' they say. 'We didn't know.' "

Ben turned and stared directly at me. "How are you going to replace that?" he asked. "You can fine them, you can make them put little trees in, you can do anything you want. But the fact of the matter is, no matter what you do for mitigation, they have won the war. Because they have cut the trees down."

He fell silent for a long moment; his eyes had moved back to whatever he saw beyond the windowpane. "I'm in it for mitigation," he said at last. "I'm trying to mitigate damage. I don't know whether I'm going to stay here. I grew up in this area. I am attuned to a rural lifestyle. I cannot tolerate the suburbs, I cannot tolerate the city. I don't even like going down to New Milford. But I do love Kent. I have emotional attachments."

I asked him what kind of emotional attachments. He grimaced, but then he replied:

"This is my grandparents' house. Their folks before them. I have tremendous childhood memories of when this was a farm. That are just great."

Such as? I pressed. Ben shook his head.

"I don't want to get into that," he said.

I pressed him some more. Finally he shrugged his shoulders.

"It's remembering," he said, without looking at me. "It's just remembering the way a working farm looks in this particular landscape. It's remembering the different elements. You had woods and pastures and tillable fields and a pond. And to a kid, that's like the whole world. He can walk all day and never see it all. And every little piece—that's the great thing about farming in Kent. You can have a three-hundred-acre farm, and have at least two dozen microunits. A little ledge here with a certain kind of vegetation, a little wetland here, a pond, a brook—everything. Instead of being one big chunk of land, to a kid, it's like secret places. All those secret places."

I drove down the mountain from the man's farmhouse, into the strong afternoon light. Now and then a winter cardinal flickered across the road. At the bottom of a steep hill, half a mile from our house, I made a right turn onto Route 341 toward Kent. The road took me past Hatch Pond, the elongated lake whose southernmost tip nearly bordered the South Kent School football field. People were ice-fishing on the pond. I could glimpse them drilling with large blue drills, in their earflapped caps and their heavy boots. Driving past this scene, not looking too closely at the vintage of the cars parked beside the road, it was possible to see it as frozen in time: it could have been the 1940s, the railroad tracks between the road and the lake still active with Penn Central passengers and freight, the Grange intact, the ice-fishermen unconscious that anything would ever change.

Less than half a mile beyond the northern tip of Hatch Pond I passed the last working dairy farm between South Kent and Kent. The blue-painted wooden farmhouse hugged the side of the road; behind it were expansive barns, rolling pastureland that climbed a gentle hill behind. A mixed herd of guernseys and holsteins grazed there, formal and elegiac against the green of the hillside grass. In late summer a patch of spectacular sunflowers bloomed in the small front yard. That was all I knew about this place: that it was a dairy farm and that we always looked forward to the sunflowers. I had never bothered to get acquainted with the farmer, his wife, his sons. Now I wondered whether they had entertained thoughts about divesting and becoming rich; whether we would see the sunflowers next summer.

I had wanted to argue with my host in the farmhouse on top of the mountain. "Aesthetics," he had said. "The appearance of a rural lifestyle." These were not the phrasings appropriate to a powerfully built young man of the land. These were the phrasings and sensibilities of advertising, of marketing—the primacy of *perception* over reality. The implications were monstrous, surreal: an entire community, town and farmlands, artificially preserved in some invisible aspic—all the secret places defended, not because of what they might generate into an organic economy, but because of how they might look to someone passing through, out of the corner of the eye, from behind the window of a speeding car.

Kent—the old "hideous, howling wilderness" of the Puritan age— as a venue. A stage-set.

And yet I could not really argue with the man. First, because I was one of those people who were changing Kent from a farming community to . . . something else. And second, because I agreed with him. As demeaning as his choice of words sounded, at some essential point there was no other option. All across America the lights of the dairy farms were going out; we would not see them go on in our time again. At some essential point—by whatever artificial means were available—one had to begin figuring out a way to save the sunflowers.

Chapter X

It was a primped, pressed, polished, styled, sprayed, creased, combed, cologned and color-coordinated collection of mostly middle-aged town advocates who bent to select their clear plastic name-tag holders at Angela Greenwell's registration table and then file into the gymnasium of St. Joseph's elementary school in Cairo on the morning of March 17, 1988.

Not to mention a sedate one. In the pantheon of legendary hell-raising conventioneers, the men and women of the Quinstate Forum were not often mentioned in the same breath with, say, a delegation of mail-order lingerie sales reps in Reno, Nevada. (One of the conferees, for example, had listed himself without detectable irony as the Executive Vice President for Kentucky's Western Wasteland.)

The Forum had been organized in 1982 by a university extension agent in southern Missouri. It was typical of many such groups around the Midwest: informal associations formed to help educators and professionals reinforce one another's efforts in community development. (Poston's talent for mythifying the ordinary had succeeded in glamorizing my expectations of the conference. When he'd mentioned the Quinstate Forum to me in a telephone conversation before I arrived in Cairo, his tones had suggested that it was a body marginally subsidiary to the Trilateral Commission.)

Most of the members signing in on this morning were professionals in what might be thought of as the healing arts of community life: county extension agents and extension advisors from Midwestern universities, tourism and historical preservation people, chamber-of-commerce representatives, clergy. There were some free-lancers: a "Home Grower–Entrepreneur," a husband-wife team who identified themselves as "Producers of Country Wood Products"; a "Producer and Marketer of Fruits and Nuts", and one "Businessman Active in Community Sports Programs".

It would not be fair to say that the Quinstaters entirely lacked a certain élan vital. Many, if not most, had dutifully marked the occasion of St. Patrick's Day with a flare of green somewhere on their person: a necktie, a blazer, a corsage, a pair of pants, sox. Before long the gymnasium—garnished with intertwined strands of emerald-and-white crepe paper by Doc Poston's Decorations Committee—resembled a reunion of the Sons and Daughters of Oz, as all shuffled toward the folding chairs in a vivid, verdurous gavotte.

Poston pressed flesh, clapped backs, recalled names (with a quick glance at the clear plastic tag), wheeled about to whisper briefly with an Enterpriser. As I watched, some television lights flared up behind him. A news team from Cape Girardeau, Missouri, was setting up to cover the event.

His instinct for style had not failed him. Disdaining any deference to St. Patrick's Day, he had shown up as the young Peter Lawford. He was flawless in a crisp navy blazer and creased gray slacks, a white button-down shirt, a red-and-navy striped tie. Again, the precise vintage of these excellently matched threads baffled me. He looked dramatic and almost inordinately alive, and I felt happy to know him; I wanted him to get up there and knock this crowd dead.

First came some formalities. As the Quinstaters settled greenly into their folding chairs, the organization's chairman, massively corsaged, promenaded to the microphone. Behind her, facing the audience from the bottom row of bleacher seats, sat the "battery of Action Committee chairmen" of Operation Enterprise. The men had on their good dark church suits; the women wore shiny fine dresses and shoes of matching color. The Action chairmen looked sensational. Each was frowning down furiously at the typewritten script clutched in his or her hands.

The chairwoman welcomed everyone to the Sixth Quinstate Forum, "established to provide an opportunity for communities in five states to share ideas, frustrations, successes and failures with each other." She declared that the Forum felt extremely fortunate to be here in Cairo and to work with this Operation Enterprise here and to participate and be a part of the effort that's here.

The chairwoman proposed that this was a good thing because people normally retain only 20 percent of what they learn through reading. But the chance to *hear* the Enterprise describe their program, she declared, would add another 20 percent retention.

"Then at 3:30 this afternoon we have the opportunity to *see* what is happening," she went on. "The tour of Cairo! So, not only the hearing but the *seeing*, we'll be doing today. So that's 50 percent!" Some of the Quinstaters were busy jotting this down.

"Then at supper we're on our own," the chairwoman continued. "But I hope that all those participants that are going to stay for tonight's town meeting will get together at suppertime and talk with each other. Because that increases the retaining of this information to *70 percent!*"

The mathematics of this were starting to make me feel a little green, myself. I glanced about the gymnasium from my folding chair and spotted a solitary, virtually unnoticed figure that turned out to be Mayor Al Moss. He stood stiffly at the end of the bleachers, behind and to stage right of the podium, a foot or two from the last Action Committee chairman. He was wearing a suit the color of split-pea soup. He did not seem to know what to do with his body. One of his elbows rested gingerly on a bleacher slab, but his weight wasn't on it. His hands were clasped, his feet were pressed together, and his mouth was a tight little noncommittal line.

"Then this evening we have that final opportunity which we can participate in," the chairwoman was telling the crowd, "and that's the *doing*. The town meeting!" She beamed toward Doc Poston, who organized a nod in return. "And that's the *90 percent* we're looking for. So as you see, throughout the day, we've got an awful lot of learning to do. And we're going home with 90 percent of what we've learned today!"

Without further taxing the Quinstaters' capacity for percentages, the chairwoman thrust a hand abruptly toward Angela Greenwell, who was seated next to Doc Poston at a card table beside the podium. "Attitude and altitude!" the chairwoman exclaimed. "Our *attitude* determines our *altitude!* And the person that I'm about to introduce has the attitude. Angela is the co-chairman of Operation Enterprise!"

With her golden hair swept into a precarious bouffant, Angela Greenwell had a little altitude to go along with her attitude as she arose to applause and stepped, with perfect posture, toward the podium. She wore an attractive peach-colored dress that caught the television light. I had expected her remarks to be brief, but her suddenness caught me a little off-guard, and, as things developed, perhaps one or two others as well.

"Thank you, Norma," said Mrs. Greenwell into the microphone. "First off, I'm going to call on Al Moss, the Honorable Mayor of Cairo."

There was a pause while Moss seemed to snap awake—gather himself—and the Quinstaters craned around to see whom they were supposed to applaud. Then Moss began to make his way past the battery of Action Committee chairmen, tugging his lapels into place and squinting into the brightness. He leaned into the microphone.

"I'm kinda like the mosquito at the nudist colony," the Mayor allowed to the Quinstaters. "I know what to do, but I don't know where to start." The line drew a beat or two of poleaxed silence, followed by a smattering of extremely forced chuckles. Moss foraged ahead.

"We been pretty busy around Cairo for the last week or ten days as yawl have prob'ly seen on TV," he said in his high-pitched banjo-twang. "We just come through a political situation with the primaries up and down the state with all these candidates runnin' up and down the state.

"I like to tell the story about—we're just simple country folks here. We all know what it means when the farmer says he's gonna bring a cow in to service—uh, the bull in to service the cow." He paused and looked sly for the kicker. "So when these fellas run up and down the state and say they wanta become public servants—we know what they got on their mind!"

In the stupefied silence that followed, I thought I detected the actual sound of what comic-strip artists of my boyhood penned above characters' heads, always in parentheses, as a "(gasp)." One or two of the male delegates managed to produce, from the deepest caverns of their throats, the funereal imitation of a chuckle. Someone released a boo. Angela Greenwell's smile, as she stood beside the mayor, could have been annealed in place with a blowtorch.

With this kind of an act to follow, it occurred to me, Doc Poston was being handed the chance to look like Daniel Webster by comparison—unless Moss, out of some half-conscious kamikaze inspiration, was trying to empty the gymnasium before Poston could make it to the podium.

The mayor was not through; he had a million of them. "I wanna clear up one other thing," he deadpanned into the glassy faces. "With a name like Moss, and I have so much green on this morning, I want you to be sure you understand—my ancestors *were* Irish; they just came through Germany!"

A rimshot, a burst of guffaws from the nightclub audience, elbows nudging ribs, spilled drinks—what was the man imagining? "And I don't know," he crowed on, "of another place where a meeting like this could be held that would be more appropriate to St. Patty's Day than the home of the St. Joseph Fighting Irish, which is this gym!"

Apparently there weren't too many grade-school sports enthusiasts among the Quinstaters, because this applause line brought no one to their feet in a rousing three-rahs and a locomotive. By this time it was beginning to dawn even on Al Moss that his patter was not exactly bringing down the house, because he abruptly switched into his toastmaster mode.

"Dr. Poston, Mrs. Greenwell, Operation Enterprise, board members, representatives of the Quinstate Forum, distinguished guests and visitors: as mayor of Cairo I want to heartily welcome you. We are honored and pleased that the Quinstate Forum has selected Cairo for its next—*this* meeting. I'm glad to be here. . . . "

We have so many natural assets, Moss went on to tell the crowd. We have location, we have water, we have river transportation, highways just north of us. *It's just got to be a matter of puttin' it all together.* Again he wanted to welcome them. He hoped they would find his city interesting, hospitable and energetic. He wished for them a very successful meeting. He thanked them very much.

Angela regained the microphone. Her smile now took on a new luster. Her next words, spoken with a tremor of pride, might well have made the retreating mayor wince a little.

"I would like to introduce to you Cairo's very own Dr. Richard Poston," she declared to the Quinstaters. "He came out of retirement to help us, and we are very grateful. I could go on and on and on talking about Dr. Richard Poston." She glanced down at the upturned face of her friend. "But he's very modest and sometimes he kicks me in the shins. So—" Angela Greenwell's eyes had gone very bright in the television light, and she seemed to lose her momentum for just a moment—"I'm going to turn the program over to Dr. Poston."

There was a respectful round of applause as Doc Poston arose, fastened the button of his blue blazer and bounded up to the podium. His thin gray face swept the crowd. I had pictured Poston addressing an imaginary audience almost from the first conversation I'd had with him, just a few nights ago. Now I was about to see him in action before a real one. My image, I quickly learned, was if anything a shade understated. Poston launched himself into an oratory that Demosthenes himself, railing into the sea, might have paused to admire.

"We are here today to address the subject of community problem solving," he shouted, his eyes fixed above the Quinstate conferees, converting the far gym wall into a vast and smoky balcony. "Nothing to which we could devote our time is more important! Everywhere these days the American community is in trouble! Giant bureaucracies blanketing our nation are spending billions of dollars of taxpayers' money! Tons of slick brochures are being published, and professional grantsmanship has become one of our most lucrative occupations.

"Yet the trouble in our communities continues to mount!"

He had brought his voice up to a quavering tenor. He marked his declarations with a stabbing index finger, and he rocked his shoulders from side to side. The Quinstaters sat upright, taking it in.

"Throughout our nation," Poston howled at them, "there has been a tendency to treat something which is basically whole, namely the human community, as though it were an assortment of parts and pieces that have no relationship to each other! And so we have a host of agencies fighting turf battles, all pulling separately instead of together, the result being that even where useful projects are pushed to completion in special areas of interest, the community as a whole is relatively untouched and unimproved!"

The old cherished phrases rolled from his tongue. *A vigorous, action-oriented interpersonal network of human relations! Men and women, young and old, of every race, color and creed, rich and poor and all in between!*

The Quinstaters stared back at him.

"This is the inner soul of real community development!" Poston shouted. "For what it means is simply this: that democracy itself, when fully activated and put to work, is the single most powerful human force a community can muster. . . . community development is concerned fundamentally, not with *things* but with *people* . . . a gradually unfolding social climate in which the most priceless resource of every community—its *people*—will not be wasted. . . ."

I glanced around at some of the faces near me, and tried to speculate which ones were pulling their retention up to 40 percent.

"This is community in full bloom, in all its glory and creativity!" Poston was declaiming in a high wail. "It is this, the sparkling essence of community bursting forth like the crescendo of a Beethoven symphony, in which the people of this flamboyant old river town wedged in between our nation's two mightiest waterways, the Mississippi and the Ohio, are now giving of themselves an effort that has the potential of blazing new trails in problem-solving for communities in trouble *all across America!*"

It had the sound to me of a guaranteed applause line, and I raised my hands. But the Quinstaters were sitting on theirs.

Poston cranked it up a little more. "The human attributes that flow from viable community life are being eaten away because community life itself is being eaten away! At a dizzying pace we as a nation are taking on the character of a fabulous mansion in which the residents are busy with their affairs, but which has termites in its supporting timbers. The local community, the basic unit in the very foundation of democratic society, is badly in need of repair!"

He produced an imaginary canvas and smeared on it a vision of the infamous city as it might have been conjured by Baudelaire, with help from George Orwell: "As the metropolitan complex spills out over the landscape in great extensions of steel and concrete, increasing millions take up residence without knowing or caring about each other, without being conscious of themselves as communities! Men, women and children go their daily separate ways, to be swallowed in the anonymous crowd! The family loses its solidarity!"

The Quinstaters pursed their lips—they'd heard about this.

"The urban inner core becomes a cesspool of racial enclaves, the urban extremities an assortment of mortgaged dwellings and impersonal population globs! Human interaction and individuality are lost to batteries of computer disks and programmed systems devoid of flesh and blood! Steadily and systematically, we are moving toward uniformity and compliance as scores of millions are reduced to spectators of the passing scene!"

Upon this tableau of modern-day lost-soul sterility and despair, Poston then laid out the bright colors of redemption.

"This is why Cairo's movement called Operation Enterprise is so utterly vital to America!" he cried. "Cairo's struggle for survival is precious because within the framework of modern times it is organizing patterns of civic behavior that enable men and women to resolve community problems by direct personal involvement! These courageous Cairoites are walking the street, talking to their neighbors, carrying the torch for that age-old American way of getting things done, building and improving their community on their own initiative!"

Silence from the folding chairs. It was impossible to judge how this was going down. (The Action Committee chairmen, seated behind Poston, took their cue from the larger audience and sat rigidly still, at parade rest.) The bloodless attentiveness of these greened-up people baffled, then began to irritate me. Here was a pioneering star of their vocation, preaching his heart out. Granted, Poston's syntax smacked a little of the caboose platform, the newsreel, the Fourth-of-July stump. At least he was using it in their behalf; he was offering them the gift of a heraldic vision of themselves. And they were wondering what to do about lunch. Two or three rows behind me and to my left, a woman rummaged idly, serenely in her handbag for something that turned out to be a lipstick. Her retentive rate seemed headed—a generous estimate—for the low 70s.

Perhaps I was reading too many of my own preconceptions into this scene. But I'd been in Cairo several days now, and some of the gothic futility of the place was seeping into my bones. The town had already struck me as having lost its visibility; it lay broken below its own tree line. Now it seemed to have lost its capacity to generate sound as well; Poston's lips moved, but no words were audible. And these were his fellow toilers in the ruins of lost community! If they could not rouse themselves to some affirmation of Poston's clarion call—if they could not work up the minimal cornball pep required of a handful of frozen-pizza vendors at a Holiday Inn district sales conference—what hope was there for igniting the imagination of a feckless, overstimulated, atomized, pleasure-driven host society? What hope was there for igniting the imagination of Al Moss?

" 'These Americans are the most peculiar people in the world!' " Poston was reciting for the Quinstaters the same quotation from Tocqueville that he had sprung on me a couple nights earlier. " 'You'll not believe it when I tell you how they behave! In a local community in their country a citizen may conceive of some need which is not being met. What does he do? He goes across the street and discusses it with his neighbor. . . .' "

Yes, he told them, *the most powerful human force yet invented for the social and physical well-being of every community in our nation is—as it always has been, and always will be—plain unadulterated democracy at work. . . .*

For if we do not find democracy in all its vitality in our hometowns, we will not find it at all. . . .

Choke it here by allowing our community problems to go unsolved, and we choke our nation. . . .

Maintain it at home, strengthen it at home, here in the place where we live, and democracy in America will grow and thrive. . . .

This is the heart of Operation Enterprise here in this old river city of Cairo at the confluence of the Mississippi and Ohio where a brave and determined people . . .

We deeply appreciate the privilege of having you with us . . .

Poston closed his speech with a clear and explicit plea. "We urge you," he cried, "to join us tonight at seven o'clock in Cairo High for one of Operation Enterprise's regular town meetings! Participate in its problem-solving deliberations, and see for yourselves how Cairo's modern pioneers are putting democracy to work!

"Thank you, and God bless you!"

Angela Greenwell shot up from her chair to lead the perfunctory applause, her hands fluttering above her golden bouffant. Everyone else in the gymnasium remained comfortably seated, as if in an aircraft that had not come to its full and complete stop at the terminal. Doc Preston waved a couple of times to the audience, unbuttoned his blazer and sat down again at the card table beside the podium.

"Thank you, Doc," Angela said, and tried a little joke. "Doc is a native of Cairo now—we know this to be true because Doc gets junk mail in his apartment!" Over the risible throat-clearing that followed, she added quickly, "And we are truly grateful."

If any of the Quinstaters were actually at work keeping their retentive percentages up high—or if any possessed a dash of gentle irony—they might have absorbed what now followed as a kind of postmodern comedy: a procession of rank-and-file Cairo citizens, black and white, all speaking in the unmistakable syntax of Doc Poston.

Angela Greenwell led off this talking-in-tongue. Glancing at a script in her hand, she told the audience: "Operation Enterprise is an all-encompassing program of community development that treats the human community as a whole living organism, every component part of which has both a direct and indirect effect on every other component.

"We have, therefore, set up a battery of committees to conduct in-depth research into every component part of our community: search out every strength, every weakness, and report their findings for public discussion at our biweekly town meetings, at which time everyone in Cairo can have his or her say in the decision-making process."

After a little more of this, Angela began to introduce the individual Action Committee chairmen. One by one, these groomed and concentrating people arose from the bleacher row and came to the microphone, clutching their prepared remarks and squinting into the unfamiliar television light.

The co-chairwoman of the Census Committee reported that throughout the conduct of the recent census, "we not only gathered vital statistics, but more important, we strengthened our bonds of neighborhood friendship." The Organization's chairwoman disclosed the results of polling the town's thirty-five fraternal orders, business groups, sororities and service clubs: "This research revealed certain deep-seated fractures that very much need to be repaired if we are to mold Cairo into the united—" she paused; squinted "—citizenry . . . that we know we must have before our level of civic performance can be evaluated to its maximum potential."

The Government and Public Services Committee chairman, a prison guard by occupation and a lone sartorial rebel in a bushy beard, flannel shirt, green tie and a blue ball cap festooned with slogan buttons, observed in a deep twangy voice that "in a democracy, when gummint fails it fails because the people—you and I—allow it to fail." He promised that, in a "co-opera-tive," nonpartisan manner, his committee would study all public services in this component of Cairo's internal social structure and "he'p ferret out" any and all problems that may exist. Findings and recommendations for action would be submitted at the regular scheduled town meetings—"thereby making it possible to pave the way for gen-u-wine citizen participation in gummint affairs."

If Mayor Moss was still in the building, this particular report probably did not gladden his day.

The Environmental Improvement Committee chairman promised a detailed, inch-by-inch examination of Cairo's physical appearance: every dump, every junkyard, every sidewalk, every alley, every park, every eyesore. "It will," recited this young building-trades contractor, "*as it were,* put Cairo under a microscope looking for bits of ugliness . . . they can find. This committee will thus be a major spark plug that will provide the citizens with a definite and visible means of working as a teammate for the complete physical redevelopment of our Cairo community."

And so it went. Economic Development: "Simply, this is a fundamental tool," quoted the young black man at the microphone. "Every other component part of our community's social structure must therefore be treated as an essential ingredient in Cairo's development effort . . . appropriate action will be proposed in our town meeting for expanding our supply of job opportunities and a systematic marketing campaign will be mounted for new business and industrial recruitment."

Retail Trade and Services: "This committee will encourage more up-to-date merchandising practices," said the divorced young minister at the podium, "better customer relations . . . it will ferret out every feasible means for making our community an increasingly interesting and exciting town in which to stop, stay awhile, and buy things. It will help spearhead our endeavor to recapture the glamour of Old Cairo as an early American river city."

Housing: "We have begun a survey of current housing conditions," reported the nun who served as chairwoman. "We will devise plans for both immediate and long-range action to make certain that every person in Cairo has a decent place in which to live."

Education: "In cooperation with our schoolteachers and administrators"—the black teacher in a purple dress ornamented with a brooch adjusted her flashing glasses—"this committee will dig out every problem and write reports of its findings for discussion at town meetings."

Jenolar McBride, as chairwoman of the Library Committee, received a special introduction from Angela Greenwell: "Miss Mc—I call her Miss McBride!—Jenolar McBride is my co-chairman of Operation Enterprise. A fantastic, beautiful, wonderful Christian person. She probably will be very embarrassed and very upset with me, but I do want to take this opportunity to say that we could not be where we are today in Cairo without her great effort!"

Miss McBride, in a royal blue suit with matching hat and heels, was barely visible as she limped slowly to the podium. The microphone loomed over her head.

There was a certain historic appropriateness in Jenolar

McBride's serving as chairwoman of the Library Committee. She did not refer to it in her brief remarks at the podium. But a few days earlier, during a stop I made with Doc Poston at the Chamber of Commerce office, I had asked her what it had been like as a young black woman in Cairo before the civil rights movement.

"Well, some of the things I was sort of . . . unaware of," she had answered carefully. "And was unaware of for awhile. I went to the public library and checked out books—took my youngster with me—without knowin' that we didn't go to the public library."

Were there separate public libraries? I'd asked her.

"Noooo—but there was a sort of a branch system. There were books in the library at Pyramid Court. And the library was very generous about getting whatever materials the teachers wanted over to Sumner High School [the black school in Cairo then].

"But I had been accustomed to going to the public library. So when I arrived in Cairo, that's where I went. And the librarian was just as cordial as anybody had ever been to me. It wasn't till I mentioned to somebody that I'd picked up these books at the public library—I don't remember who it was—that that person said, *'Did you go to the public library?'* 'Yes I did.' And who I was talkin' to said, 'Well, uh, Negroes just *don't go to the library!'* And I said"— here Jenolar McBride let her shoulders shake a little—" 'Well, *one did.'* "

Now, from below the microphone, Miss McBride was saying, "Our Cairo library is a magnificent old historic building. But it is far more than that. It is a rich center of knowledge, another institution for learning. Yet, like all other parts of our community's infrastructure, it has problems our Cairo citizenry needs to learn about and help solve.

"Research and recommendations for action to put before our town meetings for this purpose will be the job of our Library Committee, once it is activated."

Jenolar McBride sat back down to the meeting's first appreciative applause, and the parade of Action Committee chairmen continued. The Health Committee chairman, a muscular and mustached black athletic coach, noted that "Webster defines 'health' as being a condition of complete physical, mental and social well-being of a living organism—not merely the absence of a disease of infirmity. With this in mind Operation Enterprise has set an ambitious goal . . ." He averred that the Health Committee would examine "with a fine-tooth comb every practical means of providing our people with treatment and diagnostic services that they need and so deserve. It will ferret out every problem Cairo faces concerning health care, and devise specific recommendations for action to be put before our town meetings. . . ."

The Social Welfare chairman promised that her committee would "delve into" some of the most sensitive issues and human needs of the community. The chairman of the Recreation Committee opined that "one of the most vital parts of our community's internal social structure concerns the opportunity of our people to express themselves through varied forms of recreation." He noted that this "calls for facilities and activities that allow people to express their intellectual, emotional and physical energies—thus finding a pervading sense of freedom in their daily routines." He then called up an "old adage"—an adage that sounded distinctly neo-Postonian to me—that said, "the town that plays together works together."

The chairwoman of History and Cultural Development unveiled a plan whose antecedents were familiar to me from *Small Town Renaissance:* "Working hand-in-hand with our Recreation Committee, this committee will come up with reports from which we will create and produce an extravagant pageant-drama, with a cast of hundreds of Cairoites, doing our own scenarios, staging, music and costuming. We will have the assistance of a university dramatic technician, but the production will be our own. Local talent, we the people of Cairo, will tell ourselves who we are, how we got that way, and what we may yet become."

I could not resist letting my thoughts trail over the excellent array of talent in town available for type-casting in such a venture. When I snapped back to the present moment, the divorced minister, substituting for an absent committee chairman, was presenting another plan from the center of Poston's heart.

"Last summer we learned that Fort Defiance State Park could go pop as far as the State of Illinois was concerned," said the minister, boldly injecting a little of his own vernacular into the report. "We were determined not to let that happen. We learned that we could lease the park on a long-term basis, through the vehicle of a not-for-profit corporation. For that purpose, we formed the Confluence Community Development Corporation, the corporate arm of Operation Enterprise.

"Our lease has since been signed with the Illinois Historic Preservation Agency. The state is contributing a stipend every year of five thousand dollars for maintenance, and we have adopted the development of this park as one of our very major Action Projects."

The young minister summarized the plans: campsites, a miniature golf course, a children's playground, replicas of the first French trading post and of General Grant's Fort Defiance, from which the Civil War siege on Vicksburg was launched. There also would be excursion boats and water sports, an outdoor amphitheater for dramatic productions, and the remodeling of an adjacent building into a museum with a riverboat theme.

There was more: "Our plans," said the minister, "also include an eighteenth-century show-house and restaurant, done in authentic style, with vintage entertainment, such as Dixieland music and can-can dancers [here the minister rolled his eyes, drawing an involuntary guffaw from the audience] as a source of income for the restoration of Cairo into an early-American river town."

Here was some major news! For those who were able to decode it, Doc Poston was revealing the contours of his master agenda in Cairo. It was an agenda that would place him and his organization inescapably at odds with the vested interests of Cairo's power structure—meaning the wharfage magnate Bill Wolter and his sympathetic friend, Mayor Al Moss.

The little peninsula that formed Fort Defiance Park—the precise southern tip of Illinois—lay only a few hundred yards from the hub of Wolter's tugboat-and-barge maneuverings on the Ohio. Wolter considered that riverfront as his riverfront. (The Mississippi side of the peninsula was a tangle of swamp and thicket; Cairo tended to face the Ohio River.) He would not welcome interference. Nor would Al Moss likely welcome this competing claim on his authority, his stewardship of the town's economic destiny.

The good members of the Quinstate Forum did not suspect it, but they were hearing an extremely audacious, if subtle, declaration of war.

There came another burst of laughter from the Quinstaters. The chairperson of the Secretarial Committee had just successfully pulled off a little joke that she had rehearsed with Doc and Angela the day before. Noting her responsibility "to write minutes of our town meetings and also to duplicate reports of all other committees—the detailed records enable us to keep tabs on ourselves and engage in continuing self-evaluation," this gentle and sallow woman had continued: "And now I'd like to introduce you to two of our trusted committee members—Miss Cassette Recorder [she held up a recorder] and Miss Bic Pen [she held up a pen]." The crowd thought that was a thigh-slapper.

The final presenter kept the laughter going, and I began to hope there might be some ginger in the Quinstaters after all. Betty Rivers, the Treasury Committee chairman and a close friend of Miss McBride, was a self-styled comedienne. Tiny and droll, she used her throaty voice to great effect. Now she was threatening to steal the entire morning's show.

"Currently this is a *one*-woman committee," she deadpanned, looking weary. "It's very sad. I have to run so *fas'* . . . when anybody gimme any money.

"I perform the function of a *treasury,*" she read from Doc's script, then looked up. "You know what that is? And *ah*—who?! Me!—*Ah*—Ah *am* that woman!" Laughter from the audience.

"When groups' activities warrant it," she continued from the script, then ad-libbed, "Ah am goin' to get some *he'p!* 'Cause this committee has *got* to expand!" She marched from the podium to a burst of laughter and applause.

Angela Greenwell took the microphone. "This basically ends our program," she announced. "Our presentation to you. If you have any questions, we're open for questions."

There was the predictable, interminable pause, as Angela glanced rather helplessly around the gymnasium. Finally, from somewhere in the rear seats, came the dyspeptic rumble of a late-middle-aged male:

"I didn't hear anything about the responsibility of the churches in the community."

I left the Quinstate Forum at that point. I needed air. I got in my car and drove for awhile. I went north on Sycamore, the business route, passing Al Moss's boating supplies store, and then crossed the city limit by driving through a banked railroad underpass, the old Illinois Central line extending toward its Ohio River Bridge into Kentucky.

Just north of town, about a mile from my motel and on the Mississippi side of the peninsula, lay the small and rotting, strictly black settlement, the ghost-suburb, that I'd been meaning to investigate: Future City.

I turned left from the highway onto a dirt service road and headed in.

Future City was perhaps two city blocks in length and another two blocks wide. The dirt trails that served as its streets had citified names: Broadway, First, Second, New Division. A rail fence facing the main highway supported about thirty mailboxes bunched together. Behind this fence was the city—a putrefaction of shanties made from the ancient husks of trailer-homes; tar-paper shacks; corroded aluminum siding.

Cars without wheels rusted in front yards. Garbage, broken children's toys, skeletons of bicycles lay half-buried in the back. I saw dozens of prowling cats, some spavined dogs, a few limping chickens, and not one human being.

At Bridge and Second streets I saw a hellscape: a denuded building whose shingling had completely burned away; there were no panes in its windows. Near it were some old shopping carts carefully filled with debris that defied itemization; some stacked railroad ties; some cleared-out scrub brush. A little further away there stood a gangrenous molding shack of green tarpaper and exposed, rotted wood; the roof had caved in and the windows were smashed.

I thought of the Environmental Improvement chairman and his promise of "a detailed, inch-by-inch examination of Cairo's physical appearance." I thought of all the "delving into," the "ferreting out," the "fine-tooth combing" that had been promised on this morning in the St. Joseph gym. I felt the weight of immense fatigue and depression settling over me. If this was Cairo's suburb, what sort of defilement had these people fled?

Betty Rivers lived in Future City.

I put the car in gear—the lever had the weight of an anvil—and drove back toward town. At the railroad underpass, I noticed a boosterish sign that proclaimed: WELCOME TO CAIRO/THE GOVERNOR'S HOMETOWN AWARD 1986. Who came in third? I wondered to myself. The thought did not cheer me up.

I drove down Sycamore until it joined Washington at Harper's Restaurant, and continued south on Washington—past the bleached-out service stations and storefronts, past the public library and the National Guard headquarters—toward the tip. I was driving to Fort Defiance Park, to view the setting of Poston's plans for regeneration.

At the entrance to the park—a sharp downward plunge on a dirt road just off the highway—had been erected a Historic Marker:

CAIRO, ILL.—PIERRE FRANCOIS XAVIER DE CHARLEVOIX, A FRENCH JESUIT, REPORTED AS EARLY AS 1721 THAT THE LAND AT THE CONFLUENCE OF THE MISSISSIPPI AND OHIO RIVERS WOULD BE A STRATEGIC LOCATION FOR SETTLEMENT AND FORTIFICATION. NEARLY A CENTURY LATER, IN 1818, THE ILLINOIS AND TERRITORIAL LEGISLATURE INCORPORATED THE CITY AND BANK OF CAIRO.

BUT CAIRO WAS THEN ONLY A PAPER CITY AND PLANS FOR ITS DEVELOPMENT CAME TO A STANDSTILL WITH THE DEATH OF JOHN GLEAVES COMEGYS, THE LEADING PROMOTER OF THE CORPORATION.

THE AREA'S COMMERCIAL POTENTIAL AGAIN CAPTURED THE IMAGINATION OF ILLINOIS LEADERS AND EASTERN INVESTORS IN THE 1830s . . . [BUT] THE FIRST LEVEES FAILED TO HOLD BACK THE RAMPAGING RIVERS, AND FINANCIAL DIFFICULTIES SLOWED THE COMMERCIAL BOOM. COMPANY POLICY TO LEASE, NOT SELL CITY LOTS ALSO RETARDED EXPANSION. . . .

WHEN THE CIVIL WAR BEGAN, BOTH NORTHERN AND SOUTHERN STRATEGISTS RECOGNIZED THE MILITARY IMPORTANCE OF CAIRO. . . . ALTHOUGH THE CITY BUSTLED WITH WARTIME ACTIVITY, NON-MILITARY COMMERCE WAS REORIENTED ALONG EAST-WEST LINES.

—Erected by the Illinois Department of Transportation and
the Illinois State Historical Society, 1964

I proceeded down into the park.

The day was overcast, and yet there were a few pinpoints of sparkling light on the sheet-metal surface of the Ohio, off to my left. I drove toward the extreme point of the park—the point of Illinois, the rivers' confluence—where the dirt road formed a loop. Circling it counterclockwise, I could see traces of Cairo nearly hidden behind its Ohio River flood wall, not at all unlike Miss McBride nearly hidden behind her podium. The automobile bridge into Kentucky commanded the foreground of this vista; a few tugboats from Bill Wolter's operation were moored a little ways upstream from its foot. A couple miles beyond was the railroad bridge, and to the southwest I could see the old-fashioned green cornices of the Interstate 57 bridge that linked Cairo with Missouri.

A few miles upriver on the Mississippi, I knew, was yet another bridge, a relatively new span built for the divided-lane interstate spur that brought traffic from across the continent.

Four bridges. Two rivers. A superhighway. Two adjoining states. So many assets. A matter of putting it all together.

The weather turned nasty in Southern Illinois that night: a wet snow fell on Cairo. CAIRO HIGH SCHOOL WELCOME (sic) QUINSTATE TOWN MEETING THURSDAY 7 O'CLOCK HERE, read the lighted marquee at the high school's entrance. But inside, it was quickly clear that despite Poston's and Angela's repeated reminders, nearly all the Quinstaters had skipped the chance to see democracy in action. Perhaps they had wanted to beat the bad weather back home.

About a hundred townspeople had come, a better-than-average town meeting turnout. A few brought small children. They found places on folding chairs in the school auditorium, facing a row of card tables at the foot of a stage: the dais for the Enterprise high command.

If Doc Poston was let down by the absence of visitors from the conference, he kept it heroically to himself. Dressed in the same spiffy blazer and tie he'd worn that morning (he'd changed into a fresh white shirt), Poston was very much the commanding impresario. He had put together a fairly elaborate pageant—there were to be songs, a slide show, waves of Action Committee reports—and Doc whipped things along, beginning with an electrifying invocation by a local black minister named Eddie Hodge.

The theme of this town meeting was "beautification," and the first presentation was a reading from a children's storybook, *Evel Weevil*, about a messy little beetle indeed, by a woman member of Operation Enterprise. The woman accompanied her reading with some fuzzy slides of the book's illustration, and the slide machine's *whirr* competed with her somewhat self-conscious rendition.

Then the young minister arose. He was a slim Lutheran named Randy Scott. A guitar was strapped over his shoulder. Rev. Randy Scott announced that at Doc Poston's *firm* insistence—the minister rolled his eyes comically to make it clear just how firm the insistence was—he was going to sing the James Taylor ballad, "Hometown," while the Enterprisers watched another slide show, this one of color photographs depicting Cairo's physical squalor.

It was not an uplifting experience. It was a descent into the American underworld. Whoever had taken the photographs had been remorseless in his or her approach, and the bombardment of pestilent images—bashed house-windows, broken pavement, filthy and vacant-eyed children, scrofulous husks of burnt buildings and cars, garbage-strewn yards, abandoned filling stations, piles of ulcerated auto tires, growths of weeds, like dermatitis, on abandoned brick-strewn lots—none of this was enhanced by the slightest overlay of artistic technique.

The James Taylor song had many verses, but the minister ran out of them before the slide-show was finished; and so there ensued a fairly dismal interlude, slide after slide after slide, in which the only sounds in the darkened auditorium were the metronomic *skrawk, skrawk* of the ancient projector's moving parts and the mortified giggles and nervous wisecracking of the people in the audience.

The day began to back up on me; Cairo began to back up on me. My sense of gloom, which had taken hold during my detour into Future City, tightened into a kind of suffocation. Once again now the Action Committee chairmen were reciting their "reports," all placed in their mouths by Poston. Tepid, labored applause followed each speaker. Someone uttered the word "democracy," and I winced. Too much broken glass, too much rotting wood, too much anesthesia, for democracy here. Cairo's diseased past infected this small gathering, infected Operation Enterprise, mocking its mild hopes. Up at the front of the auditorium now, an Action Committee chairman was pointing with a yardstick at the slide-projector screen, where there wavered an idiotic image: some handmade signs of oak and granite. The signs spelled out WELCOME TO CAIRO. A progress report. A mission accomplished.

What kind of self-deluding ritual was I witnessing here? What varieties of personal compulsions had this monomaniacal old man succeeded in transferring to these lonely and aimless people?

The odds against Poston's mission here now struck me as incalculable, laughable, infuriating. America had receded from Cairo—if indeed America had ever really connected there—as America had receded from all its rivertowns and inland hamlets up and down the Mississippi Valley and into the West. It was the Darwinian force of technology and economics, not the Postonian force of elbow grease and moral suasion, that had changed the face of America.

Chapter XI

Several months after Dorothy Gawel's fatal accident—on a breezy and sunswept spring afternoon in Connecticut—I decided to pay a visit on her daughter Susie, who had been driving when the collision happened, and who was still recuperating at her home.

The Gawel clan was scattered among the steep hills to the east of Route 7, in the region called Flanders, immediately north of Kent. Many Gawels, or relatives of Gawels, lived not far from Carol Hoffman's eighteenth-century farmhouse, but they lived in more modest homes of far more recent vintage.

Flanders was the site of the original village. It was where Kent's proprietors first cleared their auction-bought land in 1738; it was where people lived and farmed before the iron foundaries went up, before the railroad line came through in the 1840s to draw the town down from the rise, toward the flatland and the Housatonic banks. Kent's first church had been built up here, in 1741. One could still make out the remnants of tanyards; of a "fulling mill," where cloth was taken to be moistened and pressed after it had been woven, and an Ecclesiastical Field, a triangular plot bordered on one side by a stone wall, where Kent's militia had drilled for the Revolutionary War.

This was National Register of Historic Places territory. At least ten of the houses visible from Route 7 had been built between 1740 and 1840. Some were low-slung, shuttered wood-frame houses in the Federal style that nestled behind rail fences and screens of pine and maple trees, displaying faded American flags on their front porches. A few elegant old Colonial and Greek Revival master-pieces arose out of the curving terrain, with their foundations of fieldstone, their shingled sides, their heavily detailed entrances and their gabled roof-frames. And their real-estate-agent shingles im-planted at roadside.

Neither the Gawels nor their neighbors and kin could afford to live in any such picture-book estates. Their bungalow houses sat farther up the sides of these hills, on land that, a generation or so ago, had been meadow or orchard or farmland and, not long before that, woods. Similarly, it was land that until fairly recently in the century had been owned in vast quantities by a few patriarchs.

Only in recent decades had the patriarchs found it necessary to subdivide the land, sell it in parcels to newcomers, or hand some pieces of it down to the newer generations in the family. This selling-off of ancestral land had accelerated during the boom years of the 1980s; it was perhaps the chief mechanism for the saturation, in the town, of newcomers. As the old estates and their acreage passed from kinfolk to strangers, the sellers' relatives (and, thanks to the higher taxes, quite frequently their neighbors as well) were obliged to move farther from the town center. Often the younger generations left the town entirely and did not return. Thus was Kent passing from the status of indigenous community to the status of urban colony.

"Our grandparents, and even our parents—they had so much land," Susie Gawel had told me by telephone when I'd called to see if I could come visit her. "But selling it off is the only way you can survive, or help your children set out. My grandmother gave me an acre of land, where I built the home I have now. If it weren't for that . . ." she let the thought die. "You can hang on to the land for just so long."

Susie Gawel was as close to the center of Kent's permanent, multi-generational community as it was possible to be. She herself represented the unification of two of the town's largest and oldest families, the Gawels and the Chases. A Solomon Chase is listed in the town records as early as 1787 (for an unpaid debt, as it hap-pened). One of the local mountains bears the Chase name. The Gawels came later, of course, but proliferated and sank deep roots into the land: as carpenters, schoolteachers, proprietors. "My fa-ther was one of five, my mother was one of five," Susie Gawel had told me. "These families all stayed in the Kent area. Their children are still here, their grandchildren are here, their great-grandchildren. The offspring branch out."

Less than a half mile north of the Kent town border I made a right turn off Route 7 onto the steeply winding dirt road that led up to Susie's house. It was an old stagecoach road, she'd told me—a king's highway; preserved in ancient statute from being widened or changed. Now it was bordered by metal mailboxes, and houses with television antennas.

Susie Gawel, in bluejeans, waved down to me from the deck of her small frame house as I pulled my car into her driveway, then slid back the glass panel to her kitchen and disappeared inside. When I entered the house she was sitting in an easy chair in her living room with one socked foot up on a hassock, an ice pack resting on her knee. Her lifelong friend, a cheery, whitehaired older woman named Marie Naboring, was visiting her.

I asked Susie how often she still had therapy for her injuries.

"I'm two nights a week at the doctor's office, and I go to swim therapy three days a week," she replied in a robust voice, one that may have been tuned to speaking out-of-doors—across a windy meadow, say. "It's the whole body they're still workin' on—back, neck, muscles."

She was a small, solid, resolute woman with the doe-like dark eyes of a young child, although the framed color photographs in the room around her showed, among other relatives, two strapping sons. These were Alan, the fire marshall, and Joe, her younger son. (Susie had been divorced from the father of the two boys and had chosen to retain her parents' family name, as had the sons.)

The young man whose pickup truck had smashed into the Gawel car had been convicted of negligent homicide; he'd been released from jail after serving a short term. "They're very clever," Susie observed vaguely, and without particular bitterness; bitterness seemed alien to her nature. She may have meant the young man and his relatives, or perhaps their attorneys. "They know the ins and outs of the law."

We spent a little time talking about Dorothy Gawel.

"Well, she's a native," said Susie, unconsciously keeping her mother in the present tense. "She was born here, grew up here. She's a Chase. She met my father, I guess, through high school or something. They were four years apart. They were married in '37."

"That's right!" put in Marie Naboring from her perch near the small upright piano. " 'Cause I come back up the same year they got married! Yeah, they were married in '37 'cause I come up in June!

They were married the second of June of '37 and I come up the fifteenth of June of '37! And I met her the year after!"

"And my dad's father had given my dad some property here on Studio Hill Road," said Susie. "And he, being a builder, built the house that when they got married they moved into."

"Ha! Ha!" said Marie. "That house is somethin'!"

"Well, okay," said Susie, "they got married, and then they started to have a family. They had three bedrooms—"

"They had *two* bedrooms!" interjected Marie. "When they started they had two bedrooms. Two bedrooms upstairs."

"And every time they had a child," Susie said, "another bedroom got added on."

"Yes!" said Marie. "Because John went through the—the one bedroom, in the middle, then . . . you were right, I'm sorry, there was three bedrooms!"

The women seemed to take solace in talking on about the past as though it lived into the present, and I found myself content to listen.

"But they—oh, it was really fun then," said Susie. "My mom, she used to work at a big inn in Kent, called the Petite Chalet. It was a magnificent inn. I can even remember it—it was right in the center of town, in the open lot where the Lions Club has the lobster fest."

"But she worked before," put in Marie, "when she was goin' to school. She worked before, when they was at the log cabin. Your mother worked there before she got married."

"The Chases," Susie said. "My grandfather, Sherm Chase, was a logger in his early days, and a builder also; he built this Chase Road off Route 7. He built the house there, and built many houses on that road. And they—my mom, and her sisters and brothers, grew up there. And across Route 7 there was the old Chestnut Inn, a log cabin inn, and my grandfather actually built that.

"Mom used to work after school when they were goin' to school. Her mom had severe asthma, and was not really too well. Mom was the oldest of the five. She helped out with the younger children. And wait tables at the Petite Chalet, and everything.

"So then she and my dad got married and they started to raise a family, and mom was always—she was home all the time, she didn't work outside the home. She did all the books for my dad, did the financial aspect of it. Then as we grew up, she was in with the Boy Scouts, the Cub Scouts—and the Brownies and Girl Scouts. And she was one of the original establishers of the Kent Nursing Association, and I can remember back in 1955, she was voted Mother of the Year for the whole town of Kent. And they had this *huge* ceremony, and she was so embarrassed, she hated to have any recognition, she was just, you know, a quiet person that way. She was the president of the Ladies of the Sacred Heart in our church for many years, and she was on the Elderly Housing committee. . . ."

Susie fell silent for a few moments. I took that opportunity to ask her about the geese.

"The geese," said Susie, and some of the heartiness came back into her voice. "The geese came every fall and spring. She loved the geese. My dad stocked bass in that pond over at the house where they lived"—she swept her arm up to indicate the now-vacant house just a couple hundred yards across the old meadow—"and my youngest son Joe, at eight years old, would go out and ice-fish. And he just loved it; he caught a seven-pounder once; he was thrilled.

"And—you know sometimes how you'll lose a fishhook? Well, the geese would come along in the spring. There's a rock out in the middle of the pond. Mom put a tire out there, and they would nest in the tire. One time, one of the geese got a fishhook caught in its throat. And Mom could see from her window that something was the matter. She went down and she got that fishhook right out of the goose's mouth.

"She kept in *touch* with those geese. She loved nature. Wild turkeys would come onto her lawn. We have pictures of that. And the deer, all the time the deer."

Marie, who had been quiet for some time now, chimed in: "She was just a wonderful person. Always, you know, had her door open to everybody. Everyone went up to her house in the morning—well, I did, every morning—went up to her house, even when the kids were coming along, and I was working. I'd go up and have a cup of coffee and then we'd do the crossword puzzles. *Not* crossword puzzles," Marie corrected herself, "*jigsaw* puzzles. We always had a card table with the jigsaw puzzles. The two of us. She was color-blind, so she couldn't go by color, which I went by color. She went by shape. She was great!"

Susie Gawel shifted her stiff knee a little on the hassock, and adjusted the ice pack. Her dark eyes were shiny. The memories were really working inside her now.

"When we were growing up," she said, "we had—all the property owners were relatives, really, because that's who were in the town. And we'd run a span on our little legs across lots. We'd run a span down to where the old Chestnut Inn is, Chase Road, where the relatives were, and all the way up to the top of the hill to the Peet Farm. And we'd run that whole span. On Saturdays our mothers would pack a lunch for us and off we'd go for the whole day. You'd go from one house to the other and play games and have a wonderful time.

"I can remember when this house—this house where I live now—I can remember when this whole acreage here was a hayloft, a potato lot. I used to help my grandfather. He would drive a team of horses and I'd sit on the kick behind the team, and we'd rake hay in strips. And then he would go back to the farm and unhitch the horses and—oh, I can remember lots of things! I remember running down cross-lots to the farm, and he'd be making honey, and he'd chew the honeycomb, and then he'd mix cider—jeez, we had a lot of fun with the cider!"

"We used to sell that cider," said Marie.

"The holidays were fabulous," said Susie. "The family would come. We'd always have thirty people on any holiday. Family and friends."

Marie said, looking at Susie, "We always come up to her house for Christmas, and then you all come down to my house for Thanksgiving. And go back to her house for New Year's. I was the one that made the potatoes all the time. Always mashed potatoes. Because, well, you had to have room on the top of the stove to cook all the other things."

Susie said, "But they all participated, all, everybody got together and helped one another, which was really nice. You miss that so much today. You just—" she threw out both her hands, helplessly. "You get up in the morning and you go to work and you come home at night. I mean, there's just that—that *drive*. And you don't even have time to turn around and stop."

"You don't know anyone downtown!" said Marie. "You go downtown, you don't know a soul. Before, when I'd go downtown, I knew everyone. Now I don't know hardly anyone. We're getting to be a city! This is what I don't like! I moved back here to the country 'cause I loved the country. I'm fifty-two years here. I come up here for a vacation in '37, went back, quit my job, come up here and I never went back. I love it up here."

"You hate to see the natural habitat change," said Susie.

"That's it," said Marie.

After I left Susie Gawel and Marie Naboring, I got into my car and drove around the dirt road from Susie's house to the house where Dorothy Gawel and her husband had lived. It was a fine sunlit afternoon; the yellow forsythia was out and the willow trees around Dorothy's pond had leaved into a luminescent yellow-green. As I drove, I could see the big rock that rose from the middle of the pond, and the spare tire that ringed its top. A duck was nestled in the tire.

I pulled into Dorothy Gawel's driveway. Three deer had just sauntered out of the woods behind; they stood near the tree line staring at me with their large, soft eyes. I got out of my car as slowly as I could. The deer did not run away—they had gotten used to newcomers. Dorothy Gawel's house was an olive-green woodframe with a nice sundeck that faced the pond. Skylight windows had been added—not too many years before, it appeared—and there was a huge fireplace chimney at the south end.

I walked up to the house, crossed the sundeck and peered inside through the doorway window. I could see a large wildlife mural, covering an entire wall, that some local artist had painted for her. It depicted turkeys, bluejays, a woodpecker, flying mallards, nesting ducks. The tones were oranges and browns—the colors of autumn.

Behind Dorothy's house, perhaps fifty yards distant, stood another Gawel residence, a small white woodframe. Behind that house there rose a higher peak of the mountain.

When I returned to my car, the deer had gone.

I thought about Susie Gawel, and her memories of running on a span across the Saturday haylots of her youth, a little later that afternoon. I thought of her, and I thought of Dorothy Gawel's empty house with its wildlife mural, as I drove south on Route 7 just a few miles below Kent, on a two-and-a-half-mile stretch of road between the towns of New Milford and Brookfield, a stretch that, like an open pot on a hot stove, contained—at least for the time being—a kind of steam-head of development boiling up from the south, from the Connecticut shoreline and New York.

I thought of the Gawel family as I passed the Holiday Restaurant, a Finast Super Center, a Texaco, a Dunkin' Donuts, a Carvel Ice Cream, a Gulf service station, a Plymouth-Chrysler dealership, a Renault-Pugeout dealership, a Hess gasoline, a U-Haul Rentals, the Village Market & Deli, a Discount Soda, Shepard Lodge No. 65, The Hayloft, the Blue Grotto Restaurant, a Burger King, the Stereo-Video Package Store, Michael's Deli Market, Statewide Transmission and Brakes, Power House Television Appliances, a McDonald's

(Over 70 Billion Served), a Ford-Mercury dealership, a Sonoco 24 Hours, the New Milford Diner, Andy's Auto Coachworks, Hubbard's Cupboard, Larry's Plaza Printing, a self-service BP gas station, an Oldsmobile-Cadillac-Pontiac dealership, the Diamond (Your Home Investment Center), a Val-U-Rated Used Cars, Country Homes Real Estate, the Federal Mall, Northeast Carpet, Fantastic Sam's Fish Market, Modzelewski's Body Works, Roger's Real Estate, the All Best Self-Storage, Big T Auto Parts, Robert Mark Real Estate, a Skihaus, a Bradlee's, a Parade of Shoes, McCrory's, a Super Stop 'n' Shop, a Union Savings, a Radio Shack, a Discovery, the Village Bakery, an Executive Center, an All-State, the New Milford Bank & Trust, Joey's Seafood Restaurant, a Video World, a Union Trust, the Schneider National, the Shiver Mountain Press, a Van Heusen Factory Store, a Sav-On Shoes, the Yankee Supply Center, Unicorn Books, the Bottom Line Furniture Center, the New Milford Shoe Service, a Getty Mart, the Italia Mia Pizza Restaurant, the Covered Bridge Garden Center, an attorney-at-law, the Fast Oil Change, the Expressway Lube Center, an E-Zee Rental, a Tobacco & Convenience store, the Windmill Diner, Sergio's Italian Restaurant, a Century 21, the Commercial Truck & Trailer, Katharine's Antiques, the Class Act, William Pitt Real Estate, a Tools of the Trade, an Auto Land, the New Milford Savings Bank, Big John's Breakfast and Lunch, Hays Used Cars, Hays Buick/Chevrolet, a Meineke Discount Mufflers, the Osbourne Professional Park, a Danish Furniture, a Merrill Lynch Realty, a Metropolitan Life, The Corner Store, an American Motors, a Will Rogers Real Estate, Real Tech Realtors, Bill's Bait & Tackle, the Country Folks Sweet Shop, Carlo's Auto Service, Jet Contractors, the New Milford Sign Shop, Alco's Sales, South End Auto Body, Cosmo's Greenhouse, the Wicker Outlet, the Candlewood Valley Country Club, the Valley Liquor Store, the Valley Veterinary Hospital, V&V Wood Stove, Spas and Hot Tubs, Country Chow, Hair Etc., the Maplewood Industrial Park, an Evergreen Center, Valley Marble and Slate, the Marathon Family Restaurant, the Doll House (Baskets and Gifts), the Elephant Trunk Bazaar, Platts Rustic Fences, a Carpet World, Burkes Travel Center, a TranStar, another Gulf station, Cullens Stables (Free Manure), the Connecticut Golf Center, Tower Realty Corp., Honest Engine, New Milford Block & Supply, Ryan's Marine, A Storage Solution, and several other establishments.

And the next day, a Saturday, as I ate a turkey-sandwich lunch by myself at a vinyl-and-formica booth in the nonsmoking section of the Villager Restaurant, a comfortable, locally owned eatery that traced its lineage in the town to 1820, I thought of Marie Naboring and her lament that she hardly knew anyone anymore when she went downtown. I thought of that lament while I listened to a conversation in the booth directly in front of mine.

Three people had taken seats at this booth, two youngish men and a small boy. The men had wetly combed hair and were wearing expensive jeans and the sort of pressed and brightly-colored button-down "western" shirts that New York people, for instance, buy at, say, the designer section of a Fifth Avenue clothing store for week-ends in the country. The small boy, to his credit, was wearing a small boy's clothes.

A waitress, a young girl in a blue checked dress and an apron—a 1980s version of the young Dorothy Gawel, perhaps—came over, with order pad and ballpoint in hand. One of the men asked whether there were pancakes on the menu in front of him. The young girl said there were.

" 'Cause there's pancakes and there's pancakes," the man said, to no one in particular. Then: " 'Cause, you know, I hate those thick, bready ones."

"Any way you like," the waitress told him. She poised her pen.

The man told her how he wanted his pancakes cooked. "If you do that," he told the waitress, "I'll be so happy I'll eat 'em right up!"

Then he said: "And I'd like some home fries on a separate plate, and I'd like some coffee, and I'd like to sit here and eat it. All of it."

Then his two companions placed their orders.

When the waitress had left, the man discussed Roberta Flack, whose voice was coming over a loudspeaker behind the counter, with his adult companion, as the small boy listened. He discussed her in an authoritative and familiar way, referring to her as "this lady." He said that this lady had made only two beautiful songs.

The waitress returned with the orders.

"Can I ask you a favor?" the man said to her. He pointed to the home fries. "Put those on the grill and just keep 'em there a while— 'cause those are so mushy."

He began to saw off bites of pancake and put them into his mouth, making little mews of appreciation. The three people ate without talking for a few minutes.

The child spoke for the first time. "Look at that ugly vegetable," he suddenly said. He pointed to a lithographic painting behind the counter, a photorealistic watercolor of peas in a delicate pod.

The waitress brought back the order of home fries. "Perfect," the man said, with his mouth full. "My heart is happy."

Then, abruptly, the man in the perfect western shirt spoke to the child for the first time. "Don't you wish," he asked, leaning forward a little, "that you were a girl? So you could wear bright red lipstick and look like someone had slashed a knife right across your face?"

In the few moments it took for that conversation to unfold, I had the sense that Kent, Connecticut, had edged irrevocably closer to the city to its south.

A Fiat with New Mexico plates was parked in front of the Kent Market down the street when I left The Villager. Directly across from me—across Route 7—stood Bill Litwin's newly completed Town Center, with its French windows on the bottom and its bright yellow woodframe crowning the second story: the "neo-Mall" that he had joked about. I hadn't taken a close look at it yet, so I crossed the road and walked around it for a few minutes.

A Folkcraft Instruments occupied half of the southernmost building; the rest was an Italian delicatessen. I walked inside, where a lot of people in black, soft-leather jackets were ordering food. "Mustard on your chili dog?" a counterman was asking one of them.

I looked at the tins of Tuscany toast and pure almond paste and imported small-pearl tapioca. Under the deli-counter glass I could see provoletta, and ricotta salad, and olive loaf, and Virginia ham, and smoked ham, and ham cappi, and ham deluxe. I could see dry cappi and mortadella, and salads of seafood, and egg, and artichoke. Soppresata, I could see.

All this on the ground where Gordon Casey had learned the lumber business.

I recrossed Route 7—the May sun was shining on willow and forsythia and automobile chrome—and walked east, toward the rear of an auto dealership that had formerly been Gawel Chevrolet, down a newly paved strip of road that led into Gordon Casey's Kent Green.

Here, on what had been a flat meadow at the base of the small rounded mountain that rose above Town Hall, were the low-slung, mock-Federal boutiques that had been thrown up in the past year. Each building occupied a sector of an invisible grid, an island of building and sidewalk, with narrow borders of trimmed grass, surrounded by fat tundras of black tar. There were no trees.

I stopped into the Newbury Doll House, where the clerk, a teen-aged girl in makeup, sat behind the cash register writing a letter in swirling longhand. The place smelled as though it had just been aerosoled with violet sachet. A three-story Newport dollhouse kit was going for $325, or $625 assembled. On the shelves I noticed a collection of miniature furniture, including a ceramic toilet.

At the Cobble Cookery, a gourmet food shop next door, a small girl lay on her back kicking her heels into the floor and screaming while her mother, ignoring her, filled her wire shopping basket and other customers stepped over her. There was French donut mix, duck-liver mousse in plum-wine sauce, creme de noiselle, choco-late-chip bread pudding. There was fajita seasoning and lightly salted tortilla chips and pure water-decaffeinated Tip-of-the-Andes coffee. "Awright, we're gonna need an Irish smoked salmon on dark bread," a big man in soft leather was shouting to the counter-woman over the child's tantrum shrieks. "That sounds like a great sandwich!"

I looked through the window at Clendenin's, a children's clothing shop. The clothing was riotous with announcement. THE CRAYON KID STRIKES AGAIN, screamed a $15 T-shirt, in crayon. Another garment babbled, WINTER SPORTS ALPEN SKI TEAM. A boy's Jordache Air Force shirt, complete with ammo loops, was selling for $25. A far cry, I thought, from the durable denims and T-shirts worn by Kent kids across the decades.

I walked back up the macadam strip toward Route 7 and the sector of downtown Kent that traced its roots to the nineteenth century, the railroad era. Both sidewalks along Route 7 were filled with strolling people, but they did not seem to be Marie Naboring's kind of people. They held hands and wore Polaroid sunglasses and their clothing matched. These people were not strolling the town so much as they were combing it.

Walking south toward the House of Books, I remembered a re-mark Bill Litwin had made about the way people dressed in Kent.

"I can recall the people you'd see in town," Litwin had said, "and I recall the way they dressed was rather rural. Rather rural and rather simple. *Now,* everybody wears—you know, they dress well, they act well, they drive nicer cars and so forth. Things have changed in town. People have become a little more civilized," he concluded unenthusiastically.

Chapter XII

I went back for a second visit to Cairo at the end of April. Again, I went warily. I needed to justify this journey to myself with some sentimental pretexts, some necessary lies. These seemed only prudent, like antitoxins, for anyone who had visited the town once and was not absolutely obligated to go there again.

I tried conjuring up some old sensory memories of early spring in a Mississippi rivertown, boyhood memories of scent and sunlight and girls in dresses and doors left open into the evening. I told myself that even this particular and accursed rivertown must have its aspects of purity and wholeness, of some temporary surrender into the healing breadth of Illinois in its seasonal greening. I took the view that my rush of revulsion and despair on that last March night in the little town had been partly rooted in its winter decrepitude—its seasonal aspect of saplessness and vacancy and death. Even Cairo must come alive a little in the spring, I thought; even Al Moss must start thinking baseball thoughts and drop a line in the river. Even Bill Wolter must have his Saturdays.

Yes, I had told myself as I had sat wedged among my hate-glazed fellow passengers on the overheated commuter bus that hurtled over potholes toward the fierce prosperity of Manhattan, I should go back to Cairo in the spring.

There I would find the small pleasures of the stale beer-smell of open-door taverns along Commercial in the afterdinner twilight, and of a skyful of Midwestern stars in deep night, and of crickets and honest mosquitoes, and of the invisibility of moccasins and bullfrogs down in the swamp. And I would find the smells of pollen and garden soil, and the gestative perfume of the awakening river itself. To an old town boy years exiled in a city, all this counted for something.

And yet none of that was what drew me back, not really, and I knew it. What drew me back was exactly what had repulsed me at the end of my first visit: the eerie and depressing experience of witnessing a drama that thrashed toward its inevitable sad ending in an otherwise empty theater, the director oblivious of the vanished audience.

The men and women of Operation Enterprise—not to mention the people in the town who wished them ill—were enacting a struggle for the soul of a community that in the maddened larger nation had long since been decided, and then forgotten. A vast economic Darwinism drove the destinies of towns in America, not the dreams of old grass-roots patriots nor even the petty greed of the local moguls. Weak and abandoned towns died in America, or lingered in a kind of brain-death. They were perhaps the lucky ones. The fate of the robust town was annexation into suburban madness.

All of which made the Cairo struggle all the more compelling to me. I felt implicated in the town, somehow; accountable to the very anonymity of its torment, which began to take on, in my mind, a strange kind of gothic elegance, a bravura.

And of course there was Poston.

I had been in touch with Poston. Or Poston had been in touch with me. Since my return to the East after the Quinstate Forum and Doc's gloomy town meeting, he had called me up a few times. I would lift the receiver and there would be his voice, not so much beginning a conversation as seeming to continue one—like a child awakening from sleep into an idea, it finally struck me—insisting away on whatever argument gripped his mind at the moment. Typically this would involve a project or a strategy for Operation Enterprise.

After several of these calls I began to miss sitting across some formica table from Doc Poston as he talked and smoked, gray-faced and all sucked-in below the cheekbones, conjuring his invisible audiences. And so when spring arrived in Southern Illinois, I flew to Paducah and drove back into Cairo.

. . .

Southern Illinois had indeed ripened into woodsy green. The drought that would desiccate the country that summer was as yet only a harmless cloud of dust behind a pickup truck on a bottomland cornfield. I put up in my accustomed room at Glen's Mid-America—the vomit stench had been disinfected, or had biologically degraded, since my last visit—and moseyed into town, to see what I could see.

At the Elias Tru-Value Hardware Store and Family Center (TUX-EDO CENTER FOR PROMS AND WEDDINGS, noted the marquee) I received robust greetings from a couple of Operation Enterprise regulars, Bobby McFarlane and Cordell McCoy, each reeling intently behind an armload of brand-new rakes—a reminder to me that Doc Poston's second annual community cleanup of Fort Defiance Park would commence early the following morning, a Saturday.

I drove on south through town. Cairo looked as spavined as ever, but some pink hollyhock blossoms and thick layers of wild-growing vines now served to soften the naked charred squalor of last winter. I kept on until I reached the point.

A handsome new wooden sign over the entrance to the park immediately caught my eye. It announced FORT DEFIANCE, CONFLU-ENCE OF AMERICA. Some sixth sense told me that this was a successfully completed Operation Enterprise Action Project, and that Richard Poston had a hand in the wording.

The bought rakes, the new sign—however anemic Poston's crusade might have seemed on that snowy night in March, clearly it was not dead yet.

I ate some fiery barbecued ribs at Shemwell's, where the pungent scent of hickory smoke floated out into the open windows of passing cars, and then repaired back to my room at Glen's, where I started to work the phone.

My first call was to Poston, and right away I learned, to my complete astonishment, just how alive things still were. Angela Greenwell had gotten herself thrown out of a city council meeting.

It had happened just three nights previously, a Tuesday. Angela had petitioned to speak during the visitor's portion of the council agenda. Her stated topic—a complaint that the annual Cairo Jaycees' carnival was blocking the front entrance to a downtown senior citizens' center—was a ploy.

Once she had the floor, Angela quickly disposed of her pretext. She stunned everyone, and triggered near-apoplexy in Mayor Moss, by reading aloud from a written statement on behalf of Operation Enterprise that objected to the Council's renewal of wharfage-rights leases for Bill Wolter's Cairo Waterfront Services. (Neither the statement nor its presentation to the Council had been authorized by Poston.)

The mayor did not preface his reaction with any homespun anecdotes this time. "You lied to me, Mrs. Greenwell!" he shouted, and immediately ruled her out of order. When she refused to stop reading the letter, Mayor Moss ordered the police chief to remove her from the Council chambers. (An account of the incident received banner-headline treatment in the *Cairo Citizen Plus* a couple of days later; the story was reported and written by the police chief's wife.) Apparently Angela managed a certain aplomb befitting her social status and her majestic golden bouffant even as she was being given the bum's rush. Turning to the police chief, she icily enunciated, "Is this an invitation to leave?" The chief agreed that it was.

Predictably, perhaps, the confrontation had spilled over into Poston's jurisdiction.

"Al came down to the Chamber of Commerce afterwards," Doc told me over the phone, some weariness in his voice. "I sat in the back room with him for an hour and a half or more, tryin' to reach some kind of an understanding. Now, Ron, this was a difficult thing to do, because I'm not asking Angela to change her position. If she did that, it would be devastating, because she would be looked upon by the people who respect her for having stood up that way as having lost her courage and cut a deal.

"But if they could agree to get past this controversy, get on with the total program—see, the mayor wasn't gonna supply any city equipment, or help, or anything for this big cleanup tomorrow. He was just gonna—word got out, I don't know whether he said it or not, but a lot of people have said he said it, that he was gonna kill the Chamber of Commerce. He was gonna go out and get the people to stop payin' their dues, withdraw their memberships . . . he was *absolutely furious toward Angela.* And knowin' this guy, Ron—he can be pretty vindictive when he wants."

A couple of nights later—the night before my visit, in fact—Al Moss and Angela showed up together for a summit in Poston's apartment. That meeting alone was a minor triumph for Doc in the nuances of town diplomacy.

"Comin' out of the post office yesterday, I got in my car, and there's a big honking behind me," Poston recalled, "and there's Al

Moss. So I got out of the car, and he's saying, 'How are we gonna get this thing sorted out?' So I says, 'Well, I tellya what, Al, I'll get ahold of Angela tonight, and then I'll call you.' He says, 'Well, we can come over to my place of bidniss.' I said, 'Well, I'll decide where and when and I'll give you a call.'

"I wasn't about to take her to his place of bidniss," Poston's voice continued—infinitely parsing, as usual, the labyrinthine implications of the narrative, "because of the *physical arrangements*. He'd be sitting there behind a desk. It'd be like him in the mayor's chair. That'd be bad. So the only place was my apartment. We could all sit around in a circle there. Just the three of us. So, okay, he agreed to that. I got to Angela, and she agreed to it."

But the diplomatic maneuverings were not to be quite as simple as that.

"So they came up here last night," Poston's voice continued, "and lo and behold, he brings his guy with him." Poston named a Cairo councilman who served as Moss's unofficial backup man on nearly all of the mayor's transactions. "Well, anyway, they were all here till 11:30 last night—and then in comes Carolyn!" This was a blond and bouffanted friend of Angela's, a member of Operation Enterprise who relished a good fight against the town's power establishment. "She was obviously angered and peeved: 'Well, now, what's this secret meeting you're having? What kind of a deal have you cut?' "

Poston paused to release a copious sigh that seemed to end as a yawn. "I had to talk to her until 3:15 in the morning! Her and Angela and me! Then I couldn't—I had to unwind! It took me till 4:30 to actually get in bed! Got up at 6:30; had a lot of things to do today! Then Al calls on me again this morning—"

I had been in town less than two hours, and already it was starting to back up on me. I looked at my watch—6:20 P.M. A long and lonely evening in this room stretched ahead. My reveries of scent and sunlight and open doors suddenly seemed as distant as they had in New York.

Poston was still talking: ". . . And he left. But he left smiling at me, and I said, 'By the way, Al, I forgot to tellya, we need that electronic bullhorn you have so we can make announcements to people out at the park tomorrow!' 'Okay,' he says, 'I'll have it.' "

Poston's voice had recouped some of its heartiness now. "I'd say he's still suspicious of me, but he sees me as somebody he's gotta work with. In other words, this Operation Enterprise has gained power, Ron! And I'm looked upon, I guess, as the symbol of that!"

I rang off with the promise that I'd see Doc in the morning. I'd join him at the site where the cleanup caravan would form for its drive through Cairo to Fort Defiance Park.

I sat for a few minutes on the edge of my bed, turning over the implications of what Poston had just told me. I wondered whether he had considered them carefully himself. He was right about gaining power, of course. But power in Cairo was a finite and husbanded commodity. One man's gain was another's loss. Historically in this town, entrenched power had defended itself with dreadful intent.

Now Poston was on a collision course with Cairo power. By inspiring Angela Greenwell—however inadvertently—to mount a public offensive against Mayor Moss, Doc had greatly advanced the stakes of Operation Enterprise.

Now the stakes manifestly included Bill Wolter and his control of the riverfront. By challenging the legality of the lease agreement that awarded Wolter exclusive use of the Ohio River's right bank in front of Cairo, Mrs. Greenwell had tacitly announced Operation Enterprise's designs on the same property.

Perhaps just as significantly, she had openly seceded from Cairo's power elite, in a manner almost guaranteed to abrade that circle's sense of decorum. One of Bill Wolter's few close friends was a wealthy farmer conspicuously absent from any of Operation Enterprise's gatherings: John Greenwell, Angela's husband. I did not meet John Greenwell during my visits to Cairo. My understanding was that he and Angela were rarely seen together socially.

There were two other calls on my list, and I hesitated over each of them. The first was to another source of entrenched Cairo power, the Reverend Larry Potts. I wanted to ask Potts whether I could attend his Sunday service at the Cairo Baptist Church, and also whether I could meet with him to talk about Cairo and Operation Enterprise.

I assured myself that this was a plausible and necessary contact. I needed to move outward from Poston's own orbit in the town and get to know its people on my own. Larry Potts was one of Cairo's two or three most prominent clergymen. It was only natural that I talk to him.

Except that it could not be entirely natural. Larry Potts's clerical prominence was not the entire reason I wanted to meet him—a fact that it troubled me to acknowledge.

Larry Potts was the minister who had beaten an old black man to death, in a rage, with a baseball bat, twenty years before. (And the Reverend Larry Potts had not been forced to stand trial for this act; it had been ruled justifiable homicide.) The black victim's name, Marshall Morris, had all but vanished into the maw of the nameless past; it lived on only in the microfilmed files of the *Cairo Evening Citizen* at the public library. Not even Jenolar McBride could recall having known him. And the town had permitted Potts to continue on as if no killing had ever taken place; had permitted him to go on ministering to his flock, a respected man of God, preaching a Christian gospel of love and the acknowledgment of sin to his exclusively white congregation.

Larry Potts was a link to the violent past that now lay subdued under the town's present anesthesia. I didn't know exactly what I thought I would learn from him—about Cairo, about America, about demons within—but I wanted to see him, and hear him talk, and ask him questions. I lifted the telephone and dialed his number.

A child's voice answered. A boy. Rev. Larry Potts was not in. I identified myself and asked whether the reverend might mind if I came to his church on Sunday. The boy's voice—flat, terse, non-committal—said he would leave a message. The call was not returned.

I put the telephone receiver down, hesitated a while longer, then picked up the Cairo directory and looked up the number of Bill Wolter.

I had managed to learn a little about him from newspaper files and from people in the town. The son of a Wisconsin ship-builder, he had come to Cairo in 1956 from the nearby town of Mound City, where he had started a small wharfage company with his mother's money; the company had nearly gone bankrupt. His original Cairo enterprise numbered four employees. Thirteen years later it numbered eighty-five. By the 1980s, informed people in town were figuring Bill Wolter's worth at three-and-one-half million dollars.

He had held on, through those early lean days, until the strategic location of his business began to pay off. As Doc Poston liked endlessly to point out, Cairo was "at the confluence of two of the nation's mightiest waterways." The one person in town who realized a direct profit from that fact was Bill Wolter.

Barges traveling upriver from New Orleans "split" their cargoes at Cairo: some of the scows continued up the Mississippi; the rest were taken off the fleet and reattached to towboats heading eastward along the Ohio. That was where Wolter's Waterfront Services came in.

Wolter charged $15 per day for every empty fleet that tied up on his leased Ohio waterfront. Loaded barges were billed at $20 a day, and those loaded with chemicals were billed at $42.

In addition, Wolter charged a basic rate of $115 a day for the use of one of his tugs; he also charged an hourly rate for taking a barge off a fleet, and for attaching a barge to a fleet. It added up.

But Wolter's prices were not what stuck in the craws of certain Cairo citizens. What irritated them was the extremely nominal leasing fee that Wolter paid to the city for the 2.3 miles of Ohio waterfront under his commercial control.

It was common knowledge around town that under the terms of a twenty-year lease signed in 1977—a copy of which I saw—Wolter paid twenty cents a year per lineal foot, which would total out at just under $2,500 a year. "But a more typical fee is a dollar a lineal foot," a local man told me. And indeed the city records showed that the Bunge Corporation, the soybean-processing plant just above Wolter's business on the Ohio, paid the city sixty cents a foot a year for the use of one land parcel, and $1.22 a foot for the adjoining one.

"I know some towns along the Mississippi River that charge *thirty* dollars a foot," the man insisted to me. "When you figure that those levees are paid for and maintained by the taxpayers—hell, Cairo has five sets of pumps that belong to the flood-control system; they were built by the Army Corps of Engineers. One of them alone ran up $23,000 in electrical bills last year. Wolter doesn't pay that, the taxpayers do. Seems like a real sweetheart deal to me."

The local man thought a bit, and then added, "You know Al Moss used to deliver groceries to those tugboats when he was a young fellow. He depended on Bill Wolter."

I had done a little checking among barge companies along the lower Mississippi to see how the operators felt about dealing with Wolter. Riverboat men form one of the older and more closed societies in this country; they are a hard-edged, self-reliant lot, and suspicious (if not outright contemptuous) of strangers. I heard a lot of "don't quote me"s and "I ain't going to get too deep into this"s in my phone conversations; but one observation did surface consistently, and it was this: that over the last ten or fifteen years, several barge companies had purchased their own fleet of tugboats—and had taken to performing their own taking-off and putting-on of barges—rather than meet Bill Wolter's prices.

"We got five tugs of our own now," one manager told me. "Wolter's a good fellow, got good personnel, good equipment, but—" the man considered for a moment "—it got to be a cost-conscious thing."

Not everyone in Cairo would readily agree that Bill Wolter was all that good a fellow. Doc Poston bitterly remembered a snubbing he'd received from Wolter at a Christmas party. Others puzzled over the frosty qualities of the parties at his mansion.

"My son is one of the few people that I know that's talked to him," another Cairo man told me, "and my son was very *negligibly* impressed by him. They had a sour bidniss deal. He come up to my boy who owned a buildin' here, and he said, 'Whaddaya charge to rent this buildin' and put a car in?' And my boy says twenty dollars a month, meaning twenty dollars a month *per car*. Wolter says okay, and he put several of his cars in, and then he wouldn't pay more than twenty dollars!"

Apparently the tightfistedness that Wolter displayed toward parking-garage managers did not apply to the purchase of the cars themselves.

"Wolter got the idea," the townsman told me, "I guess it was in '77, the last year they made a big Merc'ry, that he wasn't goin' to be able to get a big car anymore. And so what he bought was these *identical cars*. Merc'rys. And he put 'em in storage, and he'd drive one till it would give out—then he'd take another one out and use that one for parts. And he figured he could go the rest of his life in a big luxury car. They were all black, and they were all identical to look at from a distance, you know. And he was gonna drive these cars forever, and be a man of distinction, and all this, evidently."

I dialed Bill Wolter's number.

The coldest human voice I had ever heard came on the line. It had the quality of sheet metal. I identified myself and asked whether I could make an appointment for an interview. There was a silence on the other end.

Then Bill Wolter's voice told me this: "I know something of the people you've been associating with. I don't think I want to talk to you."

For the first time in my visits to Cairo I felt the prickly sensation of menace—direct and immediate. The Phantom of Riverlore knew of my presence in Cairo, and he knew something of my activities there. Someone had been informing him of these things. It was not too hard to imagine who that someone might have been.

I resisted the impulse, triggered by anger and fear, to slam the receiver down. Keeping my voice neutral, I pointed out that I had been "associating" with these people because these people had allowed me access to their circle. My wish, however, was to write a comprehensive account of Cairo and its concerns. A meeting with Mr. Wolter would help me to widen my scope.

There was another, longer silence on the other end. Then Wolter muttered something vaguely to the effect that he might have a little time available the following Wednesday. I said that I would call him on that day, and we ended our conversation without pleasantries.

This was to be my only contact with Bill Wolter. (When I called on Wednesday to confirm the appointment, his secretary refused to put me through.)

I hung up the telephone and sat for a while on the edge of my motel bed. It was still early in the evening. From somewhere out in the corridor, a door opened once, then closed, violently, then closed again without opening approximately five times in succession—an eerie property of hotel and motel doors that I had noticed many times before, especially at Glen's.

I left the motel—the truck tires still floated invitingly in the swimming pool—and got in my rented car and started driving north out of town on the two-lane highway that was Route 127. I had no clear idea where I was headed; I just wanted to drive and listen to the radio and think.

The sun was setting off to my left, on the horizon beyond the railroad tracks. To my right was swamp and greening forest; I glimpsed four deer on the far side of a plowed field. There were some houses where the land rose above the swamp—wooden bungalows, pickup trucks parked in their small yards. People sat out on the front steps or tinkered under the raised hoods of the trucks. Cairo's black suburbs. Some of the bungalow roofs bore old scorchmarks, and the paint was peeling. But generally the houses were more prosperous, or at least less desperate, than the houses of Future City. Some of the dirt yards had satellite dishes.

I had with me in the car a copy of a speech Poston had delivered a couple weeks previously at a town meeting. He'd mailed it to me in New York. I planned to reread it if I stopped somewhere for coffee.

The text was uncharacteristically furious. Poston had returned to the town after several weeks of traveling to the state capital at

Springfield and to Washington, D.C., where he had tried to raise foundation money for his restoration of Fort Defiance State Park as a cultural center and theme park. What he found there had moved him to a tirade.

He had begun with some standard Postonian boilerplate: the meeting point of our nation's two mightiest rivers; tonnage of commercial navigation exceeds that which passes through the Panama Canal; mainline rail service reaching out through America's heartland; access to a network of interstate highways; teeming consumer and industrial markets within less than a day's travel, etc., etc. . . . and then Doc Poston had turned explicit.

"Now we have the Memphis District of the U.S. Army Corps of Engineers ready to begin engineering studies for a commercial and recreational harbor," he told the Enterprisers. "And frankly I'm worried about what they may discover when they get here just two days from now.

"I'm wondering, do our elected officials carefully study the agendas before their meetings, listen to all sides of an issue, really research it before casting their votes, seriously think about what's best for Cairo and Alexander County—or do they simply vote on the basis of some selfish interest?

"I've heard," Poston went on, "that some people don't come to our town meetings because they're afraid of what certain individuals in positions of power might do to hurt them. I've heard it said that we must be careful not to cross certain power figures, disagree with them, or express points of view different from theirs, because if we do we'll alienate them and they'll get even by withholding support from our community effort. What is this," Poston had demanded, "the USA, the home of the brave and the free—or is this the Soviet Union?"

A hard-edged sun was resting on the horizon. Southern Illinois lay as flat and impassive as west Texas in the twilight. The plowed, doomed cornfields were already showing plumes of dust where a breeze blew; the summer's drought was setting in. On some of the fields there rose the smoke from small bonfires.

Poston's speech had continued:

"In Cairo, even today, there are those who don't like this business of democracy at work. There are those among us who, by premeditated intent, have attempted to undermine this movement; who, behind the scenes, have opposed this development effort from its inception, who actually fear the workings of American democracy because it provides room for honest differences of opinion. Some act as if they dislike our American way of having the courage to bring the ugly side of our community into the open and discuss it. . . ."

There wasn't a great deal of room for speculation as to exactly which "power figures" and "behind-the-scenes underminers" Doc Poston might have had in mind. In its own way, this speech was every bit as directly confrontational as Angela Greenwell's subsequent disruption of the city council meeting. Perhaps the speech had inspired Mrs. Greenwell. In any event, the pretense of unity and mutual respect between Operation Enterprise and the entrenched interests of the town seemed on the verge of dissolving.

Now the homes along the highway were converted housetrailers, still mounted on their wheels. I saw abandoned tractors, rusted pickup trucks: the region's history, arrested and congealed. A young hitchhiker stood on the side of the road, knapsack on his back; he looked as though he hadn't gotten out of the sixties yet. He had come to the right place. I listened to some country music on the radio.

In the last part of his speech, Poston—obviously having detected a new onset of apathy among the Enterprisers—had conjured one of his most cherished fantasies: that the eyes of the world were upon Cairo. Noting that he's learned, upon his return, that a scheduled Enterprise cleanup along the Ohio levee had drawn only forty volunteers, and that a second cleanup had been called off, he tried a little brimstone on his audience.

"I just hope the press doesn't find out," he'd scolded them. "Just imagine what the newspapers, the television and radio stations will tell the world about Cairo if now Operation Enterprise is allowed to dwindle down from the high level it reached last July when more than three hundred Cairoites . . . moved out in a seemingly endless caravan to the Point, and literally manicured Fort Defiance State Park?

"Why, the newspaper and television and radio backlash would make Cairo a laughingstock throughout the state of Illinois, and all the way to New York and Washington, D.C.! We'd never get anything in here! Bank deposits would keep on dropping! Unemployment would keep on swelling! Cairo would be finished!

"I have no idea how many metropolitan newspapers will be watching to see whether or not Cairo stands up to the initiative its people started last summer—but I strongly suspect out-of-town reporters and television cameramen will be here to write and show what they see and hear. What happens Saturday, April 30, can be either great or horrible for the future of Cairo! I have faith! But I also have to be realistic! So I'm keeping my fingers crossed."

The fateful day, April 30, was tomorrow. Such a portent this old man was able to evoke—even in the imagination of a somewhat reluctant outsider. I was happy to be out of town for a few quiet hours before the reckoning.

Passing again into the darkening countryside beyond a hamlet called Mill Creek, I saw my first elevation of ground: a ridge line. I could see clusters of houses and barns built along the low hills. It was nearly dark now, and I could make out that there were people in the houses, but not a single light burned.

I sensed something very secret here, very deep, and deceptively calm. It was hard to tell, driving north on this concrete two-lane highway in the near-darkness of this spring night, whether it was America that had receded irretrievably far, into its city clusters, from this hooded land, or whether this *was* the essential America, watchful and ancient and infinitely patient, waiting for the distant madness and chaos to play itself out, waiting for its time to come round again.

The sky turned into a kind of fierce cobalt, and Venus came out, and a full moon; and suddenly the highway in front of me was bordered with small Baptist and Pentecostal churches; and then it ascended a short steep hill, and I found myself inside a village of the sort that was not supposed to exist anymore.

It was called Jonesboro: a tiny luminous cluster at the top of the knoll. Its center seemed to be a perfect little circular park at the knoll's very crest, about as big around as a rich man's front lawn.

I pulled into the parking lot of a little place called the Family Restaurant. I had eaten barbecue in Cairo a couple hours earlier, and was not really hungry, but I felt the need to be around people, and I wanted to enter this particular enclave.

The Family Restaurant was the middle establishment in a storefront facade of three businesses. Its big front window was decorated on the inside with half-curtains. Brown's Hardware (closed) was on the left, as one faced the facade, under a lone streetlight. The White Horse Inn, a tavern with a brick front, was on the right. In the darkened windows of the White Horse were two neon signs—a Bud Lite and a Lite Beer—and a Tiffany-style lamp with the Busch insignia on it, illuminated. Behind these I could make out a wall-sized portrait of some ducks (courtesy of Budweiser), a Coors lamp and a rack of potato chips.

The White Horse seemed to be a place where you could go and have a beer.

Back behind me in the quiet darkness, and curving around the knoll, was the rest of commercial Jonesboro: a Standard filling station with its illuminated sign; a Kraft's, a Quik-Service, a Culligan store. At the intersection where Route 127 lifted up to join the circular street around the knoll was a big building of ancient brick. On its side, in faded paint, was the legend, JONESBORO WAREHOUSE MARKET, and another, MORE APPEAL TO A MEAL, and another, BUNNY BREAD: STAYS FRESH DAYS LONGER, ornamented with a faded painting of two bunnies. All of this, bathed in the faint glow of streetlights against the vast and limitless Illinois distance and the cobalt sky.

I walked into the Family Restaurant—bright flourescent lighting flooded its dining room—and sat down at a formica table toward the rear. The place was almost deserted; it was a little late for suppertime in Southern Illinois, but a couple of tables were still filled. At one of them sat a man in a chrome wheelchair and his family. The man's small daughter toddled among the tables and back into the kitchen in a proprietary sort of way. I could hear honky-tonk music thumping from the jukebox at the White Horse Inn on the other side of the wall, and at some point I realized that the White Horse and the Family Restaurant shared a common entranceway back in the kitchen; they were, to some extent, the same establishment. Knowing this reinforced my sense of enclave, and I looked around my side of it.

One wallpapered wall was festooned with photographic portraits of babies—the owners' grandchildren, no doubt. There was a salad bar, and the typewritten menu sealed inside its plastic holder highlighted the catfish and the ribeye steak. I wasn't hungry, but I ordered the ribeye from the young waitress anyway, and planned to save some room for the pie.

As I ate, two massive Illinois State Highway patrolmen came into the restaurant and sat down at the table in front of mine. Their pressed uniforms were of tan khaki, trimmed in yellow and black insignia. One of the troopers had a walkie-talkie with him, and as soon as they sat down he switched it on with an impressive burst of static and radioed in their whereabouts to headquarters. He included the phone number of the restaurant.

All of this seemed exactly right to me. It seemed right, and familiar. I wanted to stay there all evening, running forkfuls of ribeye through swabs of A-1 sauce and looking at the baby portraits on the wallpapered wall and eavesdropping on the talk of those troopers, while the honky-tonk music from the White Horse Inn came thumping from the other side. I became bemused, fascinated by the common entranceway between the Family Restaurant and the White Horse, and finally I understood why this was so: the joining took me back into a recurring dream of mine, a dream in which everything is sort of subterranean and safe and interconnected, and everyone knows and is at ease with everyone else, and things are safe: a dream of the perfect town.

Chapter XIII

At 7:59 the following morning I nosed my rented car into the caravan that had assembled at St. Mary's Park, a block or so from Bill Wolter's mansion and Dick Poston's apartment. I was just in time to join the ceremonial promenade as it headed south toward downtown and then into Fort Defiance Park, there to begin the second Operation Enterprise spring cleanup.

It was a sunny Saturday in Cairo, with the promise of a little spring heat later on. St. Mary's Park was an interesting anomaly in the bleached and crumbling little town: several dozen grassy, tree-shaded acres of graceful sanctuary for the neighborhood's children. There were swings, a baseball diamond, and even a few lighted tennis courts. (The dyspeptic rumor around town had it that Mayor Moss's son was a tennis buff.)

I counted fifteen cars. Blacks and whites were about evenly represented. On volume, though, it looked like a disappointing turn-out, even by Doc Poston's modest expectations. The mayor was not a part of the festivities, but he had sent over one of the town's black-and-white police cars, which now crawled out into the caravan's lead, its red swivel-lights flashing. Behind the police car came a white fire engine that added a little bit of show business by roweling its siren a few times. Then came a brown-and-cream van that I took, at first, to be another Cairo municipal vehicle. It had twin loudspeakers fixed to its roof. From the loudspeakers rasped an amplified recording of "Make of Our Hearts One Heart," from *West Side Story*. I thought immediately of Poston. I had not spotted him yet, but I knew that he would be plenty visible once we reached Fort Defiance.

The caravan turned on to Washington and headed south, passing directly in front of the Wolter mansion. Its Confederate flag snapped, translucent in the early-morning sunlight. I looked for someone who might fit the general description of Wolter as I had understood it, but I could see no one, not even a gardener or a manservant. The house itself seemed to have its gaze averted.

The bells of St. Mary's Church rang the hour behind us.

By the time we got to the park's entrance, the caravan had swelled to perhaps twenty cars. Poston's new sign—FORT DEFIANCE, CONFLUENCE OF AMERICA—looked quite spiffy in the spring sunshine. The roadbed leading toward the Point was dry, and we kicked up a high cloud of dust as we clattered along toward the cleanup site.

Waiting for us, under the Boatmen's Monument at the edge of the two rivers, I could see a scattering of municipal equipment: dump-trucks, a bulldozer, even a cement-mixer. The mayor may not have planned a personal appearance, but it was apparent that he had not stinted Poston on the town's resources.

The Enterprisers had fanned out and begun working by 8:30. The work force numbered maybe a hundred now, including two truck-loads and a jeepful of National Guardsmen from the post in Cairo. The guardsmen arrived wearing their laced boots and billed caps and their pressed olive-drab camouflage fatigues with the sleeves rolled up the regulation number of rolls. Some of the guardsmen were more or less just standing around, cupping cigarettes in their hands and surveying the scene from behind their sunglasses with a kind of military irony.

The scene involved quite a lot of raking. Poston was still not in sight, but the Enterprisers fanned out on their own, men and women, and began to rake long strands of dead grasses and vines into a series of heaping piles around the Point.

A strong breeze blew across the Ohio River from Kentucky and ruffled people's hair. I could see the edges of the wind-patterns ripple across the skin of the river. Several Cairo people had told me that I would be able to tell where the Ohio and the Mississippi joined; the waters formed a seam of subtly contrasting color-tones. But on none of my visits so far had I been able to make this out.

There was some traffic out on the water this morning, and I stood for a while and watched a tow pushing six barges make the tricky transition from the Ohio channel, on my left, to the Mississippi, on my right. Its line of approach seemed, by a trick of perspective, to be taking it on a collision-course with the tip of Illinois. Just when it appeared that the big snub-nosed boats were going to come grinding and clanking up onto dry land, the tow slid gracefully past, not more than sixty feet out in the channel, and began to turn north for its ascent up the Mississippi. It struck me that tow pilots had been making this same transition since well before I had been born— and steamboat pilots before them—and that some of the barges I had watched as a child, from my grandparents' front porch on the crest of a hill on the far side of Hannibal from the Mississippi, had negotiated the very maneuver that I'd just witnessed fewer than fifty yards from the tips of my shoes.

When I turned back toward the park, I saw that the work was getting serious. The guardsmen were no longer standing around. They had deployed into a number of efficient little units down at the Ohio River's edge, below an embankment of large white rocks. There, they had begun to attack some accumulated tangles of drift-wood with chainsaws, sending up puffs of blue smoke and a terrific racket. The guardsmen dragged the sawed sections of driftwood up to the level of the park, where they stacked them around the heaps of raked grass and vines. The Enterprisers raking, the guardsmen sawing—it all looked very purposeful, oddly sacramental in its solemn absorption. I began to feel self-conscious that I didn't have a rake in my hand, and to cover my essential uselessness here, I began to walk around a little.

I passed the parked brown-and-cream-colored van with the loud-speakers, and saw that it was not a municipal vehicle at all. Its sides bore the lettering of the Cairo Baptist Church. It was Rev. Larry Potts's car.

Heading toward a grassy slope, I heard a hearty voice call to me: "It's like Gandhi's march to the sea, don't you think? Making salt!" The voice belonged to one of Operation Enterprise's mainstays, a vigorous and jovial nun named Sister Lorraine, who was the princi-pal of St. Mary's Elementary School.

"That's what this is all about!" Sister Lorraine exclaimed when I drew near her. She leaned on her rake and wiped some perspira-tion away from her reddened forehead. She was a fifty-ish woman with iron-gray hair and a powerful frame. "All the struggle here! All the riffraff, and the corruption, and—how did Gandhi deal with it?

Nonviolence! That's what this is all about! We can't allow ourselves—and I told Angela that, just the other day, too—we just can't let ourselves get wrapped up in confronting the establishment! You know, we *can* overcome!" She gestured around her. "Lookit Martin Luther King!" she demanded, and inadvertently, I looked. "Lookit Jesus Christ!" She paused again, and let herself drink in the vista of Cairo people raking, dragging driftwood. "I couldn't help thinking of Gandhi while we were driving down here in the caravan," she went on after a moment. "How stupid *that* seemed to the government, to go to the sea and make salt. And how stupid this seems to many people, for us to be down here at the river cleaning up. . . . " Words failed her; she was in a kind of ecstasy. "*You* know," she finished up, with another wide gesture, and got back to her raking.

The guardsmen had a bonfire going near the Point. Greenish smoke came billowing from the dried weeds under the driftwood, and then the wood itself began to catch; orange flames shot upward, sending sparks into the breeze. Then another bonfire started, and another. Small boys wearing discount-store combat fatigues darted at the base of the fires, tossing twigs onto the piles. The wind across the Ohio blew the smoke from the leaping fires into a pervading haze that thickened over the park's surface. People's eyes were starting to water a little, and it was harder to breathe. I found myself hustling to find a place away from the direct downwind of the blowing smoke, and I wondered for a moment whether the guardsmen had miscalculated; let things get out of control.

And yet there was no real slackening in the work. I saw Angela Greenwell, a big bandana covering her gold bouffant, helping some women carry a picnic cooler toward the elevated Boatmen's Monument, and we waved. She had the look of a pleased hostess. I saw a man walking around with a pair of gardening shears; he would bend stiffly over at the waist and clip little clumps of weeds that had grown in odd pockets of the vast lot. Then he would move on, looking for another clump. Another man with a long-handled weed-cutter moved around, taking aim at stray growths and slashing. The noise of machinery grew. A small motor-grader with the lettering of nearby Mound City on its side pushed debris and branches up and into one of the bonfires.

A work-flow pattern had emerged: the rakers raked their leaves and twigs into piles. Then other workers pushed the piles into large vinyl bags; the bags were tied at the ends and stacked onto the motor-grader, and the motor-grader dumped them onto the flames.

Everyone seemed to know exactly what he or she was supposed to be doing; there was a fierce and silent coordination to the work.

I counted the cars parked diagonally at the edges of the service road. There were about forty now. This seemed to indicate a work force of considerably fewer than the three hundred people who had turned out a year ago; and yet the intensity of those who had come seemed to me terrific.

I decided to look for Poston. Someone told me they had seen him back at the entrance to the park. I was glad for an excuse to get away from the acrid haze for a little while (and glad, too, for an excuse to stop hanging around here, conspicuously useless), so I got into my car and drove back along the service road, with the Ohio on my right and the Mississippi, obscured by terrain, off to my left, until I reached the steep incline and the new Fort Defiance sign. A large National Guard trailer-truck was parked there, and the men were unloading fencepost logs from its flatbed.

Emerging from my car into the clear air, I heard Poston's voice about six feet above me. He had climbed up the rungs at the rear of the flatbed and was just then engaged in bossing everybody around.

"I'm countin' the difference between the cedar and the pine, Ron!" he called down to me. "If you put pine in the ground the termites'll rot it, but if you put cedar—" he paused and wiped his sleeve across his nose. "So there's about twenty cedar here; now I gotta figure out how many posts we need."

I asked Poston what, exactly, was going on here.

"We're buildin' a fence!" he shouted down at me. "To harmonize with the sign's wood over the entryway! This was all landscaped yesterday! There was an old metal guardrail here! Looked horrible! And look at all these nice trees they planted—" he indicated a row of young pines that bordered the small gravel parking lot at the park's edge. "They'll be fifty feet high when they—they'll be beautiful!" He shook his thin head. He was Douglas Fairbanks now, up there astride the cedar logs on a Saturday morning, the wind unfurling his blown-dry hair into thin gray wings. But in the sunlight he looked pale.

I could not help remark his wardrobe. As always, it was utterly thought-out, and of utterly fathomless vintage. This morning he wore a beige cardigan sweater, a cream-colored silk shirt, tan slacks and soft-skinned beige slippers.

"I got the wood from the Forest Service," he was shouting down at me. "They put in the pine trees and those redbuds and the dogwood down there. And then they seeded the grass. See, that was all just ugly rock and junk out there. So the whole area's gonna be landscaped, Ron! Marianne," he called from his high perch, cupping a hand beside his mouth. "I've found the cedar!"

I remarked that it looked as though the mayor had been rather generous with his city cleanup equipment.

"That was part of the peacemaking process between Angela and Al," Poston said. "The day after those late-night meetings, I went to Al, and I said, Al, dammit, this is gonna look like hell if the city isn't pullin' together with the people. You can't let that controversy over that wharfage lease have anything to do with this. So he wrote me an official letter sayin' that he'd supply this stuff. But he wasn't gonna do that at all, if I hadn't gone in there and—" he paused. "This is the kinda thing you gotta do, Ron, to bring a town like this together. You gotta be soft, sweet, tough. One minute you gotta be a damn tiger, the next minute you gotta be a—uh—a sweet lover-boy!" He guffawed, and blew his nose into a large handkerchief.

I told him I had re-read his tough town meeting speech the night before, and said that I was a little surprised at its anger.

"Yeah, well," he said, and looked out at the world from his high perch. "They needed to be told things like that." He shook his head. "See, that was immediately talked about all over town! And that had something to do with the fact that we got this good turnout today." I let that one go by without a question. "You have to keep motivatin' 'em, Ron. All communities that are dying are that way. The small town of America isn't gonna come back unless somebody goes in and motivates the people to get goin'." The imaginary audience was assembling, something told me. "The only people who can rebuild our small towns in America are the people who live there! Well, they need some outside help, yeah. But outside help isn't worth a dime if there's *no local initiative!*"

As he spoke these last words, Poston was climbing gingerly down the iron rungs of the flatbed. At ground level he ran a hand through his disorganized hair. His forehead was damp. "I guess I'm gonna have to get with the Jaycees and give 'em hell," he remarked suddenly. "They've got to get more actively, coordinatingly involved in this thing!"

The Cairo Junior Chamber of Commerce had scheduled its annual parade for that very afternoon, to coincide with its annual spring carnival. Poston was miffed that the Jaycees had had the effrontery to arrange an event that would conflict with his own agenda. The fact that the Jaycees had invited him to be the grand marshall had apparently done little to mollify him.

The irritation was not typical of Poston. The sudden edginess that had crept into his demeanor unsettled me a little. I thought of fatigue, and worse. To lighten his mood a little, I asked him what his duties as grand marshall would entail.

"Just ride in a car, wave to the people, I guess." He was looking someplace beyond me. "I dunno. I've never been a parade marshall before. But it's kind of interesting," he reflected, "that they'd ask me to *be* the parade marshall." Another thought distracted him, and he made a sudden, jerky turn, as if expecting to see someone behind him. "I better go down to the Point and have a look-see," he said. "There's supposed to be a camera crew from Carbondale down here, but I haven't seen 'em yet. Supposed to be three crews, in fact."

There were no camera crews. There would be no camera crews. I decided to let Poston reach that conclusion on his own.

I got into my car and followed Doc Poston down to the Point. It was now mid-morning. The wind off the Ohio was blowing harder, creating a pervasive blue smoke-haze from the several bonfires that now hung over the entire park. Many of the Enterprisers had covered their noses with handkerchiefs, and some of the older women were sitting down, daubing at their eyes. The haze had driven a few people away, but those who remained had not slackened in their intensity.

Angela Greenwell and some of her friends had set up a few picnic tables under the Boatmen's Memorial. I could see packages of hot-dog buns, dishes of potato salad and coolers of soda pop. Not far away, a big yellow-and-red cement mixer was churning up cement to pour inside several wood-frame borders. These would be the foundations for a series of permanent iron barbecue grills that the Enterprisers had voted to install in the park.

I left the park a little before noon. I drove up to Commercial Avenue to take a look at the Jaycee carnival. There were a few people on the street—it wasn't utterly deserted, as it had been the first time I saw it, in March—but the atmosphere was still one of vacancy, as if the life of the town had bled off from here to somewhere else.

The carnival lay there in the sunshine, in the middle of the street. It began at Commercial and Fourteenth and extended on for a couple of blocks. It hadn't opened up yet. There was a ferris wheel, a merry-go-round, some tents. Bleached red and yellow colors.

Rusty loudspeakers, some sandbags, guy-ropes. THE SWINGER, the paint on one of the rides said. No people, just a carnival. But there must have been someone in there. As I turned to walk back to my car, the loudspeakers seemed to clear their raspy throats, and the calliope went on.

There was an hour or so to go before the Jaycee parade started, so I went to a restaurant on the main road for lunch. Doc Poston was on my mind. I had not yet had a chance to spend any real time with him on this visit, except for the few minutes beside the flatbed trailer at the entrance to the park. He had seemed dangerously fatigued—he always seemed dangerously fatigued, I had realized— but the sudden petulant mood-shift regarding the Jaycees was something new. I sat in a booth sipping my coffee and trying to imagine, exactly, what it must be like to be him: to be an elderly man in a forgotten dying town, telling that town the story of itself in order to keep it alive.

It was financially tight, for one thing. I had seen Doc's threadbare apartment; I had taken note of the clothes he wore: outdated, but lovingly preserved and matched. I had seen him over a meal—he was a birdlike eater, and in fact his main consumption appeared to be coffee and cigarettes.

Once during my first visit he had told me a little about his finances. "I'm paid a salary by Southern Illinois University," he'd said. "When you retire from one of the state universities, then you go back to work for one of them, you have what they refer to as an 'earnings limitation.' They have some mathematical formula in which they compute what you can earn, and it's based partly upon what your salary was at the time you retired.

"Well, I retired as of Dec. 31, 1974. So, 1974 salaries were a great deal different from 1988 salaries. If I was a full professor right now, I would be earning at least fifty thousand dollars or more. Anyway, when they computed my compensation for this job now, it came out to eight thousand, four hundred and sixty-eight dollars and twenty-three cents a year—which works out to about seven hundred six dollars a month. If I got paid any more than that, I would lose my retirement."

I had asked Poston back then whether the university paid his expenses when he went out on the road to raise money for Operation Enterprise.

"Supposedly," he'd said. "They're supposed to pay expense accounts after a week or two. But I have expense accounts dating back from the first of November that they haven't paid yet. They now owe me about twenty-five hundred dollars." He gave a short guffaw. "They owe me in expenses more than my monthly salary."

And then Doc Poston launched into a tale that might have brought a nod of recognition from Franz Kafka.

"A big university like this, Ron, they're just as bureaucratic as a government agency! They're supposed to pay the rent on my apartment. A hundred fifty a month. That actually saves 'em a lot of money. Cheaper than a motel room. So what they did, to show you how garbled up the bureaucracy can get—they were supposed to enter into a contract with the man I'm renting from. Okay, this goes to Springfield and they say, well, this is real property, so you gotta have proof that he owns the property! You gotta have a deed from him to show that he owns it. So he gets a deed to 'em. So weeks pass; then they say, well, *we gotta have an affadavit that shows he's the person named in the deed!*" Poston broke off for a brief laughing and coughing fit.

"Well, this goes on and on—and meanwhile I thought he was gettin' his rent. But I finally found out he'd never been paid a cent. I called up the Vice President for Academic Affairs, the number two man up there, and I says, 'My god, you gotta get that rent paid!' I told him I'd found out that word was gettin' around Cairo that the university was just like any other deadbeat; they wouldn't pay their bills. So then they told me *I* should pay the rent, and they'd reimburse me right away. I paid him three hundred dollars; that'd be for October and November. Then they figured they'd put in the paper work for those two months, so what I should do is pay him another three hundred for December and January. So I did that; so I'm out six hundred dollars now. So then they find out that the paperwork they did for October and November won't work. Got messed up in Springfield, in the controller's office. And so now they have to figure out how to reimburse me six hundred dollars for that four months' rent."

Poston shook his head, sighed, and lighted a cigarette.

"So finally they got back to me with six hundred dollars. But this will be every *month* after *month*, Ron."

It had been right after this tale of woe that Poston had first declared that his job, in Cairo, was to work himself out of a job. "I'm not here to build my ego," he'd elaborated then. "I've got to build this town into a self-determining, self-sufficient unit. That's my job." Now, sitting in my booth, I thought of the people still raking away down at Fort Defiance Park—a small percentage of an under-populated town. I thought of Sister Lorraine, who had implicitly compared Doc Poston to Gandhi. I thought of Angela Greenwell, who had been moved by Poston to openly confront the town's political and social establishment that had formed the context of her life.

These people and others like them were in Richard Poston's thrall. They might find it difficult to let him work himself out of his job. Judging from his reaction to the Jaycees' competing plans, Poston might have more difficulties than he had expected fulfilling that plan.

I had been coming to Cairo in the hopes of learning something about Poston's town-development theories that might be universal; that might be applied in other failing towns around America. But now, for the first time, I began to consider a new possibility: what if Poston was not only the storyteller, but the story itself?

People—mostly black families and children—had taken up spectator positions along the parade route by the time I left the restaurant. They stood, or sat on the curb, or leaned against storefronts, arms folded. Some of them had folding chairs. It was hard to tell anything by their expressions. There were long gaps along the route with no people at all.

I drove to the point of origination, an asphalt parking lot behind a hardware store. The lot was crowded with marching bands, decorated flatbed trucks, American flags, balloons and young women in formals with silk sashes over their shoulders. I saw Poston at a distance; he'd gone home to change into his natty blue blazer. We exchanged waves. Mayor Moss, squinting, hands on hips, in shirt-sleeves, was standing beside a fire engine, and we made a little labored small talk. The topic of the cleanup at Fort Defiance Park did not come up.

The police car at the head of the column flicked on its flashing lights at precisely five minutes of one P.M.; the bass drums and cymbals started crashing, and a six-man marine color guard stepped smartly out into Sycamore Street, heading south. Next came a fire engine, and then an open convertible carrying Mayor Moss and an electrifying Cairo personality, whom I'd heard once giving the invocation at a town meeting: a black preacher with "processed" hair, a ham face, and a voice like prophecy itself, the Reverend Jimmy Hodge. The mayor and Hodge were flinging Toot-sie Pops toward the clusters of children.

Then came the grand marshall. Richard Poston rode by himself in a white Lincoln convertible. He was perched on the top of the rear seat. Both his arms were upraised, and even from a couple of blocks away I could see that he was very happy.

The parade clanked and boomed down Sycamore in the bright afternoon light. There were Congressional candidates in pickup trucks; there was a man in a Smokey the Bear suit. There was the Shannon Clanahan Mondrian High School Band, and a car with a loudspeaker that blared "We've Only Just Begun," by the Carpenters. The Cairo School of Karate came marching by. Then a white fire engine. Then a truckful of small children, singing.

The Kim Shrine Club rolled by on a truck, and the United Methodists Vacation Bible School, on an old-time fire engine painted orange. Some senior citizens rode past in a white Cadillac. Berline Jones, beauty consultant from Mary Kay Cosmetics, swept past in her white Lincoln, the famous Mary Kay logo lettered in pink on her windshield. Then came a float carrying some little kids in green: ST. PATTY'S LADS AND LASSIES. ST. PATTY'S CHURCH CELEBRATES 150 YEARS 1838–1988. YOU'RE NOT GETTING OLDER YOU'RE GETTING BETTER. Here came a Blazer wagon pulling a trailer with a piano on it. And Cub Scout Pack 105. "Lef', lef', lef' right lef'." A black Monte Carlo: THE POLASKI/ALEXANDER COUNTY MENTAL HEALTH CRISIS LINE, with the phone number. Scouts on bicycles. And the inevitable officious fat boy on his Honda four-wheeler, charging back and forth along the parade's length, talking importantly into a walkie-talkie.

And then, after a while, the parade was gone. And Cairo prepared to face another evening in spring.

Chapter XIV

I spent that spring evening in the small living room of Doc Poston's apartment, sipping iced tea and talking about life in the town with two sometime members of Operation Enterprise. Call them Pauline and Marcella. They were sisters, bashful and much given to secretive humorous glances between them, and each possessed of a deep and sinuous knowledge of the town beyond the curvature of Doc's or Al Moss's, or Angela Greenwell's knowing. Now in their twenties, they had been children in the Pyramid Court housing projects when the bullets flew at night and the buildings burned. The memories of those years and certain ambiguities in their present lives had made them shy about offering their real names for any conversation that might end up in print.

Pauline and Marcella were repositories of a Cairo that no longer existed except in memory, just as Susie Gawel and Marie Naboring held inside them a living memory of a vanished Kent. In such people, I had come to suspect, resided the last traces, however faint, of American town life as it had been understood by the people of J. Hector St. John de Crèvecoeur's time.

As Doc Poston sat hunched forward in his small easy chair, squinting from face to face and smoking and trying to keep silent—an heroic effort, in which he mostly succeeded—I asked the sisters what it had been like being a child in Cairo.

They exchanged secretive humorous looks, and after a minute Pauline spoke, in a voice just above a whisper.

"Everything was goin' along good until we started havin' the racial trouble," she said. "And that's when things started goin' bad."

"Before the trouble we used to play in the playground," put in Marcella. "Softball quite a lot. But after all that stuff breakin' out, mother was scared for us to get too far from home."

I asked what kind of house they grew up in.

"We were raised in the projects," said Pauline. "Durin' the racial problems we moved out. We were there when, first sign of dark, you had to be in the house, locked doors—couldn't have any lights on, no TV, none of that. Best thing to do actually was get up under the bed. Because you could lay on the bed and see fire passin' the windows."

I wanted to know whether it was fun being a kid in Cairo before the trouble.

"Yes. Holidays were so special," Pauline said. "It was like—goin' downtown, you had all kind of stores you could go in. Everybody had a bill, so you didn't have to worry about not havin' enough money. And it was just fun."

I asked about church life, and it was Marcella who spoke.

"Yes. Church. St. Columbus School. Segregated. Black and white churches. We were raised Baptists. But we went to three churches. Father was Catholic—we don't have the same fathers, okay? Sunday mornings, we'd go to Mass. Get out of Mass, go home, have breakfast, go to Sunday school. There we had morning service. Go home, have lunch. Go back to church in the afternoon."

When did it change?

"It changed overnight, in my opinion," said Pauline. "It was just like an overnight change. There was a lot of gettin' used to. Because we were used to layin' up with our door unlocked."

"Here's how we learned about it," said Marcella. "We got a phone call from our mother's sister in Tennessee. Sayin, 'You better get outa there. It's bad for you.' See, we weren't seein' the news what they were seein'. But when it all come to a head we wanted to go to Tennessee. Mother had got home from work. She said, 'Well I don't wanta stay here and go through this all weekend.' She made a few phone calls. They told her about cease-fire."

"Yeah. They told us how to get out of the projects with our parking lights on. And we went out of the projects and went to Tennessee. And we saw all the stuff on TV that was happenin' in Cairo."

"But finally Mother had to bring us back. She had to work."

Doc Poston had told me that the sisters had slept in a cast-iron bathtub to avoid getting shot. How many nights had that been necessary?

"Lots of nights," Pauline answered. "We slept under the bed lots of nights. There was no TV after dark. They would come through with loudspeakers, you know, and they had certain ones, they'd be up on top of the coal bins, you know, guys shootin' and stuff. They'd say: 'Don't make no sound!' You was scared. You was terrified to go to the restroom. You didn't do anything."

How old were you then, I asked.

"Ten."

"Thirteen."

"See, that's the scars, that's the stuff that you never forget," Pauline said. "I myself don't feel like it really benefited anything. Because it didn't benefit the black people the way some of 'em said it was gonna benefit. Look at Cairo now. What did it do?"

What kind of scars? Marcella shuddered.

"Nightmares. Gunfire. Could see Mother gettin' shot. My brother-in-law's best friend got shot, and it's never been explained to me how he got shot. (You remember Jerry?) And nobody can ever get the full details on how he got shot. He got killed. And that's when George got shot, too."

"You talk about scars," said Pauline. "I tell you how deep some of 'em are. After we got out of the projects? Nobody—*none of us*— ever want to move back there. We don't go there now after dark. We got friends there. We go durin' the daytime and get out. You stay fifteen, twenty minutes and you get out of there. At night you would never see me head towards Pyramid Courts. Which, it's called McBride Apartments now."

Do you hate white people now? I wanted to know. Marcella shook her head.

"No. Cause all white people not the same."

"It's a lot of people here that just cannot stand white people," said Pauline. "That's the way they say it: 'I cannot stand—I hate white people.' Because of what happened then. I guess it's all in how we were raised. Because I don't hate. I don't hate Moss. I don't like some of the things he do, but I don't hate him. And just like things happenin' in '68 or '69, I can see it clear today as to what happened. And if that same thing happened again, Moss is gonna be on that side of the fence, and we're gonna be on this side of the fence."

I asked whether the sisters felt safe from crime in the town now.

"If I was to go for a walk, I would go and be back before say nine o'clock at night," said Marcella.

"I'd ride all night long," declared Pauline with a secret glance and a chuckle. "Lotta nights that's what I do is, I ride all night long. But as far as walkin' the streets, no."

Does Cairo still have its prostitution problem? I asked. Pauline gave a bitter laugh.

"Prostitutes ain't got a chance in Cairo. 'Cause the teenage girls is givin' it to the old men, ain't nobody buyin'." Both sisters laughed out loud. "They say it's too much free stuff out there. Why should we pay somebody for it?"

Then Marcella lowered her voice and looked thoughtful.

"My son come home a couple weeks ago, he was really upset. A girl who's gonna graduate this year is pregnant. And it really bothered him. Okay, my brother, when he started his freshman year at high school, he ain't been goin' to school but about a week, and he told his mother, he said, 'Ma,' he say, 'somepin' ain't right up there at the school.' He say, 'They teachin' them girls all wrong and the guys, too.' He said over half the school is pregnant. And he was tellin' the truth."

"When I was goin' to school, you didn't come to school if you was pregnant. They sent all your schoolwork home to you; they didn't want you in school."

I wanted to know more about what it was like in Cairo before the trouble.

" . . . Lie up in the projects," whispered Pauline, half to herself. "And we'd go and fly our kites and stuff, and . . . "

" . . . Make a picnic . . . (Marcella shot her sister a glance) . . . out on the levee . . . and then you can't even stop on the levee any more."

" . . . Goin' down to Fort Defiance. Oh God, that was like takin' your kids to Six Flags is now. We 'preciated goin' to Fort Defiance. Cause that's where everybody was. You barbecued, you stayed all day long, you were there till in the night . . ."

" . . . Everybody's kids were racin' to get down there and get under a shade tree, so you could get the best tables and everything, you know . . . and like say you were down there no later than eight o'clock in the morning, and you be down there to nine o'clock at night."

" 'Cause there was lights down there and that's just somepin' we just do then . . ."

" . . . And there was a ride down there at night," offered Marcella, "and you lookit the water and everything, and walk around . . . then you'd have Lovers' Lane . . ." the sisters laughed together.

" . . . You could get out, and walk along, and you wouldn't be afraid. I used to love to go just down there to Eighth Street to the river. I liked to go and just sit. Just look out at the water. I go down there now, I'd have them doors locked and the windows rolled up and the car runnin' . . ."

" . . . And pray there's a man sittin' in the seat next to you!" They laughed again, rocking forward.

I asked them what they did in the summer.

" . . . Well, we would go crawdad huntin', and we would get them. And I mean that was a turning point event in the year. When they come. Everybody go around—every house you go in had a pot of boiling . . ."

" . . . Down at Fort Defiance, down the walkway where the water would sit off on the side, or right down close to the bank, was where you'd find 'em, and everybody—you would buy 'em from people when you couldn't catch 'em . . ."

" . . . And I mean the whole project would go down there! We used to catch frogs. Bees in jars, junebugs. Lightning bugs too: cut their tails off, make rings on our fingers. Take junebugs, tie strings on the bag and fly 'em. If you killed a snake, then everybody in the project was comin' down to look at the snake you killed . . ."

Halloween? What was Halloween like?

"Ooooh! We used to go trick or treat!"

" . . . Corn Night was the 30th," said Pauline. "All you do, you go by and you get corn. It wasn't trick or treat. You go to everybody's door and knock and holler, but it's only corn you get that night. Next night was trick or treat night, you got all your candy."

Tell me about the games you played, I asked them.

"We used to play I guess what you'd call stickball. The mothers and them got out and played with us. Can you imagine this?"

"And another game we played, you'd have to wait for the first time when it rained, and after it rained the water in the sewer would back up. The water would be so high it would come up to 'bout right here on you." She pointed to her waist. "And everybody in the neighborhood's there. And be glad when a car come along and splash you. And hoist your pants back up and everything, get soakin' wet, see? Those are the good days."

What did they eat?

"We'd usually have commodity," said Pauline. "My Mom would take the commodity food and fix it . . ."

What's commodity? I asked.

"It's what they give away. I mean they give away canned Spam durin' that time, canned beef, she used to take that beef and make barbecue out of it. Red beans. She make us like a chili pie. She was always bakin' somethin' sweet. Ever' day, we'd have somethin' sweet."

I asked them to tell me some more about their church life.

"Whoooo! We sang a lot! We worked hard! We were Sunday school teachers, we were secretaries, we had to make speeches—it got to the point where they could just call on ya and you could just go on up there and do it without any rehearsal."

"Churches now are like fashion shows," Marcella said suddenly. "Everybody's goin' to church to see what they got on. But my church—I luuuuuv my church. I am the youngest member of my church, besides the kids. There's not a lot of us—we have fourteen members—and it's not like a fashion show. You go to these other churches and like I say, it's a fashion show."

Do you believe in God? I asked.

"Yeah," said Marcella. And Pauline said:

"I asked myself that. And I'll say, 'It's gotta be.' Sometimes I have doubts. But see, I'm a sinner. I'm goin' with a married man. And I don't mean to ever change that now."

"There not enough single men to go around here now!"

" . . . We're in our tenth year . . ."

" . . . He's six-foot-four!"

"See, we been together so long, until—how would one say—I got that man trained! That man know I don't take no mess! (laughter) But—he's good. He's good to me so I can't complain. And by the same token I'm good to him and good *for* him. He couldn't even stay married if it wasn't for me. I send him *home!*"

I asked them if they thought Doc Poston's efforts in the town were going to succeed?

"Kelly's got to do a poster for school," said Pauline. "Teacher asked her class, 'Does anybody know what Operation Enterprise was?' And Kelly told me, 'I was the onliest one that raised my hand, Mama, didn't nobody else!' She said, the teacher looked around, she asked the kids, 'Where y'all been, you haven't heard of Operation Enterprise?' So that's what they're gonna start studyin' on next week, is Operation Enterprise."

Chapter XV

There was one other place I wanted to go in Cairo before I ended this return visit, and that was to Cairo Baptist Church for a Sunday morning service.

I could think of plenty of unassailable reasons for wanting to do this. The Lower Mississippi Delta Development Commission, in its interim report on the region's crisis of poverty, had specifically cited what it called "the ecumenical church" as a potential source of "bottom-up" development. "In many rural Delta communities," the report went on to observe, "churches are the best sources of information on community problems, and sometimes the only source of non-government funding. Many belong to denominational structures which can provide varying levels of financial and technical support."

Cairo Baptist was the largest and most prosperous church in town. Much of its congregation was drawn from the merchant class, or what remained of the merchant class. If Doc Poston was ever to widen the base of Operation Enterprise beyond the sixty or so loyalists who came to his town meetings, he would have to look to Cairo Baptist. But how inclined was Cairo Baptist to respond? I wanted to find out.

But there was another reason why I wanted to attend a service at Cairo Baptist, and I thought about that reason as I stood in front of the clothes-hanging bar that served as my closet at Glen's Mid-

America Motel, at 7:30, with Sunday morning leaking into Cairo the way it had leaked into the Hannibal of my boyhood. My garment bag hung on the clothing bar. Inside the garment bag was my disguise for today's expedition: a blazer jacket and creased pants, a white shirt and a necktie. Sunday best. I had hauled these clothes all the way from New York for this occasion, and now that the occasion was at hand, I lurked in front of them like the trespasser I was about to become.

Cairo Baptist was the Reverend Larry Potts's church. Potts operated a segregated private school, called Camelot, and now he ministered to the largest flock of Christians in Cairo.

Sunday had already congealed on the town, reducing the pulse of human activity, faint enough on a business day, to something like brain death. I sensed that was so without even parting the window-curtain and looking out, which would have revealed only a desiccated cornfield in any case. It was amazing how tactile Sunday mornings were in America. I was taken with the thought that I could awaken from a coma and know if it was a Sunday morning. But then, awakening from a coma in Cairo, Illinois, would probably prove to be quite a bit like not awakening from a coma at all.

On this day I would trouble Cairo's sleeping consciousness. I would make a foray into the half-dreaming realm that blurred the town's present with its past. I would visit Larry Potts's church, and look for some sign of its relationship to the town.

I had driven past Cairo Baptist the previous day. The message board beside the front entrance seemed unbeset enough by the past. It had read: THE BEST EXERCISE IS TO REACH DOWN AND LIFT SOMEONE UP.

Curiously, the very perverted innocence of that message, its terrifying absence of irony, had nearly been enough to warn me away from my clandestine visit. Whatever had happened in the Potts household that night—whatever calculus of improbable lust and deadly discovery, the unforgiving bat raining down judgment on the gardener's skull, the sudden stillness on the pastor's January floor—whatever had happened, the town had absorbed it; sponged it in; covered it over with time. Who was I to pull back the drawstrings and look in?

And yet how could I ignore Larry Potts? How could I leave Cairo without taking some account of him? More than anyone else in the town, and in symbiosis with his long-dead victim, Potts might embody the claims of the past on this place, the refusal of the past to release this time-besotted town into any kind of replenishing future.

If this were true, it suggested a bleaker prospect than I had yet dared imagine—bleak not only for Cairo but for all American places outside the rims of urban mass. I had come to believe that dying towns were at least partly a symptom of the country's dying memory of itself; its broken covenant with the riches of its agrarian past.

But Cairo's memories seemed to produce nothing except paralysis, exile, decay. The town's legacy of meanness and violence was an extreme case, but it was hardly unique. If town memory had grown so encumbered with town sin that townspeople needed to blot out the past, or pave it over with theme parks, or escape to the more tolerably anonymous horrors of the city, then the town was essentially finished in this country, except as a satellite colony of refugees from other bad memories.

I wanted to visit Cairo Baptist and see if I could gain any sense of whether Cairo's past, and Larry Potts's, lived within this enclave, and on what terms, and to what consequences for the town.

As I put on my Sunday best I tried to relieve my anxieties by recalling a little town history of my own. I thought of the preachers of my boyhood in the town two hundred miles upriver, and what they had to do with the way we lived our lives there.

Preachers had not played a predominating role in my moral development back in Hannibal. My parents had sent me to a mainline Protestant Sunday School on those orange mornings and occasionally we all went to the ten o'clock church services afterward: I lip-synched the hymns, lost the gist of the sermon and came to life during communion, when the deacons passed around shallow trays of some pillow-shaped, bite-sized industrial Host—I took several—and a Blood of Jesus that seemed the same vintage as Welch's grape juice; it came in little plastic thimbles in a perforated board.

Hell was somewhere between Hannibal and China in the middle of the earth; Heaven was a perpetual overcast with harps, and the trick was to die without too many sins on the top of your head. I was under the impression that sins accumulated on the scalp like dandruff or little grains of sand; this was no doubt because I had watched our minister baptize people by tilting them over backwards into the font, soaking their hair, while calling on Jesus to "wash their sins away." I figured that with enough shampoo and the right timing, I could eliminate the middleman, scrubbing my way to glory-land in the privacy of my own bathtub. Cleanliness was next to godliness, they said, and nobody took it more literally than me.

And yet I knew that my home-remedy plan for salvation was not foolproof. What if the Reaper showed up unexpectedly, putting himself as it were between me and the toiletries? And it wasn't a car crash or a fire that I dreaded, but something far more hideous, since the agent of my demise in this scenario would be my own innards.

Among the kid rumors and theories that circulated during my boyhood was one that struck me as just morbid enough to be true. It went this way: if you were unfortunate enough to sneeze, belch and fart at exactly the same instant, you would die.

I lived in a paralytic dread of that triple detonation, which I had no doubt would pick me off sooner or later. It was nothing for me to achieve two out of three; I did it all the time. One belch away from Eternity. I was a walking hand grenade.

And it was so demeaning. So lacking in the tragic dimension. One minute you were bending over to tie your shoelace; the next—you were history. You wouldn't even hear the last "Geshundheit."

Perhaps the worst part was that not even your memory would be free from an everlasting snicker. Even your parents, trying to work through their grief by verbalizing their feelings, might not be able to keep an entirely straight face. "Ronnie was a good boy," I could hear them murmuring quietly through their tears. "Never gave us any trouble. Never sick a day in his life." A silence; a handkerchief pressed to eye. A half-suppressed snort. "He just sneezed, belched and farted at the same time. The doctor said he never felt any pain."

Cairo Baptist Church was a graceful enough link to the town's civic past, at least from the outside. A squarish old redbrick chapel with a pyramid roof and opaque cathedral windows, it commanded the intersection where Poplar slanted into Washington at Eleventh Street, near the remains of the old town center. The cornerstone read 1894. Worshippers climbed three concrete steps to enter through double doors built into the bottom of a Byzantine bell-tower that featured an onionskin dome crowned with a cast-iron fleur-de-lis; it looked as though the architect had been trying to cover the odds of God's ethnic origins.

A newer, lower wing had been grafted onto the rear of the original church, across Poplar Street from Shemwell's Barbecue and its permanent hickory haze. The cornerstone here read 1960—about the time of Potts's arrival from Paducah, Kentucky—and added, piously, FOR ALL WHO WILL LEARN OF HIM. This was the home of the Camelot School. The new wing, L-shaped, formed a crook-armed sort of embrace, along with the original building, of a vest-pocket playground for white Christian children along Poplar Street. Here were a carousel, a swing-set, some hobbyhorses mounted on steel springs, a log playhouse and an American flag.

Most of the congregation was inside and seated by the time I arrived. A couple of men lingered on the top step, welcoming the latecomers, and I held out my hand to the one I instinctively knew to be Larry Potts: a short, balding, bandy-legged little backwoods Christian with a carnation rammed into the lapel of his too-big sport coat and a glint of hell in his narrowed eyes. I took a breath and introduced myself.

The man smiled and dipped his eyes. Nossir. He was just an usher. Now, I'd find the reverend right on in through there.

I was more taken aback by my own gaffe than perhaps the incident required. It made me feel exposed, monitored. Eyes shifting to the stranger. I croaked out some kind of apology and hurried on into the sanctuary. I took a seat to the right of the altar, at the end of a pew so slick with polish that I skidded a few inches, like a beer truck on ice.

I looked around and saw to my relief that none of my fellow worshippers seemed very curious about my presence. In fact they appeared to be bathed in a private luster. In fact, now that I noticed it, they were literally glowing. They seemed to generate light. Hair, teeth, foreheads, eye-whites; every human surface was winking and glittering with some kind of weird candlepower; they looked like shopping-mall elves at Christmastime.

It wasn't until I glanced up at the ceiling that I fully realized the radiance was reflected. Directional spotlights beamed down from the rafters. If the outside of Cairo Baptist referred to the past, the interior had been converted into a kind of futuristic bunker: half sanctuary, half studio, all lighted and wired and miked and monitored for transmission.

And it was packed. I hadn't realized that there was this much prosperous pink flesh in all of Cairo. I tried not to stare too openly at the important hairdos, the powdery pastel sport-jackets, the neckties with dimpled knots.

As had happened to me so frequently in Cairo, I felt overcome by a yawing lurch of time. This congregation looked as though it had been airlifted in from two decades ago, and thawed. I was in Any-church, in Anytown: the attentive wives in their crisp Christian dresses and their Mary Kay faces; the menfolk strong and responsible in their Christian color-coordinates and their big Christian chins; the children bunched together with their parents, clear-eyed and roseate, like tinted studio portraits of themselves.

All white.

I finally spotted the TV camera. It was a miniature remote-control job, mounted over the main entrance, aimed at the choir and pulpit. The services, I assumed, were videotaped for shut-ins and those who were away. As I was soon to discover, there was also a state-of-the-art sound system with lots of directional miking that picked up the choir, the professional-quality soloists, and the preacher. (The audio portion of the service went out on the local radio outlet.) With all that hardware on line, I suspected an unseen technical director someplace—headset phones, monitor screen, control board, the works. A broadcast center, here in the rubble of Cairo. It was eerie, to say the least.

When I turned back toward the altar, the organist was playing a prelude and Larry Potts was at his pulpit.

Whatever I had expected—clawhammer coat, a talker-in-tongues, live snakes, Hazel Motes—I found no traces in the person facing the congregation. No mark of Cain. What I saw was a man in a gray business suit, a man of about fifty, his iron-gray hair dry-blown into a kind of helmet around a strong-boned face gone a little puffy in middle age. He was wearing silver-rimmed glasses that glinted in the light.

The character clues were all in the mouth—a recessed little lip-less line, pressed back into the flesh of his cheeks by a staple-like indentation at either end. It was a mouth built to tighten down hard, if necessary, against the world.

Rev. Larry Potts might have been a banker. Or he might have been an anchorman. Or he might have been a winning small-college football coach getting ready to address a Lions Club luncheon. He could have been anyone in this Anytown crowd. He could have been me, it came to me in a burst of hard light, if I had remained in my small town and gone to the Baptist Junior College, as I had wanted.

Comprehending this, I felt the orange Sunday moving on my skin in an old and familiar way, almost too familiar. Cairo seemed to shift a little in that moment, and reveal itself, however fleetingly, less to my senses than to my memory. This recognition of Potts had the odd effect of easing the moral doubts I had felt about coming to his church and observing him in his habitat—although it drew me toward a more shadowy complicity, the implications of which I did not just then feel I wanted to pursue.

As I sat thinking these thoughts, Larry Potts had begun to address his flock informally in a soft but astonishingly resonant baritone, an engine humming low.

". . . They worked hard at it and they gave faithful attention," he was saying—referring to some of the people associated with the church's radio broadcasts. "Twenty-five years ago we began broadcasting our morning worship service, and we've only missed two Sundays all that *tam*. One, when the power was off all over the whole city, and the other one"—here Pott's voice dropped a quarter note—"when the sermon was of such a nature that I didn't want it broadcast that particular Sunday."

And there it was. The memory lived. It lived in the first few syllables of this random service twenty years of Sundays into Cairo's future. The congregation glittered, and gave no sign. No smiles wavered.

"So, twenty-five years. And many, many blessings. I hope it goes until all the years are accomplished and Jesus comes back."

He read from the church bulletin. *Adult chaperones meet at two this afternoon. Bible Study Wednesday night.* "We've come through the building of the Temple. We've worked our way that far, since the very first night nearly three years ago when we started Genesis! Now we've come through First Kings, chapters five through eight— no more tabernacles, no more wandering, now God shall have a temple! And Solomon will build it!"

Sonny will have surgery this morning; Jack's mother has broken a hip. In the pew holders you'll find mission envelopes.

Rev. Larry Potts strolled down from his pulpit.

"Boys and girls!" The organist struck a theme: "Praise Him,

praise Him, all ye little children." "I've looked forward all week long for these moments! If you'll come quickly!" And suddenly Potts, the good shepherd, arms open, was wreathed, on the altar, in children.

"Anybody learn a Bible verse this week? Let's hear yours first, Mary!"

"Jeeeesuss will never leave you!"

"Never leave you! Never's a long *tam!* . . . Nathan?"

"I have called ye by name . . ."

"I like that! Rachel?"

Rev. Larry Potts went around the children until all the Bible verses had been scoured up and offered to him, like dollops of fudge on the end of a wooden spoon. Then he displayed a book in either hand. "Can you tell me which one's the hymnbook?" he gathered his mouth into a moue of mischief. Fingers darted. "Very good!" Now Potts held up the other book, the Bible. *"That's* a himbook too! H-I-M! It's all about Him! Our Lord! Our Savior! You sing about Him. You read about Him. This is His word to us. So take good care of the hymnbook and this Him-book. . . ."

The children melted away into the congregation and a men's ensemble, in white jackets and carnations, trooped to the altar. The men did some close harmony on a barbershop quartet–style gospel number called, "I Look Away to Heaven." Each time they sang the refrain, "I look away to hea-ven (bo-bom-bo-*bommm*)," the tenor, a skinny man with a thin mustache and a bobbing adam's apple, would tilt over to his side and point toward the ceiling, wagging his eyebrows significantly at the audience. "Good Lord, I hope I'm goin' there."

Next up was a young woman soloist in an electric-blue formal dress, who flicked on a cordless hand mike and threw herself into a show-stopping, broadcast-quality gospel ballad, "In Heaven's Eyes." She sang in a kind of professionally sincere nasal shriek that must have awakened bloodhounds in Tennessee.

And then Rev. Larry Potts began his sermon.

He teased the congregation with a rhetorical question, flattering them with their familiarity over Scriptural characters: "If we could have one person out of the New Testament come and join our church this morning, who would you want? One personality from these wonderful pages. From the early church." The membership chewed this over opaquely.

The reverend then professed that if Paul came, "you'd have to get

another preacher. I couldn't handle that pressure. What a giant!"
(An old trick, but it worked here, drawing some feminine *moos* of
scolding at the pastor's excessive humility.)

It turned out that the person from the New Testament that Larry
Potts would love to see join Cairo Baptist Church on that morning
was a man mentioned in Acts, chapter four, verse thirty-six. Joseph
or "Barnabas to the Apostles." His name connoted "son of encouragement and consolation."

That was the keynote of this morning's sermon: encouragement.
The encouragement to "follow in the light of Christ, the Great Encourager."

" 'Barnabas' means 'the encourager,' " explained Larry Potts. "So
when Barnabas would come on the scene, they wouldn't say, 'Here
comes Joseph.' They would say, 'Here comes the encourager.' Like
you would say, 'Here comes the enforcer.' Or, 'the avenger.' "

Potts took his flock through Barnabas's five characteristics. The
first was that "he saw a need and he met that need"; the second, that
"he saw an outsider and he brought him inside."

I stole another look around at the worshippers in my vicinity.
These were not troubled faces, not the thin and careworn counte-
nances I'd grown used to seeing on the streets of Cairo. Here I saw
unwrinkled skin, reflective little smiles, heads tilted sideways in
keen reflection. These people were absorbed in a pleasant parable
about encouragement and consolation, while outside their cathedral windows, their town rotted and bled toward its doomsday. The
Best Exercise, it is said, is to Reach Down and Lift Someone Up. But
in this field of vision, no one was down. There were no outsiders
to bring inside. Perhaps I was wrong about the town's past, its
secret memories, living inside this bunker. Perhaps the past had
indeed been expunged, vaporized by a beam from the TV camera
mounted over the door, the standard method for vaporizing the
past elsewhere in America.

Perhaps I had misjudged Cairo Baptist Church. Perhaps it was the
town's best link with the only kind of future left to imagine in this
country: a future of the eternal time-present.

The third characteristic of Barnabas was that "he came to troubled waters and he poured calming oil on them." Acts, chapter
eleven, verses twenty-five and twenty-six: " 'Then departed Barnabas to Tarsus, for to seek Saul. And when he had found him, he
brought him unto Antioch. And it came to pass, that a whole year
they assembled themselves with the church, and taught many people. And the disciples were called Christians first in Antioch.' "

I heard Larry Potts's baritone explain that, in 1969, Cairo had needed a school. And suddenly there it was again; the memory, flooding the sanctuary like the lights from above. He said he visited an educator who, yes, "encouraged" him.

Potts went off on a rambling anecdote about a meeting at the church in July of that summer. Marshall Morris would have been dead then for eighteen months. The young black soldier would have been found hanged in the city jail cell about then. The shooting and the burning would have been just beginning in earnest.

Potts went on: He'd been minister for nine years, he feared opposition in the church; but the school was too important.

He pointed to a man in a front-row pew. He recalled how an influential woman of the church had been sitting in that very place, and how she had arisen to say, "I have ten thousand dollars that I'll contribute." Larry Potts almost sobbed about the encouragement that woman's money gave him.

The fourth characteristic of Barnabas was that he recognized a talent and he enlisted it.

I began to think that I understood a little of the enigma of this church and its many contradictions: its dreamy prosperity in the very epicenter of town death; its peculiar capacity almost to dwell in the year 1969 while shutting out its catastrophic implications for the community. I thought I even understood what bound this congregation so adoringly to its pastor, a man who, after all, though found innocent of murder, had broken a Commandment in a most bloody manner, in a moment of homicidal rage. Perhaps this bond was the easiest part of the enigma to understand.

Violence was not a rare occurrence in Cairo; perhaps it was not as rare in most American towns as our amended memories allow us to think. A woman of the town had told me that, in her neighborhood alone, there were four murderers of whom she knew for a fact. Two of them had done time. Her daughter regularly met one of the others walking his dog of an evening.

In fact, violence had long been encoded into the town's culture, and its permutations had been creative. A newspaper publisher during the immediate post–Civil War period had written affectionately of the violent practice of tweezering.

What Potts had done to Marshall Morris symbolized in its very hideousness an act of purity; an apotheosis of the racial virulence that had supplanted tweezering a century later in Cairo. Most of the virulence was anonymous, at a safe remove: shooting into the black housing projects from behind barricades, torching buildings under the cover of night. Larry Potts alone had confronted the enemy, or perceived enemy, face to face; and the slaying had been in all respects properly Biblical: primitive, by hand, with a staff. A broken Commandment for a broken Commandment.

Perhaps in this purifying act Larry Potts had absolved his flock of sin—not by calling on Jesus to wash it away, but by gathering it into himself, onto the scalp of his own head. I thought of Hawthorne's Reverend Master Dimmesdale, who had fulfilled a similar function for another congregation in another time. No wonder they loved him.

From his pulpit, Larry Potts was just now beginning to describe the fifth and final characteristic of Barnabas. This characteristic was that of finding "some good" in people. And to drive home the significance of this characteristic, Potts was digressing into parable.

He told a story of a poor child who at four years old lost his daddy, and at twenty had his wife leave him, taking their child with her. The man tried his hand at this and that, and failed at everything. Finally, he became a cook, and by the time he was sixty-five he had his wife back and was living on social security.

If this was a New Testament character, his description had so far eluded my limited capacity to identify him. But clearly this personage, whom Potts had saved for the last, was in some way central to the reverend's personal theology. Perhaps he was the key to everything, the celestial unifier of all the contradictions, all the enigmas, that lay upon this town, and upon all the lost and dying towns of America. I listened closely. For reasons I could not quite understand, but which might have been connected to my earlier sense of identification with Larry Potts, I wanted this sermon to end on a note of triumph, redemption—even revelation. I wanted all my theories to be proven wrong.

The man in Reverend Potts's story looked at his social security check made out for a hundred and five measly dollars and felt broken.

I began to suspect that the New Testament was perhaps not the pertinent text for the story we were hearing. We were back in time present. But time present certainly had its share of inspirational role models for a resourceful clergyman to draw on. I told myself that, and then I told myself that again.

The man felt such a failure he thought of suicide.

For a second I thought I knew this story. But it couldn't be. It could not be.

But when he was preparing his farewell note, he recalled his wife telling him what a good cook he was. He regained his confidence.

It was going to be. It was beyond my power.

The man then "borrowed eighty-seven dollars against his next social security check, and bought some chickens and some boxes."

"He fried that chicken as only he could," cried Rev. Larry Potts. "He went door to door, selling it!" And so Potts explained the inspirational saga—and huge wealth—of Colonel Sanders.

There was a moment of meditative silence. "I'm not talking about chickens," came Potts's consoling and encouraging voice. "Let's bow our heads."

I filed out of Cairo Baptist Church with the flow of the worshippers, under the tulip-shaped canopy, and squinted into the orange light of Sunday that had thickened on the town. It was a spring morning, Sunday all across America, and somewhere nearby, time was moving: the Ohio River, a few blocks to the east, and the Mississippi, a few blocks west, skidding along toward their joining of purpose a few blocks south, at the tip of Cairo, the tip of Illinois.

So many resources, people said about this town. So many advantages. It was just a matter of time.

That might have been true, for all I knew. But I was out of theories for a while; out of questions. I had just emerged from one of Cairo's innermost enclaves, and the revelation I had hoped for, the light that would shine down and scatter the enigmas, had not manifested itself. If Larry Potts had delivered a prophecy from inside that bunker, it had eluded me. I turned north on Poplar in search of my rented car; I had begun to confront the imminent prospect of passing a Sunday alone in Cairo.

But then in broad daylight one of those visions occurred, the sort of concurrence that leads men, even the jaded and the sick in spirit, to believe that there might indeed be a purpose to things, a design for the universe that mortal men could not comprehend.

From above the tree line three blocks to the north on Washington Street there loomed the face of a man, enlarged many times beyond human proportions. He was clothed in white, and he had a flowing beard, and he was smiling down on Cairo in a serene kind of ecstasy. Beside the face were the words, in flaming scarlet: EAT IN OR CARRY OUT . . . 9 BLOCKS ON LEFT.

I had asked for a sign about Cairo's future. And now I had it.

Chapter XVI

The morning after I attended Larry Potts's service, I waited for him in the children's sanctuary of Cairo Baptist Church. He had agreed by telephone to talk with me about the town—a decision I could not help admiring, given that he stood to gain almost nothing by such an interview, and that, judging by the clipped tone of his voice, he regarded my presence in Cairo with the same resigned distaste that had radiated from Mayor Moss. There was also, of course, the unspoken, dark matter of why the Reverend Larry Potts might have drawn the curiosity of a visitor to the town in the first place. It was astonishing, given these layers of discomfort, secrecy and suspicion, that he would agree to a conversation under any circumstances.

And yet he had agreed, and so here I was, on a Monday morning, seated at a small children's table inside the new wing of the church, listening to Potts's resonant vibrato echoing off the corridor walls down the hall as he conferred with some of his deacons.

I was in a shiny sort of room; the walls and floor seemed freshly, if not fiercely, polished. Ten rows of gleaming hardwood pews faced what might have been a small altar, but what in fact had the trappings of an audio-visual center; there was a large Sony video screen behind a puppet stage framed by a fake brick facade and a red curtain. A piano sat at an angle off to the side.

While I waited for Potts to finish his meeting, I arose and scanned the titles of the books that filled a wooden shelf against the wall—the children's sanctuary apparently doubled as the church library. Many of the titles were of the sort I might have predicted: *Brainwashing in the High Schools; How to Beat the Blahs; If You Marry Outside Your Faith; Christ and the Fine Arts; Law for the Layman; Home Sweet Fishbowl; Famous Singles of the Bible,* and so on.

Some of the others suggested a slightly more disciplined turn of mind; the dogged searchings of the self-educated man: a Strunk and White grammatical handbook; *Twenty Thousand Words; Better English* by Norman Lewis; *One Hundred Pitfalls in English Grammar; English in Action; Free-Lance Writing; The Written Word; Publicity Goes to Church; Basic Word Lists; Making Every Word Count; The Writer's Hotline Handbook; How to Write and Speak Effective English; Conversationally Speaking; Public Speaking—How to Sell Yourself;* and *Shake Well Before Using,* by Bennett Cerf.

Finally there were some titles that I would never have expected within three or four city blocks of Cairo Baptist Church: Mark Twain's Christian-baiting *Letters From the Earth;* some C. S. Lewis; some Jules Verne; a volume of Frederick Lewis Allen; a volume of Winston Churchill; and—perhaps most incongruously of all—Allan Patton's *Cry the Beloved Country.*

As I browsed, hands in my pockets, contemplating what all those titles might add up to, the Reverend Larry Potts strode into the room behind me.

He was jacketless in an off-white shirt, firmly knotted tie and suitpants. His steel-framed glasses caught the light, as they had from the pulpit the previous morning. He raked me with a glance that might have chastened an Old Testament prophet, gestured to a wooden chair across a small polished conference table at one side of the room, and we sat down across from one another. Potts's small, indented mouth was nearly invisible as he awaited my questions.

The first surprise he had in store for me came when I asked whether he had been called to Cairo by the Southern Baptist Convention. "This is an American Baptist Church," he corrected me, with just the hint of an ironic smile at my preconception. "I received my degree at the Southern Baptist Theological Seminary in Louisville, and this church contacted the seminary for a recommendation. They selected me. This was in 1960."

Changing the subject, I asked him whether, in light of Cairo's long history of tribulations—racial hatred, poverty, civic corruption, vice, prostitution—he could think of some Biblical reference to God's judgment on wicked cities that might apply here.

"Well, there are examples," said Potts, after studying me for a moment, "but I don't know that they apply. 'Course, Sodom and Gomorrah was destroyed for sexual sin. No," he went on, "I don't think God judged this town. I think he let its own ways take their courses. And men have a way of bringing about their own judgment. You abuse your body"—here his eye flicked for the tiniest instant to my midsection—"you gonna have bad health. And if the town doesn't have good leadership, it's gonna get bad leadership." He paused a beat; lowered his voice. "There are no vacuums," he said.

Larry Potts considered the question a little longer, and then went on: "It started down in the 1940s, if you really study the trend," he said. "Cairo was losin' population in the forties. Now, you mentioned a lot of the problems; you didn't mention the *union* problem. That was a bad one. We've lost some existing industries and plants directly through union disorder. Edison was here, Singer was here. They left solely because of union problems.

"But it wasn't union alone," Larry Potts continued, his voice rising a little toward pulpit-pitch, "it wasn't vice alone, it wasn't the change in the river trade alone. It was all those things. Then after it got down, then I think there were other forces and factors that contributed to its present condition."

Such as? I ventured.

Larry Potts gazed off at a point over my shoulder and began to tell a story. It was the story of an American Baptist convention he'd attended up in a suburb of Chicago not long after he'd arrived in Cairo. "And I was just a green pastor, I was just goin' to try and fit in, do my part, what I was supposed to do," he recalled, toning his voice down again. "And I was a nobody, I was the least of people at that convention. Right out of seminary, hadn't been here a year.

"And I was paged to go to a certain table in this big area, and a Mrs. [here he gave a name] was at that table. She was in charge of the state . . . human resources, or civil . . . social concerns, or something like that. And I sat down, and she said"—here Larry Potts dropped his voice even further and looked directly at me—"said: 'we want you to integrate the church in Cairo.' "

There was a moment in which I was silent, and Larry Potts was silent, and then Larry Potts went on.

"I said, 'Well, ma'am . . . I have no problem with blacks. I've played ball with them, I grew up with them, I've gone to school with them. But,' I said, 'they don't like to worship the way we worship. We're dull and dead to them. And I've already met some black pastors in town, they're good people, and I'm not gonna raid their churches. And,' but I said, 'Why Cairo?' She said: 'Never mind, we have selected Cairo.' I said, 'Why not Springfield, that's where the state office is?' And she got a little aggravated, and she said: 'If you don't do it, you'll be responsible for problems that occur.'

"Well," said Larry Potts, clasping his hands behind his helmet of iron-gray hair, "I didn't think much about it then. But over the years, I've thought a lot about it."

I waited.

"*We were set up.* We were selected, but the selection was a setup." For—? I prodded.

"For a civil rights target, and so on," murmured Larry Potts.

This woman, I said. She was a member of—

"The American Baptist Convention," Potts said. "Which is quite liberal." He paused and seemed to think about something deep inside himself. "She's dead now," he went on after a moment. "But that to me indicated that Cairo had—been chosen. Our problems were not generic. We were at a stage, an affordable stage for the state. They could afford to do things like that in Cairo, rather than in their neighborhoods and backyards." He paused again, his eyes still locked on mine. "We were at an *expendable* stage," he said quietly.

Now it was I who remained silent for a long moment before asking, Expendable in what way?

Potts spread an open palm. "Well, in that the dirt, and the problems, and the turmoil wouldn't affect *them.*"

Before I could phrase another question, he was taken with a dreamy, reflective thought:

"You know, I can understand, the convention was heavily into the civil rights thing, and I was certainly sympathetic to all of that. And they wanted to do it, though, without repercussions in their own churches, in their own neighborhoods. It's like people send money to Africa to missions, but they wouldn't welcome a black child across the street. It's hypocrisy," he murmured, "in a way. . . .

"Anyway," he went on briskly, "I think that was the final stroke in the picture for Cairo. It wasn't the cause of it. The racial thing was never the cause of our trouble. It was a symptom."

The question I wanted to ask him next was so large, and so dangerous, and yet still so unformed, after all this time, in my thoughts—the question was, of course, about the killing of the late black gardener Marshall Morris—that I sat looking at Potts for a few moments while I tried to find a way to phrase it.

Potts was tensely attentive; he seemed to read my mind, for now he declared abruptly: "If you start shootin' through old holes, I'm goin' back in my office to work." In the absolute silence that followed, he added—somewhat contradictingly, I thought—"You don't feel the pain that goes through old holes!"

I held my silence until Potts was ready to continue.

"This is not the town it's been painted to be," he said finally. "And we're not the people we're portrayed to be." He dropped his voice again. "But as long as we know that, that's all that matters."

A fresh thought seized him. "You know one day a guy named Shimei was cursing King David, and throwin' dust at him, and rocks, and"—here Potts suddenly snapped his fingers in front of my face—"King David could have had his head, just like that! And his men around him"—I thought of the male voices I'd heard down the corridor, the deacons—"wanted to take his head off! And David said"—here Potts relaxed, and his voice lapsed back into a languid drawl—"leave him *alonnnne*. I know what I am. What he says doesn't make any difference." He let the sibilance of the last word trail in the air.

"So that's what we've kinda finally had to come up with, you know?" For the first time, he smiled at me. "This is a good town."

We talked for the better part of an hour after that. The consciousness of race intruded, often reflexively, into nearly every opinion Potts had formed about Cairo—and many of his opinions, I discovered, were penetrating, even sophisticated. As I had suspected, he was no particular friend of the Cairo political establishment. "Those in control politically," he told me, "have always kept that control, rather than sharing it, you know. And it's not white from black. Those in control aren't going to let anybody get control."

The divisions he sensed most acutely were divisions of class. (I thought of the self-help books on his shelf.) "There's the upper class," he told me, "and there's the lower class. But the least division, I feel honestly, is the racial division. That's a division, but it isn't *the* division. Among the white class," he went on, in what might have been a revealing slip, "there's so many divisions. Where you bank. Which funeral home you use. Which grocery store you go to."

He defended his Camelot School—it was still in operation, but educating only twenty-five students a year now—on the ground that sudden, forced integration in Cairo had thrown the public school system into chaos. "We had token integration from '64 on," he said. "They could go anywhere they wanted to. So, most of the black students preferred to stay at their school. Sumner. Some went over to Cairo High School. The white school. And there wasn't any problem. But in '76, they closed the black schools, just without preparation or anything, just combined it. And it was as hard on the black kids as it was on the white kids. And it was even harder on the teachers. And the best ones quit. And so from '67 to '69 we just had chaos.

"And here we had our children in that system," said Larry Potts. "Well, people were leavin' town. Well, this is no way. I've either got to leave, too, or we've got to have an alternative. We chose to provide an alternative.

"And you talk about gettin' whipped. And called all-white." Potts shook his gray-helmeted head. "We *weren't* all-white. Started out that way, but anybody could come. Along the way we've had black students. And never charged more than six hundred dollars tuition at any tam. But we took a whippin' for it. I'd do it again. I'd hate to do it again. It was hard. But we had no—we had a choice. That was to leave."

I asked Larry Potts what he thought of Doc Poston's chances of success with Operation Enterprise. He considered a moment or two before he spoke.

"I don't think there's anything here that can't be fixed," he said, "if addressed. I admire Doc tremendously. I'm glad he's here. It's the only positive thing that I've seen. And he does have widespread backing."

And then Potts added, "But he hasn't tackled the real problem yet."

Which is? I asked.

"Which is gov'ment," said Larry Potts. "Anytime he's encroached upon that which local government controls, he starts to get the reaction. It's like the riverfront. He's touched a raw nerve there. He'll touch another one when he gets into the utility company. That's taboo. You don't bother that. Those who have done so have paid a price."

Why, I asked Potts, haven't you been present at Doc Poston's town meetings?

Potts sighed. "I've told Doc Poston, my tam is consumed here. And I'm not gonna sacrifice this. I can't. I don't take a day off. I don't take vacations. I've just dedicated myself to being a good pastor from here on in. It takes all my tam. I don't fish or hunt or play golf. Only thing that seems irregular is, I mow some grass around some of our property. But otherwise I'm on call all the tam. Two sermons a week, and a midweek hour-long Bible study. It's like an hour-long lecture. And then a Sunday-morning lesson to teach, that's four preparations every week.

"My wife'll tellya. I don't watch television. I don't go ridin' around, or anything. I'm there sittin' at my desk, when I'm not on the road."

I asked Potts what he thought would happen to town life in this country.

"It's happening," he said. "It's happening throughout Tennessee and Kentucky and Missouri. A Wal-Mart can go up on the outside of a little town, and the rest of the people can hang it up. And then the mall goes in thirty miles away from that, and that Wal-Mart's not gonna do well either. It'll relocate. It'll move on to the mall.

"And they're great stores. That's the best store in the world. You can get top brand at low prices. But they're movin' next door to the malls, where the traffic is."

Did he see towns that resemble Cairo as he drove around the Mississippi Valley?

"Um-hum. Sure. Name you some. Charleston over here. It can't compete with Sikeston or Cape Girardeau. Sikeston's having a hard time competing with Cape. Goin' down through the Bootheel, closer you come to Memphis. Lotta towns like this one.

"I just came back from Kansas City last week. Richmond was a good town at one time, Richmond, Missouri. And it's lost all its bidniss district. 'Cause it's only twenty miles from Independence, where there are two huge malls. That's the Kansas City complex.

"It's happening out there, it's happening over in Kentucky, it's happening down in the Bootheel. It's a common occurrence now. People gonna go where the price is better, and the selection is greater. You know, on any given day or night you can go to Cape and see half of this town, go to Paducah and see another half."

If Cairo is going to come back, I asked Potts, how will that happen?

"Jobs. Work. Creativeness. If Cairo had a theme park, for example, like Six Flags, where every young person had a job to do—entertaining, or serving, waiting tables, whatever—so he'd have money in his pocket." He lifted his voice up a little to the preaching mode. "The *love* of money is the root of all evil. *Money* is not. The *absence* of money is another root of evil. And economics"—he pronounced it *"eek-*onomics"—"are so important. The Bible is full of economics. But it needs to come the right way. This town tried to build on vice. All it got was a bad name and a wrecked future."

And then Larry Potts voiced a variation of the idea—the dream, the fantasy—that I'd come to believe everyone who lived in the town would express, if just given enough time to do so.

"If the State of Illinois were to make Cairo a showplace because it's a port of entry," he said, "and I think they'd have every justification to do so, this would be paradise. You couldn't travel the country over and find a better place to put a town. More scenic. More things to draw on."

So many assets . . .

I left Larry Potts's church this time through the rear exit of the additional wing he'd built a couple decades before. In my line of vision was the rear end of Shemwell's Barbecue with its neat stacks of hickory logs, and its ancient marquee: EAT ON TAP. I could smell the pungency of the logs.

Out on the sidewalk, another sign caught my eye, in the door window of a faded little building next to Shemwell's:

CAIRO BAPTIST THRIFT SHOP
SORRY WE'RE CLOSED

Chapter XVII

The decision by the Kent School to offer six hundred acres of its mountaintop campus property for sale to private developers did more than symbolically usher in the epoch of flash-growth in the pre-Revolutionary Connecticut town. It did more than herald a transition period in the town's history that would see the creation of sudden wealth for a few divestment-minded property-owners, including the school and a number of surrounding dairy farmers.

The effects of the announcement sounded far deeper in the community's web of economies, of class relationships, of its very notions of itself as a community. They activated a sense of crisis without known precedent in the town's 250-year history: a sense that unless a kind of resistance formed immediately, the fragile balances that made Kent a town would be forever disrupted, and what had been a town would degenerate rapidly, and irrecoverably, into a colony of metropolis.

These measures of resistance had in common one paradoxical feature: an essential grounding in the synthetic. They depended not on indigenous, deeply-rooted economic processes, but on a kind of ad hoc economic engineering: ordinances, property-transfer formulas and tax incentives that would have the cumulative effect, baldly stated, of *forcing* the town of Kent to remain sleepy, charming and rural in a surrounding context of unrestrained suburbanization.

This early resistance had its leader. While he did not exactly fit the stereotype of the charismatic populist firebrand—his idea of letting off steam, for example, was to smack bucketfuls of Whiffle balls toward the roof of his barn with a fungo bat, from a position near his outdoor swimming pool—he was to prove, over the ensuing years, a remarkably steadfast and resourceful champion of Kent's traditional patterns and character. This was the retired *Time* magazine correspondent Donald Connery, who, with his wife Leslie, had been a guest at Carol Hoffman's dinner party on the night Dorothy Gawel was killed.

The Connerys lived in a gracefully restored eighteenth-century farmhouse tucked into the hilly contours of Skiff Mountain Road—the road that would absorb the greatest impact in traffic volume if the Kent Girls School property were bought by a residential developer. My family and I loved to visit there. My sons seemed in awe of the gigantic sugar maple tree that shaded the main house, sweet and dark in summer, flaming scarlet in autumn. They tiptoed reverently through the dark horse-barn with its chestnut beams, reaching out their hands to touch the coarse flanks of the horses; and they ran through the curving pastures past apple trees toward the line of the deer-filled forest, where a waterfall was hidden amid the pines. Perhaps their greatest pleasure, and certainly mine, lay in climbing the spiraling iron staircase that Don Connery had installed inside a white stone silo at the edge of a great down-sloping meadow. He had turned the old structure into a conical library, lining the inner walls with thousands of his books. On the top landing he had built a small platformed study, with windows giving on to a tremendous view into the valley. My sons regarded this remarkable structure as their spaceship. So, in a certain sense, I think, did Connery.

Donald Connery was a lanky pipe-smoking sort of fellow in his early sixties, the kind of citizen reflexively described by his friends as "mild." The mildness was a little deceptive. True, his passions were of the sort that might comfortably have been hand-stitched and bound in calf's leather: he attended town meetings and cared about precision in language and sincerely felt that people ought to have a better understanding of geography in light of the new world being born as we approach the twenty-first century. But there was some steel in Donald Connery, and he was willing to unsheathe it on behalf of his notions regarding Kent.

He had grown up in Brooklyn, within walking distance of Ebbets Field, the son of a Canadian-born preacher and "elocutionist" and amateur inventor, and had enlisted in the army in 1944, directly out of high school. "Basic training, South Pacific, field artillery, Philippines, chasing the Japanese," was the way he curtly recalled it one day from the easy chair in his book-stuffed den. "I wasn't in the MacArthur invasion, I came along as the troops were mopping up. So we were 'mopping up' the Japanese. Isn't that a wonderful phrase? Like having a mop—we were chasing them all over the hills with flamethrowers." If President Truman had not decided to drop the atomic bomb on Hiroshima and Nagasaki, Don Connery might have been a part of an invasion of the Japanese mainland. "Mile for mile, it would have been the bloodiest campaign in history," he remarked, squinting as he took off his rimless glasses to polish the lenses. "The Japanese would have fought to the death. It would have been horrendous."

Instead, he found himself a copyboy at United Press in 1945. There he had one of those date-with-a-dame-called-Destiny experiences that seem to have been de rigueur for smart cub reporters of that era. Directed to report to the bureau chief at an early session of the United Nations in Lake Success, Long Island, he was told by the busy editor, who had scarcely looked up from his desk, "Oh yeah, good, good, we need you. Take Trusteeship, take Narcotics Commission, and fill in for Stu on the Security Council." The middle-aged man in the easy chair still glowed at the boyish memory. "I *didn't* say," he assured me, " 'Excuse me, Mr. Manning, I think you've made a mistake, I'm only a copyboy.' I said, 'Fine.' Then I went to a dictionary and looked up 'trusteeship.' Got myself a pad, and I went off and began covering the United Nations. I was doing major wire-service reporting, as a copyboy, on a copyboy's pay, with bylines all over the world—and *nobody said anything.*"

He was accepted at Harvard—he wrote his application on United Press letterhead—and graduated in 1950, in the same class as his future fellow townsman Henry Kissinger. (At that commencement exercise Thornton Wilder, the author of *Our Town,* had remarked how the twentieth century was "shifting its foundations and altering its emphases with striking rapidity," and of how disturbing it was "to have lost the feeling of belonging to one reassuring community"—observations that lodged in Connery's imagination.) He married his sweetheart, a jolly Radcliffe girl named Leslie, joined up with *Time* magazine and for the next eighteen years traveled the world: India, Japan, Siberia, Moscow (he was expelled), London, Scandinavia, Ireland, Africa.

In 1968, with four children and a comfortable bank account and a craving for permanence, the Connerys realized that they could live just about anyplace in the world they cared to. "We wanted to bring up our kids in a small town," Donald recalled. "We preferred New England. I knew about these Litchfield hills. We came to live in Kent."

The Connerys became the quintessential members of an important enclave in Kent: outsiders who put down roots. As the children grew into self-sufficiency, Leslie taught school and volunteered for the local ambulance service. Donald became a habitué of town meetings in the creaky old wood-frame Town Hall, and was always on hand for community projects and seasonal rituals. The man who had nearly been a part of a human-wave assault on Japan found something eternal in the small community, something that spoke to his soul. In his copious and tenderly written elegy to Kent, *One American Town*, published in 1972, Connery rendered "this spruced-up, well-kept and comfortable old shoe of a town" and its people through the prism of their seasonal cycles. Toward the end, he wrote, with a perceptivity that the ensuing decades ratified:

> In our own small way, like a model in a wind tunnel, we reveal some of America's contradictory forces—the consolidating and diversifying forces—which are shifting people from one part of the country to another and draining the life out of some places while swamping others. Somehow, as rural people drift to the cities and city people flee to the suburbs, as the countryside empties here and fills up there, we seem to survive and thrive. But not so other good towns, especially those deep in the heartland and the far reaches of the Great Plains. The farm-to-city movement has withered hundreds of towns that once were bustling with activity and bursting with pride. It remains to be seen whether the whole way of life they represent is going for good.

Connery's affection for Kent was affirmed early. Less than a year after he and Leslie moved into their farmhouse, on a foggy January night, its furnace room caught fire. As he wrote in his book, "The town came to our rescue . . . volunteer firemen swarming about the house, friends running with lengths of hose, strangers donning oxygen masks, shadows chopping through the ice in the pool, the first selectman going up a ladder, shopkeepers and artisans and workingmen disappearing into the smoke . . . people risking their lives for you."

The experience moved him. "It is almost too much to bear," he wrote. "Not the fire but the kindness. The involvement. The sheer humanity of it all. This is not what modern man is used to. The drift of the world is to the depersonalized city where the knack of survival is not to get involved. Avoid thy neighbor."

Now, in the late 1980s, with the prospect of flash-growth threatening to overwhelm Kent's landscape, its peacefulness, its traditions of volunteerism—all he held dear—Donald Connery saw his chance to repay his old debt to his neighbors. He seized it.

Citizens for Controlled Growth was not the original title of the organization that Connery put together—the group first called itself, with perhaps an excess of tact, Friends of Kent School—but it was the most enduring. Most of its members were people very much like Donald and Leslie Connery: comfortable landowners of a certain age, many of them transplanted to Kent from another place, all of them reasonable, temporizing folks without strong social or ideological axes to grind, who just wanted the town to go on the way it had been.

The first public stroke of CCG, in December 1986, was suitably sedate: it unleashed a questionnaire. Aimed at 1,500 postal route customers and post-office box holders, the survey probed residents' opinions about the town's rate of growth and their inclination to support a moratorium on large-scale development.

A month later several local weeklies reported the results: among the 628 replies—44 percent of the total mailing—65 percent said the growth rate was too fast. (Another 18 percent said it was just right.) An even more emphatic majority, 81 percent, said it would support a moratorium. "We think a moratorium should be strongly considered by the town," Connery told reporters, "because it will give us breathing space." He and the organization's president, a landowner named Harmon Smith, said they would press the Planning and Zoning Commission to impose a year-long freeze.

The P&Z, however, had other fish to fry. "This town is wired to go," chairman Paul Abbott was happily assuring *The New York Times*. "Under current regulations Kent's density could be doubled quite rapidly." Abbott's optimism soared even beyond that happy prospect. "There are several other large tracts of land that we are anticipating will come on the market through a death in the family or a farmer going out of business," he told the newspaper. The only dark cloud in Abbott's field of vision lay in the annoying fact that one third of the land in Kent was off the tax rolls. "We have an Indian reservation, four state parks, the Appalachian Trail, two private schools and lots of farmland," he lamented to the *Times* reporter. "That has got to influence our planning. We have too much land in trees."

That was exactly the sort of talk that drove some of Kent's native-born residents through the roofs of their endangered homesteads. "I see that as the most dangerous attitude," seethed my acquaintance, the young family-farm owner who sought to "mitigate" the development damage to the town.

"It's a suburban attitude," the man continued, spitting out the most withering pejorative in his vocabulary. "That's the attitude people bring here who've come from the small cities, the large suburban towns to the south of here." He meant towns in Long Island and Westchester County; he meant the city of New York. "Everything they think is colored by that experience. They come from a land where everybody sits on a one-acre lot. Everybody has a more or less equal piece of the pie, and the people with more than that are the wealthy people, who are privileged. The problem is, we're not talking about Westchester County. We're talking about Kent, Connecticut. They're trying to turn it into suburbia."

These prospects were not exactly lost on Donald Connery or his Citizens for Controlled Growth. Within weeks after its formation— even before its poll of local citizens, in fact—CCG had begun brainstorming ways in which to minimize the effects of the inevitable.

One strategy that emerged early involved a search for an alternative to commercial development of the girls' school campus. In the fall of 1986 CCG called a Sunday-afternoon meeting at the local public school to unveil what it called an "options report" for alternative use of the site. The options included a sale to another educational institution; some clustered residential units that would not require the leveling of certain fields and woodlands; even the construction of a "colonial or Victorian-era community village on the site."

The options report had little impact in the community. In fact it would be safe to estimate that virtually no one, outside the CCG membership itself, knew, or cared, that an options report existed. As much as Donald Connery and his friends might have wished to the contrary, the time had long since passed in Kent when like-minded townspeople would band together in a meeting hall and pore over complicated plans aimed at neutralizing a common threat—especially when that threat was as large, and amorphous, and apparently inevitable as large-scale development.

"I would say most people in Kent, by far, are apathetic,"

conceded Connery ruefully, as we sat in his den some months after these events had played themselves out. "They don't come out to the meetings that we call. We don't have really big meetings. We don't have a lot of people calling to join up."

That acknowledgment was not tantamount, however, to a concession of defeat. There was still some steel left in the town's leading revolutionary.

"So it falls back on what the British refer to as a 'ginger group,'" Donald Connery averred, with just a glint of recklessness in his mild blue eyes. "The relatively small group of people who just feel that something's gotta be done about the situation. And do it."

While Donald Connery and his friends planned further strategies to stave off traumatic growth, other people were starting to concern themselves with the traumas that had already been unleashed.

The new investment money flowing into the pockets of divesting farm-owners around Kent was by no means an unmitigated blessing. Not only did this new wealth fall short of benefitting everyone in town, it worked actively against the interests of many long-established families there. As the large farm estates suddenly became "in-play" commodities for rich development corporations, the real estate firms representing those estates started pushing the land prices upward. As the value of real estate increased, so did its tax base—and so did prices generally in the town.

These historically unprecedented increases trapped certain families as surely as a rapid rise in a region's climate would trap certain species of animals accustomed to colder temperatures. These included people who lived on fixed incomes geared to the local economy—people such as Susie Gawel, the bursar at South Kent School. These people were now finding it harder to make ends meet in Kent. Unlike Susie Gawel, on her inherited (albeit diminished) property, some old families were leaving Kent for other, undiscovered towns. And even those who could manage to cling to their native ground were facing the shock of being the last generation of their family lines to do so: their children, priced out of the market, were going elsewhere.

Not all of them, to be sure. A small group of Kent young people—Alan Gawel's crowd, as it happened—had worked out a system for circumventing the new price structures. Perhaps unconsciously, they had reverted to the practices of "loyalty," "steady habits," "harmony" and "mutual respect" that had defined the community in its Puritan era.

"We all try to help out each other," Alan Gawel told me. "The Soules are a family that's been here for awhile. Bob Soule is the fire chief right now. He has three boys, one my age—Danny—and we're all in the fire department together. Two years ago Danny's father separated some land that he had—because you can't afford to buy it—and so Danny took out a mortgage for some building material. Then we all worked with him and built a house. We worked weekends and nights. We did all the labor for nothing. I mean, that's the only way we can keep seeing each other. We all do that for each other, 'cause there's maybe ten of us that really care, we're always tight, we can do that."

What about some of the other young people in town? I'd asked Alan. He'd shaken his head.

"I don't know what they're gonna do," he said. "They just can't—you know, they're just not gonna make it."

This sort of fealty did not move the hearts of everyone in town. It certainly did not move Bill Litwin's.

"There are people who are saying, 'Our children don't have a place to live in Kent,'" noted Litwin—who, in the gold rush of the late eighties, was busily forging his own comeback with the multi-million-dollar Kent Town Center. "*Well, so what?* How long did it take you to gather enough economic stability for you to be able to move to Kent? It took me a long time. There is no God-given right, simply because you're born in a town, that you should stay in that town. *If* you can't afford it, *if* your parents can't afford to buy you or give you a piece of land"—here Litwin raised his shoulders and put his palms out—"you *may* have to go to an adjoining town where the jobs are and work your way back!"

The very notion of these indigenous people and their annoying demands made Litwin's blood boil. "The issue is always: 'Why don't we have more affordable property?' But these people who are squawking are the same ones who probably made a bundle of money selling some of their property to people like you and me!" He delivered his coup de grâce: "The only people who get involved in this town are those who have a profit motive."

And yet, even in his indignation, Bill Litwin did not lose sight of the fact that the native-born, middle-class people of Kent played an important—perhaps indispensable—role in the life, or lifestyle, of the town.

"Strictly from a superficial point of view," he allowed, "the reason you and I and a lot of other people came to Kent is because of the people we're discussing. The country people, the rural people who run the funky little cafes like the Villager. Who don't know from chi-chi." He smiled. "Or sushi.

"If Kent had developed as a rather chi-chi place," Litwin went on, "you probably wouldn't have selected it. Because what you liked was that little bit of simple rural aspect of it. Standing in line at the Kent Market. You're living out a fantasy."

This, it struck me, was only a slightly different way of saying what the local Congregational minister had once told me: "Part of the charm of Kent has always depended on a certain level of sustained poverty." And yet the two men were speaking from perspectives as different, in their way, as Kent was different from Cairo, Illinois.

The minister's name was Glen Rainsley. Tall and lean and big-boned, with thinning hair and a trimmed goatee, he had moved to Kent from Maine in the early 1980s with his wife and small daughter, to assume the pastorship of a congregation GATHERED, as the clapboard sign beside Route 7 had it, IN 1741. (The present building was far more contemporary, having been erected in 1849.)

Glen Rainsley's interest in the housing imbalances caused by the soaring prices was impeccably moral, but it had a personal dimension as well. He and his family were living, much to his surprise and chagrin, not in a house on a leafy neighborhood street in the town, but in a small parsonage, across the driveway from the church and of comparable vintage.

"We sold our house in Maine and came here with twenty grand for a down payment," he told me one morning as we drank coffee in the parsonage kitchen. "My wife and I had a combined salary of forty-two thousand dollars. We were warned that we couldn't live in the town on that salary and that down payment," he said, giving a kind of bewildered chuckle, "and we couldn't. We flat-out couldn't. That," the minister said, "got me angry."

Glen Rainsley channeled his anger toward finding out how many other people in his congregation—and out of it—were caught in the same pinch. What he discovered turned his anger into incredulousness.

"There are basically four groups of people who simply can't go on living in Kent under the present real estate price structures," he said. "The first group is older people. They've lived here forever, now they've retired, and they can't keep pace. We've lost a few of them.

"Then there are the single parents who have to work. Two years ago we counted nineteen kids in the elementary and middle schools who had to drop out because their mothers or fathers had housing problems. You see these divorced mothers working in banks, trying desperately to scratch some money together.

"Another group," Rainsley went on, "—this is a corker—is kids who've moved away from their parents but have had to come back. I know of one example that's a beaut. The mother and father are in their fifties. All their kids had left the house. Three sons and a daughter. They'd all gone and started out on their own in a house somewhere in the area.

"One by one," Glen Rainsley said, his tenor voice rising just an octave, "they have all come back. Each son with a spouse. One of them with a child. Now there are nine adults and one child living in a single-family house—which the parents had redone for themselves after the children moved out."

Rainsley had to fall silent and think about that one for a minute. Then he said, in a lowered voice, "The fourth group, and maybe this one is the hardest to understand or accept, is the young working people. Two-salary families. Even they can't afford the housing prices in this town."

I asked Rainsley what implications he thought this trickling away of ordinary working families held for the town. Again, he thought for a while, his eyes on his large hands, before he spoke.

"Let's set the moral implications aside for now," he said finally. "What happens to public services in this town? What happens to volunteers? What do you have left when you have a town full of people who will buy things but won't serve on anything? This is a retail-based community. Retail and construction. If you don't have the people to staff those kinds of jobs, I don't quite understand how Kent will function.

"Look at the village fairs in the area. They're down. Church fairs—down. Antique shows. These are part of what used to be the social fabric. Now there's no one left to go to them, or no one who can afford to."

These were among the discoveries and considerations that had led Glen Rainsley to get involved in a cause that he hadn't intended to get involved in; one that promised to consume as much of his time and energy as his pastoral duties. Glen Rainsley got involved in affordable housing.

Like "controlled growth," "affordable housing" was a concept that had swept through the United States in the late 1980s, particularly in the Northeast and on the west coast. In certain respects the two movements appeared contradictory. ("Controlled growth" hardly sounded necessary in a country where, by 1979, a median-income family could not afford to purchase a median-priced home.) The origins of affordable housing were partly in the federal tax reforms of 1986, in which the Reagan administration, as part of its general repudiation of government participation in housing programs, eliminated all tax incentives for private development of low-income housing. In New England, these tax reforms collided head-on with the onrush of wealthy second-home buyers in rural towns such as Kent. By 1987 in northwestern Connecticut, the median family income was the fourth-lowest in the state, while housing prices were the second-highest. "In the middle of this heated real estate market," as one housing professional put it, "you had all the federal tools sucked right out of the mix. Instead of low-income housing, the developers were saying, 'Yo! Condos! Shopping centers!'"

Affordable housing defined a formula for partnerships between local citizens groups and state governments to restrain prices on houses and apartments for people unable to keep up with the "bid-up" real estate prices. The Kent Board of Selectmen had formed a task force not long after the movement had gained a kind of fashionability. Its introductory report, a loose-bound brochure, sounded all the right notes: affordable housing was not just something that would be nice for Kent; it was "essential to the survival of the quality of life that makes Kent such a special place to live." It would be an insupportable loss "for the sons and daughters of longtime Kent families to be forced to move elsewhere to find housing they can afford." There was some language about "the ties that bind us together as a community."

And then the brochure got down to brass tacks—the same brass tacks that Glen Rainsley would later depend on in lieu of the "moral arguments" that few, in the 1980s, were inclined to feel moved by.

"As the town grows," the brochure argued, "so does the need for goods and services; yet who is to provide them? Stores, restaurants, local services and trades all rely heavily on a local labor pool. . . . As the population shifts to part-time residents the question arises: who will 'mind the store'?"

Another way of putting that question might have been: "Who will play the parts?" My sense, as I followed these developments from my occasional perch as a weekender in South Kent, was that in several unmistakable ways Kent was taking on the aspects of a

large community-theater project, with many directors and complicated, shifting sets. Instead of simply looking and behaving the way
it looked and behaved as an unconscious function of its accumulated history and traditions and cycles of manufacture and
service and harvest and worship and the schooling of its children,
Kent would henceforth look and behave the way certain people
wanted it to look and behave. These directors were many and
cacophonous: Gordon Casey, with his mock-Federal Kent Green
crowned with its Disney-ish Town Hall; Bill Litwin, with his Railroad-Era Victorian Town Center (containing its Italian-style delicatessen); the Citizens for Controlled Growth, with their wish for
unspoiled vistas and a "Victorian-era community village" on the
site of the Kent School girls' campus atop Skiff Mountain; the Kent
Affordable Housing Task Force, with its insistence, surely sincere,
on the presence of "regular people" as extras in the extravaganza;
and my mountaintop farmer–friend with his amorphous wish that
everyone would go away and leave the stage as it had been in the
previous century.

At any rate, several months after the Kent Affordable Housing
Task Force had issued its cautionary report, Glen Rainsley found
himself the chairman of a nonprofit organization called Kent Affordable Housing. Among the group's first goals was the acquisition
of the old town hall—a decrepit white-frame warren of offices and
meeting rooms, now abandoned, that sat on the southern edge of
town on Route 7 not far from its intersection with 341. Their plans
were modest enough: three rehabilitated living units within the
building, and three new ones added to the grounds.

"I like the symbolism of the old Town Hall," Rainsley told me at
the time.

Later I saw him in town and asked him how he and the group
were doing.

"It's not as if I can really afford the time," he replied, looking even
gaunter than he normally did. "It's a battle. Even my three-year-old
daughter detects it. You know, Daddy is out doing things. And it
would be better to have him home. And that will continue. There's
a certain energy that this place consumes."

I asked him whether he was receiving any cooperation from the
town government. He sighed and shook his head.

"I'll tell you what kind of cooperation," he said. "Right now
they're doing an entire rewrite of the zoning regulations. Our group
has asked for input into this. But you know what they say? 'No, no,
it's too expensive per hour. We don't have time for that. If you have

suggestions, you might put them on a piece of paper and send them to us.' Are these suggestions going to be raised or not? God only knows.

"In fact," the minister went on, "There's virtually *no* public input. You don't read a thing about it in the local paper. No one is asking the people of the town what they want to see in zoning, including affordable housing. I think it's sort of a closed system."

In the meantime, Donald Connery and his ginger group of Citizens for Controlled Growth—having achieved little in the way of substance in the months since it was formed—transmuted their efforts into a new phase. In February 1989 several members of CCG incorporated themselves as a new entity, The Kent Land Trust.

Land Trusts were another phenomenon of the region and of the times.

By the time Connery's group coalesced, there were nearly eight hundred land trusts across the United States, about half of them formed since the beginning of the decade. Most were administered by small, localized nonprofit groups. The plurality of them, and most of the significantly powerful and aggressive ones, were clustered in the Northeast, particularly in Connecticut and Massachusetts, where land values were higher and rising faster than in nearly any other part of the country.

Land trusts, as devices to protect scenic land, were not unique to the late twentieth century. Their origins were in nineteenth-century New England, where sedate and civic-minded organizations gained legal authority to preserve the vast estates of deceased landowners. They did not take on the characteristics of political action groups, however, until the 1980s, and when they did, the impetus sprang from the same source that fueled Affordable Housing: the Reagan Administration and its withdrawal from social spending. Not only did the federal government radically reduce its spending for land acquisition during the Reagan years: with James Watt as Secretary of the Interior, it gave every signal that even lands that had been set aside for public use—national parks, for instance—would increasingly be fair game for development. This new vacuum of official respect for the sanctity of open land brought land trusts rushing in.

Land trusts financed their operations in various ways—the larger the organization, the more sophisticated its monetary resources were likely to be—but most depended, essentially, on a resale of the land they had acquired from private owners, the terms of the resale conditioned by the trust's insistence on environmental and aesthetic standards. Some trusts, in the early days of the movement, functioned in ways that mirrored the quick-strike tactics of the developers themselves: a representative (often a lawyer) of a large, unnamed corporation, would purchase several thousand acres of some forest land in some New England county, allowing local officials to assume that the land would be used for development (and the generation of new taxes). Sometimes, to further the ruse, the representative would go so far as to apply for permission to subdivide the land. Later, after the sale was consummated, the purchaser—surprise!—would throw off his corporate cloak to reveal himself, Robin Hood–like, to be an agent for a conservancy or a land trust. As the town or county chief executive, in the role of Sheriff of Nottingham, gnashed his teeth in frustration, the conservancy agent and his merry men would be negotiating to resell the land—to the State of New York, say, as a forest preserve. (To add insult to injury, sometimes the conservancy people were able to realize healthy profits on their resales.)

Donald Connery and his group were not quite so roguish as all that in their tactics. Nor were they as absolute in their goals. They did not have the resources to prevent land from being developed altogether. Their limited and realistic goal—as my mountaintop friend might have put it—was to mitigate.

"We try to target the properties in Kent that are valuable, and might be saved from the kind of development that would destroy the landscape and the ambience," Connery said. "Then we go to these people. Maybe we get to them even before they've actively thought about selling for development. Our strategy is to pick a member of the land trust who knows those people as friends. And we go to them, to Farmer Jones who's now in his seventies or eighties, and we say, you know, 'Have you thought about the future? How would you like your two hundred acres to go into the future, even without you? What would you like your heirs to do?'

"If they say they're going to sell to a developer at the highest price," Connery continued, "We say, 'Well, terrific, because you deserve, after all these years of work, to have that money. But you don't have to sell it to a developer! You can sell it to us for the same amount. If he's gonna pay you two million dollars, we might be able to pay you two million.'

"You see," said Connery, "we might have a certain fund we could call on to pay for a bank loan. We would get a loan to buy the property. Then, with the help of a designer, or an architect, we'd figure out how a portion of that land—a third, or a quarter—could be developed, leaving the rest as open space. We're not trying to stamp out development," Connery acknowledged. "We're trying to control the process."

But as the 1980s spun along in Kent, the question seemed not to be how to control the process, but rather whether the process was still amenable to control.

In July of 1987 Leo Tobin gave up his last cow. Tobin was eighty-four. His grandfather had come over from Ireland more than one hundred years before, and started dairy farming. At about the same time Bill Litwin applied for a permit to built twenty-eight condominiums behind Kent Town Center.

Paul Abbott, the dapper science teacher who had gained notoriety as the development-minded chairman of the Kent Planning and Zoning Commission, resigned. He was replaced by a retired New York marketing professional named Paul Moroz, a whimsical and deliberate man with a goatee who had sometimes played Santa Claus for the town's children at the annual Christmas gingerbread-cookie bake sale at the Community Center. Moroz announced that the time had come to hire a professional planner for regular consulting. He said he thought it would be the only way to stay ahead of the decisions that must be made.

In January 1988 two developers new to the area acquired large parcels of land in North Kent. One acquisition saw the transfer of 210 acres for $1,610,000. The other involved 241 acres. No price was announced.

Also in that month, the original purchasers of the Conboy Farm property—the acquisition that had opened up the era of large-scale development around Kent—announced that they were offering the farm, and some adjoining acreage, to a New York development firm. The original purchasers had agreed that forty acres of the 163-acre property would be deeded to the Weantinoge Heritage Land Trust. But the prospective buyer said he would not buy the property with the land-trust agreement attached. He asked instead for a restrictive covenant.

Paul Moroz announced that the 1988 budget for planning and zoning had gone up 50 percent over the previous year's, and might go up even more in the following year. He stated his opinion that the commission should have legal help to offset what he called "a case of laymen against professionals."

In February 1988 Kent's first selectman, Maureen Brady, called a meeting to address safety and pollution concerns on the nearby Appalachian Trail. She called the meeting in response to a report from the Appalachian Mountain Club that had described the pickup of seven bagfuls of garbage along River Road, Bulls Bridge Gorge and the trail in that area.

In July of that year, John McGuinness entered a nolo contendere plea in the case of the automobile accident that killed Dorothy Gawel. He subsequently served a brief jail sentence.

In September, a local newspaper editorial, titled "The Decline of the Farm," observed that "Annabel Irving parted with her Angus beef cattle last week—and this only two years after Bill Newton stopped milking and parted with his herd. John Dubray sold off his milk cattle about four years ago and just before that Katharine Evarts got rid of her prize herd . . . Most of these lands are glittering prizes for developers."

In October, yet another New York development company purchased the Conboy property, this time for $2,146,750. In that month there were four property sales of more than $1 million each. One local family estate had gone for $2.3 million.

On one weekend in November, news got out of three local break-ins in two days.

In December, newspaper accounts warned of "urban creep" headed up Route 7 toward Kent from New Milford. A cluster-housing development had just been completed there—fifty-six two-bedroom dwellings, selling for $160,000 to $175,000. Forty-five had already been sold.

And in the late summer of 1988 a small counterveiling event occurred, scarcely noticed amidst all the greater currents swirling about Kent: a family of weekenders, the Powerses, put their house on the market and left for somewhere else. Our five-year tenure on the margins of Kent town life came to an end, as did our life as urban dwellers. We were headed for Vermont and what we hoped would be a permanent stay in a small town there—"permanent," we supposed, meaning at least enough time to change our license plates.

Chapter XVIII

By the late fall of 1989—as drug wars, racial killings and homelessness deepened the national perception of an urban breakdown—the small Illinois town of Cairo had fallen more deeply into Richard Poston's redemptive grip than anyone who lived there could possibly have suspected. I did not suspect it myself for several months after my first visits there, and then only by gradual increments. I had sensed his fundamental seriousness, of course, from the moment I'd first met him outside Glen's Mid-America, the John Philip Sousa pounding on his tapedeck, and never had an instant's occasion to doubt it thereafter. It was the *extent* of his seriousness that I was not, for some time, prepared to grasp.

Perhaps his small frame, or the gray pallor of his parchment skin, or the red fatigue at his eyes, or his atemporal lingo and wardrobe, or the pervading dreaminess of his demeanor—he never seemed to live *completely* in the moment—perhaps these attributes obscured the true force of the engines that roared inside him.

His single-mindedness was impossible to overlook. I had gone so far as to impute to him a mild tendency toward compulsion, even the faint promise of fanaticism. But nothing I knew about him had equipped me, as yet, to comprehend the absolute purity of his will. It required distance, not proximity, to gain that comprehension.

Poston himself supplied the distance.

He receded from the daily life of Cairo after May of 1988. He became a phantom. He floated above and beyond the constraints of the small town and its discontents, and began to operate on a vaster grid. No longer was he an irritating buzz in Al Moss's ear, and the sudden silence, for Moss, must have been deafening.

Doc Poston left Operation Enterprise's day-to-day functionings in the hands of his ally, Angela Greenwell, and launched himself on a quest, an odyssey, the complete terms and goals of which were known only to him.

I followed this odyssey, or parts of it, from the remove of half a continent. My own visits to Cairo had ceased as I worked out the terms of my own future, and my family's, back east. In the spring of 1988 I quit my comfortable job as a journalist in New York. Like many people I knew, I was tired of my own adrenaline. I wanted to live in a town again. Some possibilities were opening up in Vermont, and it seemed likely that by the end of the summer we would move there, leaving both New York and Kent behind. Without my being consciously aware of it, Cairo and its discontents were starting to slip into a hazy past. This was not exactly a novel fate for the town.

Poston kept in touch during that period: a letter would come in, or a telephone call. His whereabouts frequently astonished me. He traveled to Chicago, and often to Springfield, the capital of Illinois, and St. Louis, and even Washington—places that had some plausible connection to his efforts on behalf of Cairo. But as the months went on he also turned up in less explicable environs: Memphis (several times); Louisville (several times); Vicksburg and Jackson, Mississippi; Davenport, Iowa. He visited places unbeknownst to me until I examined his full travel log many months later: he blew into Indianapolis; he surfaced in Athens and West Barboursville, West Virginia; he checked in at Chapel Hill and Williamsburg and Arlington and Nashville. Lexington, he visited, and Normal, Illinois, and Morgantown, North Carolina, and Cape Girardeau. Decatur was on his itinerary, and Edwardsville, and Peoria, and Kankakee.

The Washington trips were by plane; his Chicago trip was by train. Most of the rest of his journeys he made alone in his elderly Chrysler sedan. By his own careful reckoning, his automobile travels on behalf of Cairo from early 1987 through the end of 1989 totaled 44,206 miles.

His missions varied. Speechifying—perhaps his one true recreation—was prominent among them. In Davenport he received an achievement award from the International Community Development Society. In Athens, West Virginia, he keynoted a community development conference, using Cairo as a case study. He addressed dinner meetings; he conducted workshops; he met with coalitions.

Wrangling was another object of his travels. He must have become a fixture in the state capitol building at Springfield—I could picture his bent-ahead, prowling figure—lobbying legislators ("negotiating," he preferred to call it) for funds, bequests and easements of all kinds to speed along his various schemes and projects for Operation Enterprise. In Chicago he buttonholed an Internal Revenue Service functionary to "expedite," as he delicately put it to me later, a tax-exempt status for a corporation he'd cooked up: Confluence Community Development, Inc.

The range of his attention span was breathtaking. Through all his travels and his rarified strategic planning, Poston never really relinquished control of his operational base in Cairo. A letter, sent to him in August 1988 from the vice president of a Carbondale construction company, acknowledged a recent stint of Doc's lobbying. "Dear Dr. Poston," it began, "This letter is to confirm our estimate to you for the paving of the roadway into Fort Defiance at Cairo. We propose to do the necessary grading, apply a prime coat, and 2" of bituminous concrete surface for a total cost of $36,835. I know how hard you are working to give the historic Cairo area a boost. Therefore, we have given you a 10 percent discount from a normal price on the work. . . ."

But on the great bulk of these highway journeys, Doc Poston was after something larger, deeper, more consequential, at once more corporeal and more mythical than easements or tax-exemptions or even funding grants—although funding grants were a vastly important goal in Poston's odyssey.

Memphis, and Louisville, and Vicksburg, and St. Louis were river towns. More specifically, each was a district center for the U.S. Army Corps of Engineers.

Poston was after a riverboat. Or the idea of a riverboat. And the Army Corps was just the sort of outfit that might have a spare riverboat or two lying around.

Poston's riverboat fixation represented a new phase in his strategic thinking about Cairo—or perhaps an acknowledgment of a strategy he'd been working out since he first arrived in the town. It signaled his comprehension that persuasion alone—rhetoric, speechmaking, storytelling—would not rally Cairo. His protestations of "renewed hope" and a "historic turnaround," his assurances to all and sundry that "concerted civic initiative has taken hold," that "blacks and whites are pulling together," that "people long mired in poverty are participating"—all of that was fine for the regional press and for local consumption, useful for keeping the recruits from wandering off the post. On the other hand, there was Al Moss and there was Bill Wolter, and there was the invisible aristocracy. And as long as those fixed entities held true to their nature, Operation Enterprise was going to remain—to put it in the starkest of possible terms—a kind of community therapy group, a collection of fond dreamers. And the town would slide along toward its inevitable doom.

As a grass-roots force, Operation Enterprise had peaked—arguably, it had peaked during that first cleanup of Fort Defiance Park, or during the census-taking. Although Poston never conceded such a thing, the brute reality of it was inescapable to a man of his perceptions.

If that was the case, Richard Poston was left with two clear choices.

One was to quit; to concede defeat and leave the town to recover as best it could from its latest failed dream of El Dorado.

The other, more to Poston's tastes, was to attack with reinforcements—to hit Cairo with a get-rich scheme the likes of which the little river town hadn't dreamed of since the heyday of the Illinois Central Railroad.

Such a blitzkrieg would accomplish two things. It would supply Cairo with the capital transfusion the moribund town had needed for at least seventy-five years. More strategically, however, it would create something for the long term that perhaps not even Poston himself, at first, had consciously considered. A big, splashy, successful "attraction," implanted by outside development capital—a philanthropic grant, say—would empower Richard Poston, acting of course as the surrogate for the town, to create a kind of para-government: a superstructure of economic leverage that would render Al Moss and his puppet City Council, to a certain extent, irrelevant.

The problem—Operation Enterprise notwithstanding—was that Richard Poston was not an agency, not an organization, not a bureaucracy with WATS lines and secretaries and vice presidents in charge of development. He was not even, in this area at least, an extension of Southern Illinois University, with the support systems of that institution at his disposal. He was Richard Poston, a seventy-four-year-old man with some personal letterhead stationery and a gift for getting through, and if any philanthropic funding was to come into Cairo, Poston was going to have to scare it up. Himself. From scratch.

"I always detested writing grant proposals," he wrote to me in the summer of 1988. "I don't think of myself as a grantsman, but as a community developer. Yet I must face hard reality." (As I read this I could not resist positioning myself, once again, in Poston's imaginary audience.) "If Cairo is to be transformed into the vibrant town of prosperity its richness in history and its geographical location make possible, we've got to have outside money—cash, a packaging of investment capital . . . And I'm the guy who has to go after that, bring it in, and supply the decent people with the ammunition they must have to win the victory." (Cheers! Whistles!)

I would read these letters, or hang up the phone, and imagine Poston at large on the road: Poston rampant; Poston hunched over the wheel of that old sedan somewhere outside Cape Girardeau or Wheaton, squinting and chain-smoking his Now cigarettes, Sousa on his tapedeck. Poston rehearsing his presentation like a drummer rehearsing his summer line; Poston in some eighth-floor Midwestern motel room, draping his timeless pants over a wooden hanger, checking a phone number; Poston exhausted to distraction, moving his lips, sleeping a little; the collapsible alarm clock, a shower and the hair-blower, coffee in the coffee shop, refining the pitch, confirming the appointment, clean shirt, flirting with the secretary, a handshake, the pitch, the planning grant proposal from the attaché case, so long to the secretary, check out from the Ramada, and on the road again. Like a ghost.

". . . Going for the political muscle, which will require a lot of travel, a seven-day work-week, and long night hours . . ."

"Frank Pettis of the Illinois Humanities Council has strongly urged me to write this letter," he wrote to the MacArthur Foundation in September. "It concerns a program of comprehensive community, economic and cultural development . . . I chose Cairo, at the confluence of our nation's two mightiest waterways . . . if it were to succeed in reversing that course of history . . ."

"Enclosed is the economic development proposal we discussed during our meeting in Chicago Oct. 20," he wrote to the Joyce Foundation a few months later. "As I contemplate the magnitude of what we have set out to accomplish . . . the difference it can make for the well-being of our nation . . . priceless ingredients that make our American system of free enterprise so great a marvel of human endeavor . . . "

There was an element of personal pride in these initiatives, as there was in nearly everything I saw Poston undertake. Dealing with foundations took him back to his glory years; the prestigious days of his work with the federal agencies, the presidential commissions, the days of CARE and the Peace Corps. And yet there was no escaping the realities of elapsed time.

"The contacts I once had in the foundation world date back twenty-five years," he wrote ruefully to me in September 1988, "six months to the day after the Quinstate Forum"—as he noted beside the letter's date—"and all the top executives I used to work with are gone—retired or deceased.

"This means that, in addition to having more than I have time for, I'm now faced by the monumental task of researching foundations, studying their guidelines, and cultivating new contacts. The one thing that hasn't changed in those 25 years is that no matter how you write your proposals, it's who you know that really counts. So, in effect, I'm starting all over again. However, I did get that $10,000 from the Chicago-based corporation whose name I'm pledged not to reveal, and somehow, someday, I'll get others."

If Doc Poston conceded the odds against his harvesting a significant philanthropic grant, he suffered absolutely no doubts whatsoever as to how he would use the money if it came his way. He would buy a riverboat.

His riverboat-shopping had been characteristically scrupulous and thorough—it had accounted for a significant percent of those 44,206 miles; on one scarcely untypical four-day stretch alone, in September 1988, he had tooled to Memphis, then to Vicksburg, then to Jackson, Mississippi; and then back home—and it had turned up some prospects. "The Army Corps has said they'd give us the 24-by-46-foot dredge Ockerson," he wrote from Memphis, "which they have declared surplus. I have to find a way to get it hooked to a tow to move it out of the Ensley Engineering Yard, find out what it will cost to strip out the machinery, and convert the vessel to a showboat." While there, he had also visited a private company to kick the hubcaps of an old paddle-wheeler on sale for $33,000. "I think it's too small," he fretted in his letter, "and don't know yet what it would cost to rehabilitate, but once we have the money the Corps tells me I can bring them way down in that selling price. It's called the 'Arkansas'. . . ."

In Vicksburg there was "a highly experienced riverboat man." In Louisville there was "a naval architect who has offered to help me."

But the apple of the old man's eye, clearly, lay at anchor on the Mississippi at St. Louis. This was the Belle Angeline, a replica of a nineteenth-century showboat built in 1977 as a commercial attraction, but presently shut down and lying vacant at the levee. Poston's voice had fairly quivered with covetousness when he'd told me about it by telephone.

"I went through it, Ron! It's luxurious! It's been empty four years! The operator was under-capitalized! The price is $850,000! I wanted 'em to give it to us for nothin'! Take a tax write-off! They don't think they can afford it! I've got to get some big foundation money! Think of it! We could push it by towboat from St. Louis right down to Cairo. Why, the St. Louis press and television stations would go wild over that!"

A riverboat off the Cairo shoreline, of course presupposed an *access* to the Cairo shoreline. But certain things were developing in Southern Illinois politics—abetted by a certain amount of behind-the-scenes work by Richard Poston—that seemed reasonably certain of providing that access.

The question of *which* riverboat aside, a sort of proto-riverboat had begun to form in Poston's mind, and then on enameled paper, limned with an artist's full-color illustrations: a most fantastical and plenipotent riverboat indeed; a riverboat that would unload the cargo of a separate economic structure upon the town that Mayor Al Moss and Bill Wolter presently controlled.

The riverboat even featured a human symbol, a goddess of pure Postonian proportions—at once seductive and maternal, at once anachronistic and weirdly apt: a bejeweled and full-bosomed 1890s dance-hall girl in a slit scarlet gown, a tilted chapeau, a feather boa, and black mesh stockings just above the knee.

(Dance-hall girls occupied a special niche in Doc Poston's private mythos, as I had learned by then. They were cherished artifacts of his past, preserved and displayed in the present without self-consciousness or irony. In the summer of 1988, he was already looking forward to a Poston family tradition: his annual birthday/New Year's trip to Houston with his wife Marjorie to visit their daughter. "She always takes us to the Old San Francisco Steak House, Ron!" he'd told me. "They have the Girl in Red on a swing there! And at midnight she swings all the way up to the ceiling and kicks the cowbell! They have a honky-tonk pianist! It's a jam-packed place, Ron! You have to have a reservation to get in there!")

As executed by a Cairo artist named Alice Johnston, the symbolic chanteuse posed, hand on hip, on the cover of a loose-leaf brochure titled *Cairo's History/Cairo's Future*. She was the figurative hostess of Doc Poston's dream attraction: a three-decked nineteenth-century riverboat that would be anchored off Fort Defiance Park on the Ohio River—directly, as it worked out, in Bill Wolter's watery backyard.

The riverboat, in Poston's vision, would offer an irresistible lure to many of the 2,482,000 motorists streaking past Cairo each year on Interstate 57 to the north. It would stand, or float, as the centerpiece of the town's grand resurgence; it would at once honor and illuminate Cairo's gaudy, ambitious past, and serve as the fulfillment of that past's abiding prophecy. It would invest Cairo with its destiny as El Dorado.

So many natural assets . . .

Poston's plans for the riverboat, as inventoried inside the brochure, displayed his familiar penchant for obsessive, inexhaustible detail. But they hinted, to me at least, at something more unexpected and gently fantastical than that. They hinted that a boy survived somewhere inside the old man: a boy from a long-ago and destitute time, constructing Sinbad fantasies out of the images of opulence that might have glittered, in the river's-edge distance, in the dry Missouri of the 1930s.

Poston's riverboat was a riverboat such as never plied any stream known to Mark Twain. It would need a special name to encompass its functions as Showboat–Dinner Theatre–Museum and Cultural Center. It would be stocked with all the accoutrements of pleasure that a dutiful boy grown ancient might imagine. And if some of those accoutrements struck the late-century senses as a bit outdated, not to say naive (hardly the kind of diversions a state-of-the-art marketing specialist, say, might recommend to a professional attractions-developing client), then perhaps it was the late-century senses that needed readjusting.

Poston's riverboat would have Dixieland bands. It would have can-can dancers and minstrels. There would be a restaurant on the second deck, with food to be prepared in the hull galley and sent up by dumbwaiter, unless the occasion called for steam-table smorgasbord, and a donor's fountain, to be constructed of polished limestone with waterspouts and colored lighting, would display the names of financial contributors.

The boy had licked his pencil-point and thought of everything. "On the top deck," he wrote in the brochure, "where the pilot house and management office is located, there will be an organ, a bar and cocktail lounge, and a promenade area. Speakers will enable patrons to hear the orchestra which will be playing on a lower deck."

(Orchestra. . . ?)

The second deck would contain the restaurant, "where violinists will roam among the diners, and expansive windows will afford a breathtaking view of the rivers."

(Violinists. . . ?)

The first deck would house a theater, complete with a stage and an orchestra pit. "The theater will utilize nonstationary cushion chairback seats," Poston wrote. "This will allow for expanding the size of the dining area when a major performance is scheduled. . . . The utilization of chairback rather than stationary seats will provide a showboat theater deck which can be adapted for use as a conference hall, [or] partitioned for seminars and general meetings, as well as providing space for art exhibitions, presentations and individual performances."

There would be floor lighting, a prompter, a retractable cinema screen for those seminars and conferences. "However," Poston was quick to assure, "all construction and stage design will be in the motif of the period, thus maintaining the museum's historic integrity."

The hull, below the water line, would provide dressing rooms, a staff lounge, areas for food storage, and the kitchen.

Back to the top deck: here would be the wheelhouse, the pilot and captain's quarters *(pilot and captain. . . ?)*, calliope organ and smokestacks. "The pilothouse will be constructed authentically in every detail," Poston wrote, "as will be the placing of the calliope organ. As with the first and second deck, this deck too will provide a relaxing promenade where patrons might take refreshments while enjoying the scenic quality of the rivers."

The name of the boat, by the way, would be the *CAIRO.* "The selection of the name *CAIRO* for the showboat," Poston wrote, "will serve to identify both the community and the showboat as well as the project. In time, when Cairo is mentioned, individuals will immediately be cognizant of the showboat and the historic restoration of this famous old river town."

Ah, yes: *the historic restoration of this famous old river town.* In that phrase, Doc Poston's brochure betrayed the master plan, of which the riverboat—however lovingly stocked and detailed in Poston's imagination—was simply one facet. "Phase I," as the brochure put it.

In Phase II, Poston proposed to throw a kind of restoration-developmental shell across the decaying surface of the town itself.

"Original blueprints and plats of the town have been studied," Poston wrote, "which will facilitate an authentic restoration of the city as it existed, or provide for its reconstruction as an early river town.

"As Phase I becomes functional, the revenues it generates beyond expenses . . . will be utilized for restoring or reconstructing Cairo's numerous landmark historical facilities. The intent is to restore all original buildings to the state they existed [sic] when constructed. Also, funds will be raised to reconstruct present-day business facilities to simulate the structures of the time, thereby maintaining the continuity and setting of the 1800s and early 1900s."

But not even a complete, attraction-oriented face-lifting of municipal Cairo exhausted the imagination of the boy inside the old man. (As I read through this brochure, I tested my own imagination—I tried to picture the reactions of Al Moss and Bill Wolter as they riffled through its pages.) All of this was but prologue to Phase III.

Phase III would not be containable by the town of Cairo alone. It would require the cooperation of three states.

"The Ohio and Mississippi Rivers have bound the interests and needs of this region encompassing Illinois, Kentucky and Missouri into a common bond," Poston wrote. "Therefore, the intent of Phase III is to physically link the three states by a theme park which will accentuate the historical period as Busch Gardens does or Williamsburg, Va."

The Illinois shore would represent Cairo "as it first appeared as a wilderness fort, then as a trading center and a major river hub. The Missouri side of the Mississippi River would be used to portray the westward movement that faced the pioneers. Replicas of cavalry outposts, Indian villages, mining towns and western towns would enable the visitor to grasp the magnitude of what confronted the pioneers after they left the safety of developed lands and cities. . . .

"The Kentucky side of the Ohio River would be developed to demonstrate the lifestyles found in the river cities of the South, the conditions found during the Civil War, and emphasis placed on the value of river technology and its use in the past, the present and for the future.

"Having visited the restored historical sites and the theme park, visitors will be able to return home with a greater appreciation for the traditions, the dedication and the sweat that built their heritage and freedoms."

Those heritage-appreciating and magnitude-grasping visitors would, of course, require a convenient, late-twentieth-century system for negotiating the three states and two rivers. Doc Poston's imagination was equal to this need.

"Travel through the theme park," he wrote, "would be by a tram system. This would be set up on a circuit tour. The circuit would link the three sites of the theme park as well as make stops at key intervals throughout the historically restored or reconstructed projects. Areas of historical significance in all three states will eventually be restored."

All of this—the entire dream—depended on Poston's gaining access to the riverfront. And access to a riverfront dominated by the sort of municipal-business axis that held sway in Cairo would appear, on the face of it, next to impossible. But as he developed his plans, Poston knew that a bill was making its way through the Illinois Legislature that could significantly diminish this axis's control. The bill was for a state-created port district, one that would be administered by a governing authority that would supersede the city's control.

And so as he worked toward his master revision of Cairo, Doc Poston allied himself with the port district proponents as well.

Historical significance. Heritage.
So many natural assets . . .
The contradictions and ironies embedded in this scheme were as stupendously interlayered as the overwrought hallucination of "heritage" that Doc Poston had conjured, with himself in the role of heritage-master. As I read them over—they'd arrived in a fat brown parcel in the mail one day—and thought about them, I found that I could not purge from my mind a haunting and frightful phrase that had bubbled briefly into the American argot during the Vietnam war: *"We had to destroy this village in order to save it."*

This association of that bleak apology was grossly unfair, of course, in certain perfectly obvious ways. What Richard Poston intended for Cairo was, without question, infinitely more benign than the intentions of the U.S. Army officer who ordered the application of Zippo lighters to the thatched roofs of the Vietnamese peasant village targeted for "saving."

And yet the two situations inescapably shared a common pool of

American convictions and fantasies—even a cockeyed sort of flawed optimism. One such optimistic conviction was that no human or societal predicament was too hopeless, or too complex, to be remedied by the fix of technology—of human engineering. Another was that reality was pretty much what one chose to make of it.

In Cairo's case (as well as that of the Vietnamese village, for that matter) there existed plenty of precedent to lend credence to those convictions.

Heritage attractions had become so numbingly commonplace on the American landscape by the 1980s that they seemed at times almost to form a parallel universe, a shadow-nation of artifice and illusion. A strange deadpan *urr*-society inhabited this universe: women in farthingales and poke bonnets, men in jerkins and hob-nailed boots, barefoot boys with fishin' poles 'n' patched knickers, waitresses in dirndls, bellhops in greaves and gambadoes. . . . From restored bed-and-breakfast inns to shopping-mall arcades to steakhouses to outdoor museums to dude ranches to centennial celebrations to rehabilitated commercial districts to theme parks to entire filigreed cities-within-cities, "heritage" trilled its two-note invitation to the American-in-transit: learn a little history. Have a little fun.

Roadside attractions—the schematic ancestors of Doc Poston's riverboat—dated from the dawn of America's long drift toward synthetic reality. They dated virtually from the inception of paved roads themselves. It was the automobile, of course, that made paved roads necessary, just as it was the automobile that evacuated the nation's farm and farmtown populations along these paved roads and deposited them in cities—thus creating a vast hunger, growing out of cultural memory, for the illusion of town.

During the years of the voyage out—from town to city—the road-side was a fabulous, Oz-like dreamscape, hurtling the motorist into a futuristic corridor of instant gratification and wish-fulfillment. The 1920s saw a highway culture crowded with barbecue stands shaped like pigs, duck retail outlets shaped like ducks; there were building-sized doughnuts, hamburgers and ice-cream cones. Gas stations presented themselves as outsize cowboy Stetsons; Motel cabins as tepees, restaurants as Dutch windmills, as neocolonial mansions, as derby hats. As early as 1932, the *Ladies Home Journal* was crusading against what it called "the hideous American road-side spectacle."

It was just the sort of spectacle that might have caught the secret fancy of an otherwise earnest, impoverished, romantic young man embarked on a long automobile trip west from Missouri to Montana.

But even by that early time, the road back—back to an illusory Arcadia—was already well under construction.

In 1926 John D. Rockefeller Jr. wrote a cryptic telegram to an Episcopalian minister in Virginia that inaugurated the American mania for historic "preservation," a trend that soon cross-fertilized with the less dignified aspects of roadside attractions. Rockefeller's telegram read: THIS WILL AUTHORIZE THE PURCHASE OF THE ANTIQUE WE LAST DISCUSSED AT 8. (SIGNED) DAVID'S FATHER.

The "antique" was an eighteenth-century estate known as the Ludwell-Paradise House, after two families who had owned it. The setting was Williamsburg, Virginia. The "8" referred to $8,000. The Rockefeller purchase grew, over the years, into the acquisition of eighty-eight buildings of the same period, in the area that came to be known worldwide as Colonial Williamsburg.

Williamsburg is the national shrine—perhaps the world shrine—to heritage-kitsch; its name a mantra on the lips of every travel agent, chamber-of-commerce president and development advisor in the country. Its 175 acres near Interstate 64 about fifty miles east of Richmond are a sanitized, color-coded, landscaped, period-costumed, restroomed, golf-coursed, swimming-pooled, gift-shopped masterpiece of historical airbrushing, in which visitors clutching Patriot's Passes ($25 the adult, $12.50 the child) can hop a Historic Area Bus to tool down Duke of Gloucester Street and have a squint at the various blacksmiths, coopersmiths, silversmiths, lumbersmiths, gunsmiths, wheelwrights, wigmakers, bookbinders, bootmakers, harnessmakers, milliners, tailors, bakers, salthouses, smokehouses, toolhouses, icehouses, coachhouses, privies, and a gaol. There are Dining Opportunities and Shopping Opportunities. There are four taverns. In 1988 the attraction drew 1,250,000 visitors, including three museum curators from the Soviet Union, one of whom was the director of something called the Vladimir Suzdal Restoration.

In that same year—1926—in Hannibal, Missouri, a seventy-five-year-old lawyer and philanthropist named George A. Mahan commissioned a statue to be built in the town: the first statue ever, it is commonly believed, to honor two purely literary characters. The characters were Tom Sawyer and Huckleberry Finn, and the statue drew attention to the fact that Hannibal was the boyhood home of their creator, Samuel Langhorne Clemens—Mark Twain. (Mahan had purchased and thus preserved Clemens's boyhood home in 1911, a year after the author's death.) The completion of the Mark Twain Bridge across the Mississippi River in 1936 placed Hannibal squarely in the path of the Pikes Peak Ocean-to-Ocean Highway—Route 36—and opened the little town up to a national stream of visitors during the great age of auto touring: soon Hannibal boasted a paved and lighted Mark Twain Cave, a Mark Twain Museum, and a Mark Twain Memorial Lighthouse; and, as the years wore on, a Tom Sawyer theater, an Injun Joe motel, a Becky Thatcher restaurant, a Mark Twain diorama, an annual Tom Sawyer Days celebration (featuring a fencepainting contest "sanctioned by the U.S. Congress") and a comestible, advertised on giant billboards, called Mark Twain Fried Chicken.

Twenty-four years after Rockefeller's telegram and George Mahan's statue, a movement began in Winston-Salem, North Carolina, to preserve the old original town—a community established by the Moravians, a fifteenth-century German Protestant sect that antedated Martin Luther. The brethren, having immigrated to America and founded the city of Bethlehem in the 1740s, purchased 100,000 acres in the North Carolina frontier some twenty years later and built on it a planned, German-speaking community that survived until industrialism overtook it in 1856. Its buildings survived into the twentieth century. The attraction known as Old Salem presently encompasses ninety-one buildings on seventy-eight acres within a half-mile of downtown Winston-Salem. It includes two gift shops and a bakery that turns out the Moravian ginger cookie, said to be a particular favorite of the television weatherman Willard Scott. One hundred fifteen thousand paid admission into the attraction in 1988, and its administrators estimated that another 150,000 people came to gaze at it from its perimeters.

Five years after the Old Salem movement, in 1955, heritage got cross-fertilized with packaged fantasy. Disneyland opened its gates in Anaheim, California.

As America urbanized and plowed its authentic past under a widening crust of asphalt and concrete, its strange, deadpan society of crossbred heritage attractions grew. "Preserved" or "historically redeveloped" towns and sites and centers and theme parks and outdoor museums proliferated across the land: Silver Dollar City in Missouri, New Harmony in Indiana, Old Tucson in Arizona,

Deerfield and Sturbridge in Massachusetts, Mystic Seaport in Connecticut, Dollywood in Tennessee, Roadside America in Pennsylvania, Old Town in Kissimmee, Florida; Henry Ford's Greenfield Village in Michigan. There was even, for one brief shining moment, a fundamentalist-Christian entry in the field: Jim and Tammy Faye Bakker's Heritage USA in Charleston, South Carolina.

As more and more heritage attractions entered the lists, a certain inevitable rationale began to attach to them—an economic rationale. With growing frequency these enterprises began to turn up in towns or regions or urban sectors that had lost their grip on an indigenous economy: a manufacturing plant had left, or the trains had stopped coming through, or the surrounding farms had fallen on hard times. When one or another of these calamities struck, there always seemed to appear, sooner or later, some professional with a business card that read, HISTORIC REDEVELOPMENT, or COMMEMORATION SPECIALIST, or CONSULTANTS IN RESOURCE MANAGEMENT. As "Rust Belt" and "Forgottonia" began to define large sectors of the country, "heritage" became a kind of entrepreneurial anti-venom, a commercial quick-fix. Those who did not understand history, to paraphrase Santayana, were doomed to pay admission for it.

Decaying waterfronts, forgotten neighborhoods, whole sections of cities were targeted for investment, restoration and the requisite tricking-up in period gaud: Gaslight Square in St. Louis, Old Town in Chicago (each of which eventually faded), Faneuil Hall and Lewis Wharf in Boston, Ghiradelli Square and the Cannery in San Francisco. There was Old Atlanta; there was South Street Seaport in New York.

The trend took on a a manic kind of momentum. Entire towns began transforming themselves into theme parks. Large sections of America were beginning to resemble giant dioramic cartoons. Frankenmuth, on the lower peninsula of Michigan, "went Bavarian." Its populace started to wear lederhosen and eat sauerkraut, to the presumed enchantment of tourists passing through on their way north to the upper peninsula.

But at least Frankenmuth had some ancestral connection to Bavaria. By the end of the 1980s it didn't seem to matter whether the theme related to the town's history or not, just so long as it was a theme. Tourism had grown to the third-largest retail service industry in the United States; travelers within the country were spending more than $300 billion a year on goods and services.

The implications for American towns, particularly depressed

towns, were transitional and unambiguous. Towns, in the late twentieth century, had simply ceased being what they had always been, and had begun to be something else.

No more talk, now, of summer evenings in Knoxville. No more white towns drowsing in the sunshine of a summer morning. No more of the Emersonian idea that all historic nobility rests on possession of the land. No more of Hector St. John de Crèvecoeur's notion that "we are all tillers of the earth, from Nova Scotia to West Florida" (West Florida was now the province of Busch Gardens, a roller-coastered, water-flumed, Tanganyika Tidal Wave'd Jungle of Fun in the West Florida Sun!). No more of the Town as the crucible of necessary American innocence.

No longer did the Town function as a generator of products and values and human beings into the great stream of American life. The stream had been exactly reversed: now products came from somewhere else to transform the face of the Town; now values were imported from distant marketing and merchandising centers; all so that human beings from the metropolises might now feel inclined to drift through the revised Town, and look, and spend, and move on.

The New York Times, which had begun tracking some of these stories early in 1990, quoted David Edgell, an official of the United States Travel and Tourism Administration, as declaring, "It's happening overnight."

Heritage, it appeared, was the wave of the future.

Viewed in this perspective, Richard Poston's master plan for Cairo had the ring of inevitability about it—even of genius. Here, finally, was the consolidating mechanism for all those natural assets. Here was a chance for the sordid, violent old town to rouse itself from death's doorstep and reassert its ancient prophetic claim on the nation's attention.

Here, in other words, was a chance for Cairo to cash in.

Unfortunately, it was not all that simple. The heritage of "heritage," in commercial American life, had grown as questionable economically as it had always been aesthetically—all those cartoonish town meeting halls, those frontier delis, those emasculated avuncular Lincolns and Jeffersons and Twains; all that coin-operated oratory and souvenir craft and molded-plastic logcabinry. (This was an age, after all, when the Statue of Liberty's hundredth anniversary would be celebrated with Elvis look-alikes; when a television network could "honor" the Reverend Dr. Martin

Luther King Jr.'s official holiday with an hour of singing and dancing and scarcely a mention of the civil rights struggle.) It was a forgettable age for remembering.

Not to mention a treacherous one—economically, and in certain other ways. This came home to me one day during a conversation with a convivial man named Richard Wagner. Wagner is a senior executive with the Main Street Center, which is itself a division of the National Trust for Historic Preservation in Washington. The Main Street Center was established in 1980. Since then it has worked with 550 communities in America—each of which was afflicted with either Cairo's syndrome (a crisis of poverty) or Kent's (a crisis of affluence).

"The vast majority are in the 'we-need-to-stimulate-growth' area," Wagner told me. "But as the eighties went on we began more and more to address the questions of growth management."

Wagner didn't need much prompting on the subject of heritage attractions as a panacea for the regeneration of towns.

"The interest in tourism, in the stimulation of the town as a place for tourists to come, is something almost every one of our towns gets excited about," he said. "Tourism was the Holy Grail of the eighties. It's a tremendous industry, you know—the primary or secondary one in thirty-one states.

"So it seems to make a lot of sense to develop tourism. The problem is that this thing you create, this product to attract tourists, is double-edged. It can spell the economic success *or failure* of the whole community."

I asked Richard Wagner how common it was for a community to seize on some point of local history as the thematic base of a tourism project. He sighed.

"Probably in two thirds of our towns," he said. "One of the questions we constantly get asked is, 'Should we "theme" our downtown?' A lot of towns in isolated areas say, 'Gee, we should go Wild West,' or, 'Gee, we should go Colonial.' They all point to Williamsburg. Our argument is that *except* for Williamsburg, it's not a smart thing to do. First, people tend to forget that the Rockefeller family poured about thirty million dollars into Williamsburg in the 1930s, and that the Williamsburg Foundation today is constantly reinvesting its profits. It just doesn't work in all cases, unless you have massive amounts of capital.

"But number two is, you've typecast yourself as a community. These attractions tend to create an artificial culture; it's not really Colonial, or Wild West, or Bavarian, or American, or anything else.

It's a Hollywood creation. And that simply is not healthy for the community. People," said Wagner, "don't do well when they're not allowed to *be* themselves—when they have to 'act out' their own lives."

I asked Wagner about what he called "the flipside" of his organization's involvement in towns—the syndrome of a town that has grown suddenly and unexpectedly rich.

"That's why we're in growth management," he told me. "Look what happened to Jackson Hole, Wyoming. The issue there was the merchandising of the whole town. It was targeted to an affluent market. The natives fill the service jobs, but they don't have the money to buy the stuff displayed in the downtown area. The impact on this sector of the population has been tremendous."

Wagner said that the Main Street Center's philosophy was to look at this sort of revenue—or any sort of revenue—not as an end in itself, but as a subordinate asset to what he called "ongoing management."

"We believe that an existing business district must be well managed," he said. "You can't just leave the health of a community up to market forces. You can't leave it up to the city; it has a larger agenda. You can't leave it up to the Chamber of Commerce, which also has a larger agenda and may not be specialized enough."

I asked Wagner where, then, the responsibility should fall.

"It must fall on a Main Street Organization, which we help create," he replied. "A downtown development authority independent of city control. It has to have involvement from merchants, business leaders, church people, property owners—we try to pull together all the stake-holders, both empowered and non-empowered. We go in and show the people an approach, but it's up to the local people themselves to keep it going. And one of the factors we consider carefully before going in is the matter of political will."

The more Richard Wagner talked, it struck me, the more he sounded like Richard Poston. How ironic it was, then, that the more Richard Poston had been speaking lately, the more he was sounding like the sort of person the Main Street Center was warning its clients to be wary of.

Perhaps I was jaundiced in this reaction. Just three or four years before, I had watched as my home town of Hannibal, Missouri, was nearly torn apart by a heritage project, dreamed up by a New York–based consultant (whose motto for commemorative celebrations was "pour brandy on it and light it") and designed to create a historic influx of tourists: an eight-month-long celebration of Mark Twain's Sesquicentennial birthday. Early plans—announced to the town as virtual certainties—included a riverboat regatta, a "Good Golly Aunt Polly" rock 'n' roll revue, a "Huck-sters" raft race, the Federation Internationale d'Aeronautiques helium balloon championships, an American storytellers/Mark Twain humor symposium, two musical stage productions and a folk opera based on "The Notorious Jumping Frog of Calaveras County"—not to mention weekly fireworks displays, daily parades and a total of 432 stories told in daily sessions from a specially designed Storyteller's Tree.

Between 750,000 and a million visitors would come to see all of this. Their aggregate spending would generate a quarter of a billion dollars into the deflated economy of northeast Missouri.

None of it had happened. The consultant had misread the sophistication of Hannibal, and its eager city fathers had misread the consultant's misreading. The necessary corporate sponsors did not take the small town seriously; they did not sponsor. There was a Sesquicentennial, but it was subdued and chastened and local. In the detritus of the broken promises and failed plans, Hannibal had become—briefly, at least—a seething camp of recriminations and wrecked political careers and self-mockery.

Now came Doc Poston with his plan to impose a make-believe heritage extravaganza on the dying town of Cairo.

What compounded the irony was Poston's essential decency, even innocence. For all his schemes and strategies and sermonizing, for all his lobbying and his grantsmanship and his dramatic trips to Washington, Richard Poston remained an ingenuous man, perhaps the most perfectly ingenuous adult I had ever met. (When I tested my theory on him once—my theory that he had been fascinated by some roadside attraction or other during his trek to Montana as a very young man—he turned his thin face to me, squinted a moment, and said, "I was fascinated by the land itself, Ron.") How strange that this ingenuous American should be the carrier of potential calamity to the very place he had come to save.

Of course there were the circumstances to consider. Had Cairo been much more than it was—a crushed, comatose, cataleptic little town bleeding toward an almost certain extinction—the calamity issue might have seemed a little more compelling. Given the condition of the town, the question of calamity was arguably moot.

. . .

My family and I left New York and its environs for the Champlain Valley of Vermont in the late summer of 1988. A job offer came, from a college town near the Green Mountains. My wife and I were tempted, but felt an unexpected reluctance to leave our familiar urban world. We drove our van to a chamber concert at Lincoln Center, agreeing during the trip to midtown that we would probably turn the offer down. We parked the van on Tenth Avenue. Returning from the music, in the darkness, we found a window smashed and the inside ransacked. On the way home we agreed to accept the offer.

And so we reentered American town life: not weekenders this time, but flatlanders, another invading population that was altering the very permanence it had sought. Route 7 ran through our new hometown, the same Route 7 that ran through Kent—headed toward its northern terminus at Canada. A mountain river eddied through the center of this town, then cascaded into a waterfall under the main street-bridge. There was a white-spired Congregational Church at the crest of a hill; a village green; a sprawling redbrick nineteenth-century inn; a small warren of brick storefronts; a couple of cozy restaurants tucked down in the hollows; an old-fashioned ice-cream parlor; a movie house; a railroad line that carried long freights through a tunnel near the Episcopalian Church at night. There was also a nearly intolerable problem of traffic congestion; an affordable-housing crisis; a struggle for survival among the surrounding dairy farms; an even more afflicted rural underclass; an intractable class warfare (flatlanders against the locals, in its simplest terms) that expressed itself in bitter fights over public-school budgets; and a pervading sense of political helplessness against the large forces of development, bureaucratization, ceaseless and bewildering change.

It was in this ambiguous setting that my family and I cast our lot, and became townspeople.

I did not see Poston for another year—I'm not certain I ever expected to see him again. We continued to keep in touch. He had given himself over almost completely to finding an endowment for his transformation of Cairo. The town meetings in Cairo had gone into suspended animation; the Enterprisers, along with those who opposed the Enterprisers, had little choice but to wonder what he would do next. He had escalated his travels; he moved mainly by air now—he'd landed a modest development grant from a foundation—from his home in Carbondale to Chicago and New York and Washington, systematically combing the major foundations: Ford, MacArthur, Joyce, Hitachi, World Neighbors. When we talked by telephone now, it was all facts and figures. "According to the Rand-McNally Commercial Atlas, Ron," he'd be likely to shout by way of salutation, "there's 3.9 million population living within a radius of 125 miles of that point at Fort Defiance! And effective buying power in 1987 of $57.5 billion! If we develop this according to these plans, Ron, the flow of new money into that area can be absolutely *staggering!*"

The next time I saw him was in the summer of 1989, at a restaurant on the Upper West Side of Manhattan. He had jetted in one hot day to make his case at the Ford Foundation. I had come back to the city on some journalistic assignment or other, and we met for lunch near Lincoln Center.

Poston hurried into the restaurant and began talking almost before he had sat down, as though we met for lunch every day. He was dapper as always in his pressed blue blazer of indeterminate age, but today he was flushed and almost giddy with scandal—he'd been approached by a pimp in Times Square, and he could scarcely wait to tell me about it.

"You were actually approached by a pimp?" I repeated, as he suavely lighted a cigarette. He seemed smaller and more husklike than ever in the honking cacophony of the city, and it had struck me how easily the pimp might have been a mugger, or worse, and how casually catastrophic the consequences.

"Oh, yeah!" he replied, and some of the delight drained from his face; he had misinterpreted my concern, I think, as incredulity. With injured dignity he added, "I wouldn't think that's unusual, is it?"

I pressed ahead. "What did he have to offer?"

"Said he had a *whole bevy of beautiful girls,*" Poston exclaimed—tickled, perhaps, to have encountered a pimp who spoke the same grandiose argot that Poston himself favored. "He just kept on describin' the girls, Ron! And, 'Come on, I'll show ya,' and I was just, 'No thanks, no thanks'! And I kept tryin' to push him away, and he even took hold of my arm! He wasn't roughlike, or anything—*friendly!* Very, extremely, exceptionally *friendly!*" Poston guffawed. "He just insisted he was gonna sell me on one of those girls!" He guffawed again. "I says, 'Oh, no. I haven't got time!' " This triggered another guffaw. I sensed at that moment that Poston was as happy as I'd ever seen him.

The adventure with the pimp, however, was as nothing compared to the great saga of Poston's wangling an appointment from the Ford Foundation, and then making the trek to New York to consummate it. Tightly condensed from its original telling, the saga went this way: Poston wrote a letter of petition to Ford's director of urban poverty programs, a man named Robert Curwin. (Poston recited the two-page letter from memory for me, verbatim.) Unbeknownst to Poston, Curwin was traveling in Asia when the letter arrived at Ford. But when he telephoned Curwin's office a few days later to follow up, he caught the attention of Curwin's secretary, whose name was Bobbie Silver. (Initially unapproachable male executives and their ever-sympathetic secretaries were archetypal figures in Poston's crowded personal mythos.)

"Her response was very enthusiastic," Poston assured me at the restaurant, as I ate and he smoked. "I offered to send along a copy of one of my books about kids and poverty, *The Gang and the Establishment.* She said, 'That'll be right down his alley!' And she would see that he got it, and mark it to his attention. She refers to him as 'Robert.' I said maybe she'd like to read it as well, to which she responded very positively. I said, 'Mrs. Silver, I gotta bring you a rose!' "

Complications ensued. Curwin and Poston spoke by telephone several weeks later and agreed on a meeting. The date was set, and Poston bought an airline ticket from St. Louis to New York—"one of those nonrefundable things that you can get for, you know, a big discount." Mrs. Silver called back: something had come up. Could Dr. Poston change the date?

"I said, 'Well, Mrs. Silver, I've got this ticket here'—I said, 'Well, I'll tell ya, let me see if I can rearrange things.' I call my travel service. They can't change the ticket because TWA won't allow 'em. I called everybody at TWA. Called the Ambassador Club; I'm a life member; I was in it back in the early days when they started the Ambassador Club. It was by invitation only, and no dues. And in St. Louis County it was a bottle club, because it was illegal to sell liquor by the drink at airports in those days. People kept their bottles in the club. Herb, the big, fat bartender—he was the man to see.

"So I called the Ambassador Club. I get all the way back to their corporate headquarters somewhere in New York. Naw, absolutely can't do anything about it. Okay. So then a few days later I'm up in St. Louis on another business. So I go out to their division headquarters in Earth City, that's west of St. Louis. I go in there and I see the man who's the regional manager. I'm sittin' there, Ron, just outside his office, he can see me, I've sent my business card in, it says, Professional Community Development, Southern Illinois University. So when I go in he says, Well, he says, what would a professor be wanting to see me for? He says, One of two things. Either you're raising money for the University, or, he says, you've got a nonrefundable ticket." Poston gave vent to a large guffaw.

"We talked, I betcha, for at least forty minutes or more, gettin' real friendly, and he's askin' me what I'm doin', and I'm tellin' him about the Cairo thing, and all that—and so then he finally says, Well, you know, rules are rules. Now, if you buy a ticket to see the St. Louis Cardinals play baseball tonight, and you decide you're not gonna go till tomorrow night, they're not gonna refund you the money on that ticket. He says, A rule's a rule. Yeah, I know, I says. He says, Now, you're a perfectly intelligent person, he says. I understand, I says. And so finally after we talked on and on and on, and we got into this thing about civic initiative and the development of community, and all that, we get talkin' about some of the things he's been doin' in St. Louis, and finally he says, 'Patty!' he yells out. She's the assistant manager. She comes in. He says, Patty, what is the most common problem we have with clients? She says, Wantin' to get changes and refunds on nonrefundable tickets. He says, That's right. And that's what this character wants. He says, Patty, go take care of this guy. Says, For some reason, he's different."

The Man Who Would Save Cairo leaned across the table toward me, his black eyes alive with triumph. *"I got his bidniss card!"*

But Poston's triumph over TWA and the Ambassador club proved a hollow one. He was never to hear from Robert Curwin at the Ford Foundation again.

Chapter XIX

It was during Richard Poston's season of grand touring—his season of long absences from Cairo—that his simmering but discreet feud with the town fathers flared at last into public view.

In his maneuverings to carve out a physical foothold on the Ohio riverfront, a foothold essential to every hope he had for his theme-park superstructure over the old town, Poston had finally crossed a line into enemy territory. As soon as he crossed that line, his enemies struck. The line was the one that separated Poston's Operation Enterprise agenda from the entrenched business and political interests of Mayor Al Moss and the wharfage-services magnate Bill Wolter. The warfare that resulted carried all the way to the Illinois Legislature.

Poston's maneuver aimed at nothing less than stripping Wolter of his comfortable riverfront leasing contract with the City of Cairo, and of his influence in determining the use of river frontage not under his direct control. It would accomplish this by removing the riverfronts themselves from city control, and placing them in the hands of a regional port authority. The problem was that although there existed thirteen such district authorities in the state, no such body had penetrated the enclosed fiefdom of Alexander County. So Poston would have to get one created.

In point of fact it was not Richard Poston who dreamed up the idea for an Alexander-Pulaski County Regional Port Authority. He simply attached himself and his organization to it, and lobbied for it, and made it inseparable from his own goals. (And, in so doing, erased whatever doubt may have existed that Moss and Wolter would throw themselves full-force into its opposition.) The original notion had come from one of the region's rich storehouses of rugged individualists: a retired restaurateur, Democratic party regular and amateur gadfly named Jack Sneed.

Sneed was one of those people who refer to themselves as "taxpayers" in ways that give governmental bureaucrats gooseflesh. He had gained a measure of local notoriety around Southern Illinois back in 1981, when he brought a lawsuit against the State of Illinois over some trees of his that state workers had uprooted and killed during the construction of Interstate 57 north of town—the same Interstate that Poston envisioned as a tourist lifeline into Fort Defiance State Park and beyond. "They sent me some money," was the way Sneed liked modestly to refer to his victory. The money he was sent was in the amount of $2,170. Not the sort of sum, perhaps, to bring the U.S. Treasury to its knees, but enough to bring Sneed to the attention of certain politicians of the region, including a Democratic United States Congressman named Ken Gray.

"I was asked by Ken Gray's office for my thoughts," Sneed later recalled, "on how to help bring this area out of the economic depression it was in."

One of Sneed's first thoughts was to build a miniature Panama Canal.

"I recommended that we have this concrete canal, five miles in length, that would connect the Mississippi and the Ohio several miles above Cairo," Sneed told me. "It would create about ten or eleven miles of additional wharfage. But it would do something else as well. See, we're on the northern edge of the Sun Belt down here. We'll never have the problem of our rivers icing over, at least not one that would amount to anything. We could bring small seagoing ships all the way up here to a Cairo Harbor, and into this canal I proposed. The import-export trade would be a tremendous tool for economic development, and it would take a lot of the clout away from people like Bill Wolter. Of course the thing is that Wolter would benefit as much as anybody else on something like this, if he'd only realize it."

Sneed's idea caught on as a political issue. As early as 1987 a young Democratic state representative named David Phelps, running hard for reelection in 1988, had taken up this idea of a port authority as his cause.

In almost no time, Sneed discovered that he had an enthusiastic behind-the-scenes ally named Richard Poston.

It was not the five-mile concrete canal part of Sneed's brainstorm that attracted Doc Poston's attention. The truth was that Poston thought a five-mile concrete canal across the Southern Illinois flatlands was a fairly crackpot idea, and if you pressed him on it, he did not have all that many sterling things to say about Jack Sneed himself—Sneed, after all, had some annoying potential as a rival idea-man.

The concept of a slackwater port for seagoing vessels at Cairo was something else again: it appealed to Poston's fondness for the big sweep, the grand gesture, and it confirmed his well-exercised rhetoric about Cairo "at the confluence of two mighty waterways." What really brought him to full attention, though, was the obvious fact that such a vast undertaking would need its own governing body. It would require a port authority. And a port authority meant that much less municipal authority for Moss and Wolter.

In specific terms, a port district created by the state legislature would require an authority with a range of powers. It would take the form of a twelve-member board, and would regulate dock and harbor lines, anchorage facilities, bridge operation and even the speed of boats in the harbor. It could build and maintain levees. It would be able to invoke eminent-domain on property it wished to acquire. It could form an import-export trading company. It could sell revenue bonds and apply for various public loans. It would have the power—though none of the thirteen existing port authorities in Illinois had ever chosen to exercise it—to levy a five-cent annual tax on each resident.

It could even extend its control from the waterfront to the small public airport that lay just outside Cairo. The airport, as it happened, was the subject of much dark speculation and suspicion among local people. Many of them remembered, with a mixture of scandalation and perverse pride, its chief unspoken function back in Cairo's heyday as a vice center: the depositing and collecting of gamblers, gambling spoils and prostitutes. In the late 1980s people liked to suggest, without coming right out and saying it, that the airport's sinister uses had not abated; that it continued to be a pickup and drop-off point for all sorts of illicit commodities. "You can get off an airplane in that airport and in less than five minutes be in one of the rivers or on Interstate 57, which connects to 55 and 64," one knowledgeable local woman pointed out to me. "That airport sits in the middle of a soybean field. If you turn your lights off when you land and take off, nobody will know you've been there."

This was the flavor of the community—in part, at least—that an Alexander-Pulaski County Port Authority would be obliged to supervise.

Poston's entry into the debate was, characteristically, a cavalry charge. "I have completed a nationwide random sampling survey of six hundred forty-one companies," he shouted at me over the telephone one summer day in 1988, "which got a fantastic, almost *unbelievable* response! Twenty-eight percent replied, Ron! Usually those things get thrown in the wastebasket! *Thirty-one* companies, each of which employs 500 or more people—add those together, that's a minimum of 15,500 people; these are not peanut companies, Ron—*thirty-one* of 'em have said, We will use that harbor if in fact it is constructed!

"But Wolter is fighting it!" (Here Poston's voice assumed a trembling note of incredulity, as if that reaction on Wolter's part were the last thing in the world he would have expected.) Mildly, I asked him why he supposed that was so.

"Why? Because he's afraid this will destroy his power base! You can have a thirst for money, or you can have a thirst for sheer power, to control people!" (Poston's voice thickened a little; I could hear genuine rage building.) "To grip 'em by the throat and make 'em do as you say!" (Now he was as angry as I had ever heard him.) "Now, that's the kinda—I can't answer that question, 'Why would he be against this,' because it's so incredi-ble! It's unanswerable!"

There was a short silence on the line while Poston gathered himself. Then he said, "He and Moss—now, they wouldn't be fighting all this so hard, Ron, if we weren't gettin' somewhere. That is a beautiful index of our progress! Because if we weren't gettin' anywhere, if the people weren't beginning to come out of their shell, and stand up like Americans should, they'd pay no attention to us. See?"

By June of 1988, David Phelps's port district bill had already enjoyed a wild and wooly political career. It had died as a proposed bill the previous year. Then it was pulled from the table on the last night of the June 1988 legislative session and slipped into a more comprehensive bill that was passed and presented to the Republican governor, James Thompson, for signing. But instead of signing, Thompson had begun to line-item veto. When he had finished, he had line-item vetoed the bill out of existence—except for one item: the Alexander-Pulaski Port District.

The Illinois House voted 117–0 to accept the governor's vetoes—and his exemption of the District. Only a Senate vote remained. Now the outcome appeared to be inevitable, automatic.

But then the ancient wheels of Southern Illinois politics began creakily to turn.

Voices arose—indignant voices. One voice belonged to Allen Moss. "It's a bad bill," the Cairo mayor fumed to a reporter for the *Southern Illinoisan* newspaper. "It adds another level of bureaucracy that we don't need." Moss followed this declaration by reading from an open letter from the district manager for the Bunge Corporation pointing out that Alexander County comprised one of the poorest regions in the state, and that a port authority would simply be another unnecessary taxing agency.

These images—of a port authority as *bureaucracy* interested mainly in *taxation*—formed the dual warhead of a sudden new ground swell against the plan. Neither Moss nor his comrades-in-protest had anything to say about the state senator's claim that such an agency might well oversee a multimillion-dollar boom in economic development along the Ohio River in Alexander and Pulaski counties, a boom based on access to worldwide trade from the Illinois shoreline. (Nor did they address the "taxpayer subsidy" countercharge raised by the man who thought up the whole scheme, Jack Sneed—that as things presently stood, Cairo taxpayers were subsidizing Bill Wolter's leased levees and thus his wharfage business, allowing him to get by on that twenty-cents-a-foot price structure year after year. Wolter consistently refused to comment to the press; on one occasion, he ordered a reporter to be firmly escorted from his office.)

A woman named Lynn Koch suddenly entered the picture, seizing hold of the anti-District campaign with a crisp professionalism and zeal not necessarily typical of Southern Illinois politics. Lynn Koch skillfully coordinated a shock wave of alarming letters and telephone calls to Illinois legislators from both parties. She also supervised the presence, at public hearings, of large blocks of citizens who testified against the measure. Many of those citizens tended to be members of Laborers' Local 773 in Cairo, invited to the hearings by their boss Eddie Smith—a Democrat, as it happened. Most of those workers were employed by Waterfront Services, owned by Bill Wolter, the patron of the Republican mayor,

Al Moss. Moss himself showed up at several of the hearings, insisting on one occasion that a district would not only fail to stimulate the economy, it would cause existing businesses to move. "We've got a full house here," he declared. "Nothing here is available for a port district."

Lynn Koch was a former high school teacher from the small neighboring town of Metropolis. She had taken a master's degree in something called "professional services" at Murray State College in Kentucky and, after her teaching career, went to work in the town as a management consultant. Among her consultancy clients was a political candidate named Bob Winchester—the Republican who eventually lost to David Phelps in the race for the state senate in the 1988 election.

Whether by coincidence or something perhaps a shade more deliberate, Ms. Koch's anti-District offensive provided an excellent opportunity to hand her defeated client's rival, David Phelps, his political hat—and in the process to put the quietus on the crusty Democrat partisan Jack Sneed. (Sneed's attitude toward Wolter could be likened to Poston's, without the softening tact and restraint.)

"I've got a lot of Republican clout," she allowed to me several months after that clout had been convincingly demonstrated. As she portrayed it, she had unleashed her clout only after grave deliberation, and only in the cause of rescuing a cowed and deceived grass-roots community—the same grass-roots community, as it happened, that Richard Poston was then busy rescuing, only from the other side of the controversy.

"I first became aware of a port district plan while I was doing legislative research for Bob Winchester," she told me. "When I pulled the legislation for that item, I thought, 'No one in my district knows anything about this.' That red-flagged it for me. So I called Mayor Moss. He said, 'What port district? I don't know what you're talking about.' I took the legislation down to the mayor, and he read it, and he said, 'You know, I remember seeing six or eight months ago in the paper there was a potential for a port district, but no one talked to me.' "

Such late-blooming comprehension of political issues was not exactly a rarity with Al Moss, especially in matters in which Dick Poston was involved. But in Lynn Koch's view, Moss wasn't the only person in the dark this time.

"We began to ask questions," she told me. "No one knew about it. None of the local mayors. Nobody—nobody knew about a port district."

Here Ms. Koch began to sound positively indignant. "That bill gave a twelve-member board total control over the Ohio and Mississippi rivers! Every piece of freight would have to pass through that port district! No business could be transacted that did not go through that board! They could put a surtax on every barge that comes down the river! There's a little district in Louisiana that's doing this! Five dollars a barge!

"The board would have very broad powers. It could take control of the airport, hire its own *police force* to police the airport! Surtaxes, back-door referendums—*this twelve-person board could do anything it wanted to do!*"

Not as long as Lynn Koch had anything to say about it. All she needed was empowerment. Empowerment came in the person, not of Al Moss, but of Bill Wolter.

"When I talked to the mayor, he said, 'Talk to Wolter, he'll know,'" she recalled. "I did, and Bill hired me—himself and several other industrial managers along the river. It was about this time that Doc Poston surfaced, by the way. He was saying that a port district would help him do his marina, that riverboat plan of his."

Lynn Koch swung into action shortly after the 117-0 vote in the Illinois House. Her target was the state Senate.

"I came home and organized a grass-roots function," she recalled. "All the people from the river industries contributed to it. Tons of letters went out. We made a lot of phone calls. We contacted everyone we needed to. We got the votes from the Republican party. We needed five Democratic votes." She paused. "There was some arm-twisting."

It all paid off. An image quickly spread in Southern Illinois: not an image of a bold new apparatus to attract seagoing vessels and the trade they would provide—trade that might revitalize one of the nation's most chronically depressed regional economies—but rather an image of a monster; a monster of bureaucracy and taxation.

In December 1988, to the shocked disbelief of Richard Poston, the Illinois Senate decided, by a margin of four votes, to defeat David Phelps's bill for a Port District.

Al Moss crowed his triumph to the *Southern Illinoisan*. "I think they just thought you create a port district and everybody's gonna die and go to heaven," he said. "But it doesn't work that way."

Poston was devastated. The Ohio riverfront seemed finally to be beyond his reach, and with it, his hopes for saving Cairo. In its death throes, the violent and sorrowful old town had managed to gather itself for one final blind swipe at its perceived enemies. That the wounding blow had fallen ultimately on the town's own chest was an irony without charm for Poston, because he and Operation Enterprise had been crushed in the process.

There would be no purchase of the Belle Angeline. There would be no Showboat–Dinner Theatre–Museum and Cultural Center, and no historical restoration of Cairo flowing from the riverboat's appeal to those 2,482,000 motorists sweeping by on Interstate 57; and there would be no heritage theme park sprawled across three states resulting from the success of the town's restoration.

The last person to leave Cairo, turn out the lights. . . .

The 44,206 miles. The laboriously composed letters of application to foundations, the audiences at Ford and MacArthur and Hitachi and Joyce. The speeches and the exhortations. The Quinstate Forum and the cleanups at Fort Defiance State Park—"How stupid that seemed to the government," Sister Lorraine had cried, thinking of Gandhi, "to go to the sea and make salt"—and that first triumphal entry into the town, on that February night in the Cairo attorney's living room—"The applause was spontaneous. . . . all eyes focused on me. . . ."

His alliance with the civic-minded Angela Greenwell—"I thought, *finally, a group of people were alive,* you know, *in Cairo!*" she'd told to me—and the formation of Operation Enterprise, with its battery of committee chairmen and its town meetings . . .

"We can change the face of America, Ron!"

Done for.

This was not the way the movie was supposed to end.

By August 1989, Al Moss was openly stalking Operation Enterprise. It had come down to this: Moss, pressuring the group to remove a marker it had constructed along the side of U.S. 51 on the north entrance to the town. The marker read: WELCOME TO CAIRO.

"That sign was put up by our Environmental Improvement Committee," Angela Greenwell told me later. "It came out of the enthusiasm generated at the Quinstate Forum, the enthusiasm to clean up the town. Since it was on a state right-of-way, Doc had gone all the way to the Illinois Department of Transportation to get permission."

The marker was made of red Missouri granite. Besides the "Welcome" legend it included an outline of the state of Illinois. After volunteers from Operation Enterprise had spent several hours getting it into place, an emissary of the mayor appeared on the scene and told them the marker constituted a traffic hazard. It was a question of liability insurance, the emissary explained. The city could not place additional liability on the taxpayer. A complaint would have to be lodged with the state Department of Transportation. In the interests of the town.

Angela Greenwell alerted the media. A couple of days later her smiling face appeared in the *Southern Illinoisan,* with the granite marker in the background. CAIRO WELCOME SIGN ISN'T GREETED BY ALL, said the headline.

"When this hit the news," she said afterward, "Al realized he was in the spotlight, and he backed off. He said it was a problem between the DOT and Operation Enterprise."

The mayor's retreat may have been prompted equally by Mrs. Greenwell's pointing out that a nearby sign on the same stretch of road, advertising Al's Boat and Trailer, presented a similar hazard.

But Moss took the occasion to get a lick in at Poston and Operation Enterprise. "They're seeking to stir things up constantly," he told the newspaper, "to hide the fact that they're not accomplishing their goals."

Chapter XX

I drove back down to Kent on a wet late-autumn day a little more than a year after my wife and I had listed our house for sale and moved the furniture in it up to Vermont. I wanted to see a few old friends, find out how things stood in terms of growth and containment of growth, and (I'd brought my camera) spend a few hours reacquainting myself with the willowy hills and gorges of the old howling wilderness. Perhaps I would drive the four miles down 341, past Hatch Pond to South Kent and photograph the house that was no longer ours, and Bernie's goat pen across Bull's Bridge Road, to show my sons how things looked in a place where they had spent so many happy times.

We had left at the beginning of a lull in the town's development—a lull precipitated by a kind of supernova burst of buying and selling toward the end of the decade. The lull had given us some anxiety: the house we had won by bidding against another buyer to its top market price had languished in the listings for several months, as had some other hopefully priced properties we knew of. After its seven-year spree of real estate binging, Kent had gone a little stunned. Woozily, its silk hat askew and its white collar undone, the town was patting its pockets, feeling for the aspirin, trying to remember what time it was and what sort of party it had been.

The time, as it happened, was exactly two hundred fifty years after the town's founding, and Kent indeed looked a little as though it were at the dregs of a blowout party. The wet leaves clinging to the pavement made me think of confetti. Bill Litwin's yellowish Town Center, conspicuous and out-of-scale with the other buildings on Main Street, still had the raw and unwrapped look of some giant centerpiece. And as I approached the northern limit on the downhill curve of Route 7 from Flanders, I could see a rainsoaked banner that read KENT'S 250TH ANNIVERSARY CELEBRATION, 1739–1989 sagging over the intersection of 7 and 341 at the far end.

Donald Connery had dressed up in a powdered wig and tricornered hat and played George Washington earlier in the year, I happened to know. At a commemorative ball at Kent Center School, Connery had delivered Washington's first inaugural address to a crowd of similarly bewigged Kent people. (Connery had told me by telephone before the ball that he was toying with the idea of hitting the assemblage with an updated version of the address, couched in twentieth-century jargon; but as nearly as I'd been able to determine, he had not followed through on that threat.)

Connery's Kent Land Trust had gone into a temporary hiatus because of the drop in real estate activity. Connery had turned his civic consciousness, temporarily at least, to other concerns: he'd mailed me an outline for a series of books he intended to write with his wife Leslie, a children's series designed to combat what the old globe-hopping journalist saw as a crisis of geographic illiteracy. He and Leslie were in fact out of town on the day of my visit—in the early stages of what he'd called "a year-long odyssey," in search of material for the books.

The Kent School girls' campus on Skiff Mountain—the sale property that had triggered the wave of reaction to over-development a couple of years before—still hung above the town, on the market, its fate uncertain, another consequence of the lull. Some people I knew had told me not long before that there had been a flurry of sprucing-up activity in the buildings, and that Kent people assumed it would soon be sold to a developer, with concussive effects on the town.

I looked up Gordon Casey in his Main Street office and asked him why things had cooled down in Kent. His answer was characteristically blunt.

"Everybody who had a house put it on the market for a ridiculous sum," he growled. "The buyers were all second-home buyers. Finally the market just reached its limit—people had gone from 'greedy' to 'very greedy.'"

I asked Casey whether things were likely to heat up again. "Yeah," he said, and shrugged. "Now, people are learning they'll just have to go back to 'greedy.'"

I spent a little while with Glen Rainsley in his kitchen across the driveway from the Congregational Church, where over a cup of freshly ground coffee I learned that the Kent Affordable Housing Corporation, the affordable-housing group the minister had helped form, had not made a great deal of progress in finding any sites. In fact it had not made any progress. Rainsley was preparing a letter to the Board of Selectmen formally requesting that the village donate its old Town Hall to the group. He did not seem optimistic about an early decision. The slowing down of real estate action in Kent was not exactly deepening anyone's charitable impulses. Meanwhile, the exodus of ordinary people continued. A longstanding resident of the town, a waitress for many years at the Fife 'N' Drum, was preparing to move to North Carolina because she could no longer afford to live in Kent.

Back in my van, I took a turn down through the village, along the section of Route 7 designated as Main Street. In the parking lot of the Fife 'N' Drum I glimpsed a woman in a deeply woven wool skirt, leather boots and leather gloves—she held one glove in a gloved hand—emerge from a Celebrity Estate station wagon and begin to stride purposefully toward the restaurant's adjoining gift shop, which specialized in candles, "antiques," spices, scented soaps, large stuffed bunny rabbits and pewter mugs. No supplicant for affordable housing, she. Farther along, parked at curbside beside the Villager Restaurant and Foreign Cargo and Country Clothes and Kent Video, I saw an array of shiny new cars, their skins bright and polished in defiance of the wet day. There were baskets of flowers hanging from some of the trees.

When it was time, I turned my van around, drove back north through the center of Kent and up into the hills of Flanders. I made a right turn on a familiar little steep-winding road and climbed toward the crest, toward what once had been unbroken meadowland where children had run on a span. I was keeping an appointment with the one person I had really wanted to spend some time with on this visit. I was headed for a meeting with Alan Gawel.

.   .   .

In all my years as a weekender in South Kent, I had never had an extended conversation with Alan. There would have been virtually no protocol for it. Weekenders did not have conversations with permanent residents of Alan Gawel's generation, or of any generation, unless it involved a delivery of firewood, the snowplowing of a driveway or—in Alan's case—the investigation of a reported fire.

But I had come to care about the Gawel family, or what was left of it. Gawels were part of Kent's past, and, through Alan and his brother Joe, Gawels would be part of its future. Somehow it was important for me, a weekender who had passed some time in the town and then left it behind without a trace, to understand that continuity, and to honor it. I felt as though that continuity had touched me: I would never cease being affected by the memory of Alan's voice coming out of the beeper-phone in Leslie Connery's waistband that night at Carol Hoffman's dinner party, performing an old Gawel family function, summoning ambulance volunteers to an automobile collision, not knowing he was announcing the death of his grandmother.

He waved to my approaching van from the rear deck of his mother's house at the top of the old stagecoach road, then disappeared inside, just as Susie Gawel had waved and disappeared several months earlier. When I stepped through the entrance to the kitchen—the sliding glass panel was open—Alan was getting some Cokes out of the refrigerator.

He was a slightly built young man with close-cropped hair. He wore an unassuming but neat white sweater and blue jeans, and he moved with a certain erect dignity, almost a gravity, that I had rarely observed in Kent, and almost never in anyone of his age. It was the prideful bearing of a professional public servant. The bristles of a new mustache were forming on his upper lip. But the family giveaway was in his eyes; they were soft and deerlike, his mother's eyes.

We sat at the formica table in his mother's kitchen, Cokes in front of us, to talk. The small house was quiet. Susie Gawel, still in pain from her injuries in the crash that killed her mother Dorothy, was at a physical-therapy session. From the kitchen wall, among appliances, came the intermittent rasp and static of a squawk-box: Alan's link to his obligations. At age nineteen, he had become the youngest fire marshall in Kent history—in Connecticut's, as far as anyone knew. He had also done some part-time work in nearby New Milford as a volunteer fire and ambulance dispatcher, the job he was working the night his grandmother died. Now, three years later, Alan Gawel had taken on an additional responsibility. He was the business manager of a new "911" regional dispatching center, a clearinghouse for fire and police emergency calls in Litchfield County.

"We serve thirteen towns," he told me in his quiet but purposeful voice. "The center is twenty miles away, in Litchfield. I applied for the job last November—which, when I applied, I didn't think I would get it, being my age, you know, to be in charge of a whole center like that. I interviewed about twenty-five people that applied for dispatcher jobs. And then I hired eight. I manage the place, and I do a dispatching shift also. I figure the best way to stay in touch with everything is to actually do what you're managing. And I also enjoy that quite a bit, so that was part of the deal—that I stayed a working dispatcher."

I asked Alan what the source of his love for this sort of work was. Did he recall being a child and thinking about being a fire marshall some day?

"Not fire marshall," he corrected me gently. "Fire*man*. Fireman, policeman, you know. I grew up with my whole family being involved in the fire department quite a bit. Uncle Bill, Mom's brother, was in the fire department. My other uncle, Tom, who lives just up the road, was in the department for a while, and he'll still help out when anything is needed. My other uncle, John, he held all the positions right up through—he was chief for about four or five years. Then he ended his term as chief and became the first ambulance chief for the fire department, and then he started the ambulance service."

Alan wasn't finished. "My great-uncle, Walt, was my grandfather's brother, and he was in the fire department—he was assistant chief, chief, all the way through. He owned the Chevrolet garage in town. And the other one would be my grandfather, who was assistant chief, captain, lieutenant. My grandfather and another man built the firehouse in 1951, the one that's there now."

Alan's 911 managerial duties—augmented by his desire to dispatch—demanded forty-eight-hour weeks, in bursts of three-day stints of twelve hours each. As Kent's fire marshall—an eight-hour-a-week part-time job in the official description—Alan found himself putting in as many as forty additional hours to satisfy his obligations: inspecting buildings for conformity to the Fire Code, and investigating buildings and other sites where fires had occurred. I suggested to him that he must spend a lot of hours on the road. He grinned with what seemed genuine modesty, and nodded.

"Yeah, quite a few miles," he said. "The town of Kent is pretty well spread out. This morning, for example, I had a local burning permit to do just around here. Then I had to go to a meeting at a local manufacturing establishment, explain some stuff about emergency lighting and stuff. From there I had to go to Kent Center School to help them with a fire alarm—evacuate the building and so forth. From there I had to go all the way down to Kent Hollow, which is ten miles one way, to inspect some brush piles; then back to town to look at a new office place that's going in. Then I had one more burning inspection that I did about twenty minutes before you came. And then"—he gestured matter-of-factly—"the meeting with you."

But his day was far from over. "I'm crew chief on the ambulance," he said, "so I have an ambulance meeting at 5:30 with my crew, 'cause we're on this weekend. Just review with them what we're gonna do, what's goin' on. And I have tons of stuff, building plans, to be reviewed."

I asked him whether this level of volunteer commitment was typical of his friends in the town—the same small group of comrades who banded together to build houses for one another and otherwise look after the common good. For the first time, a cloud passed over Alan Gawel's open young face.

"It's changing," he said, not looking at me. "You know, when a call comes, we drop everything we do, including our jobs. That's just the way it was always done in Kent. Even when I was just starting, only five years ago, it used to be no problem. Your employer paid you even when you went on a call.

"*Now,*" he said, and gave an exasperated shrug, "we have guys right in the middle of town, their bosses won't let 'em go, unless it's an actual house fire!"

I asked him what had changed.

"They lose money!" Alan said quickly. "Everything's on the dollar. I mean, it's just—when my Uncle John was fire chief, he had the Chevrolet garage. A fire call would come up and the garage would be *emptied.* There'd just be the secretary there. Everyone who was a mechanic was a fireman. Now, we have other garages in town where we have two or three firemen working—and they're not allowed to go! This one garage was just bought by somebody from out of town about a year ago. And he doesn't let his guys go unless it's an actual big structure fire. Then he says, Okay, you can go. And the point is"—Alan Gawel spread his hands—"you know, by the time it takes for us to get there, it very well *could have become* a big structure fire, even though the call didn't come in as that.

"And the new people that come in to live here," Alan went on, "they just expect it! Our fire department is totally funded by donations. The fund-raising work it does. There is no tax money. And the people that come in, the weekenders, whose thirty false-alarm runs a year we're goin' for, the automatic alarms or whatever, *they* think it just comes out of their taxes. They don't make that hundred-dollar donation when we come out."

I asked Alan whether he felt a sense of loss about that. He nodded and took a long sip of his Coke.

"It's hard," he said. "We try to encourage as many younger people as we can; you know, my age and younger—I'm getting to be one of the older active guys, fast!—people my age, that I went to school with. There was about two or three years of us. We all came into the department together. About nine or ten of us that came in." He was talking faster now, remembering, as his mother had remembered running on a span. "It was our parents and grandparents that were part of it, had run the department, and we came of age so we all came in, and you might say rejuvenated the department with some new blood. But the point is—" words failed him for a moment "—times change. Just the fact that your employer doesn't even give you time off any more, you know, how can you go? Even if he says you can go but you're not getting paid, well, if you want to live here you've got to be able to afford to live here." He was rushing now, and his thoughts started bunching up on one another. "If you want to live here you *can't* afford to live here! A lot of people can't work in town! Even if you live here you can't work in town here because you can't make the money to live here. . . ." he stopped, a little confused by his own sudden outpouring, and shook his head.

What is it that keeps you in Kent? I asked him.

Alan Gawel shrugged. It was possible he'd never considered the question before. "I think just the heritage," he said after a moment. "My great-grandfather and great-grandmother, they came in and farmed and owned all this property, and—I just like the town. I'd like to see what the town—I'd like to take—" here he spread his hands out again, as if he were about to grasp something "—I'd like to be a *part* of the town. Make it grow and change. I've been out to a lot of other towns, and I like different things about each town, but . . . I just really like this town."

Without quite knowing that I was about to do it, I asked Alan about the night of his grandmother's death. He put his clasped hands on the surface of the table and stared hard at something a little off to the side of me.

"I was workin' in New Milford," he began. "Dispatch center. Got a call, took the call, it was my job. It was about a quarter after ten. It was for a motor vehicle accident. A woman called up and said there was a big crash outside her house. And she believed people were hurt. So I went ahead and toned out Kent—dispatched the fire department and the ambulance—and sent out the alert tone that alerts everybody, not knowing what had happened at all.

"Then when the fire chief got there he called for another ambulance, so I knew it was a serious accident. I notified the state police, said it was serious, then I went back. I was going about my normal business and the phone rang and it was Dean, his father's the plumber. He says, 'The accident, I'm down here and it's your mom and your grandmother.' I said, 'Are you sure?' He says, 'Yeah, and your grandmother's not doin' so good.' He said, 'But your mom seems to be OK, I talked to her.' Then I heard Joe, my brother, sign on; he was an officer at that point."

Alan picked up the drained Coke glass and turned it around in his hands. "We had just picked my grandmother up that day. Coming back from Florida. We picked her up, and we were talking on our way home about flights and people crashing, and about how statistics showed that you bein' in a car crash are more apt to get killed. We had just talked about that. It was weird. Then we came home and her and my mom went shopping, and I went to sleep for a few hours before I went to work."

After he learned who the victims were, Alan Gawel set about alerting the network of Gawel family and neighbors of the family, the people who lived out on the fringes of their parents' and grandparents' town, up in the Flanders hills.

"I called my uncle up here, and he had an answering machine on. I left a message. Then I called my Uncle John; they said they already knew and they were on the way. Then I called up our neighbors up the road. Said, 'You gotta go down and wake up my uncle, tell him there's been an accident. Meet me at the hospital.' They said okay."

Alan took a breath. "Then at that point I heard our ambulance radio saying we're bringing in two people, one of 'em was a female in her late 60s, early 70s, they were givin' CPR [coronary-pulmonary resuscitation]. I got up and left my work and drove down to the hospital in New Milford. I pulled in the same time as the ambulance. And they were still doin' CPR. But I knew when I saw her goin' out of the ambulance, bein' an emergency medical technician, you know, you can tell, you know when there's a chance and when there's not a chance. And her chest was crushed, and there was no way.

"So they worked on her, then the doctor had me go out of the room. And they worked ten, fifteen minutes or so. Then they told me that my mom was talking. And so I knew that was a good sign, and they said they thought she was going to be okay. Then my uncles started coming in, then the doctor came out and told me they couldn't do anything for my grandmother. She had died.

"I was ready for it at that point, because I knew. When I heard the radio transmission I just knew."

After a few minutes I asked Alan if he could recall what kinds of things were going on in his mind that night.

"I just couldn't believe it was happening, you know," he said. "But—my grandmother, she was really special, and she always . . ." he paused to get control of the words. "You know, we grew up—my mom was divorced, you know, real early. So when we grew up it was me, my brother and my mom. And my grandmother and my grandfather. And we have all, as you see here, lived on the hill together. Our whole family. And so we were all close that way.

"And she always was very strong in the Catholic Church faith. And always taught us that. All the way on through. So when I heard the radio transmission, I knew what was gonna happen. I was ready at that point. And just, knowing her faith and stuff, you know? It was real weird, because I was thinking about what we had talked about in the car. She was always ready for it. She always knew that she believed in God, that whatever He wanted was what He was gonna do, and He would always take care of her. And take care of us, whether it was good, bad or otherwise, it was what He wanted, and that was the way it would be done."

Alan looked back at me with his deerlike eyes, a creature of the countryside whose habitat had changed. When he spoke again, he had restored his grandmother to the present tense. "And I just really—I guess she's always taught me to believe in that, and so that's just the way I think about it."

The curving two-lane road on which Dorothy Gawel had died—Route 7 between Kent and New Milford to the south, the so-called "Highway to Heaven"—remained an unimproved, narrow, low-visibility hazard, despite the high level of accidents, the anxiety over safety expressed by local residents, and the election victory of a state senator who had campaigned on a promise to "push through" a bill for widening and straightening. In one of the wealthiest states of the Union, a state that had experienced several years of exploding property values, there was not enough money in the Department of Transportation treasury for such work. (On the other hand, the dreaded "Super 7," the projected Interstate extension that would disgorge a daily tidal wave of fast-lane traffic at New Milford, languished for similar reasons.) As Kent approached its twenty-first-century incarnation as an outpost of neo-suburbia, it would continue to be linked to the outside world by early twentieth-century roads—quite in keeping with Kent's rapidly becoming an abstracted image as a bucolic farm village, but lethal. Occasionally someone, like the Gawel family, would pay a price for this.

I caught up on a couple last-minute developments in Kent, before I got back on Route 7 myself and headed north to my newly adopted hometown in Vermont. One piece of news was that the Planning and Zoning Commission was preparing to challenge a plan that would give owners of open land a reduction in taxes. The plan had been devised to encourage landowners not to sell their property to developers.

"I think some landowners, who have an inappropriate farmland classification, are getting a free ride," one commission member told a local newspaper reporter.

The other development was that Kent's older people could no longer look forward to their senior citizen meal program, a volunteer operation of the Nutrition Center housed in the community center. The program—one of Dorothy Gawel's many areas of involvement—had shut down. A check of the old structure had uncovered thirty-four violations of the fire code. The official who made the check, and who had been obliged to issue the recommendation, had been Alan Gawel.

Chapter XXI

It was not until November of 1989—the beginning of the Christmas season in my family's new hometown in Vermont, a time when groups of bundled-up parents and children went caroling through the downtown streets after dark, and every house and tree and retail store in the community appeared connected by strings of light—that I heard again from Richard Poston. He called with whooping ecstasy in his voice to tell me that he had found his messiah, his savior of Cairo.

"He's read my books, Ron!" the old stentorian tenor boomed into my receiver. "He's one of the leading people in the country at putting towns back together! I met with him for over an hour in his office in Columbia, Maryland. He's coming down to Cairo in January for an on-site inspection tour of the city. It looks like we're finally gonna get this thing going, Ron!"

It would have wounded him to know how remote it all seemed. It was snowing in Vermont, a clean northern snow. My children were learning to ski. Thanksgiving had just passed. It was a season of glowing dinner parties in fine old houses outside town, of church drives for the needy, of kids leading indulgent parents through open-houses at the public schools; a time when the town's prosperous storekeepers festooned their windows with wooden soldiers and miniature handmade villages—a Dickensian season.

It was not a time to be thinking of lost towns, or the Lower

Mississippi Delta, or very much at all about the bloody collapse of order in the cities that foretold a coming set of aftershocks in American towns. It was pleasing to imagine for a while that everywhere it was as it seemed to be here: no glut, no decay, no violent uprooting of community. It was pleasing to imagine for a while that all America was a kind of New England yuletide theme park.

But now here was Doc Poston's voice on the telephone, bringing it all back.

He had found an angel for his miracle in Cairo. He had connected against all possible odds. One of his incessantly launched flares, his continuous fusillade of letters and telephone calls across the country, pleading for funding, for expertise, for a conference, a meeting, for attention of any kind on behalf of his cause in Cairo—one of these had caught someone's interest in the East. Someone had read his "Laboratory for Community Development" paper and circulated it to some colleagues in the town-planning game. Eventually it had landed on the desk of a titan.

The titan's name was Leo A. Molinaro. For nearly twenty years until his retirement in 1987, Molinaro—a former professor of philosophy at the University of Wisconsin—had been the president of the American City Corporation. American City was a subsidiary of a corporation that was to Richard Poston's scale of endeavor as the National Aeronautics & Space Administration would be to the endeavors of Icarus. It was a subsidiary of the Rouse Company.

The Rouse Company had begun in Baltimore, Maryland, in April of 1939, as a mortgage-banking firm known as Moss-Rouse. The firm's experiences in aligning home buyers and developers with the appropriate financing sources—banks, insurance companies—inspired one of the partners, James W. Rouse, to try his luck at development himself. He re-formed the company in 1954, after separating from Hunter Moss, and began the direct financing of shopping centers, apartment buildings and hotels. By the early sixties James W. Rouse & Company was so successful that it began to contemplate developing entire communities from scratch. The Village of Cross Keys, on sixty-four acres inside municipal Baltimore, materialized. An entire city followed—Columbia, Maryland, begun in 1962 on 16,000 acres in Howard County, and since grown to a size of 60,000 people, 38,000 jobs and 1600 businesses and industries. (Columbia had not stopped growing by the end of the 1980s; its target population was 100,000.)

In the meantime, Rouse was busy on several other fronts. It created Faneuil Hall Marketplace in Boston in 1976 and The Gallery at Market East in Philadelphia the following year. The 1980s saw a string of famous Rouse creations: Harborplace in Baltimore, Santa Monica Place in California, South Street Seaport in New York, Union Station in St. Louis, and others. Rouse's trademarks were an intensely rational (some critics said antiseptic) urban design, a highly complex and disciplined organizational force, and an insistence on profitability that could at times strike the romantically inclined as verging on voracious. But no one questioned the Rouse Company's expertise. When Rouse decided to undertake a project, concrete and steel and glass resulted. The company was simply the best in America, and perhaps in the history of the western world, at doing what it did.

The American City Corporation was Rouse's statement of civic conscience. Formed as a subsidiary in 1968, it offered the Rouse expertise to towns and cities in need of economic reviving. Under Leo Molinaro's direction, American City had consulted to more than a hundred fifty cities and states and countries. Besides the United States and Canada, the company's client roster had been drawn from South America, Scotland, England, Tanzania. Molinaro had lectured on urban policy for the Brookings Institution and had served on the advisory committee of the School of Architecture and Planning at Princeton.

In 1987, Molinaro founded his own development advisory corporation, Molinaro/Rubin Associates. The firm's offices were on Little Patuxent Parkway, in Columbia, Maryland—the city that Rouse had built.

Poston's connection with Leo Molinaro had led to what Poston was pleased to call "a ninety-minute telecommunications conference" with the great man. That led to a request by Molinaro to see some of Poston's accumulated documents. "I sent him our census report, the historic drawings of the riverboat, all kinds of stuff—it cost me *fifteen dollars to send it by Express Mail,* Ron," Poston had boasted to me. Then, in mid-November of 1989, Poston had flown out to Columbia for a meeting with Molinaro. At that meeting he poured out his dream of the Showboat–Dinner Theater–Museum and Cultural Center that would enlarge, over time, to a three-phase "heritage" transformation of Cairo and the countryside on the far banks of the two rivers. Molinaro, elegant and Florentine, had listened to all this.

Doc Poston's sense of destiny fulfilled was hardly diminished when he received a warm letter from the great developer not long after he'd returned home. Molinaro had closed with an offer that must have made Poston dizzy: an offer to come to Cairo with some of his associates and evaluate the town. If certain guidelines could be fulfilled—involving a reliable data base, the convening of the townspeople involved, the feasibility of the "development arithmetic," among others—then Molinaro/Rubin would undertake its legendary program toward the consummation of Doc Poston's redevelopment dream.

Or so the letter seemed to imply. Embedded in the congenial prose were a number of cautionary notes: Molinaro mentioned the "ruthless attention to the discipline of financial feasibility" at one point. Then there was the matter of the price tag: Molinaro did not offer a formal estimate for his company's services, but totalling up the typical costs of the various tasks that needed to be performed, one could easily arrive at a top-range bill of $420,000 in consulting fees alone, before a single penny of actual development money was spent.

As a gesture of sincere purpose, Molinaro had subsequently sent two of his associates at the firm—a "land planner" named Mark Papa and a research associate named Adele Levine—to do a quick site inspection of the town in December. Molinaro himself would make a personal grand tour during a two-day visit in the middle of January—all on the understanding that nothing was finally agreed-on, that the byword at this stage was caution.

What Leo Molinaro could not know, quite yet, was that he was dealing with a man for whom caution was now about as pertinent a concern as transcendental meditation. Richard Poston was burning. The salvation of Cairo was no longer simply his goal; it had melted into the marrow of his self-identity. As I was about to discover, the past year of his solitary travels and grant-proposal schemings and his increasing bitterness toward Mayor Al Moss had taken its toll: it had aged him, reinforced his fixations, deepened the seams in his face, given him a stare. Leo Molinaro's flicker of interest had ignited some dry timber inside the old man. His fired mind had leapt ahead of conditional considerations. The epic movie inside his imagination was unspooling toward its triumphant climax: Doc Poston and his new ally, the distinguished Leo Molinaro, had forged a partnership and begun their sacred quest to change the face of America.

I traveled back to Illinois on a blustery January Sunday. This time my connections took me to a tiny airport outside Carbondale, Poston's home and the site of Southern Illinois University. I would spend the night as the guest of Doc and his wife Marjorie. On Monday morning Poston would commence the unification and deployment of the institutional forces he had worked so tirelessly to assemble for the transformation of Cairo: Southern Illinois University and Molinaro/Rubin Associates. He had cajoled Benjamin A. Shepherd, the university's vice president for academic affairs and a sympathetic liaison within the SIU administration, into organizing a faculty roundtable to meet with the Marylanders and consider possibilities for a working partnership.

Monday would be a grueling but decisive day. Poston would arise before dawn and fly in a university plane to St. Louis. There he would greet the arriving consultant and his colleagues and escort them back to Carbondale. In the afternoon he would introduce the planners to the SIU faculty committee. If things proceeded as Poston hoped, this meeting would end with a declaration of common cause and the onset of the nationally recognized prototype reconstruction of a dying American town.

In any event, on the following morning, a Tuesday, Poston would drive Molinaro and his people the sixty-five miles down to Cairo for a grand tour of the town and talks with some of its leading citizens.

Those leading citizens would not include Al Moss. The mayor of Cairo had found himself suddenly beset by a crush of previous engagements. Poston had expected that. But he had not been prepared for a gratuitous flourish by Moss, the effects of which humiliated him, then enraged him, then worked their way into the core of his fixations: in response to a friendly letter of introduction from Molinaro, which referred to the forthcoming Cairo visit, Moss had written back, asking the great man for references.

Poston met me at the airport, smoking, a trench coat thrown over his customary cardigan sweater and silk shirt. His black eyes seemed to have drawn even closer together since I'd seen him last, and the vertical lines had cut more deeply along his thin cheeks and jowls, creating little columns of bunched flesh, like sausages.

A touching and eerily time-warped scene played itself out inside the little terminal, a scene out of Poston's own schematic vision of small-town America: a young soldier, returning from combat, was coming home. The youth had been a part of the United States military invasion of Panama. Stepping through the glass doors ahead of me, hurrying past Poston, the uniformed hero was greeted by a cheering committee of relatives and friends—cheers, balloons, weeping, flashbulbs, a home-made banner of welcome.

At another time, Richard Poston might have seized on this vignette as a parable about the richness of American community. Today, he gave no sign he had noticed it. He scarcely bothered even to greet me, but steered me rapidly through the small building and into the parking lot, launching into a detailed inventory of procedural concerns regarding Monday's meeting. I had grown familiar with this extraordinary singlemindedness of Poston's; this screening out of amenity or playfulness or simple pleasure. It would take me a day or two to comprehend how much deeper this austerity had seeped into his being.

That afternoon I saw Poston in his own habitat for the first and last time. Marjorie Poston had created a spare, but warm and sunlighted nest out of the ranch-style brick house they had built at what was then a woodsy edge of Carbondale in the 1950s; the neighborhood still retained maple and willow trees, a habitat for birds. Poston's study was downstairs, and there I found an intact mausoleum of 1950s-style gracious living: a curving wet-bar with barstools, some *art moderne* sofas and lampshades and ashtrays, even a copy of *Pageant* Magazine in mint condition (and featuring an article on one Richard Poston). There, too, were his immense files, and his scrapbooks: I saw the black-haired young community developer addressing banquets, being bussed by jolly-looking clubwomen in hats and nametags; I even saw a modestly cheesecakey photograph of the young Marjorie—a viewing that prompted Poston to tell me again how, on the night he met his future bride, he'd stood outside her residence hall in Washington in a trench coat, smoking; he'd flipped the cigarette butt aside and muttered to himself, "I'm gonna marry that girl." Poston's den was the editing-room of his life's movie.

I enjoyed one of Marjorie Poston's home-cooked chicken dinners that evening, and for an hour or so the two of us were fairly successful at holding Doc to a convivial line of conversation: his son and daughter, his travels around America, the old days at SIU. But as the evening darkened and a thick, wet snow began to fall outside, the small talk faded and Doc Poston turned brooding. So much was riding on the next couple of days. The meeting tomorrow had to go just right. There were certain people who would like to take control of that meeting, use it to inflate their own self-importance, and that could be disastrous! The only hope was that he, Doc Poston, could control the agenda. If it got out of control, why . . .

Poston had long since left the house by the time I awoke the following morning. Marjorie told me he hadn't slept much. The night's wet snowfall had clung to trees and telephone wires, turning the college town into the Hall of the Ice King, but already the snow was melting under the warm sunlight of a false spring; the footing promised to be treacherous. I had breakfast and read the morning papers at a campus eatery, visited with some of Poston's colleagues in the sociology department, and at mid-afternoon headed for the building where the conference would be held.

After a forcefully optimistic introduction by vice president Shepherd—"I think it's evident that the campus has placed a high priority on a rather significant and sizeable public-service initiative. I can envision a multi-faceted partnership . . ." Poston took the floor. As usual, he was the sartorial star of the gathering. In this company of corduroyed academics and a few shiny-suited state politicians he was the perfect boulevardier; he'd put himself together in a pressed gray suit, a starched white shirt, a black necktie and a black pocket square. It was as if he'd chosen a wardrobe to flout the deepening grayish pallor of his own skin, the dark thatches of his eyebrows and the hard stare of his close-set eyes. But when he spoke I heard the weariness inside.

It was a mass love affair he was having with Cairo, he told the group, and I was shocked to see for the first time how used-up he was. His voice had lost all its pitch; it was weak and breathy. The worn phrases sounded more threadbare than ever; they came out like verbal index-cards, culled almost at random from the disheveled files of his brain.

Very intimately involved, Poston was going on; the men around the conference table were listening respectfully, arms folded. *Maybe till four o'clock with a wife, listenin' to her, and the next mornin' to the husband. That's all I can call it, a mass love affair. I been with hundreds of communities from the state of . . .* he paused, seemed to grope for a memory . . . *Washington to North Carolina and all through . . .* another pause . . . *the Tennessee Valley area, and most of 'em have recovered nicely.* He paused again, rummaging his mind. *Cairo is on the critical list and I hope it does make it.* He introduced Molinaro.

Leo Molinaro smiled and inclined his head. He was all in gray, too, but somehow it was a different gray; his suit was the spun silken gray of corporate authority. His hair was white, like Poston's, but it was smoothed back over his head so that it shone under the muted lighting of the conference room like a cloud with a silver lining. A small streamlined man with deep-set eyes, Molinaro made elegant circles as he talked with his open hands, and his voice was creamy with professional charm.

The development principles in all small towns are fairly clear, he told the assembled professors, and with Poston gazing at him, his bony hands clasped tight on the table, Molinaro outlined those principles. Molinaro's first principles turned Poston's gaze into a fixed stare.

The developer stressed the importance of a tripartite harmony between a town's public, its economy, and its government. So long as one point of an ailing town's triangle was missing, Molinaro would never, he made it clear, participate in that town's rehabilitation. "And I, representing the perspective now of private development, *would run, not walk, to the nearest exit.* You cannot come into a community with warring factions."

He went on to cover some other principles: learning how to work at scale, paying strict attention to physical development—quoting Winston Churchill on how the environment shapes us and not the other way around, a respect for the ecology, "erecting a vision," and the "development arithmetic."

Molinaro spoke with enormous reach and scope; he was by turns hard-headed, philosophical, ironical, droll. He made little obsequies to the assembled professors, little shrugs and circlings of his hands, assuring them of their equal expertise in these matters; but he spun out a great encompassing rhetoric that left no doubt who was the real authority in the room.

"The big question for small towns in general is," he declared, "what is their role in the twenty-first century?" His discussion of the future of small towns in America was dramatic. His was a grim view. The loss of small personal shops to large generic companies has left neighborhoods without a soul. Molinaro saw this. "Individual enterprises—remember Main Street used to be filled with Joe Smith's hardware, Frank Brown's haberdashery? Forget it!"

"Grass-roots democracy," averred Leo Molinaro, "what Dick Poston has been talking about, is being challenged by the cynicism and the avarice and the size of other governments."

I stole a glance at Doc Poston across the table to see how he'd responded to this little bow to his own vision. Whatever I'd expected wasn't there. His thin face had not relaxed from the dark, fixed expression it had assumed when Molinaro had alluded to the parties-of-interest question near the beginning of his remarks. I knew Poston well enough, I believed, to be sure that Moss was on his mind; that in his anxious state he had begun to process

Molinaro's comment into a crisis that could abort the entire project at its inception. I also knew him well enough to be sure he was not enjoying this relinquishment, however temporary, of an audience.

Molinaro was asking his rapt listeners, rhetorically, what attitudes currently exist about small towns. "Except for realists like Dick Poston, we get *sentiment and nostalgia,* not science and technology." The future of small towns would be in the latter.

For Molinaro, Cairo could "define a new set of disciplines in community renaissance—"

Now I glanced at Poston again, because this new tack in Molinaro's remarks struck me as a good deal more troubling to his intentions than any contretemps involving Al Moss. Was Leo Molinaro saying that Cairo's future would depend on a rejection of sentiment and nostalgia in favor of some as-yet undefined commitment to technology? What, exactly, did that imply for Poston's riverboat/heritage theme-park vision?

Molinaro suggested they figure out their goals, and I noticed that this remark brought Poston, the original goal-setter, back to attention. "If Cairo is going to try to be a planned community, instead of an unplanned mishmash, . . . it's going to have to have a *very hard data base.*"

Poston couldn't hold himself in any longer. He nearly shouted: "That's what we *want you to tell us!* What kind of data we can help you gather, Leo!"

Molinaro was suddenly all self-deprecating shrugs and smiles, remarking Poston's possible impatience with his philosophizing. Poston's response was low and thick: "We're after two different things, Leo."

It was at this point that I began to see how it would go between the two men, and what the discharge might portend for Cairo. Poston's naked, raw-nerved ardor clearly caused something in Molinaro to recoil. Molinaro's technocratic dryness—his languor seemed to blot light from the air—triggered deep discomforts and suspicions in Poston. Knowing Poston's feverish fixations, his lack of sleep, I began to fear, for the first time, for his health.

Molinaro had drawn himself back at Poston's outburst. As Poston's colleagues looked on, he now subjected the old man to a little seminar in the nuances of data. Molinaro explained to Poston that data, without a framework in which the data would be used, was what Francis Bacon had called "ant-knowledge." This would not do. He, Leo Molinaro, required *"bee-*knowledge." "Ant-knowledge," came Molinaro's modulated, humming voice, "are these discrete pieces of information that people pile up incessantly and uselessly. You know—*nolum organum.* Francis Bacon said that so clearly, and we have just forgotten it. Bee-knowledge, you bring it back to the hive and you work it over and you produce honey."

I could see Poston's dark eyes darting, his jaw working. I braced for a tirade. But he merely said, hoarsely: "I think you're gonna be surprised, Leo, at how much of that we have got."

Molinaro was all smiles and spread palms. "That's terrific," he said. "I'm glad to hear it." He paused. "I haven't *seen* it." He looked directly at Poston, who was blinking back at him. "That's what I'm telling you. That all the things I got in your package are very exciting, very interesting, but they are either the first-blush-of-enthusiasm products"—he inclined his head philosophically—"which is *important;* I mean we must let people express themselves." And then Molinaro let the hammer fall. "But the level of data-gathering is still, to me . . . you know, *I couldn't use it as an investment advisor."*

It was hard to tell, from the faces around the conference table staring at Leo Molinaro, how much damage was being done here. The corduroyed professors were dreamily absorbed in the hum of Molinaro's discourse. It was not clear whether they comprehended that the air had changed. From my own perspective, the change was like a cold wind rushing in. Its temperatures, to be fair, had not been set by Leo Molinaro. They seeped through him from an America that Doc Poston, with his quaint prescriptions and his Rooseveltian syntax, had never seen coming. It was a chill born of such loss and such cauterizing of grief that a thousand Postons, orating and exhorting for a thousand years, would never thaw it. It was the glacial chill of economic determinism.

Somewhere in Molinaro's suave formulations, all the context had been obliterated. Somehow it had become, not an American town, nor the idea of American towns, that hung in the balance here—not redemption—but a question of investment opportunity.

Not that Poston himself was necessarily a model of modesty and moderation. My God, I thought, how many times, during his endless monologues over the past two years, had I wondered whether anyone in the world could out-know-it-all him? But that was beside the point now. It was Poston, and not Molinaro nor anyone else at this table, who had gone into Cairo alone. Poston, who had by himself persuaded black and white people from that racially diseased town to sit down together in voluntary common cause for the first time, perhaps, since Reconstruction. Poston, who had stood up to the dark menace of Cairo's business and political bosses and, perhaps more impressively, encouraged a number of defenseless people of the town to stand up as well. Poston, who had told a fabulous story to that town about itself, and in telling it, inspired his hearers to believe it and enact it. Poston, who had organized the great community adventures—the cleaning up of Fort Defiance Park, the taking of the census, the creation of the welcome sign—that had already entered the town's local folklore. Poston, who had created a master vision, however flawed that vision might prove to be, for bringing the town back from the dead through a celebration of its heritage. Poston, who traveled the 44,206 miles in search of an ally who could help him implement that vision; who had seemingly discovered such an ally, and had paid that ally, out of a hard-won foundation grant, to come to Southern Illinois and devise a plan of action with the university.

And now it was Poston who sat in full view of his university colleagues, being elegantly upbraided by that putative ally because his data base would not attract an investment advisor.

"I can't make the case without a very, very deep and hard-edged data base," Leo Molinaro was purring pleasantly to Poston.

The old man's voice was an angry rasp, but he kept to the point: "It's that kind of data, Leo, that these people are assembled to help you get."

But Molinaro had been seized with a fresh thought. His upraised palms described circles. "There's another whole industry that's developing that the people of Cairo may absolutely reject," he informed the architects and the demographers and the sociologists. "But—" he shrugged, and named it.

"Storage. Storage products for industrial products /"—here Molinaro had the decency to lower his voice—"industrial wastes."

It was hard for me to be sure I'd heard Molinaro correctly. I glanced around the table to gauge responses. From the corner of my eye I could see Vice President Shepherd, a hard smile on his face, begin violently to shake his head. "It is one of the very, very fast-growing industries," said Leo Molinaro. "Or businesses, or whatever you want to call it. They're looking for dying small towns. Who are looking for one last way of making a dollar."

Vice President Shepherd adjourned the meeting shortly after that.

It was a ghastly trip to Cairo the next day. Poston drove; he insisted on driving, although he was nearly frantic from lack of sleep. He had spent another fitful night, this time thrashing back through the contents of the committee meeting. In his delirium, he had fixated on one of Molinaro's "development principles," the one about the need to identify the essential parties of interest. Through the night, Poston had rehearsed all his grievances against Mayor Moss, and scarcely had he collected Molinaro and one of his aides from the Holiday Inn before he launched into a rambling inventory of those grievances—just exactly the wrong note, as I had tried to warn him at breakfast, on which to begin this day.

I rode in the passenger seat in the front; Molinaro and the aide, a thin young man in a purposeful suit, sat in the back. Poston, his wispy hair for once imperfectly hotcombed, seemed to me at the edge of a nervous breakdown. Hunched over the steering wheel of his old red sedan, smoking cigarette after cigarette with the windows rolled up and the heater on, he railed against Moss as he thrust the car ahead, skidding to stops at red lights on the service highway leading to the Interstate, nearly missing the turnoff when it came.

His Moss-tirade eventually dissolved into other preoccupations. Molinaro had questioned his data-gathering yesterday; now Poston tried to rehabilitate that hallmark of his early triumph in Cairo. He veered down old corridors of thought. Fragments from his mental file of set speeches began to tumble out into the smoky atmosphere of the car. "We had a picnic of appreciation, for all the people who'd worked on the census, Leo," he called hoarsely into the stony silence in the rear. "All two hundred twenty-five of 'em. I couldn't remember a time when so many Cairoites, from all walks of life, both races, had come together to undertake such a . . . complicated and . . . oh, tremendous project as that was. The margin of error would be less than one percent, it was much more complete than the U.S. Census would be, and I could give you some reasons why that's true. . . ."

Molinaro abruptly interrupted this to inform Poston that he had been counting trucks. "I wonder whether there would be an opportunity to create a full-service truckstop in Cairo," he called to Poston over the din of the motor and the whoosh of the heater. "These have become very big-business lately; they make a lot of money. . . . "

Poston, absorbed in his furies, did not quite take in the scale of truckstop that Molinaro had in mind. "Well, we have a truckstop, Leo, near the hotel where Mark and Adele stayed." He referred to the Molinaro aides who had visited the town in December.

If Molinaro understood Poston's confusion, he did not immediately choose to clarify it. "They didn't mention it," he called smoothly, "and Mark is very much aware of truckstops. So it didn't register with them. . . ."

I saw Poston's dark eyes darting in the rearview mirror. "Well, it's there," he snapped.

"Because these things are full-service truckstops," Molinaro was continuing. "A multi-million-dollar a year business. Just the telephone revenues from one year can be $2 million."

Poston's face was an unlovely bruise as he peered ahead at the road. "Well, I'll show you the truckstop," he muttered.

"What I'm saying is," came Molinaro's purring voice, "we're not tapping into the technology of the transportation system—"

"Well, I'll take you right by the truckstop! There's a truckstop right there, all right. And I'm surprised that Mark and Adele didn't see it, they stayed right—"

"They're sensitive to those things." Molinaro's voice was reasonable, infinitely temporizing. "Mark has actually designed a truckstop, a prototype that we have. I just think, Dick, that there are more things on heaven and earth than what Mr. Moss will or won't support, or a tourism industry will or won't support, and so on. I think we ought to look at all of those details, that's all."

Poston had begun to grasp what Molinaro was suggesting: Cairo, not as a national showcase of American Heritage regeneration (and a shrine to Richard Poston's vision of community development), but as the truckstop capital of Little Egypt—a step or two higher on the evolutionary scale, at least, than the industrial-waste storage repository Molinaro had invoked at the SIU meeting. Ducking his head in a little closer to the steering wheel, Doc chose his words, holding himself in check. "Yeah. well, I sure agree with that, Leo. Wholeheartedly. A hundred percent. But I still think that their greatest immediate economic asset"—here I started to picture the imaginary audience gathering again, and could not stop myself from mouthing the rest of the sentence from memory—"is their *richness in history and their location at the confluence of those two . . . rivers.*" I mentally noted his last-second edit from "mighty waterways."

Molinaro was ready for this, and pounced. "But how do you make that into an economic asset?"

Poston burst in, his voice raw: "Tourism today in Illinois is one fifth of the entire state product! And they expect—"

"Do you know who they count in that, Dick?" Molinaro's voice was a hum of pure reason.

"I don't—"

"They count the twenty million people who go to Chicago."

This was galling. Poston, the facts-and-figures man, the expert who had guided Operation Enterprise to its census-blanketing of Cairo, was thrown on the defensive by this outsider's statistics. It wasn't mere dignity he was suddenly fighting for now. His entire rationale for Cairo as a tourist center, the rationale that had brought Molinaro here as his ally, was under catastrophic cross-examination.

"Well, they've got 'em broken down by county!" he parried, rasping.

"All I know is"—Molinaro's tone was unperturbed—"we did the tourist count for Navy Pier in Chicago, and the overwhelming pro-portion of tourism for Illinois is in Chicago."

Molinaro and his aide were now peering out the rear window at a flock of ducks that had settled on a clear lake.

"They're very high on tourism down here!" Poston declared. "Illi-nois has an annual budget of ten million dollars—"

"Oh, boy!" Molinaro was admiring a particular duck that his aide had pointed out by extending a bony finger. But the flock rose up and flew away.

We passed the truckstop as we exited Interstate 57 near the north-ern tip of Cairo. It had a new name now, but I recalled it quite vividly as Glen's Mid-America. Leo Molinaro gave it one glance and made explicit what he had been hinting at earlier: "Our truckstops are about a hundred fifty acres, and they'll park five hundred trucks, and they'll have several different kinds of computerized cleaning and washing services; they'll have forty, fifty, sixty—*that's* the state of the art."

Poston, half hearing this, was making an effort to play the expan-sive civic host. As we drew nearer the Cairo city limit, he began pointing out the more notable landmarks.

"That tall building," he called out, gesturing off to the right, "that was a famous house of prostitution. These shacks over here, that's all Future City! And here's the 'Welcome' structure the people of Operation Enterprise put up here not too long ago as one of their community projects. Oh, there's one of the new businesses! A new funeral home! Just moved in just recently—just brand-new! Here's the sign—you see that? *'Welcome to Cairo'!*"

"I see it," came Molinaro's voice, dryly.

The town looked as bleached and skeletal to me as it always had:

wide streets, no traffic, whitened-out abandoned stores and drive-ins, cyclone fences, rubble. An eternal Sunday afternoon. Cairo was still nearly invisible above its own tree line. I tried to imagine all of this from Molinaro's eyes, and then I didn't have to, because I could hear him murmuring to his aide:

"No density . . . everything's a parking lot . . ."

"This is the courthouse here," Poston shouted on. "And here's one of the old historic buildings on the left. And on the right, there's some . . . very old buildings. And that's the library, that's a *very* historic building; it's been restored. And next to it is the U.S. Customs House, which was build in 18—let's see, it's got the date on it up there. Very historic."

Our destination was the Cairo Chamber of Commerce, where Angela Greenwell and a delegation of chamber-women were waiting to greet Molinaro and show his party around town in a van. But as we drew near, Doc Poston, raw with fatigue, could not resist trying again to thaw Molinaro's rapidly crystallizing coolness toward the project.

"What specific type of data would you need to determine whether or not this nineteenth-century showboat dinner-and-entertainment house would pay off?" he asked over his shoulder. When there was silence, he pressed on: "You'd need to know the cost, and what potential income it would bring . . . where the income would come from—"

There was a hiss of whispering in the backseat.

"Give us a list of those things, and we'll get goin' on that real quick, Leo." Poston's tone had veered close to pleading.

Molinaro released a sigh—one of many he would release on that day. "We've talked," he replied with exaggerated patience, "about this whole question of data gathering, and the main point that we've concluded is that the team that actually is going to gather the data has to be working as a team, because it has to ask each other, Why do we want those things? How are we going to use them? *Not,* how do we *generate* these things, who's going to go out and *do* it?"

This brief seminar struck me as just a little opaque, not to say a little patronizing; but Poston's response was immediate and eager: "We're right on the same wavelength, Leo."

"Well, therefore, giving you a *list* would be a bit artificial—"

"All we want to know—"

Poston was maneuvering for some sort of document that would keep the administration up at Southern Illinois University involved in the project. Molinaro had been at pains, at SIU on the day before, to stress the necessity of exactly that sort of academic involvement. But on this morning the urgency of the matter seemed to bore him.

"—A laundry list that *any*body could provide . . . it would be printouts that wouldn't mean anything . . ."

It was at this point that Leo Molinaro alighted from Richard Poston's car under the canopy of the old Gem Theater, to be greeted by a flock that had gathered to behold the savior of Cairo.

Besides Angela Greenwell—resplendent in a swirling bouffant—and her coterie from the Chamber of Commerce, Molinaro's welcoming party included an impressive cross-section of Southern Illinois mass media. Two television cameramen, balancing mini-cams on their shoulders, danced for position in the middle of Eighth Street; behind them, holding down their complicated coifs against the January breeze, hovered two high-heeled, red-coated, dark-haired young TV correspondents, each from a station in a nearby town. There were a couple of print reporters clutching notepads.

Molinaro's reputation (thanks entirely to Poston) had preceded him. UNION STATION DEVELOPER EYES CAIRO ran the banner on one area newspaper; another began its Sunday story, "Operation Enterprise is getting nibbles from one of the nation's biggest development firms on its idea to bring Cairo's river heritage back as a tourist attraction." The stories bore the traces of Poston's assistance—"Poston shipped papers, plans and other documents to Maryland in a $15 Federal Express package," one article reported solemnly; another mentioned the "90-minute teleconference"—and they also bore the traces of his unquenchable fondness for the dramatic flourish. " 'We're dealing with some very high-powered people here now,' " one article had him saying. " 'You just mention the name Molinaro/Rubin to a lot of investors, and that just about does it.' "

If Leo Molinaro's finer sensibilities recoiled against this sort of media-mongering, he was doing his heroic best to conceal it. Springing lightly from Poston's backseat, smoothing his hair and buttoning his topcoat, he offered only a perfunctory greeting to the Chamber of Commerce delegation before allowing himself to be trapped by the pretty young TV correspondents for on-the-scene interviews. I could not pick up the conversations from where I stood on the windy street, under the marquee of the abandoned Gem, but if Molinaro mentioned truckstops with multimillion-dollar pay-phone revenues or the possibility of an industrial waste-storage project to the cameras and microphones, it didn't survive any of the final edits.

The television crews followed Molinaro around town that day, taping him as he inspected the confluence of the two mighty waterways at the windswept tip of Fort Defiance State Park; staking out office buildings while he lingered inside, conferring with a banker or a state's attorney or a newspaper editor or a minor city functionary; zeroing in on him when he emerged. One of the stations had sent its own van, and it actually drove alongside the Chamber of Commerce van as it rolled down Washington Street, so the cameraman could get actual footage of Leo Molinaro in transit through Cairo.

Poston tagged along, smoking, almost unnoticed, on the periphery of the action for once in Cairo. He waited in anterooms and on outside steps with everyone else while Molinaro conducted his discussions. He looked watchful of Molinaro, worried, disheveled. Two days of virtual sleeplessness showed in the redness of his eyes.

Late in the afternoon Molinaro returned to the Chamber of Commerce for the last interview of the day, with the only representatives of "official" Cairo who had agreed to meet with him: City Councilmen Cordell McGoy, the young black prison guard who had risked Mayor Moss's annoyance by his stalwart membership in Operation Enterprise, and Darryl Hoppe, the at-large member and the only truly independent one. Hoppe was a soft-mustached, earnest young white man employed as a schoolteacher in Charleston, Missouri, a few miles across the Mississippi River. Hoppe, whose job made him economically immune from the sort of intimidation that was rumored to beset Moss's political opponents, had declared himself a mayoral candidate in the 1991 elections.

The two men presented themselves in the stark Chamber of Commerce conference room—an elongated folding table, a refrigerator that contained some soft drinks, a few old black-and-white photographs of the city on the walls—in crisp attire: McGoy wore his starched white prison-guard uniform shirt with badge and green trim; Hoppe had on a freshly pressed sport shirt and matching slacks. The room quickly filled up with cigarette haze as Poston, then Angela Greenwell and several others produced their smokes. Hoppe, a careful and soft-spoken man, made an attempt to act as the town's quasi-official greeter in Moss's absence.

"First of all I want to thank you for comin' down," he murmured at Molinaro, "just as happy as could be to see you here. We have worked as individuals with Doc Poston and his group, and have made a lot of accomplishments. We're awful proud to have done what we've done.

"We're all willing to put forth an effort . . ." he faltered, and Molinaro waved the effort at amenities aside. "What's the total City Council membership?" he asked coolly.

It went like that for awhile. Molinaro's questions established that the municipal government lacked a city manager or a business manager; that it had a planning commission (inert); that there was an economic development committee created by the mayor (it had not bothered to meet in six months); that an industrial fund existed in the city budget (but no one knew how much money was in it); that the town lacked a hospital or a health clinic; that there existed, nominally, a merchants association (but the town only had about eleven merchants left). With each new admission of paralysis or lack of information, Leo Molinaro's eyebrows seemed to raise another centimeter or so, and Doc Poston's dark thatch seemed to lower by a similar measure over his burning, narrow-set eyes.

It was Cordell McGoy who abruptly broke through the sterile drone of data-based questions and answers. I would never have expected it of him. A silent but alert young man, McGoy had suffered perhaps more than any other citizen of Cairo the agonies of divided loyalties since Doc Poston had come to town. McGoy had lived through the shootings and the burnings of the 1970s. Like a surprising number of young Cairo black people—the two sisters who had slept in cast-iron bathtubs, for instance—he had emerged without a permanent crippling rage. An intensely proud man, he had never thrown in his lot with the black resistance that was the United Front. He was a citizen of Cairo. The ruin and rubble of the beaten town affronted his sense of human dignity. He did not want a blood-reckoning with the white power structure. He wanted simply for the town to heal itself and get on.

And yet McGoy's soul was not free. He was a city councilman. Being a councilman meant voting on issues affecting the town, and voting on these issues meant intersecting with the political will of Al Moss. Moss was a Republican. So was the governor of Illinois, who acted on recommendations for patronage jobs, such as the job of state prison guard.

Thus it was that Cordell McGoy's vote on council matters very frequently completed the three-vote bloc of Al Moss's faction. Sometimes these votes were innocuous. Sometimes they were politically charged.

Just at the moment, Leo Molinaro was inquiring about the city's credit rating. Now Cordell McGoy seized control of the conversation. Erect in his chair, crisp in his starched uniform shirt, he addressed Molinaro without preliminaries in a firm, clear voice.

"From 1987 on, Operation Enterprise has done a yeoman of a job!" he declared. His fist on the conference table was clenched. "The programs are committed! A lot of people have weakened from pressure over the past year or so, but in their hearts they still know what's right! Even myself! I look for the region to grow from the programs of Operation Enterprise! 'Cause if Cairo grows, the region will grow! Today, at work, they saw you guys on television"—there had been a press conference after the meeting on the SIU campus—"and they're all poor, common people that work at the prison where I work at! And they saw that, and they picked up the newspaper today, and they said, Oh, my God, good things for Cairo, you know, we're gonna get positive publicity. But they were so enthused! The people that lived in the rural areas of Johnson County, Polk County, Hardin County, Pulaski County—they said, Oh, my, look what happened to Cairo. They had enough sense to know that if Cairo grows, the region will grow with it!"

Molinaro spread his hands, palms up, and opened his mouth to reply, but Cordell McGoy wasn't through.

"Operation Enterprise brought people together morally, spiritually and physically!" he declared. He was speaking rapidly now—a small-town private man out of his element, in a situation now where he'd never been; self-conscious, but forging on. "We had holdin' prayers on Easter Sunday! We had workin' together black and white! The racial problem here is not what it used to be! We can sit down and work together! I never saw anything like it! And Operation Enterprise helped that because they brought people out regardless of what color you were! It's what you can do for the community! The people came out and got involved! And that was the best thing I saw in Cairo out of my thirty-eight years here!"

McGoy paused and breathed in through his nostrils, gathering himself to force out what had next come into his mind.

"I'm not tryin' to brag, or make an impression," he began. "But—" he paused again and then said it: "—*it put me permanently in church!* Okay? Really!" His gaze was fierce, his chin was high as he addressed Molinaro. "I mean I was *off and on!* My wife's been a Catholic for thirty-seven years! She always dragged me in twice a month! And once I started gettin' involved I seen the spiritual need and where you had to go to get things done. I *joined* the church a year and a half ago! And been there ever since; I don't miss a Sunday! And I have to attribute a lot of that to Operation Enterprise!"

McGoy halted as abruptly as he had begun, breathing hard, eyes dancing and distended. Poston and Angela Greenwell were staring at him. There was a moment when something large might have taken hold in that threadbare room in the violent and sorrowful old town, and then Leo Molinaro defused it by inquiring smoothly about the possibilities of building a black business community, and the conference went back to being a conference.

But later when I thought about that last visit of mine to Cairo, and the peculiar, evanescent nature of the defeat I witnessed then—all of Poston's dreams of heritage and renewal, his riverboat Xanadu, his grandiose scheme to change the face of America; all of that being sucked like so much tobacco smoke into the antiseptic maw of Molinaro's formulations—it was during these thoughts that I understood the large thing that had in fact happened in that room.

A common man had spoken up, in his own words, for the soul of the town. This had not happened during any of my previous visits to Cairo. Until Cordell McGoy's moment, it had all been Richard Poston: Poston's speeches, Poston's exhortations, Poston's scripting of everyone else's lines at the Quinstate Forum, Poston's fund-raising letters and press releases and master schemes for redevelopment. The town itself had been mostly mute. Poston's audience. Given that silence, I'd often wondered whether Cairo, passive, submissive, was in fact nothing more than a venue: an empty stage to which an elderly dreamer could come and rework his old fantasies of town redemption.

But now a common man had spoken up. The script no longer belonged exclusively to Poston. Through Cordell McGoy, the town had made its first sounds with its own voice. In that scene, perhaps, Doc Poston's long-unspooling inner movie had reached the only finale truly worthy of the plot. The hero had dissolved himself into his following.

It was nearly dark on Eighth Street when the conference broke up. The television crews and the reporters had long since gone home. We left the little storefront, with its dim fluorescent glow, in ones and twos, buttoning overcoats, holding down hairdos, lighting up fresh cigarettes. Save for our dispersing group, the town, in its winter twilight, devoid of traffic, seemed as eerily depopulated as it had on the late-winter day when I had seen it for the first time.

Molinaro's whispering young aide had departed in mid-afternoon to catch a plane. Now Molinaro and I folded ourselves inside Doc Poston's old sedan for the drive across the Mississippi River bridge and into Missouri. Poston had reserved rooms for us at a motel about ten miles into the state. The three of us were to have dinner there together—the plans had been made on a more optimistic day—and in the morning Poston would collect us and drop us at the Cairo airport, where an SIU plane would fly us off to St. Louis and our connections back East.

The drive was not as dreadful as I had feared—Poston droned and Molinaro, in the backseat, feigned deafness—but the inevitable showdown between the two men came at dinner.

We ate inside an overlighted little all-night bunker across the asphalt parking lot from the motel itself. (It happened to be a truckstop sort of place, in point of fact.) The waitress brought oval plastic plates filled with microwaved catfish and "fried" chicken. Poston never saw the food. I don't know what he saw; his eyes were swollen nearly shut with exhaustion, and he was seething for a last fight. He charged, then begged Molinaro for an outline, a list of questions, a scrap, anything on paper that he could take back to Southern Illinois University. Molinaro was the picture of rueful forbearance. Eyes lowered, he picked in elegant distress at his catfish dinner, murmuring between painful silences that evaluations were difficult; that sheer enthusiasm alone would not go at the bank; that the numbers were very complicated. "I'm not so sure you're not starting at ground zero," he remarked to Poston at one point, to which Poston responded, in as desolate a tone as I had ever heard from him, "Then I've wasted the past three years of my life." It was at that point that I suggested the two of them might prefer to be alone; I asked the waitress to put the remains of my chicken dinner in a styrofoam carton, and took it to my motel room, where I sat, feeling as far from home as I can remember ever feeling, until I fell asleep.

The last image I have of Richard Poston is from the following morning. The vantage point is the window by my seat inside the small university aircraft that is warming up to fly me and Leo Molinaro from the Cairo airport to St. Louis. Doc is standing at the end of a cyclone fence, and he is looking in at us, and he keeps looking, past any comfortable interval, keeps looking until the propellers fire up and the plane begins to move, and the expression on his face is precisely the expression of a shattered boy.

It did not take much altitude before the totems of the late twentieth century lost definition and the tangled Illinois shoreline of the Mississippi began to look about as it must have looked when Dickens steamed past, or Father Hennepin. Leo Molinaro was flipping through the business section of *The Christian Science Monitor*. My thoughts drifted to the after-dinner tour that Poston and I had taken nearly two years earlier, in Al Moss's car with its enormous flickering dashboard. I thought of Moss and the town he had painted on the black nighttime canvas, a town with two waterways, so many natural assets, no history, no Negroes, no legacy of hopelessness or evil; a town still waiting for its metamorphosis into El Dorado. I thought of Donald Connery up in Kent, and the town he had painted in his book, a spruced-up, well-kept and comfortable old shoe of a town, with its volunteer firefighters and shopkeepers and artisans and working-men, all disappearing into the smoke.

Neither of those towns existed anymore. Their present-day phantoms, one disfigured by poverty, the other by affluence, floated along the uncertain, desperate paths ordained for them by the century. It struck me that at some moment in the future those paths would converge, and at the point of convergence there would rise the fabulous architecture of a dreamtown, and a window where one could purchase a ticket for admission.

And then I stopped thinking about these things, because the city had begun to gather its mass on the horizon below the small plane, and the city was our destination.

Epilogue

At 8:00 A.M. on a Tuesday morning in June 1990, Mayor Al Moss was stunned to encounter three visiting agents of the Federal Bureau of Investigation. The agents shut down the Cairo City Hall until noon as they examined records relating to the use of federal money—money received from the Department of Housing and Urban Development—for housing rehabilitation in the town.

The Illinois Legislature voted to legalize riverboat gambling and began receiving license applications for five locations on the Mississippi and Illinois rivers. The law permitted each licensee to operate two boats. A Philadelphia couple named Marvin and Ronnie Ornstein, who had operated a hotel and a casino in Haiti, among other places, applied for a license in the vicinity of Cairo. Several dozen citizens of Cairo traveled to Springfield, the state capital, to register their support of the application.

"We've had casinos for eight years," Marvin Ornstein told me when I talked to him and his wife on the telephone. "We understand the gaming business. With two boats per license, you have the capacity for five hundred players on each. Each boat can be on the water four hours at a time. Let's say you start your first boat at eight A.M.; your second boat goes out at ten. Last boat goes out at midnight, comes in at four in the morning. If you take those parameters—four dead hours, two boats, four trips a day apiece—well, twelve hundred times four is forty-eight hundred per boat; that's ninety-six hundred players a day, max.

"That doesn't count the people coming into town, hoping to get on a boat. I'm optimistic, but who knows. Let's say ten thousand people in town a day. You figure your ancillary factors. We'll put up a land-based facility: tickets sold; place for people to redeem chips on land. We'd need a large building for this, a large holding area for food and beverage—maybe a thirty-thousand-square-foot building.

"A hotel would definitely be in our plans. You could go on and on. We're talking a minimum twenty million dollar investment."

I asked the Ornsteins about the fears some people had expressed regarding the possible civic effects, on Cairo, of turning the vicinity into a gambling center. I mentioned Doc Poston's fear that such a development would be tantamount to handing a drink to a recovering alcoholic.

"Fears?" said Marvin Ornstein. "There will always be pluses and minuses. Gambling does attract some negatives." He paused a moment on the line. "If I was living in Cairo and had a family to raise, yeah. There are some tough areas. It's there. No question about it.

"If Cairo was running smoothly—yeah. If I were there myself, maybe I would vote against it. But—" he paused again, and groped for the right way to put it. "In Cairo, there's too many positives," he said finally.

"If it's gonna happen, it's gonna happen anyway," put in Ronnie Ornstein.

Doc Poston did not stop searching for his own savior of Cairo, the development expert who would implant, not gambling, but a commercial attraction based on heritage. In the early summer of 1990 he called me up to say he'd found a marketing consultant in Memphis, one Ronald P. Schillinger, who had done work in London, Japan, Australia and Indianapolis. Poston had managed to extract yet another modest foundation grant to underwrite a visit from Schillinger to the town.

"The doctor is looking at it from his viewpoint," said Schillinger when I telephoned him—apparently he had not understood the honorific connotation of "Doc"—"and I'm looking at it from mine. I'm looking at Cairo's potential. I'm looking at the town as a product.

"You take all the elements of the product and say, 'What is the best way it can serve the people?' The doctor says he's never heard this viewpoint before.

"The buildings, the rivers, the layout of the city," Schillinger went on. "All services related. Then you add the human element, the people, because the product is dead without people. Then you say, 'How can I use this community?'

"I truly believe," continued Ronald Schillinger, "it's one of the greatest potentials in the United States. The question is how can we bring modern technology into this community. . . . Williamsburg is a good example."

So many assets . . .

A little later I thanked Ronald Schillinger very much for his time and his courtesy in answering my questions, and hung up.

Preliminary analysis of the 1990 census, released late in the summer, showed that rural America had suffered even greater population losses during the 1980s than had been expected. The rural losses—highest in the Mississippi River Delta, the Appalachian mountains and in certain regions of the Northwest—were so acute that analysts predicted a transfer of nineteen of the country's 435 congressional seats from rural to urban districts.

The devaluation of rural America was perhaps symbolized in the plight of Butte County, a farming community about sixty miles north of Sacramento, California. In September 1990 Butte faced the prospect of becoming the first county in American history to declare bankruptcy. Butte's 185,000 inhabitants had struggled since the state's Proposition 13 slashed property tax revenues twelve years earlier. A state loan of $11 million eventually staved off disaster—at least for the time being.

Counties in Kentucky, Oklahoma and West Virginia were said to be facing similar catastrophes.

A notable anomaly in the statistics was Detroit. Early figures showed that the city's population had dropped below one million people—down from 1.2 million in 1980. Suburban migration absorbed most of a middle class, black as well as white, that had been edging out of town since the race riots of the 1960s. With its miles of abandoned and decaying neighborhood houses, its hemorrhaging of jobs, the deeply segregated patterns of its remaining people (a "remnant population," in the words of one local public-policy researcher) and its gathering mood of despair, Detroit began to take on the horrifying aspect of a gargantuan ghost town—a scaled-up version of Cairo.

Indeed, as the towns and farm communities languished, American cities, where most of the rural population had drifted, seemed locked into an irreversible, murderous slide toward chaos and barbarism. In this phenomenon, New York City was the reigning symbol. After enduring a summer of vicious semiautomatic gunplay that left eight small children dead and wounded (several of them in their living rooms, the bullets ripping through doors and walls), the city was traumatized over the early-September slaughtering of a twenty-two-year-old visitor from Utah who had come to see the U.S. Open tennis tournament: the young man was stabbed to death in a subway station as he tried to defend his parents from a marauding gang looking for money to pay its way into a Manhattan discotheque.

The New York Times reported that New Yorkers were afraid to be rude to one another anymore. Bouncers at the fashionable all-night clubs turned away patrons on peril of their lives; sometimes the rejected party returned with lethal force. The new mayor seemed mesmerized into silence; jingoistic radio talk-show hosts screamed for genocide on flagship-station airwaves.

The terror worked itself into conduits less given to hysteria: Cynthia Heimel, the voguish "Tongue in Chic" columnist of *The Village Voice*, wrote in the Sept. 4 issue—apparently with literal truthfulness—that she no longer wanted to get out of bed. A few days later, Anna Quindlen, an Op-Ed columnist in *The Times*, declared that the city was going mad. As evidence, she offered the image of her affluent West Village neighbors—bankers, lawyers, television personalities—streaming out of their apartments at dawn's first light, carrying their plastic garbage bags for the approaching sanitation trucks. These people could no longer set their trash outside the night before, Quindlen explained, because the neighborhood's homeless people would tear into it. New York had become, she wrote, "a city in which people are disposable, and not even the garbage is safe."

And yet the anticipated second wave of middle-class refugees from New York into the Connecticut countryside had not materialized by the autumn of 1990. The economics were against it. A recession had taken hold in New England—the worst recession in the United States, according to the Times. Five New England states had suffered job losses in the previous year, the only states to do so. Connecticut's rate of job growth had stood at only 0.1 percent—

the seventh worst record in the country. Personal and business bankruptcies had nearly doubled. An economist with the First National Bank in Chicago, quoted in *The Times,* predicted that New England would remain at the bottom of all regions for growth in the 1990s.

Kent, Connecticut, had settled deeply into its period of stasis. The Kent School property on the top of Skiff Mountain road remained on the real estate market, and still no buyer emerged. The school forged ahead with its construction plans for the main campus on borrowed money.

In Kent, real estate transactions reflected this economic malaise. Activity remained sluggish. The Town Center, Bill Litwin's optimistic "Madison Avenue" commercial development project of just a few years before, languished well below full tenancy. Among the few applications for space there, as the summer drew to a close, was from a videocassette dealer.

On October 27, 1990, Gordon Casey died at his home in Kent at age sixty-five. "He was Kent," remarked a local restaurant owner.

Among the few examples of entrepreneurial success in the area was Alan Gawel. His emergency-dispatching telephone service grew in response to ever-increasing demand. There was almost unlimited growth potential, it seemed, in emergency.

RON POWERS is a journalist, novelist and nonfiction writer. His criticisms of American broadcasting have appeared in several newspapers, magazines and books, as well as on television. In 1973 he won the Pulitzer Prize in criticism for his TV columns in the *Chicago Sun-Times*; in 1985 he received an Emmy for his commentaries on "CBS Sunday Morning."

Far from Home is his second nonfiction book about American town life. The first, *White Town Drowsing*, is also published by Anchor Books. Powers hails from Mark Twain's hometown, Hannibal, Missouri, and presently lives in Middlebury, Vermont, with his wife and two sons.